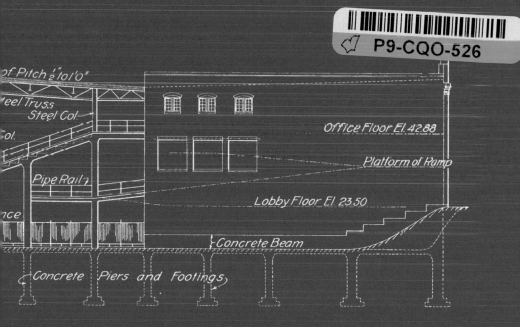

of Pitch ½" to 1'0"

eel Truss

Steel Col

ol.

Pipe Rail

nce

Office Floor El. 42.88

Platform of Ramp

Lobby Floor El. 23.50

Concrete Beam

Concrete Piers and Footings

End View of Grandstand Showing Steel Roof

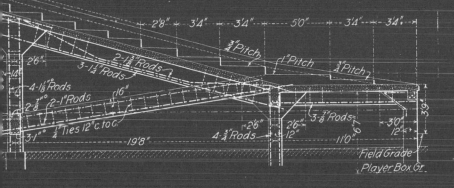

2'8"   3'4"   3'4"   5'0"   3'4"   3'4"

¾" Pitch

2'6"

2-1¼" Rods

3-1¼" Rods

1" Pitch

¾" Pitch

4-1⅛" Rods

16"

2⅞"° 2-1" Rods

3-⅞" Rods

3'9"

3-1"° ¼" Ties 12" c. to c.

2'6"

2'6"

3'0"

3-1"°

19'8"

4-¾" Rods

12"

11'0"

6'7"

12"

6'7"

Field Grade

Player Box Gr.

FENWAY 1912

ALSO BY GLENN STOUT

*Young Woman and the Sea: How Trudy Ederle Conquered
the English Channel and Inspired the World*

The Dodgers: 120 Years of Dodgers Baseball

Yankees Century: 100 Years of New York Yankees Baseball

*Red Sox Century: The Definitive History of Baseball's Most Storied
Franchise*

The Cubs: The Complete Story of Chicago Cubs Baseball

EDITED BY GLENN STOUT

The Best American Sports Writing™, 1991–present
(series editor for annual volumes)

The Best American Sports Writing of the Century
(with David Halberstam)

Chasing Tiger: The Tiger Woods Reader

Impossible Dreams: A Red Sox Collection

Top of the Heap: A Yankees Collection

Everything They Had: Sports Writing from David Halberstam

BY GLENN STOUT, CHARLES VITCHERS, AND ROBERT GRAY

*Nine Months at Ground Zero: The Story of the Brotherhood
of Workers Who Took On a Job Like No Other*

FENWAY
◆ 1912 ◆

THE BIRTH OF A BALLPARK,
A CHAMPIONSHIP SEASON,
AND FENWAY'S REMARKABLE
FIRST YEAR

Glenn Stout

Houghton Mifflin Harcourt
BOSTON   NEW YORK
2011

For information about permission to reproduce selections from this book,
write to Permissions, Houghton Mifflin Harcourt Publishing Company,
215 Park Avenue South, New York, New York 10003.

www.hmhbooks.com

Library of Congress Cataloging-in-Publication Data

Stout, Glenn, date.
Fenway 1912 : the birth of a ballpark, a championship season,
and Fenway's remarkable first year / Glenn Stout.
p. cm.
ISBN 978-0-547-19562-9 (hardback)
1. Fenway Park (Boston, Mass.)—History. 2. Boston Red Sox (Baseball team)—History.
I. Title. II. Title: Fenway nineteen hundred and twelve.
GV416.B674S76 2011
796.357'640974461—dc22   2011016068

Book design by Brian Moore

Printed in the United States of America

DOC 10 9 8 7 6 5 4 3 2 1

*To the fans in the stands—particularly the bleachers—
who still remember entering Fenway Park for the first time,
and to those who have yet to have that pleasure.*

Contents

Introduction

FENWAY PARK CHANGED my life.

I grew up outside a small town in central Ohio and was never really a Red Sox fan as a kid, but my awareness of major league baseball happened to coincide with the 1967 "Impossible Dream" team. I recall watching Billy Rohr on the news the day after he almost threw his no-hitter and seeing his hat fall off after nearly every pitch. The 1967 season was the first I followed, eagerly waiting for the newspaper every afternoon so I could devour the box scores from the night before. During the World Series I remember running off the bus and down the driveway to watch the final innings on television. I can still see Julian Javier's game 7 home run over the left-field wall seal Boston's fate as Jim Lonborg, pitching on two days' rest, fell heroically to Bob Gibson and the Cardinals. Later that fall my parents bought me a baseball bat that is still too big for me to use, but one I absolutely had to have just because it had Carl Yastrzemski's signature burned on the barrel.

For some reason I have never understood, baseball grabbed me as a kid and has never let go. If I wasn't playing or looking at baseball cards or reading baseball books, I was spending hours drawing ballparks and fields, measuring the distances precisely and to scale. At one point I even began elaborate plans to reconstruct Jet Stadium, home of the local minor league team, the Triple A Columbus Jets, out of Popsicle sticks. I never built my scale model, but getting lost in a ballpark, even one of the imagination, has always been easy for me. It was so again as I wrote this book.

Jet Stadium was nice, but while growing up I never had an opportunity to live in a city with a ballpark, and I wanted to see major league baseball the real way. So in the fall of 1981, in the midst of a recession, only five months after graduating from Bard College in upstate New York with a degree in creative writing and finding myself back home in Ohio pouring concrete, I sold my trombone, packed up the Dodge Dart, rented a small U-Haul trailer, and drove.

New York and Yankee Stadium were too scary. Chicago, despite Comiskey Park and Wrigley Field, was still the Midwest and too close to home. But I had friends in Boston, and Boston had Fenway Park. So after a drive of almost eighteen hours, including a detour to Manhattan to pick up my girlfriend, I pulled up in front of a $225 a month studio apartment far out on Commonwealth Avenue across the street from the Terrace Motel.

There were no jobs in Boston then—this was before nearly twenty-five years of nonstop economic growth changed the face of the city—and after a month we were down to counting spare change. When I accidentally dumped a bowl of spaghetti on the floor, we ate it anyway. On Christmas Eve I got a job as a security guard at minimum wage and worked double shifts through the holidays to make the rent.

Boston was different then. Everything was gritty and worn. There was broken glass everywhere. The sidewalks outside every bar were stained with vomit. There were no yuppies. Boylston Street was abandoned at night. Punk rock still had a chance.

I lost the car on unpaid parking tickets but survived the winter, and in the spring my girlfriend nabbed a job at Boston University. We scammed our way into some subleased staff housing in Kenmore Square, and I wrote papers for BU and Harvard students for extra money. In 1982 I made $6,000.

But that was plenty. I was right around the corner from Fenway Park. The first time I walked up the tunnel in the bleachers, a batting practice home run by Reggie Jackson almost hit me on the head. Ten dollars got me into the ballpark and left enough change for three beers. For another $10 I could go to the Rat, see some rock 'n' roll, drink two or three more beers, and careen home in five minutes. I probably went to two dozen games that year, plus a few more after the ushers abandoned the gates to the bleachers after the third or fourth inning and I walked in with the panhandlers and drunks who collected empty beer cups for a teaspoon of swill.

I was poor, but I had baseball. Walking up that runway into the bleachers that summer changed my life. It was my grad school. I majored in Fenway Park, Kenmore Square, the Del Fuegos, poetry, baseball, and books. I fell in love. I saw, watched, learned, got curious, did research, read, stopped dreaming about writing and started doing it. I went to work at the Boston Public Library and discovered that Red Sox history lives in thousands of reels of Boston newspapers on microfilm. My universe stretched from Kenmore Square to Copley, with Mass Avenue as the axis. The City paid me to go to library school. I got lucky, stumbled on a story, sold it to *Boston* magazine, and have never been without an assignment since, doing the work I still do today, writing.

None of this would have happened without Fenway Park, none of it at all. And that is what makes a ballpark different, and what makes Fenway Park different, because it is a place that can change your life, and sometimes does. Almost a hundred years ago it changed the lives of almost every baseball fan in Boston, and each season, as another generation of fans discovers it, Fenway Park changes their lives as well.

Fenway Park, as you will soon learn, was a different place in 1912 than it is now, and it was even a far different place in 1982, when I attended my first game, but that is part of the reason it is here today.

Although it has become a cliché to make the claim that Fenway Park is still recognizable today as the same park that opened in 1912, that is true only in the most limited sense. If a contemporary Red Sox fan were somehow sent back in time and deposited in Fenway Park on April 9, 1912, it is unlikely that any but the most knowledgeable rooter would recognize it at all. For while Fenway Park still occupies the same basic footprint today as it did in 1912, virtually every other notable structure and feature of the ballpark has been removed, recast, renovated, or otherwise changed.

And that is, oddly enough, the biggest reason why Fenway Park still exists today. Since opening in 1912, Fenway Park, more than any other major league ballpark, has evolved and adapted to changing expectations and needs. Apart from the Jersey Street facade on what is now called Yawkey Way and the concrete-and-steel infrastructure of the grandstand—of which little more than the skeleton remains visible today—every other part and portion of Fenway Park has changed. It is not the same shape, nor does it retain the same outfield dimensions as it did when it first opened. Neither the pitcher's mound nor the bases, nor home plate, are in the same precise place as they were on opening day of 1912. Today Fenway Park is nearly as changed from the original as old Yankee Stadium was changed after the 1974–75 renovation of that classic facility. In fact, one can make the case that the other concrete-and-steel parks built within a few years of Fenway Park—Ebbets Field in Brooklyn, Tiger Stadium in Detroit, Redland Field in Cincinnati, Shibe Park in Philadelphia, Forbes Field in Pittsburgh—no longer exist precisely because they did not change quickly enough or dramatically enough.

Fenway has survived not *because* it has been preserved in the original, but because it has *not* been preserved, because until quite recently it was never treated as special enough to preserve, and because the ball club has rarely hesitated to make practical changes to extend its useful life. Even in recent years, which have seen the greatest changes to the park since the 1933–34 renovation, few of the visible changes, formally speaking, have been about preservation. Virtually every change has been about adaptation, providing modern-day amenities and maximizing profit within the original footprint of the park or else expanding that footprint to include property and provide services that were not part of the original plant.

Fenway has never been static, locked away in some cabinet like an antique. Even its most distinctive features, like the left-field wall, have changed so much over the past one hundred years as to be virtually unrecognizable from the original. It is a *living* place, one that has changed, and will continue to change, across eras, evolving and shaping the collective memory of generations. And that, I think, is why each of us identifies so closely with Fenway Park, because every time we encounter it we experience it in our own way. My Fenway Park is neither "Nuf Ced" McGreevey's park of 1912 nor Ted Williams's of 1939, nor Carl Yastrzemski's of 1961, nor that of an eight-year-old boy or girl walking into the ballpark for the first time in 2012. And for that reason it belongs to us all.

That is why Fenway Park *matters*, because as each of us has changed and grown, so has Fenway Park. That is why it is still here today and why, after one hundred years, each time you walk up the ramp from beneath the stands and out toward that sea of sunlit grass, Fenway Park remains the most special kind of place there is—a place that can still change your life.

—Glenn Stout
Alburgh, Vermont

FENWAY 1912

Prologue

Who sows a field . . . is more than all.

—John Greenleaf Whittier

O N A N E A R L Y October morning in the fall of 1911, Jerome Kelley rose and, after his customary cup of tea, left his home on Palmer Street in Roxbury and began his walk to work.

The morning was cool, yet the air was crisp and carried a hint of winter. As he turned up Ruggles Street the smell of breakfast cooking drifted from the houses and small apartments of the Village, the close-knit Irish American community nestled around the foot of Tremont Street. A few sleepy horses already plodded slowly down the street, pulling carts, carrying ice and other necessities of the day. In the distance automobiles coughed and sputtered as the city began to awake. On the stoops and front porches, older men—and even a few women—already sat watching the day unfold, puffing on their pipes. Wearing his cap, work pants, and plain thin jacket, Kelley gave a nod and quick word to the other workmen he saw as he walked through the neighborhood before reaching Huntington Avenue and turning north.

Boston. In the Village it was easy to pretend—almost—that you were still in Ireland. Not that anyone would mistake the Village for the green fields of Erin, for apart from the small gardens squeezed into the back lots, there was nothing green about the Village, yet it was a place where everyone knew everyone else, and if you were not already related, well, after the next wedding you might be. If a fellow had the time he could spend all day walking down the block, stopping at nearly every house, catching up on the news of the day, and then drop into McGreevey's saloon on Columbus Avenue for a beer to soak up even more information.

But as soon as Kelley made the turn onto Huntington Avenue it was as if he entered another world. Streetcars screeched and rattled up and down the middle of the street, while the sidewalks bustled with activity. Now most of the faces he saw were those of strangers.

Here Boston was on display. Virtually every block of Huntington Avenue featured another of the city's cultural assets: The Museum of Fine Arts. The Opera House. Symphony Hall. All had been built in the last ten years, and in the clear autumn air the grand buildings stood magnificent and austere, perfectly framed by the colorful gardens and fading greenery of the nearby Back Bay Fens, Frederick Law Olmsted's masterpiece of architectural landscaping and engineering.

Kelley was impressed—everyone was—but he was not overwhelmed by the scene, which was now so familiar to him that he barely noticed. After all, while many of the men in Kelley's neighborhood had worked on those buildings as they were being built, few felt welcome inside once they were completed. The buildings were for the well-to-do, the Brahmins who until recently had run Boston and still had most of the money. Workingmen like Kelley, particularly Irish workingmen, well, they worked for the people who built the museums.

As Kelley walked up the Avenue that October morning his mind was not on the opera or the symphony or the great masters, but on a building that, to him, was more beautiful and more important than any of the grander edifices. For each of the last eight years this particular building had provided both his livelihood and his lifestyle, a place that many of his friends in the neighborhood considered a second home.

As he passed Tufts Medical College at the corner of Rogers Avenue he saw a ramshackle, wooden cigar stand, and then a towering, rough-hewn wooden fence, heavy with paint, bearing the scars of a hundred handbills and a huge advertising sign for "Dr. Swett's Original Root Beer." He then turned down a dusty footpath that paralleled the rough fence. Until recently there had been a large wooden sign that arched over a walkway and read "Huntington Avenue Base Ball Grounds." Since 1904 he had gone there nearly every day, summer and winter, to work on the grounds.

But the sign had come down recently, and no one had bothered to replace it. It was obsolete anyway. The park was closing—it was now a "base ball grounds" in memory only. The next event at the park would be a charity soccer game. Baseball season was over, and not just for 1911. For the Huntington Avenue Grounds it was over forever.

Kelley had not been looking forward to this day. The Red Sox had finished the regular season only a few days before, drubbing Washington 8–1 to inch into fourth place ahead of the Chicago White Sox, but still some twenty-four long games behind the pennant-winning Philadelphia Athletics. Each day since then, as always, Kelley had kept an eye on the weather, waiting. He had one last job to do before the soccer players chewed the field to pieces.

Kelley, age forty-one, had come to Boston from Ireland more than twenty years before and had lived much of the time since with his widowed sister Rose. At first he worked in a nearby piano factory, laboriously stringing wire through the tuning pins. It was honest work, but dreary. He much preferred to be outdoors, and when an opportunity arose to work at the ballpark in 1904, he had jumped at the chance. Since arriving in the States, like most of his neighbors, he had become quite the baseball fan.

For most of the past eight years the weather had determined his work. So, too, would the weather define this day. But instead of forecasting whether he should water the grass or send his men out with push mowers and rakes to cut the grass and smooth the dirt, on this day the weather told him that the time was right, not to prepare the field for a game, but to strip the park of the only feature that would travel the short half-mile across the Fens to the new home of the Red Sox, now just a sea of mud and bare earth along Jersey Street.

The infield. Nearly every day for the last eight years Kelley had groomed and worried himself half-sick over that diamond-shaped piece of turf, making sure it was watered and fertilized and free of rocks and weeds. While the outfield turf required little maintenance apart from a good cutting once or twice a week, the infield, just under

ninety feet square, was different. It was in the infield that games—
and livelihoods—were won and lost.

Kelley knew full well that a simple ground ball that found a pebble
or a bump could cost the Red Sox a ball game, and him his job. When
Jimmy Collins, the old Red Sox third baseman, had chosen to leave
the bag and play his position on the turf, digging in with his cleats
until he exposed bare ground, Kelley had dutifully patched over and
seeded the bare spots, time and time again, without complaint. And
when Tris Speaker, Boston's fleet young outfielder, had dragged a
bunt down the first-base line only to watch it roll foul, Kelley had
been out on the field after the game before the stands had emptied,
adding a bit of dirt to the baseline, tilting it ever so slightly toward
the field, making the transition from dirt to sod, brown to green,
smooth and nearly seamless. And when Heinie Wagner, the shortstop, had bobbled a ball and shot him a dark look afterward, Kelley
had made sure to walk the line that the ball had taken from the bat,
feeling with his foot and then his fingers for a soft spot or a stone,
adding a sprinkling of earth here, tamping down a rough spot there.
It had taken eight years to get the infield looking the way it did now,
lush and green and, since no ball had been played on it for the last
week, thick and healthy. Grass grew best this time of the year, favor-
ing the cool days and nights over the scorching heat of the summer.

That was why, of all things, only the sod of the infield of the Huntington Avenue Grounds would make the half-mile journey to the
site of the new park. Although groundbreaking had taken place only
a few weeks before, on September 25, Kelley's first task there, even as
workers were already leveling the site and installing drainage pipes,
had been to lay out the infield. And today, Kelley's last day at Huntington Avenue, his task was to take the old ground and lay it down
in the new place. He would then water and feed it through the fall
before covering it over during construction so that when the snows
melted and spring came and a new ballpark burst forth like a daffodil,
the infield would be trim and green and smooth.

He had already spent several days at the new place preparing the
soil, raking it over and over again, sifting the loose dirt through a
wire sieve to remove rocks and roots, adding loam and clay and sand

in the right proportion, turning it over again and again. The work crews clearing the site had erected a fence around the infield to protect the space so no wheelbarrow or workman would tread across the bare ground and scar it with ruts or divots. It was ready now, and all Kelley had left to do was supervise the removal of the sod from Huntington Avenue and truck it to its new location.

He gathered his small crew of men and tools and handcarts and made his way toward the field, stopping just short of fair territory. Only a week after the end of the season the field already looked a bit ragged. Sawdust was pressed into the ground around home plate and the pitcher's box, left over from Kelley's effort to make the field playable on its final day, when a deluge had soaked the field overnight. Tufts of new grass had already sprung up in the dirt portion of the infield, and the outfield turf, left untended, was long and shaggy. Pigeons swooped and flocked beneath the grandstand roof, the only spectators amid the empty seats, and a few stray papers swirled before the dugout. The breeze still carried the smells of the ballpark — a mix of peanut shells, tobacco juice, and cigars that over the last decade had penetrated the fibrous wood and now remained, even when the crowd was gone.

Kelley and his crew worked slowly and methodically as they cut the sod into strips, loosened it from the soil beneath, then used a sharp spade to cut the strips into squares. The work was familiar, not unlike the cutting of sod many of them had done in Ireland, where for generations men had worked the bogs, peeling back the surface to uncover peat, which they had cut and stacked and dried to burn for fuel.

It took most of the morning to remove the sod and wheel it to the horse carts waiting behind the grandstand, but by noon the work was done and the green space that had once been the focus for thousands of sets of eyes and the home for legends like Collins, Buck Freeman, Chick Stahl, and Cy Young was now stacked in layers, like the pages of a history book.

One after the other, as Kelley and his crew climbed on board, the wagons pulled out and followed one another up Huntington Avenue, then down Massachusetts Avenue toward the new place. Thousands of Bostonians had spent much of the summer obsessed with what had taken place on the field, but now they were oblivious as it passed by them.

Less than an hour later, the wagons turned onto Jersey Street and made their way down the rutted pathway to a bare open lot dotted with piles of rock and debris. Knots of workmen wielding shovels and wheelbarrows scurried about amid surveyors eyeballing grade stakes and men rushing in and out of a makeshift construction shack, carrying plans and barking orders. The site was on the edge of what had once been a mud flat occasionally overrun with brackish water, the ancestral holdings of the Dana family, whose roots in and around Boston predated the American Revolution. The filling of the Back Bay and the Fens, finished only a little more than a decade earlier, had turned the useless marsh into raw land, undeveloped and potentially lucrative. And for most of the last decade it had sat there, undeveloped, used as an occasional dump, awaiting its fate as Boston grew out to meet it.

Kelley's men steered their wagons to the small fenced-off area on the southwestern corner of the property, near Jersey Street, opened a gate, and began unloading their precious cargo. As they laid the sod a few workmen stopped and watched for a moment as, piece by piece, over the course of the next few hours the bare ground, apart from a narrow strip that ran from the pitcher's mound to home plate, changed from brown to green. As it did the emerging infield made it possible to imagine a grandstand rising around it, then the outfield and a distant outfield fence, followed soon by the five senses of a ballpark: the crack of a bat, the smell of cut grass, the taste of plug tobacco finding its place in your cheek, the feel of a worn glove wrapping the hand, the sight of long cool shadows cutting across the infield, and the muffled hum of the crowd slowly filling in the space between the wisecracks of the players.

Square by square, a new page was turned open to the sun. Something was passed from Huntington Avenue to the new place. It would soon take root there and then, in time, flourish every spring.

· 1 ·

1911

The lovers of the game in this part of the country already begin to realize
the important part in the sport that an ideal home for the game plays.

—*Boston Globe*

THE RED SOX needed more than a new ballpark.

On the first day of September, 1911, with the Red Sox trailing the world champion Philadelphia Athletics 3–1 and two outs in the ninth inning, pinch hitter Joe Riggert worked a walk from A's star pitcher Eddie Plank. As the fifteen thousand fans in attendance at the Huntington Avenue Grounds began to stir, Boston outfielder Harry Hooper followed with a sharp drive to left. When the ball cleared the infield and struck the ground for a clean base hit, the crowd cheered. After being shut out in the first game of the doubleheader, it appeared as if the Red Sox just might rally and take game 2.

A's outfielder Harry Lord fielded the ball on a hop and looked toward second base, where he expected to see Riggert pulling in safely. But instead of making the smart play and stopping at second, Riggert, running like a kid on the sandlot in a hurry to get home for supper, inexplicably headed toward third.

The cheers stopped. Lord calmly took aim and fired the ball to third baseman Frank Baker. He waited for Riggert's obligatory slide, applied the tag, and mercifully ended the game.

A few boos and catcalls echoed over the grounds, but most of the crowd filed out in near-silence. In the ramshackle press box that sat atop the grandstand roof, veteran *Boston Globe* baseball writer Tim Murnane sat before the typewriter and tried to sum things up. A former professional player himself, Murnane, known as "the Dean of Baseball Writers" and "the Silver King" owing to his shock of silver hair, was usually gentle on the Red Sox players. In the 1870s and '80s, Murnane had played in the National Association, the National League, and the Union Association, all considered major leagues at the time. His voice was the most authoritative among Boston's baseball scribes. He well understood the players' lot but had no patience for stupid play.

On this afternoon the Red Sox, by dropping both ends of the doubleheader to Philadelphia, had fallen from third place to fourth—trading places with the Yankees—and now seemed determined to take dead aim at fifth place. Over eighteen desultory innings the Red Sox had scored but a single run as the Athletics, despite being outhit by Boston, showed the difference between the two clubs by winning 1–0 and 3–1, each time putting the game away late by taking advantage of a Red Sox miscue. To make matters worse, Boston shortstop Charlie "Heinie" Wagner sprained an ankle while running the bases, an injury that knocked him out for the rest of the season.

The old ballplayer had seen enough for one day and started typing the ending to the running game story he had constructed over the course of the contest. Riggert, wrote Murnane, had "spilled the beans by trying to make third" and had been out "by a city block." It was, he accurately concluded, a "bonehead play."

There had been a lot of spilled beans and bonehead plays at the Huntington Avenue Grounds over the past few years, and there was now little doubt that the 1911 season would end just the way most of the previous seven seasons had ended, in disappointment. The Red Sox, once the flagship of the American League, were adrift and directionless, listing back and forth in the middle of the pack, a team with no identity and apparently little hope for the future.

RED SOX DROP TWO GAMES

Sad In The Morning
Worse In The Afternoon

American League president Ban Johnson had created the circuit in 1900, and in 1902 he declared that it was now a major league and that he intended to go to war with the only major league at the time, the National League. One key to the success of Johnson's effort was the placement of a franchise in Boston, virtually next door to the existing National League team, as one of the new league's flagship franchises.

Johnson, a man whose ambition, ego, and self-confidence matched his girth, made the success of the new Boston team a priority. He ran the league like his own personal fiefdom and initially owned a financial stake in every franchise. For the first two decades of the league's existence he had near-dictatorial powers, which he was not shy about employing. By selecting, as he often did, not only who could own or invest in a club but who they could employ as manager and players, Johnson had the means to manipulate the standings. In order for his new league to succeed he needed the new Boston club to get a leg up on Boston's long-established National League team. The best way to do that was to make the team a champion.

Together with Charles Somers, Johnson's toady and financial benefactor, who helped finance the new league and served as the titular leader of the AL's Boston franchise, Johnson led a raid on Boston's potent National League club, a recent dynasty. He signed away many of its best players, including star pitcher Cy Young and third baseman Jimmy Collins, a devastating blow to the established club. The two men also built a new ballpark, the Huntington Avenue Grounds, on land leased from the Boston Elevated Company.

It was an audacious move, for the new park sat just across the railroad tracks from the Nationals' home, the beloved but increasingly decrepit South End Grounds, but it had worked. The combination of a good ball club, a new and spacious ballpark, and an admission charge of twenty-five cents—half of what the Nationals charged— had proven to be an unstoppable combination. The Americans, as most fans called them at the time, were a powerhouse.

After the 1902 season Somers, who lived in Cleveland and was also an investor in that club, cashed out and sold the club to Milwaukee attorney Henry Killilea, another Johnson crony. He agreed to take over until Johnson could find a compliant local owner. It proved to be a good investment. In 1903 Boston won its first American League pennant and the first "World's Series," as it was then called, defeating Pittsburgh. By then Boston's National League team didn't matter much anymore—Boston was an American League town.

Johnson knew it was a good time to sell again. The Nationals had been vanquished, and the Boston Americans would never be more attractive to a Massachusetts man with some money. Of course, Johnson really didn't give a damn about Boston anymore. Now that Boston had won a title, he intended to make his New York team the next American League champion, even if it hurt Boston.

Johnson found the perfect patsy, someone who would virtually guarantee that no matter what Johnson did to help New York, he would receive little criticism from the generally boosterish local press.

The sucker was John I. Taylor and his father, *Boston Globe* publisher and Civil War hero General Charles Taylor. The younger Taylor was not unlike the progeny of many other rich and influential men of the age. While not quite a complete ne'er-do-well—Taylor had briefly worked in the family business, twiddling his thumbs in the *Globe*'s advertising and editorial departments—he much preferred enjoying the fruits of his family's bank account and resulting social status. Taylor liked to sail, ride and show horses, raise Irish terriers, shoot skeet, play whist, and enjoy every other pastime appropriate to a man of his station, much of it breathlessly reported in his father's newspaper. He wasn't a bad fellow and could be a great deal of fun after a few cocktails, but he fancied himself as more of an athlete and sportsman than he really was.

Boston's world championship baseball team had been a boon to local newspapers, and in 1903 John I. Taylor had fallen for the club like it was a prize Irish terrier. He also needed something tangible to occupy his time, so in April 1904 the General indulged his son, put up the $135,000 sale price, and installed John I. Taylor as club owner and president. The younger Taylor hadn't a clue as to what he had bought or what to do with it, but he liked the company of the players and could often be seen at the Huntington Avenue Grounds. He liked to sit on the bench during batting practice before moving to his box near the end of the dugout for the game, close enough to the action for the players to see his reaction and for Taylor to hear their earthy conversations.

He had a grand time watching in 1904. Despite the best efforts of Ban Johnson, who arranged a suspicious midseason trade that sent one of Boston's better players, Patsy Dougherty, to New York, Boston still won the pennant. On the final day of the season Boston defeated New York when star pitcher Jack Chesbro threw a wild pitch that cost him the game and his team the pennant. Boston then managed to retain its status as world champion without playing a single game when the National League champion New York Giants, in a fit of pique, refused to play them in the postseason.

The club's success made Taylor, who had very little to do with the creation of the roster besides signing the checks, think he was a genius. So in the off-season he began meddling with the roster and made several questionable deals against the wishes of player-manager Jimmy Collins. At the same time Boston's stars began to show their age. The team slumped to fourth place in 1905 and rapidly slid downward from there. When Collins criticized Taylor, the owner froze the manager out and over the next season or two refused to make any substantive trades at all out of pure spite. In 1907 he finally traded Collins away, a move that sent Boston's Irish fans into a frenzy and newsboys selling the *Globe* in certain sections of the city scurrying for cover. Meanwhile, some very real tragedies further harmed the club. In 1905, after being injured in a carriage accident, catcher Lou Criger became addicted to morphine. And in 1907 Collins's replacement, player-manager Chick Stahl, whose record of emotional instability had made him a strange choice for the job, was blackmailed by a former girlfriend who had become pregnant. Stahl couldn't take the scandal and committed suicide, drinking carbolic acid while the team was at spring training at West Baden Springs, Indiana. His death rocked the club, which would go through another four managers before the end of the season.

While Taylor stewed, the Red Sox landed with a thud, finishing in last place in 1906 with a grim record of 49-105, and in seventh place in 1907. Apart from a brief foray into the first division in 1909, the Huntington Avenue Grounds had become a place where Boston fans went to watch baseball, but not to watch *winning* baseball. In a sense the park became the turn-of-the-century equivalent of Wrigley Field, a pleasant place to be but rarely the site of any significant drama concerning wins and losses.

For many fans the real action took place in the stands along the first-base line, which effectively served as an open betting parlor. Many of the same faces sat there every day, oblivious to the score, wagering on such things as strikes and balls and pop-ups and ground-outs, bets that didn't depend on wins and losses.

In the first few years of his ownership Taylor's most significant contribution to the ball club was to change its name. Before the 1908 season he announced that the team would wear red stockings and henceforth be known as the Red Sox. The name harkened back to the glory days of the sport, when the original Red Stockings of Cincinnati had relocated to Boston and given the city its first championship club. It was hardly an appropriate name for Boston's current collection of has-beens and never-would-bes, but up to that time neither fans nor sportswriters had ever been quite sure what to call the team. They usually called them "the Americans" simply to differentiate them from Boston's National League team. Other names, both awkward and colorful, like the Pilgrims, worked in newspaper headlines but were rarely used by the fans in the stands.

The only thing the club had going for it was that the National League team was even worse, and the South End Grounds even worse than that. The double-decked wooden park had once been one of the game's most distinctive venues. But in 1894 it burned, and even though the park had been rebuilt, the new facility lacked the charm of its predecessor. The Red Sox, despite all their troubles, were first in a league of two, and that seemed good enough for John I., if not the Boston fans. They were simply there, the flag in the corner of the gymnasium, hanging listless and limp.

But by 1911 the team was not completely talentless. By chance and serendipity, the Red Sox slowly began to acquire a new core group of players that would soon become at least the equal of the 1903 champions, if not better.

Traditionally, most professional ballplayers had come from New England and the Northeast. That was where baseball first became popular and where the game was well established and where boys and young men could still be found on nearly every empty lot or town square tossing a ball around. But as professional baseball spread there was growing demand for young players, and the Red Sox faced increased competition in their own backyard. That, combined with the expansion of the American League to the west as far as St. Louis and Chicago and as far south as Washington, D.C., led some teams, including the Red Sox, to look for prospects ever farther away in parts of the country where there was less competition for players and a greater chance to nab a real prize. It wasn't part of any great plan on Taylor's part, but an instance of innovation inspired by necessity. By accident, the Red Sox became one of the first teams to take advantage of these relatively untapped new markets. It soon paid off.

The first of this core group to wear a Boston uniform was Texas native Tris Speaker, a man who grew up doing all the things easterners imagined a Texan did—hunting, fishing, roping cattle, and busting broncos. A natural right-hander, Speaker learned to throw with his left hand after breaking his right when he was thrown from a horse. A good student, Speaker enrolled after high school in Fort Worth Polytechnic Institute, where he played on the football and baseball teams, making a better impression there than in the classroom. In 1906, after he was spotted playing semipro baseball at age eighteen by Doak Roberts, owner and manager of the Cleburne Railroaders in the Texas League, Speaker became a professional. He failed to make it as a pitcher before finding his place in center field, where his speed and arm stood out. Roberts sensed Speaker's raw potential and almost immediately tried, without success, to sell his young prospect to the majors before finally getting the attention of George Huff. The Boston scout, who also served as the athletic director of the University of Illinois and in the wake of Stahl's suicide had actually served as manager for a brief period in 1907, signed the nineteen-year-old outfielder for about $750.

The dour-looking young Speaker was as raw and tough as the leather of a new baseball mitt. He could run but not yet hit. After a brief appearance for Boston near the end of the 1907 season, at age nineteen, when he played tentatively and seemed overwhelmed by both the competition and the city, he was released.

His career could have been finished, but nothing stuck in Speaker's craw more than failure. In the off-season he tried to latch on to another club, but no one wanted him. He even showed up at the New York Giants' camp in Marlin, Texas, in the spring of 1908, but was rebuffed by manager John McGraw.

That didn't stop him, for behind Speaker's dour countenance was a true Texan, a man who felt it was his duty, if not his birthright, to succeed. Refusing to accept the end of his career, Speaker boldly showed up at Boston's spring training headquarters in Hot Springs, Arkansas, without an invitation. Even though he wasn't under contract, the Red Sox let him work out with the club and at the end of spring training found a use for him. They essentially used Speaker to settle their debt to the Little Rock team for allowing the Sox to use their ballpark, paying the rent by handing them Speaker. When Speaker flourished later that year, the Little Rock owner graciously allowed the Red Sox to reclaim the player they hadn't wanted a few seasons before.

Speaker, however, never forgot his shabby treatment in 1907 and used the release as motivation in 1908. When he returned to Boston he was a changed man, both on and off the field. He was now deadly certain of his ability, aggressive in the outfield and at the plate and on the bases, and intimidated no more. In 1909 he earned a starting berth in Boston's outfield, hitting .309, and over the next two years demonstrated all five baseball tools—the ability to run, throw, field, hit, and hit with power in an era when doubles and triples mattered more than home runs. Success only increased his swagger, although even teammates who did not particularly like him personally, like outfielder Duffy Lewis, respected him. Lewis called Speaker "the king of the outfield." By the end of the 1911 season Speaker, twenty-three years old and a muscular 5'11", was on the cusp of greatness. Those who had doubted him a few years before now didn't dare touch the chip on his shoulder.

Another outfielder arrived by a similarly circuitous route. John I. Taylor was married to Cornelia Van Ness of San Francisco, and while visiting relatives in California after the 1908 season he met with Charlie Graham, manager of minor league Sacramento. Graham convinced him to take a chance on young Harry Hooper, a California State League outfielder whom people were comparing favorably to Ty Cobb. That was mostly hype, for Hooper shared neither the Detroit outfielder's abrasive personality nor his monumental talent, but Hooper was still a skilled player, with a superb arm, good speed, and an occasionally potent bat, a table-setter and defensive whiz, the perfect complementary player, and one of the few Red Sox players who got along with almost everyone. While it would not have been possible to win a championship with a team of Harry Hoopers, it was impossible to win without a player like Harry Hooper.

He was a recent graduate of St. Mary's College with a degree in engineering, had a good job with the railroad, and didn't necessarily need to play baseball. Taylor, who was already thinking of replacing the Huntington Avenue Grounds, helped entice Hooper to sign with the Red Sox in exchange for $2,800 — more than his salary with the railroad — and the vague promise of an off-season engineering job working on the plans for a new ballpark. Hooper did the math, signed a contract, and made his Red Sox debut in 1909, one of only a handful of major leaguers at the time from the West Coast.

The Red Sox had also recently signed another player from the West — Kansas native Joe Wood, who despite going only 7-12 for Kansas City in 1908 had gotten the attention of big league scouts with an impressive performance in an exhibition game he pitched for Kansas City against Washington. And after the 1909 season, during another trip west, Taylor signed a second St. Mary's product, outfielder Duffy Lewis. Pitcher Charley "Sea Lion" Hall, although not originally signed by the Red Sox, was also from California. In fact, his family came from Mexico and his real name was Carlos Luis Clolo, a fact he wisely kept to himself in light of the intolerance of the era.

By 1911 the addition of these players had changed the face of the organization, which until then had been largely representative of New England. Catcher Bill "Rough" Carrigan was a native of Maine and a graduate of Holy Cross College; a favorite of local fans, he was a man equally comfortable at Mass or in a sidewalk brawl. Pitcher Ray Collins had been raised in Vermont and was a direct descendant of William Bradford, the second governor of Plymouth Colony. He was so proud of his heritage that when asked his nationality on a survey by *Baseball* magazine he proudly identified himself as "Yankee." Infielder Larry Gardner was born on a dairy farm in Vermont, and first baseman Hugh Bradley was a native of Worcester, Massachusetts. Together, these New Englanders and their western teammates formed much of the core of what would soon become a championship club.

But this was 1911, not 1912. Despite the presence of some bona fide stars like Speaker, who rapidly became one of the best players in the game and, with Hooper and Lewis, part of the best young outfield in baseball, there were reasons why the team had yet to gel and entered September fighting to play .500 baseball.

Those reasons had little to do with talent and everything to do with personality and prejudice. The team did not mesh. The club was a minefield of cliques and alliances that divided the squad by age, geography, heritage, and, most notably, religion.

Carrigan led one faction made up of mostly Catholic, older, eastern, and New England–born players, a group the press referred to as "the KCs," in reference to the Catholic fraternal organization the Knights of Columbus. The insurgents, known collectively as "the Masons," included the younger, Protestant players primarily from the South and the West.

The Masons were led by Tris Speaker and Joe Wood. The two young players had become fast friends as soon as they met. They shared a similar background, had strong personalities, carried themselves with the cocksure arrogance of youth, and were clearly the most talented of the younger Red Sox. One rarely saw one without the other, for each had been the subject of some hazing when they first joined the club. While Speaker had been warmly welcomed by veterans like Cy Young and Lou Criger when he first joined the Sox, many other veterans treated the rookie with the traditional disdain and probably found him easy to mock—compared to his eastern teammates, Speaker, although nominally a college man, lacked sophistication and spoke with a pronounced Texas drawl that his older teammates found hilarious.

Wood had it even tougher. It was widely known that Wood had begun his professional career playing for a barnstorming "Bloomer Girls" team, a club of mostly men in drag, which made the slender, finely featured pitcher an easy target of barbs and teasing. He was thin-skinned and quick to anger and did not shrug off such slights easily. He had, wrote one reporter delicately, only a *"fairly* cool head."

In fact, when Wood arrived in Boston in July 1908 after beginning the season with Kansas City in the American Association, his reputation for arrogance nearly matched his reputation on the mound. He knew he was good, and before he had ever won a game in the big leagues he was acting as if he had already won a hundred. He reacted to the hazing and ribbing of veteran players with defiance. "Too much boosting," wrote one reporter, "has had a bad effect on the youngster." Much of his attitude was an act that masked his insecurity, but it made him a target of club veterans, some of whom were already jealous of his talent on the field and his popularity among the young ladies who sat in the stands. Just a glance from the boyish Wood was enough to make a local maiden swoon.

Although Wood was bright and would later serve as baseball coach at Yale University, as a young man he was hardly an Ivy Leaguer. His father was an attorney with a marked sense of adventure, a man who had dragged his family all over the country and who had even taken a turn as an Alaskan prospector. Wood, who had grown up primarily in western Kansas and Colorado, was himself very much a man of the Wild West. He refused to take crap from anyone and already had his own ideas about the world. He was suspicious of easterners in general, had little regard for Catholics—unless they were female—and, like many white men of his time, got a kick out of treating African Americans poorly. Even among players of the era, many of whom shared the same ideals, Wood stood out for his cruelty. Veteran sportswriter Hugh Fullerton observed that Wood "talked out of the corner of his mouth and used language that would have made a steeple horse jockey blush. . . . He challenged all opponents and dilated upon their pedigrees."

Wood didn't endear himself to his older teammates by his work on the field either. In both 1909 and 1910 he'd missed part of the season because of injury. His absence in 1909 had been self-induced: he hurt his foot wrestling with Speaker during spring training and missed half the year. As he sat out day after day his older teammates concluded that he was soft, and late in the 1910 season there were rumors that John I. Taylor considered Wood a malcontent and was thinking about trading him away. He may have been thinking that again during spring training in 1911 as the team worked itself into shape in

Redondo Beach, California, and Wood hurt himself once more—this time while fooling around on the slide at the pool in the Redondo bathhouse. Wood had talent to burn and threw hard, but he was wild. Over his first few seasons he often pitched just well enough to lose, then blamed others for his defeat, and he often complained of a sore arm. Entering the 1911 season, he was at a crossroads in his career— he had yet to back up his tough talk on the pitcher's mound. He was getting a reputation as a player with a hundred-thousand-dollar arm but only a ten-cent head.

Speaker shared Wood's attitudes and personality, but had an easier time fitting in. At age twenty-two, in 1910, he had hit .340. His stellar play was impossible to deny, and even among the KCs he rapidly earned a kind of grudging respect and was given a wide berth. His friendship with Wood may well have been responsible for keeping the pitcher in Boston after the 1910 season. The two men were roommates, and there was no need to rile the team's best player.

Not that the KCs were, on the whole, any more endearing. Catcher Bill Carrigan earned his nickname "Rough" by being one of the toughest players in the league. Base runners slid into home plate at their own peril, for Carrigan never gave way, on or off the field. In one celebrated incident Detroit outfielder George Moriarty announced his intention to come home and then did, prompting Carrigan, despite being outweighed by thirty pounds, not only to stop him cold but to spit in his eye afterward for daring to test him.

Apart from their time on the field, the two groups rarely mingled. They were just different and came from different cultures. The KCs were more working class, went to Mass together, and found Hibernian Boston familiar, while the Masons were more independent-minded and stuck with each other. Still, a few players defied convention. Duffy Lewis, although a Californian, was also Catholic and a rambunctious member of the KCs. Larry Gardner, despite his New England heritage, was aligned with the Masons, and Harry Hooper, a Catholic, had friends in both factions. American League rules at the time disallowed dressing at the ballpark so that the sight of players traveling to the game in uniform would help attract a crowd. Red Sox players generally gathered up Huntington Avenue at the Putnam Hotel—"Put's," a hotel and rooming house where twenty Red Sox players boarded during the regular season—to prepare for the game. They left together but traveled to the ballpark in separate groups, some walking the short distance and others going by carriage, usually divided between the Masons and the KCs. Even the long train rides that marked every road trip failed to bring the players together—compared to the hard-drinking, hard-partying KCs, the Masons were near-teetotalers. The two groups would not even mingle to play cards. The more pious in both groups imagined that only practitioners of their religion could enter heaven and suspected members of the other faction of all manner of diabolical behavior. Virtually every move the team made was seen through this lens by at least a few players in each group, from selecting a team captain to deciding who would pitch or even pinch-hit. They were a team in name only.

The situation became so dire between the two groups that the tension may well have played a part in first baseman and Mason Jake Stahl's retirement from the game following the 1910 season, a year in which, at age thirty, he had led the Red Sox in home runs, triples, and RBIs. Although he took a lucrative executive position at a Chicago bank for his father-in-law, the circumstances of his return in 1912 and his dismissal in 1913 suggest that the religious friction on the club may well have played at least some part in his initial decision to leave baseball for banking. At the same time John I. Taylor made several circumspect statements concerning the makeup of his team and his determination to rid the squad of troublemakers, a threat that underscored the level of dissension on the club.

Yet even in the midst of such disarray, there was some hope. The Red Sox were by far the youngest team in the major leagues. Only one regular, infielder Charlie Wagner, was thirty years of age or older, and entering the 1911 season, only two regulars in the lineup—Carrigan and first baseman Clyde Engle—were over twenty-five. During the 1911 season both Harry Hooper and Duffy Lewis hit .300 for the first time and showed signs of becoming as good offensively as they were defensively, while twenty-one-year-old Joe Wood, although still pitching .500 baseball, stayed relatively healthy all year, twirled a no-hitter, and struck out nearly a batter an inning. If the club could just come together on the field, they seemed destined to continue to improve. There was, at least potentially, a lot to look forward to.

But John I. Taylor either didn't see it, couldn't see it, or didn't care anymore. For more than a year he and his father had slowly been extricating themselves from active management of the Red Sox. While they didn't want the responsibility of ownership, they did want to retain a chunk of the profits.

Their solution was ingenious. For several years Ban Johnson had been convincing and cajoling American team owners into building newer, bigger, and safer ballparks. Not only were the old wooden parks safety hazards, prone to fires and increasingly difficult and expensive to insure, but the use of wood restricted the size of the grandstands. Once a wood structure reached thirty or forty feet in height it became so heavy that the need for more support beams and joists dramatically cut into the amount of usable space that could be created. It became ever more difficult to provide more seats where fans wanted them the most—around the infield and behind home plate.

In the spring of 1911 Johnson gave the press a statement that was more or less a "state of the game" address. He made clear that one of his goals was for each city to have a ballpark that included

> well kept fields of such dimensions that a fast runner may complete
> a circuit of the bases on a fair hit to their limits in any direction, and
> sited with mammoth fireproof stands, crowded to their capacity....
> In another year—two more at the farthest—every scheduled game
> in the American League will be contested on grounds owned by the
> home club and provided with concrete and steel structures for the
> accommodations of the patrons.

Less than a week later that desire was underscored when the old wooden park in Washington was severely damaged by a fire.

The Taylors were more than agreeable to meeting Johnson's goal and building a new ballpark—as his contract negotiations with Harry Hooper intimated, John I., in fact, had been meeting with an architect periodically since at least 1908. Besides, the lease was up at Huntington Avenue, and as Boston sportswriter A. H. C. Mitchell reported earlier in the summer of 1911 in *Sporting Life*, on some days as many as 5,000 fans turned out for the game and then went home disappointed, for the Huntington Avenue grandstand seated only 2,500 people and many potential spectators refused to attend if they had to sit in open stands elsewhere, exposed to the elements and lower-paying riffraff. On such days, wrote Mitchell, "all the seats were sold days in advance and speculators reaped a harvest."

In June 1911 Taylor announced that he hoped to build his new park on just over eight acres of land in the Fenway section of Boston, just east of Brookline Avenue, bounded by Lansdowne Street to the north, Ipswich Street and property owned by the Fenway Garage Company to the east, and Jersey Street to the west, a plot of land first made coherent in 1898 when Jersey Street was first laid out. General Taylor had acquired rights to the property some four months earlier, on February 26, at a public auction for $120,000. Known as "the Dana Lands," the property was part of a parcel that had originally been owned by attorney Francis Dana, a native of Charlestown, a leader of the Sons of Liberty, a delegate to the Massachusetts Provincial Congress in 1774, a member of the Continental Congress in 1777, and in 1778 a signer of the Articles of Confederation. As of yet there was no street bordering the southern edge of the property, nor would there be until Van Ness Street was laid out simultaneous to the building of the ballpark. The first public drawings of the park, in fact, do not show the street at all, as early plans were simply to extend Ipswich Street past the park. John I. Taylor eventually named the new street after his wife, Cornelia Van Ness, but the name would not become official until after the 1912 season. Before that it would be popularly known as "Auto Road": it provided access to what would be a small parking lot used by players and fans. Prior to the Taylors' plan to build a new ballpark, there had been tentative plans to develop the land for residential use by laying several streets between Van Ness and Lansdowne, but the ballpark halted these plans (see illustration 1).

Privately, however, the Taylors still placed some conditions on their willingness to build a new park. For one, they did not want to go into debt to finance construction. Second, the location of the park had to serve two purposes: not only did it need to be convenient for the fans, but it needed to be convenient for the Taylors. The family and others in their social circle owned a great deal of land in Boston, particularly in the Back Bay and the Fenway. With the building of the Opera House, the Museum of Fine Arts, and other cultural institutions, as well as the completion of Olmsted's park, real estate in the area was rapidly increasing in value. Property values between Massachusetts Avenue and Longwood Avenue, encompassing both sides of Huntington Avenue, had risen more than 50 percent in the previous two years, and as Charles Restarick wrote in the *Globe* in December 1911, "The main defect in the Fenway up to this year has been the lack of building operations in this vicinity." The new ballpark would spearhead a change in those conditions. The Taylors formed the Fenway Realty Company to market their holdings, and a ballpark in the area would help give the area a new identity—as yet the only commercial use of the "Fenway" name was by a line of chocolates. The city of Boston, whose major officeholders and officials traditionally received free season passes, had already promised a convenient trolley and subway line.

While the Taylors could easily have financed the new park themselves, ever since buying the team they had paid a healthy premium each year to the Boston Elevated Company, which owned the land on which the Huntington Avenue Grounds was built. The arrangement was not lost on the Taylors—the company had probably made just as much money off the team as they had, all with far less risk and many, many fewer headaches. That apparently gave the father and son an idea.

They decided to sell the Red Sox—or at least part of the team—and turn the day-to-day management of the club over to someone else. The club was already profitable, but the real carrot on the stick in any sale was a new ballpark, which would not only promise increased revenue for the new owner but allow the Taylors to use the proceeds of the sale of the club to finance the new park themselves on land they owned and then lease the facility back to the club. That meant that even after they sold the team they would still participate in any increase in profits, as well as pay rent to themselves and receive an annual payment for the park from a new investor. There was virtually no way they could lose money on the deal.

Naturally, Ban Johnson already had some potential buyers lined up, all of whom were close personal friends. Washington manager Jimmy McAleer, a tall, rail-thin ex-outfielder who played with National League Cleveland for most of the 1890s, led the list. McAleer, known as a great fielder but not much of a hitter, had thrived during the era of "inside baseball," when offense was generated by the bunt, the stolen base, and the hit-and-run play. For him to become owner of the Red Sox would require its own kind of "inside baseball."

McAleer first ingratiated himself to his master in 1901, when Johnson asked the recently retired Youngstown, Ohio, native to serve as manager of Cleveland in the American League's inaugural season. Later, when Johnson went into direct competition with the National League and declared that his league was its equal, McAleer assisted Johnson in his player raids on the National League and in 1902 was rewarded by being named manager of the AL's new team in St. Louis.

McAleer had since followed Johnson's directives as if he were a base runner dutifully following signs flashed by the third-base coach. He soon became one of Johnson's trusted confidants and toadies and even went on hunting excursions with the league president and his personal secretary, Robert McRoy, at Chicago owner Charles Comiskey's Wisconsin hunting lodge. The annual outing often included other movers and shakers in the baseball world and made McAleer part of a select social circle, that of the baseball magnate. He was one of many men who hovered around Johnson, hoping to feast on fallen crumbs. McAleer made it clear that his real goal was not managing a team to the World's Series as much as it was working in the front office as the president and owner of his own team—being around Johnson, he had quickly learned that was where the real money was.

When McAleer first heard that the Taylors were considering selling out, he balked at making a bid when he learned that they planned to retain part of the team. He was tired of being dependent on others. But over the course of the summer, as Johnson periodically checked in on the Taylors and their plans for a new park, McAleer slowly came back into the fold. In reality, he was in no position to set conditions, for he didn't have enough of his own money to buy the team outright. He could raise only $50,000, just one-third of the Taylors' asking price.

That was where Johnson's influence came into play. The league president was a master at making sure his owners owed him, both figuratively and financially. Robert McRoy conveniently was able to provide another $25,000, and Johnson had several other Chicago investors lined up waiting in the wings to make up the difference. They included C. H. Randle, a director of the South Side State Bank, and H. W. Mahan, founder of both the Drexel and South Side Banks and chairman of the board for the Washington Park National Bank. Mahan was no small-time banker, but a major mover in Chicago who listed his home address in the alumni directory of the University of Illinois as simply "the South Side State Bank." It just so happened that Mahan's daughter, Jeanie, had recently married Jake Stahl, the former player-manager of the Senators and ex–first baseman for the Red Sox. Stahl had retired from baseball after his marriage and was working for his father-in-law as vice president of the Washington Park National Bank. Although the involvement of the Chicago men in the sale was unofficial and nothing more than a rumor, an interesting alliance was beginning to take shape.

None of the men were Bostonians, like the Taylors, but they were all Johnson loyalists, which was even more important. And Johnson was savvy enough to realize that McAleer's and McRoy's surnames would play well in the Hibernian Hub. By early September, as the Sox slumped in the standings, the two groups began to negotiate in earnest.

The Red Sox appeared ready to pack it in. Just a few days after dropping the doubleheader to Philadelphia on September 1, Boston dropped another one to New York, launching the Yankees into a tie for third place. Even worse, they lost catcher Bill Carrigan, who broke his right ankle sliding into second on a force play. After the contest John I. was so angry and so upset—fifth- or sixth-place teams were not worth as much as a third- or even fourth-place squad—that he released pitchers Walter Nagle and Eddie Karger, who had combined to lose the second game, 5–1. Nagle, a Californian, had only recently been acquired, but Karger, a Texan, had pitched more than three hundred innings over the past two seasons and in 1907 had hurled a perfect game for the Cardinals, albeit in only seven innings owing to a prior agreement between the two teams.

The move sent shock waves through the Boston clubhouse, especially among the Masons, and particularly after Taylor announced that the two pitchers would be replaced by Buck O'Brien, a player as Irish as his name. The spitball artist and native of Brockton, Massachusetts, had recently had some success with minor league Denver.

With Wood laid up again with a sore arm, the ball club did not respond with honor. In a story headlined "Fading Is the Last Chance of the Crippled Sox," *Boston Post* beat writer Paul Shannon accurately noted that "their ability to fight seems gone . . . the former prides of the Hub are nestled lovingly in the vicinity of sixth place . . . with the 'also rans.'" Manager Patsy Donovan threw in the towel and began experimenting with kids. By September 13, when the Sox fell to McAleer's club, 3–1, in Washington, Shannon's observation proved to be prophetic. Boston had fallen all the way to sixth place, four games below .500 and more than twenty games behind first-place Philadelphia. The only bright spot had been O'Brien. On September 9, only one day after crossing the country from Denver, he shut out Philadelphia, 2–0, and a few days later won another game in relief.

The victories represented quite an accomplishment for the pitcher, who at age twenty-nine was ancient for a rookie. In fact, he had only been playing professionally for two seasons. Prior to that he had been toiling in a Brockton shoe factory pitching semipro ball until he learned to throw a spitball—a pitch that drops dramatically just as it reaches the plate. The new pitch suddenly made him stand out and in 1909 finally earned him a professional contract. He had received a tryout with the Sox the previous spring, but a sore finger had led the team abruptly to release him in Denver on the way back east. Shortly after joining the Sox in 1911, O'Brien heard some of his teammates discussing their collegiate backgrounds and offered that he, too, had earned a degree, "a BS from Brockton—boots and shoes." The KCs welcomed the fun-loving, self-deprecating former factory worker like a long-lost brother, but the Masons mourned Karger's departure and thought O'Brien was a flash in the pan.

Meanwhile, Taylor, McAleer, and Johnson were trying to get a deal done, and even though they had a basic agreement, the final details had to be roughed out in person. Both the Sox and the Senators had a few off-days, so after McAleer's club deposited Boston in sixth place, McAleer hightailed it to Boston.

He was met there by Johnson and McRoy, and they checked into one of Boston's finest hotels, the Parker House, where the following morning they received a visit from the Taylors. The party then retired to the opulent Algonquin Club on Commonwealth Avenue in the Back Bay, a private club that members still tout as "a peaceful haven for Boston's leading citizens to conduct business [and] socialize with family and friends."

At 2:00 p.m., they took a break from the fine china, and everyone went together to the South End Grounds, where they watched the first-place Giants beat up on Boston's pathetic National League franchise—everyone, that is, except Ban Johnson, who still found the notion of stepping into a National League park during the regular season completely odious. The Red Sox got into Boston by train at 3:00 p.m., and many of them went straight to the ballpark as well. The Giants, led by feisty manager John McGraw and Christy Mathewson, one of the greatest pitchers in the game and probably baseball's most admired player, were on the verge of winning the first of what would become three consecutive pennants. Most observers considered them the best team in baseball, and they were impressive, battering the Boston club for the fourth straight time, winning 13–9.

After the game the group met Johnson back at the Algonquin Club and resumed the negotiations. Most of their time was not spent crunching numbers but squinting over blueprints. The Taylors invited their architect, James McLaughlin, to give a presentation about the new ballpark, sweetening the pot and, they hoped, whetting the appetite of Johnson, McAleer, and McRoy to get a deal done.

As McLaughlin gave his presentation the men were indeed impressed. The grandstand at the new park was designed to hold nearly 11,400 fans. Although that was less than half the number that baseball's biggest existing park, the double-decked Polo Grounds, could hold, it was nearly five times the number that could sit in the grandstand at the Huntington Avenue Grounds. There would be room for as many as another 8,000 in a separate, roofed pavilion and space for perhaps 5,000 more fans in the center-field bleachers, making the park's official seated capacity 24,400. Even if the new team failed to draw much more than the half-million or so fans who attended games at the Huntington Avenue Grounds in 1911, the Sox would be able to charge them much, much more than before. The plans, although modest in many ways, still spelled profit, and that was a language everyone understood (see illustration 2).

Still, there were *t*'s to cross and *i*'s to dot, cigars to smoke and cables to be sent back and forth to the Chicago investors, so it took another day, until the afternoon of September 15, for a final agreement to be reached. By then McAleer had to rush off to rejoin his team before missing any games, while Johnson and McRoy hustled back to Chicago, smugly satisfied.

The sale was announced by proxy in a written statement distributed by the Taylors. It read:

> Negotiations connected with the sale of an interest in the Boston American League Baseball Club have resulted in the purchase of a half interest by James R. McAleer of Washington and Robert McRoy of Chicago.
>
> As both these gentlemen have been actively engaged elsewhere they will not be able to come to Boston until the beginning of the year 1912. At that time they will come to Boston to live and join in the active management of the Red Sox. Both are versed in baseball and have marked ability, and they ought to greatly strengthen the organization.
>
> Plans for a new ball park which will be a credit to Boston will now be formulated and the work pushed ahead at a rapid rate.

RED SOX DEAL GOES THROUGH
McAleer And McRoy Buy Half-Interest

In English that meant that because McAleer was still the manager of the Senators he would not take over until the club was officially reorganized under the laws of the state of New Jersey, where the Red Sox were officially incorporated, but in practical terms he would begin making most decisions as soon as the season was over. The sale price for the half-share was reportedly $150,000, meaning that the Taylors' original $135,000 investment in the team had more than doubled. While they would still retain a half-interest in the team, they would essentially become silent partners. They would, however, build and own a new ballpark. While that plan had previously been just a rumor, it would now become a reality. The ink was hardly dry before work began on the new park, beginning with clearing the Jersey Street property. The site was virtually empty, home to only a small church and the Park Riding School on Ipswich Street. Although a series of garages occupied the north side of Lansdowne Street, the lots immediately to the west, south, and east were completely unoccupied, the land as open as the Great Plains.

The only other item of interest concerned the manager of the team. It was widely believed that Donovan was done and that McAleer— or perhaps just McRoy and Johnson—would name a new manager. It was not long before the name on everyone's lips was Jake Stahl. His return would solve two issues. Upon his retirement he had still been one of the best first basemen in the league, and the current Sox first baseman, Clyde Engle, was the lightest-hitting man on the team. Even though there had been no public announcement concerning Stahl's investment in the club, it did not take long for the rumor mill to get going, and McAleer acknowledged that Stahl "is the man I want and I intend to see him after the World's Series is over." McAleer even admitted that "I have sunk line, sinker and hook into the Red Sox club and if my investment is not a success I am stone broke." Having Stahl on board would be some insurance against that, but when asked, the banker remained coy about returning. Owning a piece of the team was not payment enough for Stahl. He still wanted a contract that recognized his on-field talents and had no intention of going to Boston to lose either baseball games or money.

Meanwhile the Red Sox, as if relieved to be freed from the Taylor regime, suddenly and somewhat inexplicably began playing their best baseball of the year. In a doubleheader on September 16 against Cleveland, Wood and O'Brien both tossed shutouts, sparking a run that saw the Red Sox win thirteen of their final nineteen games, including their final six, the longest streak of the season. The streak lifted the club from below .500 and sixth place to a final record of 78-75, fourth place, as over the final three days of the season the team managed to vault past both New York and Chicago.

While some of their success had to do with the opposition—they avoided the first-place A's and everyone else was merely playing out the string—some was due to the pitching of O'Brien and the sudden emergence of Joe Wood. He seemed to be inspired not only by O'Brien's performance but also by the release of Karger, Carrigan's injury, and some rest. Before shutting out Cleveland, he had gone nearly two weeks since his last appearance on the mound, and he then went another nine days before pitching again, beating St. Louis 9–2 and striking out eleven. A week later, against the Yankees, he was even better. Despite the fact that the game was called after eight innings because of darkness, he shut out the New Yorkers and struck out thirteen, the highest total in the league that season and a performance he punctuated by striking out both the first three hitters he faced and the final three. No one noticed, but over the last three weeks of the season the Red Sox were the best team in baseball.

That was not all that went unnoticed. On September 25, over on Jersey Street, work began on the new ballpark. The club didn't bother with holding a grand ceremony marked by speeches or politicians or ribbon-cutting or golden shovels. With opening day barely five months off, that would have been a luxury, since there was work— a lot of it—to be done. Workers from Charlie Logue's construction company got busy clearing the site, grading the property, erecting a construction house, and moving equipment and materials on-site as surveyors began laying out the foundation and other structures, driving stakes into the ground, and marking them with bright strips of ribbon.

On September 29 papers were passed that transferred the property from the Taylors to the Fenway Realty Trust, whose trustees included both General Taylor and John I., as well as Ashton Carr, the vice president and treasurer of the State Street Bank, and Arthur Wise, an attorney whose firm bought the bonds that were issued to finance the building of the park and would soon make them available for purchase. The trust was capitalized to $300,000, divided into

3,000 shares worth $100 each. The mortgage securing $275,000 in nontaxable bonds was recorded on the deed, presumably to provide construction funds in advance of the bond sale.

FOR DEVELOPMENT

Fenway Park, New Home Of Red Sox, Transferred To Three Trustees For Improvement

While the baseball world turned its attention to the pending World's Series between the Giants and the Athletics, on the last day of the season, October 7, the Red Sox played in the Huntington Avenue Grounds for the last time.

Had it been just another game, it never would have been played, for it rained hard the night before and the field was a quagmire. But John I. Taylor had declared it "Kids' Day," promising free admission for children, and several hundred young ruffians took advantage of the offer. They were nearly alone. Most fans held little sentiment toward the old park and chose, in the cold damp weather, to stay away. Only 850 brave souls saw the old park off, and most of those were more interested in clambering beneath the grandstand than watching the game.

Jerome Kelley and his crew did what they could to make the field playable, brooming away puddles and spreading sawdust everywhere. Scattered throughout the stands were a few notable figures who had seen the first game played at the old ballyard, including General Arthur "Hi Hi" Dixwell, who had turned over the first spade of earth when the park was built and whose signature cheer had earned him his nickname. These men mostly chatted among themselves about times gone by, as if oblivious to the ball game on the field.

The game went quickly, taking only eighty-two minutes to complete as Charley Hall kept the Senators at bay and little-used outfielder Olaf Henriksen became the hero of the day with a third-inning, bases-loaded triple that broke the game open. Tris Speaker was carried off the field after an errant pitch hit his leg just below the kneecap, and he was taken back to Put's by ambulance. Joe Riggert knocked out the final Boston hit in the old park, an inside-the-park home run over the center fielder's head in the bottom of the eighth to make the score 8–1. Washington threatened in the ninth, but after Germany Schaefer singled—the last hit at Huntington Avenue—Kid Elberfeld hit a ground ball to Larry Gardner at third. He flipped the ball to second baseman Jack Lewis, and the game was done.

On his typewriter Tim Murnane tapped out an epitaph:

The park was considered one of the best to see a ballgame, as the light was good and the grounds roomy. The old stand and bleachers will soon be torn down and nothing left to show where once fierce battles were fought to the music of loyal fans.

In saying farewell to the Huntington-av Park, it will only mean a welcome to the magnificent new home the Boston Americans will occupy next season in the Back Bay Fens, just as handy as the old park, too . . . Goodby season of 1911. Goodby to the Huntington-av Grounds.

Hello, Fenway Park.

◆ 2 ◆

Hot Stove

The stand is a single deck structure with a roof of mill construction
on a steel frame. The deck is reinforced concrete throughout,
the roof being carried by steel columns bolted to the tops of
reinforced concrete columns carrying the deck. The only wood
used is in the movable folding opera chairs, roof joists, sheathing,
office interiors and screed to which chair legs are attached.

—Engineering Record

I T WAS JUST another job.
As architect James McLaughlin bent over his drafting table in late September and early October of 1911 in his office on Atlantic Avenue and made a few last minor changes to the plans he had worked on, off and on, for more than two years, he probably did not hazard to think that anything about this most recent venture would prove to be of lasting significance. It was just another project, albeit a unique one: he had never designed such a structure before and would never do so again. It was neither the largest nor the most lucrative project of his career, nor the most demanding. During his lifetime it would bring him little acclaim and serve as nothing more than a footnote to his career.

It was perhaps most notable because of the name of his client, General Charles Taylor, and his son, John I., of the *Boston Globe* Taylors. McLaughlin knew that if he pleased them it would certainly help open some doors for other notable clients. Yet that was just as true when McLaughlin dealt with a school committee over the building of a schoolhouse, or a church board over the building of a church or parsonage.

This is not to say that as McLaughlin bent over his table and worked on the design he did not give the project his full attention—he did. His career was just beginning to flourish, and he treated every project with the same care and attention regardless of its size. But this job, a home for the Red Sox, was different from anything McLaughlin had ever done before or would ever do again.

McLaughlin was thirty-seven years old in 1911 and in the last few years had established a reputation as one of Boston's leading young architects. Born James Earnest McLaughlin in October 1873 in Halifax, Nova Scotia, he was the fourth of seven children of Mary and James McLaughlin, both of whom had been born in Ireland. McLaughlin's father was one of the first portrait photographers in Halifax, but after he passed away the family immigrated to Boston, in 1885, settling with thousands of other first- and second-generation Irish in Lower Roxbury when they rented a place on Homestead Street, only two miles south of the Huntington Avenue Grounds. A good student, McLaughlin thrived in his new country. By 1898 he was already trained as a draftsman, but it is unclear precisely how he became an architect. Until the turn of the century few schools provided training in architecture—the Massachusetts Institute of Technology offered the first degree in architecture in 1865. Many architects learned the profession through a combination of apprenticeships, self-study, and even mail-order courses. At any rate, by 1900 the U.S. census listed his occupation as an architect. About the same time he opened his office on Atlantic Avenue under the name James E. McLaughlin, presumably to differentiate his work from that of the notable architect James McLaughlin of Cincinnati.

His Irish heritage served him well, for after the election of Hugh O'Brien as Boston's first Irish mayor in 1884 the Irish took full political control of the city of Boston. Government contracts, which had previously been nearly impossible for anyone with an Irish surname to obtain, suddenly became available. Fear of fire and the cost of insurance for wood-frame buildings, combined with a growing population, inspired a spate of new construction throughout the city, and

McLaughlin was able to take advantage of the situation. In a short time he began to win contracts to design schools and other small municipal buildings, using more modern construction methods based on steel, concrete, and brick instead of wood. McLaughlin generally earned a commission of between $3,000 and $8,000 for each building he designed. But just because McLaughlin designed public buildings did not mean he was a hack—he was a student of architecture, and there was a healthy competition for such projects. McLaughlin followed design trends closely, and his buildings, while classically based, often acknowledged contemporary design trends that set them apart.

Most of his early work demonstrated what was known as the Georgian Revival style and featured predominantly brick exteriors. One job begat another, and in only a few years McLaughlin was well established in his field. In 1908 he married Mary Ratigan, and the couple, who would never have a child, soon took up residence on Reservoir Road in Chestnut Hill. The young architect was not only a good businessman but a good citizen, and he did his civic duty by serving on several charitable boards, most notably those of St. Elizabeth's Hospital and other institutions connected with the Catholic Church. McLaughlin was also active in the Boston Society of Architects.

If McLaughlin had an architectural philosophy, it was this: his buildings were neither pretentious nor florid, but conservative and practical. While McLaughlin's designs were essentially utilitarian, at the same time they were precise, balanced, aesthetically pleasing, and built to last. His structures were, in a sense, organic to themselves— no portion of them appeared superfluous, out of place, or out of proportion. His building materials were purely New England—besides red brick, limestone and local granite dominated the facades of the public buildings he was most known for, yet through the use of subtle raised brick panels, recessed centers, and other strategies, he managed to give the otherwise plain faces textural interest. As he once wrote in an album he created to introduce his firm's work to prospective clients, McLaughlin's goal was to "construct and complete the buildings within the amounts appropriated," to deliver "results that are satisfactory at minimum cost, without sacrificing design, utility or other requirements," and to create a "design in harmony, with . . . carefully designed interiors, and inviting, non-stereotyped exteriors."

Most of his buildings fit well into their surroundings. Little about their design overtly called attention to them; they seemed to have always been there, either as a part of the original building or a part of the neighborhood. That explains why McLaughlin's work, while still on display in virtually every Boston neighborhood and in many other cities and towns in eastern Massachusetts, has been overlooked by architectural scholars. Over time the ubiquitous nature of his work has made it almost invisible, and all but forgotten.

The Taylors became aware of McLaughlin through his work for the city. When McLaughlin was approached by John I. Taylor and first commissioned to design a new ballpark, he was given certain conditions. Although McLaughlin's initial drawings referred to the park by the generic name of "Boston American Base Ball Park," by the fall of 1911 it was common knowledge that the name of the new ballpark would be Fenway Park, for as Taylor explained, "It's in the Fenway section of Boston, isn't it?" All Boston ballparks to date had been commonly known by their geographical location, such as the Dartmouth Street Park (aka Union Park), which served as the home field for the Union Association club in 1884; the Congress Street Grounds, which was occupied by several teams from 1890 to 1896; the South End Grounds; and the Huntington Avenue Grounds. There was no reason to treat the new ballpark any differently. Besides, the name was already familiar. Owing to its location adjacent to the Fens, the Huntington Avenue Grounds itself had occasionally been referred to as "the Fenway Park," even within the pages of the *Globe*. Officially calling the new place "Fenway Park" was like putting on a comfortable old shoe.

Other conditions were more germane to McLaughlin's task. The park had to fit within the confines of the eight-plus-acre plot of land acquired by the Taylors. For continuity purposes, the playing field had to retain a similar orientation to the sun as the Huntington Avenue Grounds. Had that not been the case, it would have been possible to place home plate either in what is now the right-field corner or, less likely, the left-field corner. In either case right field, not left field, would have been Fenway's short porch (see illustration 1).

For insurance, safety, and economic reasons, the main grandstand had to be fireproof, made out of concrete and steel. Even though concrete construction, loosely defined, had been in use since the Roman Empire, steel-reinforced concrete construction, which allowed concrete to be used on structures much larger than before, had only been in use since the 1850s. Only in the last decade had the technology been developed that was eventually used in Fenway Park, which used reinforced concrete to create columns and girders that supported concrete floor slabs, resulting in a fireproof superstructure that was strong but also much lighter and cheaper than all-steel construction.

None of these issues gave McLaughlin any cause for concern. His work for the city of Boston had utilized modern concrete-and-steel, fireproof building techniques, including the use of reinforcing steel and concrete forms. And there was more than enough room on Taylor's parcel to site a ball field, including seating areas and office space for the club. The outfield dimensions were of absolutely no concern whatsoever. Had there been any thought that the field was too confining—particularly in left field—the field's orientation could have been slightly reconfigured to satisfy those fears, or a larger lot could have been obtained. But it was plenty deep for the era—the accepted world record for hitting a baseball had been set a few years before in Cincinnati by Reds outfielder Mike Mitchell, who, using a fungo bat, managed to drive a ball 413 feet, 8½ inches in the air. But in reality, under game conditions in the Dead Ball Era, any drive much more than 300 feet in the air was considered extraordinary, and few outfielders played more than 250 feet from home plate. In Cincinnati's new park, Redland Field, the fence nearest to home plate was still 360 feet away, a distance so great, according to one paper that "it is doubtful a ball will ever be hit over the fence."

Under these conditions the size of the lot selected by the Taylors was more than sufficient to hold a ballpark. The shape of the plot of land and the resulting ballpark was not, as John Updike once famously, but incorrectly, described it, "a compromise between Man's Euclidian determinations and Nature's beguiling irregularities," for at the time Fenway was built, apart from a few buildings on Lansdowne Street, no other buildings bordered the parcel. Fenway Park's footprint was created by a surveyor's transit, not by livestock wandering the streets. The Fenway Park site was surrounded on three sides by raw land and empty, undeveloped lots. In the end the new park was built from the borders of the property inward simply to use all available space, not because concerns about the dimensions of the field required that it be so spacious. Had there been any desire to make Fenway Park symmetrical, it could have easily been done. The notion that Fenway is misshapen owing to the restriction of surrounding streets is a perception that developed long after the park was built, when the "lively ball" came into play, the game expanded, and the city grew to surround the park, making Fenway appear today as if it is crammed into too small a space.

Yet over the course of McLaughlin's discussions with Taylor about the new park, the club owner, who in turn was discussing the project with Ban Johnson and others, kept vacillating over one significant issue. Both during the original construction and during the Fenway Park reconstruction of 1933–34, the press reported that the original foundations for the park were built to support a second deck, yet as originally designed and built the park featured a grandstand with only a single tier. Taylor probably went back and forth on the issue, weighing the cost of a second deck against its economic benefit, before reaching a compromise with his architect. Although McLaughlin's final design would include only a single tier of stands, the foundations put in place would be sufficient to support a second deck in the event that the club ever decided to add one in the future. That single decision, more than any other, has allowed Fenway Park to remain viable to this day, for it has allowed the park to evolve in ways that would have otherwise been impossible.

In Boston's Back Bay and the Fenway, building foundations were not insignificant, and indeed, their design and construction remain challenging even today. The amount of filled land and the height of the water table make building there complicated. Inadequate or ill-designed foundations can sink and settle in the water-laden earth, causing entire structures to become unstable. To counteract the effect, many buildings built before the turn of the century, like the McKim Building of the Boston Public Library, were supported, not on stone or concrete, but on wooden pilings set below the water table to prevent dry rot. Other buildings essentially float on a sealed foundation bathtub or were built on caissons, a sealed watertight structure that allows excavation to take place until a stable surface is reached.

Fortunately, Fenway Park was not built on filled land. Still, an abnormally high water table due to the proximity of the Charles River made the park's foundations an early concern. Like those of most other structures in the area, Fenway's foundations were probably overengineered to compensate for the ground conditions.

Taylor also pared his ballpark back in other areas. In a sense McLaughlin was directed to design only half a park. Taylor's main concern was with the park's best, most lucrative seats, those that could be built around the infield. He did not think it was worthwhile to build a similarly grand structure for the cheaper seats that looked out over the outfield. And given that he was in the process of selling the team, it would not have been particularly cost-effective either. He was in no rush to spend any money that would not pay off for him. As a result his investment in the park was designed to produce the greatest number of high-paying seats with the least expenditure possible. For that reason, as originally designed by McLaughlin, the grandstand abruptly stopped only halfway to the outfield fence in left field, at the end of what is today section 27. There was room, if needed, for additional stands to be built farther down the baseline at some later date, a possibility that the grandstand design already accounted for. Down the right-field line the grandstand also came to an abrupt stop at the end of what is now section 14. But since the dimensions of the property were more spacious on that side, a second set of covered stands featuring a concrete-and-steel roofed pavilion above wooden bleacher-type seats was built down the baseline, angled ever so slightly toward the infield and meeting the outfield fence just inside fair territory in right field. This "pavilion," as it was known, featured seats that were cheaper than those in the grandstand and set at a steeper pitch. It was also separated from the main grandstand by an alleyway—not unlike a moat—both to prevent lower-paying fans in the pavilion from reaching the higher-paying seats in the grandstand that were closer to the action and, in the event of a fire, to isolate that structure from the main grandstand.

Under these restrictions, McLaughlin did what he could to create a handsome structure. He clearly studied other ballparks and stadiums built during the era, for Fenway Park echoes ballpark construction elements and design features then in use elsewhere. The structural design of the grandstand was inspired by the reinforced-concrete grandstands of new football stadiums at Syracuse University and Harvard University, while for visual inspiration he turned to the ball parks in the two major league baseball cities closest to Boston—New York and Philadelphia—and Cincinnati's Redland Field, which was being built at the same time as Fenway. The New York Giants' Polo Grounds featured the largest concrete grandstand in baseball, while the Yankees' Hilltop Park (officially known as "American League Ballpark"), although built of wood, featured separate, uncovered pavilions, in concept very similar to what McLaughlin eventually built. Also influential was Shibe Park, the home of the Philadelphia Athletics, built in 1909 and touted as "the largest and best appointed baseball park in the world." The exterior of that park looked, not like a ballpark, but like some grand building: it featured a French Renaissance facade consisting of brick and arches and a Beaux Arts–inspired tower at the park's main entrance, which sat on a street corner directly in line with the pitcher's mound and home plate. Extensive wings that stretched down both streets, parallel to the baseline, contained the grandstand, and the building and the grandstand shared the same roof.

Unfortunately, such a grand structure was not practical in Boston. The construction time frame was too narrow to allow the erection of such a large building, and the shape of the lot, the orientation of the field, and the fact that the parcel did not sit on a square corner made the construction of a building like the one in Philadelphia impossible. Yet McLaughlin still managed to make part of the ballpark look like a building.

His solution was to create an illusion. Only a portion of the structure, a triangular-shaped wing that housed the team offices, would look like a building when viewed from the street. The remainder would look, well, like the grandstand of a ballpark, albeit one faced with brick and featuring open arches behind the upper stands. The wing containing the offices would also be off-center to the larger structure, not evenly balanced behind home plate but down the third-base line, essentially parallel to that side of the infield. The ballpark's front door, in effect, would actually be a side entrance.

It was not a particularly elegant solution, but then again, given

Taylor's requirements, there was very little room for elegance. Still McLaughlin tried to come up with an aesthetic response. The only other area where McLaughlin could express any real creativity was on the facade of the office wing that faced Jersey Street.

Beginning in 1901, the influential furniture maker Gustav Stickley, a proponent of the Arts and Crafts style, began designing homes. The designs of the Wisconsin-born child of German immigrants, who probably never attended a professional baseball game in his life, would nonetheless prove to be an inspiration for Fenway Park.

Stickley featured his designs in his magazine, *The Craftsman*, and these homes soon became known by an architectural style of their own—Craftsman. Craftsman-style homes were usually built with materials native to the region, and their decorative details often depended on the exposure of structural elements. The variety of these structural elements, combined with the various building materials, created textures that were revealed under changing light conditions, creating interest in surfaces that might otherwise appear bland.

Over the course of McLaughlin's early career the influence of the Arts and Crafts movement became more and more pronounced, for even as he built structures that can correctly be identified as Georgian Revival and, later, as in the Commonwealth Armory, Gothic Revival, his materials and ornamental use of texture on the Jersey Street facade echo the Arts and Crafts and Craftsman aesthetics.

For the veneer of the office facade McLaughlin chose Tapestry Brick, a patented, rough-faced red brick design made by Fiske and Company of New York, and a Stickley favorite, but one rarely used on the exteriors of his homes. Not only did the dark red brick provide a nice contrast with lighter-colored building materials, but the rough face was inviting, changed under differing light conditions, and could be treated like a mosaic and arranged in design patterns, either alone or in combination with concrete.

When the park was first built, it is important to recall, there were no buildings across the street or trees to block the sun. The building faced southward and thus was exposed to an ever-changing display of light as the sun crossed the sky every day. The face of the building was designed to take advantage of these changing conditions.

Although it would be incorrect to say that Fenway Park is a Craftsman building—its architecture is far too eclectic and utilitarian to fall easily within a single definition—it nevertheless exhibits elements and echoes of the Arts and Crafts and Craftsman movements. McLaughlin might also have been inspired by the nearby Fenway Studio Building, artists' studios and residences built in 1905 at 30 Ipswich Street, an influential building whose ornamentation architectural historians have determined is derived from the Arts and Crafts movement.

It was a fortunate choice. The facade, while handsome, does not call attention to itself, yet by incorporating such forward-looking design elements, it has aged without becoming dated. In contrast, Shibe Park's French Renaissance facade, even when new, looked like a product of the previous century. Fenway, even today, seems merely quaint.

McLaughlin used one more sleight of hand in regard to the scale of the park that has helped preserve the charm of Fenway Park over time. When Jersey Street was first laid out, the roadbed was raised to keep it from flooding, leaving land on both sides of the street—including the plot upon which Fenway Park sits today—approximately ten feet lower than the street. Rather than see the difference in elevation as an obstacle, McLaughlin used it. The Jersey Street office facade rises only thirty feet above street level, capped with a three-foot-high false wall that increases in height to nearly nine feet at the top of Fenway Park's "nameplate" on a cement panel above the park's main entrance.

Yet inside the park the roof of the original grandstand was *forty* feet above field level—one enters the park and travels ten feet down to the field. It seems impossible from outside, but the office floors on the second floor of the team offices are at the same exact level as the wide promenade at the top of the grandstand. The effect helped maintain an exterior scale that appears in tune with nearby neighborhoods, evoking a nearly residential feel, and is much smaller than the scale of the grandstand itself. Moreover, moving from the street through the gate and into the park feels like entering a completely new space, one far different in scale and dimension than that of the surrounding streets outside (see illustration 1).

As McLaughlin sat at his desk early in the fall of 1911, however, his ballpark was still nothing more than a pile of drawings. Now that the ownership issue had finally been decided, the task was to turn those plans into reality. The Taylors had already hired the Osborn Engineering Company of Cleveland and civil engineer L. Kopczynski of the Concrete and Expanded Metal Construction Company of Cambridgeport, Massachusetts, to provide engineering and other needed technical expertise. Osborn had worked on several other concrete-and-steel ballparks and was an obvious choice to help translate McLaughlin's sketches into sound and detailed plans. Kopczynski was familiar with local contractors, and his company's workers were among the most experienced reinforced-concrete workers in Boston. The New England Structural Steel Corporation of Everett, Massachusetts, was already at work fabricating steel and would provide the ironworkers needed on the project.

To provide extra manpower and oversee construction Taylor selected Charles Logue and the Charles Logue Building Company to serve as the general contractor. Like McLaughlin, Logue was an immigrant, a native of Derry, Ireland. Stowing away at age thirteen, he landed in Newfoundland before making his way to Nova Scotia. While boarding there with a family, he tried to break up a dispute and was shot in the hand, losing a finger. He returned to Ireland, where he learned carpentry, and then immigrated again, this time legally, to Boston in 1882. He formed his own company in 1890, just in time to take advantage of the Irish takeover of Boston's political machine and the resulting flood of building contracts suddenly accessible to Irish firms. A large man with a thick beard and forearms that spoke of a life of labor, Logue did good work at an honest price and soon earned the trust of those who held the power in Boston politics.

In recent decades it has become something of a cliché to refer to Fenway Park in religious terms, as a kind of shrine. Yet the observation is in some ways accurate, because to Charles Logue building was something he did in the service of God. The commissioner of public school buildings in Boston under his close friend Mayor John "Honey Fitz" Fitzgerald, Logue and his wife had sixteen children, including two sons who became priests and two daughters who became nuns, and they were lauded by the Church for having such a large and exemplary family. Logue became close to Cardinal William O'Connell and was perhaps best known as a builder for the Archdiocese of Boston. He supervised the construction of dozens of churches in and around Boston, as well as many buildings on the campuses of the Catholic universities Boston College and Holy Cross in nearby Worcester, Massachusetts. A pious man, Logue attended Mass every day and died in a church, succumbing to a heart attack and passing away in the arms of his son while working on the scaffolding of St. Mary's Catholic Church in Dedham, Massachusetts.

He may well have been selected to serve as the general contractor for Fenway Park owing to his close relationship with O'Connell— the archdiocese owned a sizable property almost adjacent to Fenway Park on Ipswich Street, and it was both good policy and good politics in Boston to stay on good terms with the Church. Although Sunday baseball was banned, the ball club lusted after these lucrative dates and at some point in the future would need the blessing of the archdiocese if the restriction was ever to be lifted. It just made sense to keep the Church happy.

Logue and James McLaughlin got on well with each other, Logue providing the practical solutions to the structural and aesthetic demands of McLaughlin's design, while McLaughlin ensured that Taylor's wishes were reflected in the final product. Neither man was either hot-tempered or impatient, and from a construction standpoint Fenway Park was not overly challenging. It was like working on any other building.

NEW HOME OF THE RED SOX; PLAN IDEAL IN EQUIPMENT AND LOCATION

Baseball Park Will Contain 365,308 Square Feet Of Land With Stands Of The Most Approved Type

As the days grew shorter in October McLaughlin spent less and less time in his office, at least during daytime hours. Most of his time was spent at the ballpark overseeing his project, huddled with engineers and foremen around a potbellied stove to stave off the seasonal chill in one of two cramped construction shanties built in foul territory between the fenced-off infield and the first-base grandstand.

Boston's fans and players also prepared to spend the winter hud-

dled around the stove, for as soon as the players made a final visit to
John I. Taylor to pay their respects and pick up their final paychecks,
the "Hot Stove League" began in earnest. The new ownership and a
new ballpark were only the first changes that would take place before
the Red Sox took the field to open the 1912 season.

As soon as they collected their paychecks, most Red Sox players
scattered. Not a single player called Boston home in the off-season.
For some, like Duffy Lewis and Harry Hooper, it took nearly a week
to travel to their homes on the West Coast.

The last two players to leave Boston were Bill Carrigan and Tris
Speaker. They had been left behind at Put's to convalesce. Carrigan's
broken leg was still in a cast—he had not left the hotel in weeks—
and Speaker was still laid up by the pitch he took off his lower leg in
the season finale. It was awkward for the two men, who were forced
by circumstances to share an apartment for about a week, but in the
long run it may have been for the best. Without the other Masons
and KCs to egg them on, the enmity between the two took too much
energy to sustain, and with each man hobbled, they were dependent
on one another. Carrigan finally had his cast changed on October 10
and was allowed to begin to move about on crutches, but it would be
another three weeks until doctors would allow him to travel to his
home in Lewiston, Maine. Speaker, meanwhile, recovered rapidly and
was looking forward to the World's Series. The *Globe* had signed him
up to ghostwrite a column on the series. In truth, that meant he had
to do little more than watch the Series and nod in agreement with
whatever the *Globe* man wrote under his name, but it was easy money.

He was not the only Boston player for whom the postseason meant
opportunity. With a week between the end of the regular season for
the Athletics and the start of the World's Series, the American League
champion Athletics wanted to stay sharp. Manager Connie Mack
asked Jimmy McAleer to put together an all-star squad to scrimmage
the A's, and McAleer asked both Larry Gardner and Joe Wood to play
for a team that also included such luminaries as Tiger outfielder Ty
Cobb, Yankee first baseman Hal Chase, and pitcher Walter Johnson of
the Washington Senators.

It was quite an honor for each player to be selected for the team,
which had the added benefit of giving McAleer a chance to get to

know each man a bit better heading into the 1912 season. Each player made the most of it. Gardner more than held his own at third and knocked a series of hits off the champions, and even though Joe Wood was defeated, 3–2, in his only pitching appearance, he held the champions to only five hits, a performance that seemed to underscore his late-season surge. After the A's beat the Giants in the World's Series, four games to two, Wood's stock rose even higher, since his effort compared favorably to those of the Giants' pitchers in the Series, even the great Christy Mathewson.

The A's six-game victory was no upset, but the Giants, behind combative manager John McGraw, had usurped the Cubs as the National League's best club, and baseball reporters considered them to be a team on the way up. The Red Sox, however, were not overly impressed. Speaker, Wood, pitchers Ray Collins, Charley Hall, and Eddie Cicotte, and a few other Sox had faced the Giants in 1909 in a postseason series that Boston had won handily, four games to one. Although Wood had been Boston's only losing pitcher, he had actually earned a draw with Mathewson in the first game, giving up only six hits to the ten Boston earned off Mathewson, and he lost only because of Boston's porous defense. Speaker had been particularly impressive, hitting .600 for the series and battering Mathewson as if he were a rank amateur. Murnane called him the "twinkling star" of the contests and offered that the Sox had outplayed the Giants "in every department." Just as the Red Sox had believed that they were better than the Athletics at the end of the regular season, Speaker let his teammates know after the 1911 Series that the Giants were intimidating in name only.

As the last leaves dropped off the trees, the attention of Red Sox fans, management, and players now turned to other matters. Charley Hall had fallen for a Roxbury girl, Marie Cullen, and they married in mid-October. At the reception at the bride's home the guests were entertained by the Red Sox Quartet, a barbershop singing group made up of Buck O'Brien, first baseman Hugh Bradley, and pitchers Marty McHale and minor leaguer Bill Lyons, who were filling in for occasional tenor Larry Gardner, already back home to Vermont. Later that fall the quartet played the New England vaudeville circuit, including B. F. Keith's theater in Boston, where a receptive reviewer noted that "if they wish to foreswear baseball as a livelihood there is a rosy career awaiting them as singers."

While the players whiled away the winter, Red Sox management was focused on building—both the ball club and the ballpark. Shortly after the end of the World's Series, McAleer traveled to Chicago, a trip that served two purposes. There was that annual hunting trip with Johnson and about three other baseball big shots, which always included attending to a bit of baseball business beforehand. But Chicago was also the home of Jake Stahl, the man McAleer wanted to manage his ball club. Before leaving for Wisconsin McAleer met with Stahl and tried to convince him to sign on.

McAleer wanted Stahl both to manage the team and to play first base. In theory Stahl was not averse to either proposition, but he demanded some extra incentive to leave the cushy and cash-rich confines of his Chicago office. Namely, he didn't want to be McAleer's employee as much as he wanted to be a partner—he wanted a piece of the team. His father-in-law was already on board to be a part owner, and Stahl knew that McAleer was still a bit stretched financially. Besides, if Stahl's father-in-law backed out for any reason, the whole deal could fall apart. In this negotiation Stahl was the hammer and McAleer the mere nail.

In theory McAleer was receptive to the notion. Stahl was willing to invest as much as $15,000 of his own money in the team. But in addition to sharing in the profits, the banker also wanted a hefty salary as player-manager. McAleer balked at his price.

Stahl had McAleer by the short hairs, however, and he knew it, for with each passing day it became more and more important to have a manager in place. Although no contracts could be sent out until the team was formally reorganized after the first of the year, Stahl would have a big say in the makeup of the team and his input was vital.

When McAleer left Chicago for the north woods he claimed to have Stahl all signed up, but when word of that got back to Stahl he denied it, saying, "Matters stand where they did three weeks ago." The two men remained at odds after McAleer returned to Chicago, and in early November he headed back east, still without Stahl's signature on a contract.

But McAleer was more Red Sox figurehead than the final answer.

Ban Johnson still pulled the strings, and soon after McAleer boarded his train Johnson apparently got involved.

He knew McAleer needed Mahan's investment, and on November 10 he delivered player-manager Jake Stahl—and $15,000 of his money, representing a 10 percent stake in McAleer's ownership group. Even though Stahl would receive much of his investment back in salary, the agreement made his father-in-law happy and kept the sale from falling apart.

While McAleer was trying to build his team, the Fens echoed with the sounds of construction—hammers and steam engines, saws and steel rivets. Opening day was a little more than five months off, but there had already been a great deal of progress. Ever so slowly, a ballpark was starting to take shape.

It was important to prepare the playing field as quickly as possible, both in order to allow the ground to settle and to begin seeding before winter set in, and much of the first phase of construction focused on these goals. Even before Jerome Kelley relocated the infield sod from Huntington Avenue, engineers and surveyors had laid out the dimensions of the grandstand and crews had already been at work bringing the field to grade. The property sloped downward from the northwest corner to the southeast, and workers first had to excavate earth from the northwest and northern edge of the property to level the field. Then, before Kelley laid out the infield, a network of drainage ditches had to be put in place beneath the playing field.

The drainage system made use of the natural fall of the land from the north to the south and sloped toward several catch basins, near the base of where the grandstand would be, that were tied in directly to the city sewer system. Two-inch vitrified-clay drainpipes crisscrossed the outfield, and as the system inclined toward the infield, the size of the pipe increased, eventually feeding into six-inch trunk lines that ran into the catch basins.

The natural fall of the land is why Fenway's dugouts still often flood after particularly intense downpours. The topsoil sits on a layer of silt approximately twelve feet thick. Beneath the silt is hardpan, a soil layer nearly impervious to water, that slopes from left field toward the first-base line. The hardpan is below the water table, which means that even during dry weather water still seeps along the upper surface of the hardpan, seeking its own level, draining toward the first-base line. Periods of heavy rain can still overwhelm the system, leaving water to back up through drains and flood the dugout and other areas beneath the stands.

Most of this trenching work was done the old-fashioned way, with picks and shovels and calloused hands accustomed to the labor. Mechanized, gasoline-powered excavation machines were just coming into widespread use, either smaller, portable machines on wheels that could be driven or hauled into place or machines supported by towers and operated by the use of draglines. These more modern excavation systems were probably used at Fenway Park only to bring the field to grade and dig foundations for the grandstand.

By October 15, 1911, not only was the drainage system in place, but a layer of loam had been spread over the field. Now it was time for Jerome Kelley and his crew to take over. They overseeded the entire field, save the skinned portion of the infield, with a blend of grass seed designed for the New England climate: quick-growing fescues mixed with perennial rye and more resilient bluegrass. The rye sprouted quickly and held the soil, allowing the slower-growing fescues and bluegrass a chance to take root. That way, as soon as the ground thawed in the spring, grass would begin to grow and the whole field could be overseeded once again. After spreading the seed, Kelley's crew then rolled the field to set the seed, covered the bare earth with straw to prevent erosion, and applied water. In less than a week the first few tufts of green began to show.

While work was being done on the playing field, work was also beginning on the grandstand, where there was no less pressure to get the job done before winter. The entire grandstand was designed to be built of reinforced concrete—concrete poured into forms and supported and reinforced with steel bars popularly known as rebar (reinforcing bar). Once temperatures dropped below freezing the mixing and pouring of concrete would become problematic. The pavilion, however, was less complex, consisting of simple steel-frame construction. But both the grandstand and the pavilion required the same basic foundation structures—load-bearing columns set into the ground on concrete-reinforced piers and extended footings. Although the size and spacing of the columns varied somewhat, owing to load, in general the columns were fourteen to twenty-four inches square and spaced eighteen to twenty feet apart throughout the entire footprint of both the grandstand and the pavilion. This meant that workers had to excavate and then construct at least 150 foundation piers.

In the center-field bleachers, however, no such permanent foundations were built. The wooden structure with its myriad of columns and supports sat on wood piers set into the ground. Within a decade they would rot to such a degree that the city of Boston would deem the structure unsafe.

The soil that would later prove problematic for drainage was nevertheless a godsend when the permanent concrete piers were constructed. Sample excavations revealed that the layer of hardpan was of sufficient depth to support the weight of the grandstand—up to four tons per square foot. After each pier was excavated carpenters created wooden formwork for that pier—essentially a box, flared out at the bottom—braced to withstand the weight of wet concrete without deforming. The interior was laced with rebar wired together, not unlike a series of nesting baskets, which added strength to the concrete.

The concrete column extending upward from the pier was also created by wooden forms. Four steel bars, 1⅝ inches thick, extending from the footing, ran vertically through each column up above the surface grade, where subsequent columns could then be built vertically upward to the concrete deck slab. As the structure rose, each column was then connected and cross-braced to those around it by concrete-reinforced girders.

Workers excavated and then poured the piers and columns first, beginning at the third-base end of the grandstand and systematically working toward the first-base side. They did not, however, build the grandstand up in layers, like a cake. Rather, as the concrete of the first piers and columns set and cured—a process that took, depending on the weather, between four and six days—forms were stripped, the piers and columns were backfilled, and the next level was built in sequence until the structure reached the level of the sloping deck that would form the floor of the stands, only three feet high at the edge of the field but forty-two feet at the rear of the stands. The structure rose like a wave from third around toward first, the columns and girders along the third-base line already extending into the air while piers were still being excavated and poured down the first-base line. As construction extended above the surface grade hordes of workers erected scaffolding to allow other workers to rise with the structure, and to enable carpenters to build formwork both for the columns and for the "false work": the forms beneath the deck slab that created and supported the underside of the seating deck during construction. Thousands of board feet of lumber, primarily pine, was used to construct the forms. Virtually every original concrete surface in Fenway Park, except for the floors, was once encased by wooden formwork. In fact, there are still places in Fenway Park today where it is possible to see the wood grain from the formwork on columns, girders, and the underside of the grandstand deck, even though much of it has recently been obscured by other structures and paint.

Now that Stahl was on board, McRoy and McAleer began planning for spring training. Although the Sox had trained in California in 1911, that was primarily due to the wishes of John I. Taylor. McAleer saw no reason to cross the country, so in mid-November he traveled to Hot Springs, Arkansas, the traditional Red Sox spring home, to secure a ballpark and hotel space. McAleer planned to open camp on March 10, and he arranged to share training facilities at Majestic Park with Cincinnati, at least until the Philadelphia Athletics left town, at which point the Sox hoped to take over the Athletics' Fogel Field. Sharing facilities and switching fields would not be much of a hardship, for at the time players trained more by taking long hikes and mineral baths than they did on the field.

WORK ON PAVILION AND GROUNDS GOES ON APACE

By the start of December the piers, the footings, and the reinforced-concrete structure of the grandstand were complete and workers were rapidly forming the underside of the deck and the accompanying ramps—an innovation not yet used in any other big league park, where fans entered at the bottom of the stands, then climbed up aisles to their seats. McLaughlin's ramps allowed fans to enter at street level and reach the grandstand either by going through openings at the lower end of the grandstand or by wending their way up ramps to the top promenade and then walking down to their seats. Because fans could exit the park in reverse by the same means, the stands could be cleared more quickly. Tests later indicated that the entire grandstand could be emptied in only five minutes.

After the formwork was completed, the next major construction stage, the pouring of the concrete deck, ideally had to take place all at once. In any large construction project "continuous" concrete pours are preferable to pours that stop and create a seam between poured sections, which can weaken the entire structure. (In the 1911 construction of the Polo Grounds, for instance, the concrete for the entire grandstand structure was a continuous pour that took six full days and nights.) But that is not to say that the deck surface would be an unbroken surface. Even cured concrete expands and contracts according to changes in temperature. To allow for this expansion joints were built into the plan for both the deck slab and the ramps.

After the false work and scaffolding were complete, the undersurface of the deck slab was interlaced with rebar. By a few days before Christmas the slab was ready to pour. The procedure was so unique that a contingent of more than fifty members of the Boston Society of Civil Engineers traveled to Fenway Park on December 20 to witness the process.

Unlike today, concrete was not mixed and then hauled to the site by truck. Instead, a concrete plant was built on-site—probably on Jersey Street—where cement, sand, and an aggregate of crushed stone and water were mixed together in a 1:2:4 mix—one part cement to two parts sand to four parts stone. Water was then added, and the ingredients were mixed by a mechanical mixer and transferred—dumped—into a concrete dump bucket. The wet concrete was hoisted to the appropriate place and the concrete emptied into wheeled sidecars or dump buckets—essentially wheelbarrows, but with much larger wheels and a much greater capacity. Workers then manhandled the dump bucket into place and, where possible, simply dumped the concrete onto the deck. Then workers raked it into place and agitated the concrete to remove any air bubbles.

But since the deck was sloped, in many places it was not possible to dump the concrete directly into place. There it would be dumped into chutes, and workers then had to force the concrete down manually, using shovels not unlike canoe paddles, for even when wet, the concrete was too viscous and the angle too flat for it to flow completely on its own. Once the concrete was in place, more skilled workers used a series of floats and screes to create an acceptable surface, "floating" excess water off as the concrete began to cure. When the surface hardened it is likely that it was covered with some combination of straw, manure, and canvas to protect it from winter's chill (as the straw and manure rotted they created heat). By the time Fenway Park was complete, more than 7,000 barrels of cement—more than 2.6 million pounds—had been used.

For the workers on-site pouring concrete was dirty, messy, heavy, dangerous work. Every scratch from the sharp edges of the rusty rebar carried a threat of tetanus, and walking and climbing through rebar made it easy to trip and fall. Even the concrete itself was dangerous. It contained lime and when mixed with water created a caustic and heat-producing chemical reaction. Wet concrete left in contact with the skin can cause serious burns, and the reaction also quickly degrades clothing and leather. While working in concrete, most workers spent the day wearing heavy, knee-high rubber boots and praying that the form carpenters knew what they were doing. If a form blew out in the midst of a pour, workers could be buried. Shoulders and arms ached from the burden of shoveling the heavy mixture, which typically weighed 150 pounds per cubic foot, and workers labored in continuous shifts until the pour was complete. Records are unclear about whether or not the entire deck was done in a continuous pour (the pavilion was done separately), but even if the task was broken into several pours, several long days of work would still have been required. For this, the workers earned perhaps fifty cents an hour.

While McRoy wrapped up his duties as Ban Johnson's secretary and McAleer and his attorneys prepared to take official control of the club, the Boston Nationals, Boston's other team, served notice that they had been paying attention. Ever since the American League had fielded a team in Boston, the Nationals had been relegated to second-tier status, a third-rate team playing in a fourth-rate facility.

Now, with the Sox ready to open a new park, the Nationals began to rouse from their slumber. James Gaffney, a member of New York's Tammany Hall political machine, purchased the club. Former player John Montgomery Ward was elected president, and on December 21 the club made some changes.

First, Ward announced that henceforth the team would no longer be known as the Nationals or the Doves or the Rustlers or any of the other unofficial names they had been dubbed with over the years. Instead they would be known as the Braves. Ward explained that new owner "James Gaffney is one of the grand sachems of Tammany in New York, and is known as one of the 'braves.' Therefore Boston Braves would have the true fighting ring that the fans would take to." The Tammany Hall building was in fact named after a Native American, Chief Tammany, and so the political activists who met there and became New York's foremost political machine were called "Braves." The nickname continues to this day, used by the Atlanta Braves, although few fans realize that the name originally referred to a machine politician, not a Native American.

Knowing that the old South End Grounds would appear positively decrepit when compared to Fenway Park, Ward also announced that the Braves would embark on some substantial renovations. Although it would not become public knowledge for another two weeks, the club was making plans to build a new park of its own, Braves Field. The building of Fenway Park provided the impetus that would help lead to a Braves pennant in only two short years.

For now, however, McAleer and company were far more concerned about a Boston Red Sox pennant, and they were eager to get going. All they needed to begin making concrete plans for the 1912 season was the formal reorganization to take place at the club's annual meeting on January 3, 1912. Construction was ahead of schedule at Fenway Park. Thus far the weather had been mild, and it had not yet snowed in Boston.

On the final day of December, however, a blizzard struck. The temperature plummeted to just above zero, the beginning of a cold snap that would last for more than a month. The major concrete work at Fenway had been completed just in time. It would be nearly two months before weather conditions allowed the concrete treads that would support the seats to be poured atop the deck.

WINTER OF OLD DAYS RETURNS
All New England Hit By Biting Cold

When McRoy and McAleer met with the Taylors, their attorneys, and other officials on January 3, they hoped a variation of that headline—*"Winners* of Old Days Return"—would soon be written in regard to the Red Sox. McAleer was elected president and McRoy treasurer, while John I. Taylor was selected to serve as vice president. Those three men, along with General Taylor and John R. Turner, an attorney from Jersey City, New Jersey, formed the board of directors. Turner's residency allowed the corporation to operate under New Jersey's more favorable corporation laws. After the papers were signed the group toured Fenway Park and met with the press. McAleer made the expected optimistic pronouncements about the upcoming season and then began the real work to prepare for the 1912 campaign.

The first order of business was to draft and send contracts to the forty players Boston had in reserve. "I am satisfied," said McAleer, "that the Red Sox will be in the hunt." Even though he hoped that a few valuable new players might emerge during the spring, he seemed relatively satisfied with the roster already in place, particularly the outfield and the pitching staff. The only real question marks concerned who would back up Carrigan behind the plate and who would play shortstop and second base. Gardner's postseason performance against the A's had secured his spot at third, and manager Stahl was already an improvement at first base. If Charlie Wagner remained healthy enough to play short, Steve Yerkes, who lacked Wagner's range and arm, could settle in at second base.

While McAleer and McRoy tended to the contracts, Charles Logue had his hands full at Fenway Park. The major next stage of construction was the grandstand roof. As soon as workers cleared the grandstand deck of snow and ice, structural steel to support the roof had to be put in place.

Before the development and widespread use of portable cranes powered by steam, diesel, or gasoline, structural steel was lifted and put in place by the use of a "guy derrick," a tall mast capable of being rotated, supported by guy wires. A boom nearly the same height as the mast was attached to the bottom of the mast by a pivot and to the top of the mast by a cable. The boom was then lowered and raised by mechanically withdrawing or extending the cable through a series of pulleys. In this fashion the boom was lowered, large steel columns and girders were attached to it by steel cables and slings by iron-workers, and as the boom was raised closer to the mast the steel was hoisted into the air while ironworkers worked lines attached to the steel to keep it from swinging out of control and damaging either the mast or the boom. The load could then be spun into place and the boom lowered (the origination of the phrase "lower the boom"); the ironworkers would then bolt and rivet the steel in place.

BUSY DAYS AT RED SOX' NEW BALL PARK
Huge Grandstand Is Being Erected Rapidly

At Fenway Park the erection of the structural steel to support the grandstand roof began with what was then section L just beyond third base, known as section 27 today. The steel was staged along the edge of the grandstand; then upright steel columns were lifted and put into position, atop foundations and anchors, and bolted into place. Ironworkers, using the hot rivet method, then attached each column to the next one with horizontal girders.

The mast and boom used at Fenway were each nearly one hundred feet long, which allowed the boom radius to approach half that distance—nearly fifty feet—in every direction. After all work was done within that radius the guy derrick was taken down and re-erected in another place. In all likelihood two sections of the grandstand could be built before the guy derrick had to be moved. No more than two guy derricks at a time were in use—the proliferation of cables needed to control each one precluded using more.

Once the structural steel columns and girders were in place, it was a relatively easy process to plank the roof, although it would be spring before it could be made waterproof. While workers persevered, the weather was brutal: over the month of January temperatures rarely rose above single digits, and ironworkers riveting steel together hung in the air in wind-chills of thirty below zero or less. As they fought frostbite the front pages of Boston newspapers were screaming with headlines detailing the lengthy Lawrence textile strike. A new Massachusetts law had recently reduced the workweek for women and children from fifty-six hours to fifty-four. Mill owners responded by cutting pay, leading some twenty-five thousand workers to strike, the first mass job action in New England, and causing the state to call in the militia. Laborers at Fenway Park, toiling away in the bitter cold for up to twelve hours a day while earning a top salary of only thirty dollars or so per week, paid close attention.

No one in the city was thinking about baseball. Men wielding shovels and horses pulling plows struggled to keep Boston's streets clear of snow. For the first time in several years Boston Harbor was virtually frozen over. Every morning young boys filled the dock basins between the wharves on Atlantic Avenue, skipping school to play hockey.

Nevertheless, day by day Fenway Park took shape, and as the player contracts trickled back to Boston the 1912 Red Sox began to come into focus. Spring was in the air.

3

Hot Springs

The members of the Red Sox team are in pretty fair condition, for when
not able to work out on the field they receive great benefit from their
long hikes over mountain roads and the warm baths later. These baths
take all the soreness out of the players' muscles . . . this fact alone makes
Hot Springs the best place in the country in which to train ballplayers.

—*The Sporting News*

OT SPRINGS.

The mere mention of the name brought a smile to the faces
of the Red Sox players and the Royal Rooters, the rabid Red
Sox fan club that followed the team. For as the winter's snow and
cold locked up the boats in Boston Harbor, talk of spring training
delivered the promise of warmer days ahead and the sound of baseball
being played again. Since holding their first spring training in 1901
in Charlottesville, Virginia, the Sox had tried a variety of venues, including Augusta and Macon, Georgia; West Baden Springs, Indiana;
and, most recently, Redondo Beach, California. But players and fans
alike recalled the two sessions the team had spent in Hot Springs,
Arkansas, in 1909 and 1910, with the most fondness.

Hot Springs was, well, *Hot Springs*, a resort town renowned not
only for its forty restorative 147-degree mineral baths, which had
earned it the nickname "the National Spa," but for everything that
came with it—fine hotels, sumptuous restaurants, the splendor of the
nearby Ouachita Mountains . . . and casinos, dance halls, dogfights,
painted ladies, quack doctors, and cures for the Hot Springs strain of
"malaria" that the savvy recognized as venereal disease. Decades be-

fore Las Vegas was anything more than a spot on a map of the Nevada desert, Hot Springs, Arkansas, was the gambling and vice capital of the United States.

Corruption allowed it to happen as local officials gladly accepted bribes to look the other way. The result was an exciting yet violent place where, as Tim Murnane once noted, "shooting people was a regular and popular pastime with the best citizens." In March 1899, in fact, Jimmy McAleer had been in town for spring training and witnessed the infamous "Hot Springs Gunfight," when the police department and the county sheriff's department, each of which backed a different gambling faction, shot it out on the streets in one of the most notorious episodes in Arkansas history. McAleer told Murnane that when he left his hotel after the shootout, "he saw seven dead men laid out on the sidewalk."

As soon as McAleer took command he began to formalize his plans for the spring, securing time at one of several ballparks, making reservations at the Hotel Eastman, and lining up exhibition games with the other teams training in town. Although McAleer had not returned to Hot Springs since the gunfight, now that he was in charge of the Red Sox he felt that the benefits of training in the resort city far outweighed any potential distractions. In fact, the distractions, along with the relatively mild weather and the baths, were the main reason why several major league teams chose to work out there. In 1912 the Sox were joined by three National League teams, the Pirates, the Phillies, and Brooklyn. Spring training was no exercise in incarceration but more an excuse to break out after the confinements of winter around hearth and home and work the kinks out of muscles gone soft. Besides, it was easier to entice contract holdouts to give in if they knew they were going to Hot Springs for a month as opposed to a place like Macon or Augusta. A happy club presumably worked harder, and there was plenty to keep the players happy in Hot Springs, from the notorious dance hall and bordello known as the Black Orchid to the local opera house, the Oaklawn racetrack, and the tourist traps, like the alligator farm and ostrich ranch, that flanked Majestic Park, where the Red Sox planned to train. Just about every player on the team would return with a "bouquet" of ostrich feathers from one of the three hundred birds on the ranch and a staged photograph posing on a stuffed alligator, the least dangerous of the 1,500 reptiles that roamed the site.

After a winter spent away from the ballpark, most Sox players were looking forward to such distractions and the excitement they entailed. Charley Hall, Duffy Lewis, and Ray Collins had all married, while Hugh Bradley and the other members of the Red Sox Quartet had toured New England. Bill Carrigan had gone home to Lewiston, Maine, and looked after his business interests, which included a cigar store, and built the strength back up in his broken leg.

A number of players wrote to *Boston Post* writer Paul Shannon detailing their winter activities. Larry Gardner was in Enosburg Falls, Vermont, "leading the customary country life," farming and hunting. From New Rochelle, New York, Charlie Wagner admitted that in 1911 "my wing was never right . . . but my arm feels all right now." If true, that was terrific news, for it meant that Wagner could return to shortstop and answer the biggest question in the Boston lineup. Joe Wood wrote from his home in Parker's Glen, Pennsylvania, where he and his father looked after their Woodton Poultry Farm, that he had spent as much time as possible hunting and "tramping through the fields and woods" and that "I feel hard as nails." Boston hoped so, for his annual bout with a sore arm was something the club could do without. Wood also asked Shannon to squash a story that intimated he was about to get married: "About that marriage dope, I wrote you last week asking you to contradict the story." As the team's most eligible bachelor, Wood was constantly tied to one local maiden or another by the papers, and he was in no hurry to tie the knot and stem the flow of scented notes to his mailbox or the quiet tappings on his door.

Now that McAleer was in control, other clubs soon called, proposing player swaps and trades. Former Boston third baseman Harry Lord, a recent fan favorite who was dealt with Amby O'Connell to the White Sox for two warm bodies, had flourished in Chicago. White Sox owner Charlie Comiskey hoped that McAleer might be enticed by the prospect of bringing the Maine native back to Boston and asked for Tris Speaker in return, but McAleer was no fool. Lord was a good player, but Speaker was already great and getting better.

Signed contracts for the 1912 season soon began trickling back in.

Even those players who thought they deserved more money had virtually no leverage when it came to contract negotiations. Their only option was to refuse to play altogether and hope that might spark a trade to a team more likely to meet their contract demands, but even this was unlikely to happen. If a player wanted to play, he more or less had to accept what was offered. About the only way to express displeasure was to sit on the contract for a few weeks and hope the club responded by upping the ante. More often, however, teams waited out the holdouts until they came slinking back.

McAleer, however, did make one deal. It seemed to be an insignificant transaction at the time, but it would soon pay huge dividends.

Near the end of the 1910 season the Red Sox had drafted pitcher Hugh Bedient from the roster of Fall River of the New England League and then took the hard-throwing young sidearm pitcher to spring training in California in 1911. He had first drawn the attention of scouts in 1908 when, while pitching for a semipro team in Falconer, New York, he struck out forty-two batters in a twenty-three-inning victory, a performance that resulted in nineteen contract offers from professional clubs. He was impressive in the spring of 1911 for Boston, but the Sox chose to stick with more veteran hurlers and Bedient was sent to Providence for more seasoning.

Since Bedient was not on the Boston roster, Providence was able, in turn, to send him to Jersey City in the Eastern League. His record in 1911 for Jersey City was only 8-11, but on a team that lost nearly twice as many games as it won, Bedient stood out, and he impressed Boston scouts. Now the Sox wanted Bedient badly, but so did several other clubs. A bidding war over his services seemed likely.

Boston had an enormous advantage. Hugh McBreen had served as club treasurer under John Taylor, and after McAleer took over the Red Sox, McBreen bought into Jersey City. He spurned offers of as much as $6,000 for the pitcher and instead accepted Boston's offer of seven ballplayers, but no money, in exchange for Bedient. The deal would prove to be a bargain for the Red Sox.

Even though most Red Sox were not planning to leave for Hot Springs until March 6, a few started trickling in a month ahead of time. Bill Carrigan, eager to test his leg, was the first to arrive, followed closely by youthful Dr. Fred Anderson, a spitball artist who had nearly made the club several years earlier, only to choose a career in dentistry instead, a decision he now regretted. McAleer planned to go to Hot Springs soon as well, but before he did he wanted to make sure that work on Fenway Park was on schedule.

While the January cold spell had made it impossible to pour concrete, work elsewhere on the ballpark had progressed nicely. Underneath the grandstand, in areas that could be temporarily heated, masons used hollow tile brick to build partitions and create rooms for the umpires, storage, concessions, and other uses. The clubhouses for each team, complete with shower baths, had been roughed in, as had the team offices. Now that the weather had broken, the pace picked up considerably, and work resumed on the stands.

Concrete workers began to build forms and pour concrete for what were known as the "treads," or steps, upon which would sit thirty-two rows of grandstand seats, not including the box seats. Tied to the main structure by reinforced steel, the treads had a design that was unique in several ways. For one, instead of using stone aggregate in the concrete mix, workers used cinders, which lowered the weight by nearly one-third, from 150 pounds per cubic foot to only 110 pounds, reducing both the cost and the weight load on the deck. The size of the treads also varied. Toward the front of the grandstand, where seats would be more costly, each tread was forty inches in width, giving patrons ample leg room. But as one went higher up in the stands the width of the treads narrowed, first to thirty-two inches and finally to only thirty inches, a variation that would trip up generations of fans. Each tread step rose from between eight and eleven inches and for drainage purposes was angled ever so slightly back so that water ran down toward the field, where it could be carried away by drains at the base of the stands. Each box seat section was truly a box, separated from other seats by a poured concrete wall and from other boxes by a pipe rail. Unlike today, the box seats did not go all the way down to field level—the floor of the first row of box seats sat three feet above the field.

As the stands rose from the field the slope of the grandstand deck gradually became steeper. The Fenway Park grandstand utilized what is known as a "rising floor," not one built at a uniform pitch from the field to the back of the stands, but one that was slightly concave.

At the base of the grandstand the pitch was only 15 percent, but as the stands went higher—roughly every eighteen to twenty feet, or each time a pier was crossed—the pitch was increased by one degree. The top section sat at a twenty-degree pitch in relation to the field. The result was better sightlines and more seats, and the back of the grandstand stood six and a half feet higher than if the grandstand had had a uniform pitch.

Increasing the pitch in this manner also allowed the grandstand roof to match the height of the pavilion and, by keeping the same roofline, made it appear more like it was part of the same overall structure (albeit separated by an open alleyway between the two stands). Despite its appearance, the pavilion was a completely separate structure, and while Fenway Park was credited as being a concrete-and-steel ballpark, that was true only in regard to the grandstand. The pavilion rested on concrete piers, and the roof was supported by structural steel columns that started at grade, but the pavilion stands were not supported by or built of reinforced concrete.

The rest of the pavilion, including the seats, was built of wood, some recycled from the Huntington Avenue Grounds. The old wooden pavilion structure at the Huntington Avenue Grounds had been carefully taken apart, and much of the lumber was reused in the construction of the stands for the Fenway pavilion. Apart from the steel roof supports, the pavilion was really nothing more than a glorified section of bleachers, with bare wooden plank seats resting atop a maze of robust wooden scaffolding, as prone to fire as the old Huntington Avenue Grounds. That was the reason the pavilion was separated from the grandstand by the alleyway (the vestigial remains of which are still partially visible in Fenway Park today by the gap known as "canvas alley"), which served as a firebreak between the two structures. Although the roof of both the grandstand and the pavilion, made of wood planks and sealed with tar, was highly flammable, it was continuous and had no firebreak so that fans would stay dry during rain showers. That meant that a blaze in the pavilion could easily spread to the grandstand by way of the roof. Claims that Fenway were fireproof were, in reality, relative.

Unlike the main grandstand, the pavilion stands were built at a uniform pitch. Photographs that appeared in newspapers clearly show that the back portion of the stands, but not the roof, towered some six or eight feet higher than the main grandstand. This made for a much denser seating area in which each row was only about two feet in width—six inches narrower than the least spacious seats in the main grandstand. As a result, in roughly the same surface area as the grandstand, the pavilion held more than forty rows of seats as opposed to thirty-two rows, exclusive of the box seats. Patrons in the pavilion were cramped and uncomfortable from the start.

By the end of February the weather had warmed enough that even though much of the ground was still bound with frost, the first few sprigs of grass were springing up in the outfield and the infield was beginning to turn green. Charles Logue and James McLaughlin still had their work cut out for them, but barring disaster, the park appeared certain to be ready by opening day, of which there would be several. Although the Sox would open the regular season in New York playing the Highlanders on April 11, they were scheduled to christen Fenway on April 9 in an exhibition against Harvard University. Fenway Park was then scheduled to open officially on April 18, when New York came to Boston, and the club had planned yet another opening celebration—a dedication—on May 16 to take full advantage of another opportunity to pack the stands.

While work continued at Fenway Park, Jake Stahl became the next man to arrive in Hot Springs. He was anxious to get started, not only to evaluate his team but to get in shape himself. He knew that his success as manager would depend in part on his performance on the field. Before his retirement he had been considered one of the best first basemen in the game, just a notch or two behind the Yankees' Hal Chase. He still thought he could be one of the better players in the league, and the addition of his bat to the Red Sox lineup represented an enormous upgrade—if he returned to form.

Along with Lewis, Hooper, and Speaker, Stahl was one of a number of Red Sox players who either had earned a college degree or had spent time at a university. Yet more so than the others, he was a true scholar-athlete whose belief in the ethic of "a healthy mind in a healthy body" was even reflected in his name. The son of a Civil War veteran, Stahl grew up in Elkhart, Illinois, and worked in his father's store before enrolling in the University of Illinois, eventually earning a law degree. In class Stahl was known by his given name, Garland, a moniker that seemed to reflect his studious approach and unimpeachable reputation, and that was the name he used when signing autographs and legal documents. Yet in the schoolyard, on the gridiron, or on the baseball diamond, he was known as Jake, a good sport, and an athlete who, while always playing fair, was also tough and hard. He earned All-Conference honors in football in 1900, his junior year, and hit over .400 for the baseball team while playing all over the diamond.

Whatever name he chose to go by, he looked and acted the part to perfection. In his business suit as "Garland," wearing reading glasses and poring over bank figures in a ledger while taking notes in a handsome, florid script, Stahl, apart from his athletic build, was indistinguishable from other men of his class. But when he wore a football jersey or placed a ball cap on his head, his strong jaw, clear gray eyes, and robust frame reflected a steely resolve that earned the respect of his somewhat more earthly peers. He preferred to lead by example, but when challenged, did not back down. Stahl stood a full 6'2" and weighed over two hundred pounds, making him one of the biggest players in baseball for the era.

If he had a weakness as a player, it was that he chose not to call attention to himself and his accomplishments. Baseball writer Francis Richter noted: "If Stahl could get a case of swelled head and begin to think he is really as good as he is, he would be the greatest of them all . . . [only] modesty has held him back." He joined the Red Sox directly out of college as a catcher, recommended to Boston by University of Illinois athletic director George Huff.

Stahl's personal modesty served him well in the early days of the American League. While his intelligence could have set him apart, his reticence in calling attention to himself endeared him to his teammates—Stahl was no "egghead," but a regular guy. Traded to Washington, where Ban Johnson was running the franchise, Stahl impressed the league president with his unique combination of brawn and brains, and despite his relative youth Johnson named him manager in 1905. The club seemed to turn a corner, but then collapsed in 1906. Stahl, who hit only .222, took it personally, saying, "If I'd been able to hit .300 this year, as many of my friends predicted, we'd have been up in the first division, but I was a frost." Washington promised

Stahl he would be traded back to Boston, where he knew he'd get playing time, but reneged and traded him instead to the White Sox. Stahl felt that he had been lied to and as a matter of principle refused to report to the White Sox. Although he had just married his college sweetheart and begun an apprenticeship at his father-in-law's bank, he was clearly torn over his choice of career. He could not stay away from baseball and soon purchased the semipro South Side Baseball Club in Chicago, a team for which he played first base.

Try as he might, Stahl could not walk away from the game, particularly given the sense of failure he had felt with Washington. Traded to New York in 1908, he ended his holdout and reported to camp, making the team and earning a starting spot in the outfield. In midseason he was finally traded to Boston, where for the next two and a half seasons he thrived, reviving his career as a hard-hitting first baseman and his reputation as a first-rate baseball man. Apparently satisfied that he had proven to himself that he could succeed in professional baseball, he chose retirement after the 1910 season.

For any other player a second voluntary walkout would probably have spelled the end of his career, but Stahl was still a friend of Ban Johnson. That relationship and the fact that he convinced his father-in-law to invest in the ball club paved the way for Stahl's return. While that gave Stahl a sense of security unique among all baseball managers this side of Connie Mack, who owned the Athletics, Stahl was sensitive to the perception that he was riding his father-in-law's coattails. He knew that he had to earn the respect of both his players and the fans by his play on the field.

To that end he had spent the winter working out at his old alma mater, the University of Illinois, trying to drop the twenty pounds or so he had added sitting behind a desk. Just before leaving for Hot Springs, he went on a late-winter hunting trip in northern Illinois that left him slogging through waist-deep snow for two days, with only a couple of rabbits to show for his effort. Stahl was accompanied to Hot Springs by his wife and child, one of only a few members of the team to bring his family south.

With his arrival spring training officially began, and from then on Stahl, not McAleer, would be making most of the personnel decisions. There were not many to make. The outfield was set, and if Wagner's arm held up so was the infield. Carrigan, Hick Cady, Les Nunamaker, and Pinch Thomas gave the club four fine catchers. For position players Stahl needed only to select a few utility men from among such contenders as the multi-talented Clyde Engle, infielder Marty Krug, slugging first baseman Hugh Bradley, and outfielder Olaf Henriksen. The pitching staff was nearly set, since Wood, Ray Collins, Charley Hall, Buck O'Brien, and Eddie Cicotte were virtually assured of jobs. The Red Sox expected to carry only twenty to twenty-two players, which left room for only seven or eight pitchers. Fred Anderson, Hugh Bedient, Larry Pape, Jack Bushelman, Casey Hageman, and a few others would vie for the final spot or two.

Although the weather was cold and wet when he arrived in Hot Springs, Stahl was otherwise delighted. Majestic Park, while soggy, was otherwise in fine condition, and the team made the decision to train there the entire spring rather than move to Fogel Field after the Phillies left. John I. Taylor had built the park in 1909, and it held up under the weather much better than Fogel Field or Whittingham Park, the spring home of Brooklyn. Fred Anderson had already taken a turn on the mound with the "All-Americans"—an ad hoc team of early arrivals from AL clubs who were scrimmaging against the "All-Nationals," their NL counterparts—and had pitched well. But Stahl and Carrigan chose to wait a bit before taking the field themselves. Instead they joined former Red Sox pitcher Cy Young, who was in Hot Springs by force of habit before heading off to join the Braves in Augusta, Georgia, on a three-hour jaunt in the mountains.

STAHL PLANS LONG HIKE

Will Take Other Red Sox On 24-Mile Jaunt Today, If Weather Is Not Right For Ballgame

Young had ten years and a good twenty or thirty pounds on his younger companions, but he showed why he had won a record 511 games in the major leagues, including 190 for the Red Sox. His arm may have been worn thin—he would soon retire and not appear in another big league game—but his legs were in midseason form. Wearing a rubber shirt during one three-hour morning romp to force a sweat despite the snow flurries, he left Carrigan and Stahl in the dust. After lunch, when Young wanted to do it again, both Stahl and Carrigan begged off. But a few days later, when Stahl saw his first pitch of the spring, he was in good enough condition that he still knocked it off the center-field fence, serving notice that Boston's offense would be a bit more potent in 1912.

Such performances brought cheer to a dedicated group of Boston fans who accompanied the club south, Boston's vaunted Royal Rooters, who arrived in Hot Springs in force only a few days after Stahl. Even by Hot Springs standards the loud and lively Rooters stood out. They were unlike any other group of baseball fans anywhere else, before or since.

They were led by the self-described "thirty-third degree" baseball fan Michael "Nuf Ced" McGreevey, the garrulous owner and proprietor of Third Base, the baseball-themed saloon on Columbus Avenue that served as the informal clubhouse of Boston baseball fans. McGreevey, who earned his nickname from his colorful manner of ending arguments—banging his hand on the bar and hollering, "Nuf ced!"— originally helped create the Royal Rooters in the 1890s as supporters of the National League club. For the next decade they followed the team with a passion that bordered on obsession, elevating their heroes into something like gods. In McGreevey's saloon, where photos of the players hung on the walls and watched over the proceedings, the season never ended: there the Hot Stove League kept burning during the off-season and baseball—along with local politics—was a four-season pursuit. When half the players jumped to Ban Johnson's new American League team, the Rooters rapidly followed suit. They didn't root for the laundry but for the men who wore it, and players like Jimmy Collins, Cy Young, and Chick Stahl had their full devotion.

Made up of a who's who of movers and shakers in Boston's Irish community, including John "Honey Fitz" Fitzgerald, the mayor of Boston, the ad hoc group of businessmen, politicians, and sportsmen was united not just by their Irish heritage and their love of baseball but also by their love of gambling. They took advantage of every possible opportunity to unite the two pursuits. Led by McGreevey, the Rooters traveled together by train; announced their presence at every contest by arriving en masse in a parade, fronted by a hired band; then sat together in the stands, singing their signature fan song, "Tessie," at every opportunity, chanting and cheering throughout the contest. As the group grew the Rooters not only followed Boston teams on road trips but began to make annual excursions to the World's Series, looking for both fun and favorable odds. They soon became the best-known group of fans in baseball, as much a part of the Boston baseball scene as any player. Nuf Ced became better known than most big league ballplayers. And like the players, once spring was in the air McGreevey and his band could not wait for spring training and often showed up en masse. At times McGreevey himself was even signed to a spurious contract, given a uniform, and allowed to work out with the club.

In 1911 relatively few Rooters had managed to make the long trip to California for spring training, but now that the club was back in Hot Springs, dozens made the journey and more were showing up every day. After all, that was where the action was, and on March 5 they got plenty as Hot Springs provided a graphic reminder that it was still equal parts Old South and Wild West.

Late that morning, while the kitchen staff at the Arlington Hotel cleared tables, washed dishes, and began winding down breakfast service in order to prepare lunch, an African American kitchen worker began to argue with a white coworker over a late breakfast order, a dangerous undertaking for an African American in the South. The fight seemed to be over when the African American, who had left the kitchen, suddenly returned with a shotgun. He blasted his white coworker and then fled as the rest of the staff ducked for cover.

According to one newspaper, word that a black man had killed a white man "brought out infuriated white residents en masse," including every Red Sox player in town, the Rooters, and a larger contingent of players from Brooklyn and Philadelphia, who had already started formal practice. Angry residents, players, and fans congregated on the street outside the hotel, then fanned out into mobs of vigilantes and raced through the woods on the outskirts of town, rousting law-abiding African Americans from their homes and chasing after a phantom no one could find. It was a minor miracle that no one was killed as ballplayers and Royal Rooters alike, wading through the thickets, sometimes emerged to find themselves looking at the barrel of a rifle pointed at their heads. When they all grew tired and bored after a few hours, they trudged back to town in search of a hot meal, a drink, and a place to tell tales of personal heroism. The suspect, who had been hiding in the hotel the entire time, turned himself in before he could be lynched.

Larry Gardner, Buck O'Brien, Hugh Bradley, and Olaf Henriksen and even more Royal Rooters all gathered in Boston on March 7 and left together for Hot Springs on a train with team secretary Robert McRoy, with stops scheduled for New York, Philadelphia, Washington, and Cincinnati, where they expected to pick up a dozen other players on the way. But poor weather was slowing train travel, and their arrival in Hot Springs was delayed until the evening of March 10.

They were not particularly happy when they disembarked. Not only were the players cranky from the trip and disappointed in the damp Arkansas weather, but the Hotel Eastman was packed to the gills, forcing the players to bunk three or four to a room. They exercised together on the lawn of the hotel the next morning to work out the kinks caused by several days of train travel, and they finally took the field together for the first time on March 12. The players were so anxious to get started that they talked Stahl into a scrimmage the next day matching the "Regulars" against the "Yannigans," even though a few regulars — stars like Hooper, Lewis, and Joe Wood — sat out and Tris Speaker had yet to show. Nevertheless the Regulars escaped with an 8–6 win. As the weather allowed, Stahl planned to hold both morning and afternoon workouts so the players could catch up.

Only two days later they played their first spring contest against the Phillies, losing 12–2, a performance that surprised no one, for the players had barely unpacked and most were still sore from the first few workouts. The contest shared little with spring training games of today. Only a few hundred fans showed up to watch, some sitting in ramshackle bleachers and the rest scattered around the perimeter of the field. Some fans were so close that just about any drive that split the outfielders reached the crowd for some kind of ground rule hit.

Perhaps the most intriguing spring participant was thirty-eight-year-old Jack Chesbro. The one-time star for the New York Highlanders had pitched and lost to Boston on the final day of the 1904 season, throwing the wild pitch that, despite his record 41 victories that season, delivered the pennant to Boston. The wear of pitching more than 454 innings that season had left Chesbro lame, and he never again approached that standard. In recent years the Massachusetts native had been reduced to playing semipro ball for spare change. But when he asked for a spring tryout with Boston, the Sox agreed. Stahl and McAleer both hoped he would return to form, but after only a few days it became obvious that Chesbro was better off staying in the bush leagues. Not only did he pitch poorly, but he hardly put in any effort. He flatly refused to break into a trot while flagging balls during batting practice, hardly a way to impress Stahl.

RED SOX WALK, AND THAT'S ALL
Grounds Too Wet And Wind Too Bleak

The way the weather was behaving, there was precious little time for batting practice, for it rained nearly every day and Stahl felt fortunate if he got the team onto the field at all. His biggest challenge was keeping his squad busy, and he scrambled to find outlets for their energy. Early workouts often consisted of hiking, playing catch, taking spring baths, and pursuing pastimes like bowling, billiards, and skeet shooting. Those activities did not do much to get the team in shape but did help the otherwise divided squad forge some slender bonds of trust that had been lacking the previous season. Meanwhile the Royal Rooters whiled away the hours in gambling parlors and brothels or spent their time kibitzing in the hotel lobby, pastimes they liked nearly as much as baseball. Things could have been worse, though. Down in Augusta, Georgia, floodwaters encircled the city, leaving the Boston Braves temporarily isolated, with no way to leave town.

When the weather finally began to improve somewhat in Hot Springs, another cold snap in Boston caused a temporary halt to all pouring of the concrete treads at Fenway Park. As Murnane noted, "As soon as it stops freezing nights work will be rushed 24 hours a day." They had little choice, for a portion of the old grounds had already been sold by the Boston Elevated Company to a real estate developer who planned on erecting apartment buildings where Cy

Young had once been acclaimed "the King of Pitchers." Fenway Park had to be completed, or else the Red Sox would have to go begging to the Braves for a place to play, something certain to make Ban Johnson apoplectic. Fortunately, the freeze let up after only a few days, and work at the park took on a more frantic pace.

About the only real concern the club had was over outfielder Tris Speaker. When he had received his contract at his home in Hubbard, Texas, he had snorted and sent it back unsigned. He was fully aware of his worth and didn't entirely trust McAleer. Some years before, when Speaker was playing in the Texas League and McAleer was manager of the St. Louis Browns, McAleer had expressed some interest in the outfielder, only to conclude that Speaker wasn't ready for the big leagues. While McAleer's snub eventually helped Speaker land with Boston, the outfielder still remembered the slight and wanted to make sure McAleer knew it.

Yet even a player as great as Speaker had little leverage, and as A. H. C. Mitchell of the *Boston Journal* reported in *Sporting Life*, Speaker "likes a little talk about himself." There was plenty of that before he finally made a leisurely arrival in Hot Springs on March 18, met with McAleer, and after a bit of public grousing signed a contract worth around $9,000 a season.

Although the weather continued to be problematic, the pitchers at least were able to get in their work, something that might have been a blessing in disguise. Unlike 1911, when several players left California with sore arms, everyone was still sound. When the weather cooperated the Yannigans faced the Regulars, and the club paired off with the Phillies for several more games, but it was not until the final few days of March that Stahl finally had the time to do some fine-tuning.

One cause for concern had been his pitchers' appalling lack of concern over stolen bases. In an era when nearly every player in the league was a threat to steal and two hundred stolen bases for a team was about average, in 1911, under manager Patsy Donovan, Red Sox pitchers had concluded that holding runners on was not worth worrying about. Stahl thought otherwise.

On March 28, with the field too wet to hold a full workout but the slick infield perfect for sliding, he ordered a special workout for pitchers and catchers. Duffy Lewis, Steve Yerkes, and a few others whom

Paul Shannon described as "not chiefly remarkable for high speed," took turns attempting to steal second. As they did, Stahl instructed pitchers on "a movement that would keep the runner from getting a flying start." In other words, he had the pitchers practice throwing from the stretch position.

The strategy was apparently almost foreign to Joe Wood, and one that he saw little need to master. As Stahl worked with the pitchers, Wood hardly paid attention. When it was his turn to take the mound, he didn't hide his disdain and loafed through the drill. After all, he was the great Joe Wood. What did Jake Stahl know about pitching, except that he couldn't hit it?

While statistics of records such as stolen bases by opponents are incomplete, the fact that Wood reportedly exhibited little concern about base runners may well have been a contributing factor to his relatively disappointing performance thus far in his career. Before 1912 a disproportionate number of runners Wood allowed on base scored, possibly owing, at least in part, to his indifference to holding runners close.

The rest of the staff, cowed by Wood's brashness, followed his lead and also loafed through the practice session. Meanwhile Lewis, Yerkes, and a few others were running themselves ragged, and Cady and Carrigan and the other catchers were growing tired of wasting their time.

Stahl was steamed. Coming into spring training, he had been concerned that because many of his players still knew him as a former teammate they would fail to give him their full respect as manager. Now Wood's insolence was making it abundantly clear that Stahl had been right to worry.

He had seen enough. Yet he did not challenge his player with words or threats of violence. Instead, like a football coach teaching his team a new play, he just kept ordering Wood and his teammates to do the drills over and over and over again, daring them to refuse. Eventually the displeasure of the base runners and the catching staff shamed Wood and the other pitchers into taking the workout more seriously. Shannon reported that it took Stahl "a half an hour" to get through to Wood before he finally began following instructions. That was important, not only for teaching Boston pitchers a better way to deal with base stealing but for demonstrating that even though Stahl was a former player, he was first and foremost the manager of the team and the players—even the almost great Joe Wood—had to listen to him. As Shannon noted, "It was rather disagreeable medicine for some twirlers who have had their own way of doing things in the past, but it showed pretty plainly that Stahl means business."

Stahl found it necessary to put his foot down once more the next day when he started working with his team on signals, not only to the batters but to base runners, fielders, and pitchers. Once more, the pitching staff, apparently following Wood's lead, seemed indifferent to his instructions and tried to test Stahl. This time, feeling more secure, the manager dressed everyone down, as Shannon reported, "calling the men into account."

He also made an important decision. According to custom at the time, apart from selecting the pitchers, setting the batting order, and giving signals to the hitters, many managers exerted little authority on the field during the game. The team captain was usually responsible for making defensive decisions, such as whether to play in or out, and the positioning of players.

Another player-manager would unquestionably have taken that authority himself. After all, Stahl was going to be on the field anyway.

Instead, Jake Stahl made a decision that was both political and, from his perspective, sensible. Charlie Wagner was the most experienced man on the team, and now that his arm was working again, he would be in the lineup every day at shortstop. No one else on the club—and few others in the game—knew the American League as well as Wagner. Stahl defied convention by naming Wagner team captain and made him solely responsible for giving signals on the field.

No one in baseball had ever heard of such a thing. A writer in *Baseball* magazine commented, "Memory fails to recall a duplicate. . . . As all men know, a playing manager is always captain of the team as well." The decision was emblematic not only of Stahl's willingness to flaunt convention but of his desire to bring the team together. By both asserting his authority and then ceding some responsibility to Wagner, Stahl was letting his team know that he was focused solely on winning, not on who was in charge, and that even he, the manager, was willing to take orders if it would help the team. And if the team came first, how could Joe Wood or anyone else take a different approach?

Stahl's recognition that he needed to bring a divided club together would soon pay dividends. By the end of the month both the craps games and the harlots had grown old and tired, and everyone who had been so eager to get to Hot Springs only a few weeks before was now eager to leave and start the season. Paul Shannon's April 1 report reflected the dreary mood at the Hotel Eastman. It began: "More rain, more profanity, more vain longings for the getaway . . . No chance for practice, no opportunity to leave the hotel. More enforced confinement to the lobby and the air is charged with electricity . . . there is more grumbling now than ever the much maligned Redondo Beach Hotel provoked." Indeed, the Mississippi River was at flood stage, and the Sox, who were scheduled to leave by train for an exhibition in Nashville and then Dayton before going to Cincinnati to christen the Reds' new park, had to stay put. The games in Nashville and Dayton were canceled, and the game scheduled for April 2 in Cincinnati was postponed because most of the field was underwater.

The team stayed three extra days in Hot Springs, waiting for the weather to clear. Over the final week Stahl and McAleer had made most of their final roster decisions, which had included cutting loose the pitching dentist, Fred Anderson. But Stahl was still expected to lop off another two or three of the remaining players before opening the season. In something of a surprise, Stahl was still carrying ten pitchers, including Hugh Bedient, and all four catchers. Some observers thought that slugging first baseman Hugh Bradley, who hit .406 with four home runs in the spring, had played well enough to earn a starting berth, but Stahl himself had responded to the challenge by hitting a robust team-high .514 with eight extra-base hits, second only to Speaker.

Tim Murnane liked Boston's pitching, but offered that "I don't see how they can head off the Athletics . . . every member of the Connie Mack crew will play his head off for one more whack at the big money." He figured that the Red Sox had a shot for second place and would battle it out for the runner-up slot with Cleveland, Detroit,

and the White Sox, while Washington, St. Louis, and New York, as
usual, were expected to stumble down the cellar steps.

BOSTON TEAM LUCKY TO GET TRAIN
AWAY FROM HOT SPRINGS

Boston newspapers were already running advertisements for the
April 9 exhibition game between the Sox and Harvard at Fenway
Park. Two years before, a similar exhibition at the Huntington Avenue Grounds had drawn 7,500 people, and the club hoped that, with
the new park as an added attraction, they would draw even more fans.
Murnane thought at least 12,000 fans would turn out if the weather
was good.

As yet, however, Boston's new facility wasn't ready for twelve fans,
much less twelve thousand. Everywhere one looked, from dawn to
dusk and even later, there were carpenters and construction workers
swarming over the facility, which seemed to change minute by minute
as they rushed to finish. Although the treads were finally all in place
and the pavilion was more or less finished, the wooden bleachers in
center field had yet to be completed, and workers were still spreading
slag, a hot mixture of coal tar and cinders, over wood planks to make
the roof waterproof.

But the field was beginning to turn green, particularly in the infield, where Jerome Kelley's attentiveness was paying dividends. He
had his men working on the field every possible minute, overseeding,
aerating, watering, filling holes, patching grass killed by the winter's cold, and chasing away workmen who tried to take a shortcut
by walking across the outfield. Fenway Park was beginning to look
like a ballpark, but it wasn't quite there yet. The stands had no seats,
a protective fence still surrounded the infield grass, and while the
ticket office on the first floor of the office building behind the third-
base line on Jersey Street was nearly ready for business, the smell of
fresh paint wafting through the corridors, the team offices were not
even close to being finished. They were framed in, but there was no
plaster on the walls or doors on the hinges. Beneath the grandstand,
it was still too wet and cold to pour a concrete floor, so every time

a laborer walked up the ramp from beneath the stands he left a trail of muddy footprints. Charles Logue and his subcontractors were everywhere at once, already checking off minor tasks that could be put off until later in favor of those that were absolutely necessary for the opening of the park to the general public.

Most significantly perhaps, the perimeter of the park had yet to be fully enclosed by a permanent fence. The grandstand provided a barrier around the infield, but carpenters were scrambling to fence in the park parallel to each baseline and around the outfield. Putting in a wooden fence was yet another example of cost-cutting, for it would have been relatively easy to build concrete poured walls. That is what had been done in Philadelphia, at Shibe Park, but it was more expensive, and now it was too late anyway. On April 1 all the things that would change Fenway Park from a construction site into a ballpark — the seats, the scoreboard, and other creature comforts — were still missing. It would have been possible to play a game on the field, but it would have been almost impossible for anyone to enjoy it. And there was only a week until the exhibition against Harvard.

April 4 in Hot Springs dawned bright and warm and clear, baseball weather for the first time all spring on the team's last day in town. The Red Sox managed to get in a hard two-hour workout that morning before scrambling back to the hotel just before noon to pack. It was finally time to head north. At 1:30 p.m., twenty-five players, forty trunks of belongings, Mr. and Mrs. Robert McRoy, Ray Collins's new bride, four Boston sportswriters, and a few remaining Royal Rooters boarded the train bound for Memphis.

Twenty-four hours later they arrived in Cincinnati to discover that the Reds had failed to secure them a practice field, so after traveling all day they found themselves confined once more to their hotel, with no opportunity to loosen up. Yet even if they had found a field, they wouldn't have been able to use it: Boston's supply of bats had been left in a car that left the train in Memphis. Stahl threw a fit, and club secretary Robert McRoy fell on his sword and took the blame. Although McRoy sent a telegraph to arrange the shipment of the bats to Cincinnati and sent the team's trainer, Joe Quirk, out to buy more bats just in case the shipment didn't arrive in time, the incident was

still an embarrassment for the club secretary and caused much snick-
ering among the players. So far Boston's new owners had done little
to impress their new employees.

Bats in hand, the Red Sox finally took the field in Cincinnati on
April 6, helping the Reds christen their new ballpark, Redland Field,
which had replaced "the Palace of the Fans." Along with Fenway
Park, Ebbets Field in Brooklyn, and Navin Field in Detroit, Redland
Field was one of four new concrete-and-steel parks scheduled to open
in 1912. It was a handsome facility that featured a double deck around
the infield and a single-deck covered pavilion that extended down
each foul line. Of all the concrete-and-steel parks of the era, Redland
Field, which was renamed Crosley Field in 1934, would change the
least over the course of its history before finally being replaced (by
Riverfront Stadium in 1970).

Redland Field's most distinguishing feature was the so-called terrace in left field, a feature that at first drew little comment. The terrace was a gentle, gradual slope six feet high that ran the length of
the left-field fence to make up the difference in grade between the
field and York Street, which bordered the park beyond the left-field
fence. There was little concern that the gradual rise would bother
outfielders. With the fence 360 feet away from home down the line,
most observers thought it unlikely that anyone would ever hit the
ball that far.

The park wasn't quite finished when the Sox took the field to warm
up before the contest. Even as the game began nearly fifty workers
were still laying sod in the outer reaches of the outfield, but the field
was so big—420 feet in center field—that the workers were virtually
out of play for hitters. Although the weather was fine, if still a bit
cool, the grounds were still wet, and in some places it was downright
muddy. Reds manager Hank O'Day stood on a keg of nails for much
of the game to keep his feet from getting stuck in the mud.

His players, however, never got unstuck. Veteran Bobby Keefe
took the mound for Cincinnati opposite Joe Wood, and the game was
scoreless for the first three innings as Boston showed some rust.
After all, they'd hardly had a chance to play over the previous ten
days. But in the top of the fourth Harry Hooper walked, was sacri-

ficed to second by Yerkes, and then Speaker rolled one up the terrace
to the wall in left-center, scoring Hooper, the first of two Boston
runs in the inning.

The Sox added two more in the fifth and led 4–0 after six innings
as Joe Wood toyed with the Reds, striking out six and giving up only
four hits. Boston broke the game open in the top of the seventh when
Jake Stahl cleared the bases with a drive that hit the fence down the
left-field line. Buck O'Brien mopped up, and the Sox escaped with an
easy 13–1 victory.

The Reds evened the score the next day—in what was Boston's
twelfth and final contest of the spring, including intrasquad exhibitions—winning 6–2 as they took advantage of some sloppy pitching by knuckleball ace Eddie Cicotte and some sloppier fielding by
backup shortstop Marty Krug. He did himself no favors in his effort
to make the team, but in Boston's defense, the Sox were just anxious
to finish the game so they could leave Cincinnati, leave the spring
behind, and start the 1912 campaign. They boarded their train at 6:30
p.m. and were scheduled to make Boston the following evening at
8:00.

At long last, they were going home. And for the first time in their
history home meant Fenway Park . . . if it was ready.

4 ·

Opening Days

The sight of the great, mildly sloping stands, dotted thick
with the straw hats, was breath-taking. This was baseball
gone to heaven . . . Fenway Park is a miracle.

—*Boston Globe*

EARLY IN THE AFTERNOON of April 9, 1912, the electric
streetcars that rumbled through the streets of Boston toward
the Fens began to become more crowded, and the passengers
more lively. The streetcars were filling up, not with grim-faced businessmen on their way back to the office after a lunch break, but with
men—and a few women—with smiles on their faces, chattering ex-
citedly to one another despite the gray skies and stray snowflakes
that swirled to the ground outside the window.

While the map of Ireland was contained in the lines and con-
tours of many of their faces, some of the younger passengers spoke
in distinctly patrician accents. Normally, these two strains of Boston society rarely intermingled, but on this day both groups—the
civil servants and clerks and the students of Harvard University in
Cambridge—were headed to the same destination, Fenway Park, for
the very first time. At 3:30 p.m. the umpire's call to "play ball" would
christen the new park and begin a new era.

Most came by streetcar in a system that crisscrossed much of
eastern New England and made it possible to travel from Nashua,
New Hampshire, to Providence, Rhode Island, without ever stepping
aboard a railcar. As yet, there was no subway service to nearby Kenmore Square, and on the cold gray day few fans felt like walking very

far to the park. Those arriving aboard the Ipswich Street cars stepped off at the Jersey Street stop, while those on the Beacon Street line stopped at Deerfield, a short walk away. The ride cost only a nickel.

Many in the crowd were a little surprised by what they saw—a grandstand faced with brick and concrete that stretched down Jersey Street and wrapped around the corner. The stands then continued toward Ipswich Street, surrounded by a rough plank fence that ran from the end of the stands on Jersey Street, paralleled Brookline Avenue, and ran nearly a hundred yards down Lansdowne Street before turning just short of Ipswich Street and running back down the new street (Van Ness) to meet the end of the pavilion. Although there were clearly more people on the street around the new park than usual, and those who were there were obviously excited, few other baseball fans seemed eager to sit in the stands in early April and watch Harvard play, brand-new ballpark or not. The real cranks among Boston fans had seen the park as it was being built. There was little mystery about its contents, for only in the last few days had the view from the surrounding streets been blocked by a permanent fence. Almost every household in nearby Roxbury knew someone who had been working at the park, and until recently it had been little problem to wander into Fenway Park and take a look up close, as long as you stayed out of the way of the workers and didn't try to pocket a handful of nails or abscond with a toolbox or a stray piece of lumber.

Most of the fans arriving at the park from Cambridge had probably never even been to that part of the Fens before. All the museums were on the other side of Olmsted's park. In contrast to those magnificent edifices, Fenway Park looked almost foreign, like a fortress on the edge of the prairie, mostly surrounded by open space and raw land.

Yet fans who attended that first game still had a few experiences upon their arrival at Fenway Park that subsequent generations of Red Sox fans would find familiar, at least those fans who sat in either the grandstand or the pavilion. Those without tickets to the game queued up at the Red Sox ticket offices at the north end of the Jersey Street facade and waited patiently for tickets as they turned away from the wind. Then, depending on the seat they'd purchased, fans were directed to one of several gates. Patrons with tickets for the pavilion or the bleachers had to walk around the park, either down

Jersey Street to Van Ness to enter the pavilion or around the other way, up Brookline and then down Lansdowne Street, to find a seat in the bleachers.

For fans who had tickets for a seat in the grandstand or a box, the experience was much the same in 1912 as it is today, albeit without the carnival-like atmosphere that now inhabits Yawkey Way. The Jersey Street facade is one feature of the park that has barely changed over the years: fans today still see the name "FENWAY PARK" cast in hollow relief in concrete atop the rooftop parapet, just as the first fans to arrive at Fenway Park did in 1912. Entering the park through the gate in the facade alongside the club offices, fans handed their ticket to an usher and then entered the park. Although Fenway would soon boast eighteen turnstiles—a new feature for Boston fans, turnstiles would both help control access to the park and allow a more accurate count of those in attendance—they would not be installed for another week.

Beneath the grandstand one had the feeling of entering what then seemed like an immense, dimly lit cavern, the walls and roof of which—the underside of the grandstand—were faced with concrete. The floor was dirt. Not until 1914 would the Red Sox find the time—and the money—to cover the compressed earthen floor with concrete. For the first two years of Fenway's existence fans walked on ground beneath the grandstand, slipping in the mud during wet weather while kicking up dust in the heat of the summer.

Beneath the grandstand were also what then seemed almost an extravagance—two toilet rooms, a large one to accommodate men and another, much smaller one for women, with two similar, but smaller facilities also available up off the promenade. Once again, concrete dominated. The trough-like urinals were made, not of slate or porcelain, but of concrete. In the men's toilet they lined three sides of the room, allowing for dozens of male fans to use the facilities at the same time.

Signs directed fans to the ramps that led to the grandstands, and once each fan began to step toward the light pouring in through the short tunnel atop the ramp, time stopped. Even on this grayest of days the green vision of a baseball field, contrasted against the dank interior of the ballpark, seemed illuminated and inspired wonder, particularly on this day when each spectator first gathered the experience of arriving at Fenway Park deep into his or her own heart. Despite the gray skies, the view was breathtaking. It may have still felt like winter outside the park, but to look out upon the field was to see the summer still to come.

On the field Jerome Kelley and his men had been working overtime, and it showed. From near ground level the field—particularly the infield—appeared to be a vast expanse of pale green, as if the calendar had suddenly been flipped forward a month. Not until fans climbed higher up in the stands could they see just how sparse the grass was, for outside of the infield, bare ground dominated. The construction shacks had been removed from the field only a few weeks before. At the farther reaches of the park—in front of the outfield fence and before the bleachers—there was virtually no grass at all. Over the last week or so the work to finish the bleachers and erect a fence to enclose the outfield had left the perimeter of the field rutted and pockmarked with footprints.

Even as the crowd arrived in a steady stream Kelley's men still circled the field, chalking the foul lines, working with rakes, brooms, wheelbarrows, and shovels, smoothing the ground here, filling a hole there, brushing away a puddle of water or prying up a stone that winter's frost had heaved to the surface. Ready or not—and in many ways it was not ready—Fenway Park was about to host the first game in its storied history.

In the grandstand, almost oblivious to the crowd, crews of men were still methodically bolting together seats and fixing them to the treads of the grandstand, working from the lowest rows up, but only a few thousand seats were in place. Thousands of permanent seats and seat parts were still stacked on pallets beneath the stands, wrapped and protected against the weather, and would not be installed until after the exhibition game. In the concrete boxes down front, each separated from the next by a pipe railing, workmen carried stacks of opera chairs up the ramps from below the stands, snapped them open, and arranged them in neat rows. There were no fixed seats in the boxes, nor were there ever intended to be any.

The men worked quickly, but even as the first patrons wandered the stands and took their seats, they were not rushed. Although the Red Sox had optimistically hoped that Boston fans would be so curious about the new park that many thousands would turn out for the first game at Fenway Park—even an unofficial one—by April 9 it was clear that was not going to happen. At Wright and Ditson's sporting goods store on Washington Street in downtown Boston—George Wright of the Red Stockings was one of its founders—and the Harvard Athletic Association in Cambridge, tickets had been on sale for weeks. While the ninety-five private boxes had already been sold for the season at the cost of $250 each, on this day many seats in the first tier of boxes were available for $1.50 and those in the second tier were going for $1.25. A seat in the grandstand cost a dollar, with the first ten rows available for reserve, while a bleacher seat in the pavilion went for fifty cents and a place in the distant center-field bleachers was a quarter. Ushers wearing white jackets and red caps stood at the ready to assist patrons, wiping the moisture from the seats of fans with high-priced tickets while simply pointing the way for those with seats in the pavilion or bleachers.

INVITE OLD TIMERS TO RED SOX OPENING

Yet despite the fact that it was the first game and the ball club had touted the appearance of the "Old Timers," a who's who of Boston baseball players, professional and collegiate, from the 1860s onward, the public had evinced little interest in the game. The same men had all been honored at the Huntington Avenue Grounds near the end of the 1908 season with great success, but on this day the presence of men like Tommy Bond, who had starred for Boston in the 1870s, drew few extra fans to the ballpark. McAleer's scheme to milk a big crowd for the exhibition was a financial failure, perhaps the first sign that he would have trouble reading the desires of Boston fans. Most cranks seemed content to wait another week to see a real game that counted in the standings.

While McAleer might have been disappointed, the men putting the seats together were not. Had anything close to a capacity crowd turned out, thousands of fans would have had nowhere to sit, but with the poor advance sales and even poorer weather, the few seats in place were more than sufficient for the crowd at hand—half the tickets purchased had been for the pavilion and the bleachers anyway.

Not only were those arriving at Fenway on the afternoon of April 9 dyed-in-the-wool fans, but many of them, wisely, were dressed in wool themselves. Although the weather forecast called for "fair and warmer" conditions, that was a relative description. At any rate, the sky told a different story. The temperature had dropped below freezing overnight and had climbed only a few degrees since, to the mid thirties, and in the stands it was as damp and raw as the deck of a cruise ship dodging icebergs and plowing through the icy waters of the North Atlantic. Nothing about the day indicated that it was adequate for baseball. On any other day, in fact, the game probably would have been canceled.

None of this made the Red Sox players particularly eager to play. They had arrived in Boston the previous evening after traveling all night by train from Cincinnati. The journey had created some anxiety among the players, for as the train rocketed eastward chunks of broken ice still choked the Mohawk River and the lower valleys were all flooded, the result of a quick thaw and the torrential rains that had inundated most of the country all spring. Even though the sun broke through outside Albany, revealing farms and fields just beginning to turn green, as the train rose through the Berkshire Hills the ground turned white and summer still felt some months off. Not until the train approached Worcester, where native Hugh Bradley had been greeted by a large crowd, did bare ground show itself again. Still, the scene outside the windows of the train gave little indication that they would be playing baseball against Harvard in a little over twenty-four hours.

When the train finally appeared at Back Bay Station just after 9:00 p.m., nearly an hour late, hundreds of fans had gathered to meet it. A great cheer went up not unlike that which would have greeted a conquering army, a roar that nearly drowned out the sound of the steam engines.

As each player stepped from the train, carrying his grip, he was surrounded by cheering fans and well-wishers who stuck out their hands, hoping for a handshake and a quick word while offering their best wishes for the upcoming season. The players patiently put up with the reception but at the same time slowly pushed their way

through the crowd and out into the street. They were tired of traveling and just wanted to unpack.

It was then that the Red Sox received word that everything, perhaps, was not quite what they had expected. After hearing all spring
about their great new ballpark, they were told not to report to Fenway Park the following day, but to the Park Riding School on Ipswich
Street, where their uniforms would be waiting for them. The clubhouse at Fenway Park was still unfinished, and the club had made
arrangements for them to dress at the school. For the time being they
would walk to the park in uniform, just as they had when playing at
the Huntington Avenue Grounds.

They responded with rolled eyes, tired sighs, and knowing nods
to one another—first McRoy loses their bats, and now McAleer was
making them change in a stable. With that bit of news stuck in their
craw, the players drifted off, some boarding streetcars, others grab-
bing one of the jitney cabs that waited outside the station, and still
others choosing to take grip in hand and walk home in order to work
out the stiffness from being cooped up aboard the train for more than
twenty-four hours.

By habit, half the players had already made arrangements to stay
at Put's on Huntington Avenue, even though it was not quite as convenient to their new home as it had been to their previous one. A like
number, however, had decided that it was time to abandon Put's for
something a bit more convenient to Fenway Park. Close to a dozen
players had secured accommodations in advance at the Copley Square
Hotel; from there they could walk to Fenway in good weather in
about twenty minutes or take the trolley, which would deliver them
to the ballpark in just a few short minutes.

On the day of the game, after a late breakfast, most players began
making their way toward the riding school a few hours before the
game, arriving in groups of two or three, making the somewhat un-
familiar trip for the first time. They were pleased to discover that
they would not actually be dressing in the stables; the school, which
catered to bluebloods and their offspring, contained sizable and comfortable dressing quarters. Each player found his uniform waiting,
and they teased each other as they dressed in their regular-season

uniforms for the first time, looking to trade pants and shirts that were too big or too small. They were in no rush and lingered at the school until the last possible moment, playing cards, stuffing their jaws with tobacco, and engaging in the easy banter of the clubhouse. The field was in no condition for much more than a cursory work-out, and besides, the Harvard nine were in no rush either. Though they were excited to play on a major league field, the weather was no different in Cambridge, and the team had dressed in uniform at the university before traveling to Fenway Park. In fact, the contest would be the first time all year that the Crimson had even had the opportunity to play on a real field at all. Thus far most of their practice had taken place indoors or at Soldiers Field. They had yet to play a game outdoors.

While an editorial in the *Globe* prophesied that the contest would create "a moving picture worthy of the brush of one of the Old Masters," that was far from the case when the players from both teams took the field for a few minutes of warm-ups, tossing the ball back and forth. The crowd, some warmed by the free coffee the ball club distributed under the stands from enormous urns and others by the contents of the flasks tucked into their coat pockets, gave the players of each team an enthusiastic cheer. The Red Sox were dressed in their home whites, the name "Red Sox" emblazoned across their chests in red, and they wore plain white woolen caps and white socks with a broad red stripe that circled the calf and gave them their name. Not that fans could see any of these details yet, for as the players warmed up most of them also wore heavy, red woolen sweaters to ward off the chill.

With the regular season scheduled to begin in New York in only two days, on April 11, Stahl selected twenty-five-year-old Casey Hageman, who had joined the team along with Buck O'Brien from Denver late in 1911 and was still fighting for a place on the final squad, to pitch the exhibition. The remainder of the lineup was made up primarily of regulars—Harry Hooper, Steve Yerkes, Tris Speaker, Jake Stahl, Larry Gardner, and Duffy Lewis. Marty Krug played shortstop. In the cold weather Stahl was still protective of Charlie Wagner's arm and did not want to risk injury in a mere exhibition. For the same reason he held Bill Carrigan back and instead penciled Pinch Thomas, the fourth-string catcher, into the lineup. Like Hageman, he was still trying to make the club and was thrilled to have one more chance to prove himself to his manager.

After warming up for a few minutes with his catcher down the first-base line, Casey Hageman of the Red Sox walked to the pitcher's box at 3:30 p.m. As he stood waiting for the umpire to call for him to throw the first pitch to begin the game, his teammates jogged out to their positions and the crowd cheered them enthusiastically. For a moment or two the players stood and just took in their surroundings, getting their first good look at the park from the perspective they would bring to it for the remainder of the season.

In front of them sat the immense grandstand, stretching a full 510 feet from one end to the other. The stands held barely a thousand shivering fans, most wearing caps or homburg hats and heavy coats. A mesh screen stretched from the grandstand roof to protect fans in the section of seats immediately behind the plate from foul balls, but it stopped before reaching the box seats. Those fans would have to pay attention to stay safe. The base of the stands did not present a smooth parabola behind the plate, as it does today, but instead formed a series of shallow angles as each section of stand met another.

Only the lower ten or fifteen rows of the grandstand had seats. In the remainder of the stands the treads, looking like giant stairs, sat empty. In the occupied box seats at the front of the grandstand sat the swells, the VIPs and old-timers resplendent in formal wear and long coats, hands buried deep in pockets.

At the base of the stand on each side of the infield was a concrete dugout, Boston's on the first-base line and the visitors' on the third-base side. Each dugout was only forty feet long, five feet wide, and three and a half feet deep, which put the floor of each dugout well below field grade. On this very first day those floors were already covered with water, reflecting a drainage problem that has not fully been resolved to this day. The roof of each dugout was cantilevered reinforced concrete, with no external support. A long slat-style bench ran the length of each dugout, a concrete support column in the center nearly divided it in two, and an open pipe rail fence in front of the dugout prevented fielders from falling in when pursuing pop flies. A set of concrete steps at the far end led to the field, and the near end was open to the space between the stands. Once the clubhouse was finished, the players would be able to go back and forth without mingling with the fans. For now there was barely enough room for everyone to sit.

Atop the grandstand, directly behind home plate and looking somewhat like a covered bridge, was a wooden press box, about the same length as the dugout, containing accommodations for up to sixteen telegraph operators. Access to the press box was gained by a set of stairs at the back of the grandstand, the only stairs, apart from those in each dugout and those in between sections of the stands, in the entire park. Inside sat the pioneers of Boston sportswriting— Tim Murnane and Melville Webb of the *Globe*, Walter S. Barnes and Ralph McMillen of the *Boston Herald*, Herman Nickerson and A. H. C. Mitchell of the *Journal*, and Paul Shannon of the *Post*, all staking out the seats they would occupy for the remainder of the season. The press box also contained—or would soon—a desk and a keyboard that would be used to operate the new electric scoreboard, which had yet to be installed in left field. Although the players could not tell from the field, the roof of the grandstand sloped back toward the street, where the outside facades created a four-foot parapet designed to prevent foul balls that landed on the roof from rolling to the street. At the time most foul balls, even those hit in the stands, were retrieved by ushers and put back in play. The ball quickly turned dark from grass stains, dirt, and spit, a factor that was often taken into consideration when selecting a starting pitcher—the combination of cloudy days and dark baseballs made the ball hard to see, and fastball pitchers harder to hit.

Past first base was the open-alley firebreak some ten to fifteen feet wide between the grandstand and the pavilion, where another thousand fans or so sat crammed together in the lower sections of the wooden bleachers. Nearly 250 feet long, the pavilion itself did not precisely parallel the first-base line but was tilted slightly toward the field, so the most distant corner of the stands (section 6 in Fenway today) encroached on the field and created the beginning of the outfield wall. By today's standards, it was not far off—barely 300 feet, if that, from home plate down the line. At the front end of the pavilion a bare wooden fence of vertical planks only about eight feet tall angled far back and then turned and met the center-field bleachers more than 400 feet from home plate. Commenting in the *Post* that the right-field fence was "even farther" away than the fence at Huntington Avenue, which was at least 320 feet down the line, Paul Shannon was referring to the distance in the power alley. He also made the claim that the distance to the center-field bleachers was "essentially the same" as Huntington Avenue. But true and accurate measurements to the fences at Fenway Park at the time the ballpark opened may never be known unless precise architectural plans dating to the construction surface. Even then, these distances may never be known with absolute certainty. In the era before the home run, there was no real need to know precisely how far each fence was from home plate. The urge to pin down distances would arrive with the long ball.

The center-field bleachers faced the infield, were roughly rectangular in shape and approximately 140 feet in length, and contained more than forty rows of seats. The far end extended almost to the property boundary on Lansdowne Street, while the backside of the bleachers was hard against the property of the Fenway Garage Company, almost filling the triangle between Lansdowne Street, Ipswich Street, and Fenway Park. Between the bleachers and the center-field end of the left-field wall, in dead center field, was an open area of fair ground shaped roughly like a triangle. At the back of this open space the park was at its absolute deepest, reportedly 488 feet from home plate, and an enormous flagpole just a few feet from the back fence towered over the bleachers.

From the deepest part of the park ran the left-field fence—neither green yet nor a monster—fronted by an earthen embankment not unlike that in Cincinnati, which extended from the end of the bleachers to the property line, paralleling Lansdowne Street. In an oddity, the rise drew no comment on this first day, perhaps because it had been visible in the plans for Fenway Park since at least 1911 and was considered so far from home plate that few believed it would ever come into play on a regular basis.

Although this rise—which would eventually be nicknamed "Duffy's Cliff" after Sox left fielder Duffy Lewis—would soon be turned over for use by standing-room crowds or to support temporary bleachers, this usage was incidental. The purpose of the hill was purely structural—and economic. Since the plot of land on which Fenway Park was built was higher on the Lansdowne Street side, that end of the field had been brought down to grade to make it level with the remainder of the park. To accomplish this the grade of the field was lowered along Lansdowne Street, leaving the street itself ten to fifteen feet above field grade.

To make up the difference architect James McLaughlin essentially had two options, for no one ever even gave a thought to moving Lansdowne Street. A poured reinforced-concrete fence, built atop piers built on hardpan, like that which surrounded Shibe Park, would have been sufficient both to "hold back" Lansdowne Street and to create a barrier for the ballpark. But it also would have had to be at least twenty or twenty-five feet tall to accomplish the task. At a length of nearly four hundred feet, stretching to the corner of the property (below what is now the very back of section 38 of the bleachers), such an edifice would have been extremely costly and would have used nearly as much concrete and reinforcing steel as the grandstand itself.

So McLaughlin did the next best thing. It was a relatively easy task for engineers to calculate the pressure that the difference in grade would produce on the high side. To counteract that an earthen slope—essentially a dam—was created to ensure that Lansdowne Street would stay put. Although it has often been reported that the incline was ten feet tall, anecdotal evidence based on photographs and the fact that at least seven rows of temporary bleacher tiers were later built atop the wall suggest that it may have been somewhat taller, perhaps twelve feet, and that the slope itself stretched a bit farther out toward the field—by fifteen to twenty feet—as the embankment angle appears to be somewhat less than forty-five degrees.

Atop the wall was a simple but robust plank fence that had probably been treated with both a fire-retardant and a preservative to protect it from the rain and weather; it was held fast by both horizontal supports known as "whalers" on the backside and stout wood braces that extended at nearly a forty-five-degree angle toward Lansdowne Street. The fence was not precisely on the property line but several feet south of it, so a secondary fence ran along Lansdowne Street to prevent passersby from trying to scale the wall. Upright wooden support columns were probably set in concrete far below grade.

But on this first day the fence was not yet finished. Wallace Goldsmith's cartoon drawings in the *Globe* the next day clearly show that the fence was built in two separate vertical sections, one atop the other, and that only a few of the top sections, flanking the space where the scoreboard was supposed to be, were yet in place.

The reason for the wall, of course, was to prevent people standing atop any building the Boston Garage Company might build on Lansdowne Street from seeing inside the park. But on this day anyway, with the top half of the wall unfinished, it was probably still possible to look into the park from the garage without buying a ticket. Until the wall was finished, the height of the barrier from the field in front of the embankment to the top of the fence was just over twenty feet. When finished, the wall would be approximately 35 feet tall.

That was not all a player saw that first day when he looked upon the wall. According to a Goldsmith drawing, at some point during the contest the game was watched by two spectators perched on some scaffolding that hung from the top of the wall near the left-field line — scaffolding that was either used during construction of the fence or was in place to hang advertisements over the next week. These two anonymous workmen were the first two spectators to watch a game from roughly the same viewpoint as those who occupy today's "Green Monster" seats.

If Goldsmith's drawing is accurate, as of yet there were no advertisements in place on the unfinished wall. By the time Fenway Park opened officially that was no longer the case. Although it is uncertain precisely when the wall was covered entirely by advertisements, there is no doubt that by the end of the season it was completely covered.

The left-field fence continued far into foul territory until it reached the property boundary just short of Brookline Avenue; then another tall fence ran approximately two hundred feet to meet the backside of the grandstand on the third-base side, leaving a wide expanse of foul ground between the foul line, the grandstand, and the outfield fence and occupying the space taken up by sections 28 to 33 in today's Fenway Park. Some sportswriters speculated that the area would make a fine place for pitchers to warm up, but "bullpens" as such were not much in use at the time. Since the area was not in view from the third-base dugout, where the opposing manager could see who was warming up, such an arrangement would have needed approval from the league. Besides, at some point in the future, as needed, the club planned to fill this space with seats. The grandstand, in fact, had been designed so that whenever more seats were built it could be done seamlessly and made to look like part of the original structure.

After Casey Hageman threw a few warm-up tosses to Pinch Thomas, Harvard Crimson third baseman and captain Dana Wingate stepped into the batter's box, becoming the first batter in the history of Fenway Park. A native of Winchester, Massachusetts, Wingate took Hageman's first pitch for a ball, then struck out, overmatched by Hageman's fastball.

He may well have been intimidated, and with good reason. While pitching for Grand Rapids in the Central League in 1908, Hageman threw a pitch that struck hitter Charlie Pinkney behind the left ear, killing him. Hageman was mortified and sat out the 1909 season before making his return in 1910, with Denver in the Western League, where he teamed with Buck O'Brien in 1911 to form one of the best pitching tandems in the league.

The pitcher dispatched the next two Harvard batters with ease. One of them, shortstop Dowd Desha, became the first man to make fair contact with the ball at Fenway Park, lofting a soft fly to Steve Yerkes at second for the second out of the game.

Sam Felton, the son of a railroad magnate and better known for his kicking ability on the gridiron, toed the rubber for Harvard. Although he would later be offered a $15,000 contract by the Philadelphia Athletics—which he would refuse—on this day he pitched like a rank amateur and struggled to find the plate. Harry Hooper led off for the Red Sox with a deep fly ball, then Steve Yerkes singled to right field to collect Fenway's first hit, but after loading the bases the Red Sox failed to score.

They broke through on Felton in the second when, after two walks, Hageman helped his own cause with a hit, knocking in Marty Krug, who gained the honor of scoring the park's first run. With that out of the way, the rest of the contest went fast as one Harvard hitter after another went down on strikes, the Crimson collecting only one hit, and the Red Sox, taking advantage of Felton's wildness, kept walking to first only to be stranded. Then, in the fifth inning, Hageman, a one-man team, singled in a second run to give the Red Sox a 2–0 lead. By then it was snowing, and a cold wind blowing in from the northwest made it feel even colder. The crowd had seen enough and started to drift off, and after Harvard went out again in the top of the seventh, as Hageman collected his ninth strikeout, the Sox decided they had had enough as well. Stahl waved the umpire over to the dugout and to the relief of all ended the contest.

The game, admitted Mel Webb in the *Globe* the next day, "did not amount to a great deal." Another unattributed comment in the *Globe* gushed over the grandstand, praising it for its pitch, so that "the milliner's 'art' in front of you will give you no bother," and offered that "it is a great thing to have an unobstructed view," which of course was true—and remains true—only of seats in the lower half of the stands. Local scribes, to no great surprise, gave the ballpark a thumbs-up. Herman Nickerson of the *Boston Journal* called the new park "a corker" and added, "When it is finished it will be the best in either major league circuit." That wasn't true, for Fenway was neither as spacious nor as handsome as most of the other concrete-and-steel structures built at the time, but few cities in baseball have ever been more boosterish than Boston, and that was as true in 1912 as it would be for some decades after.

BOSTON 2, HARVARD 0

Crimson None Too Easy
Sox Open New Park With Victory
Crowd Of 3,000 Shivers

The Sox were supposed to go to Worcester for an exhibition the following day, but owing to the cold Stahl called the game off. They left by train for New York and opened the season for real on April 11 at Hilltop Park against the Yankees.

The weather was much better in Manhattan, and it almost felt like spring when Boston took the field. The Sox had finished only a game and a half ahead of New York in 1911, and Boston had won the season series by the margin of only a single game, so the opening series against New York promised to provide Stahl with an accurate gauge of just how much his team had improved—or not.

The two clubs were already rivals, a relationship that over time has only grown more heated. Indeed, the rivalry dates back nearly to the birth of the game, when the fledgling Boston version of baseball, known as "the Massachusetts game," lost out in favor of New York's version. Ever since that time Boston and New York baseball interests have intermittently seemed to go head-to-head against one another, as if no other two cities are similarly connected through geographic proximity and cultural roles. Boston, considered America's dominant city at the beginning of the nineteenth century, had lost that position to New York by the dawn of the twentieth century. The Hub has since taken great pride in bettering New York at anything.

But the rivalry was also more than symbolic. Much to the consternation of Ban Johnson, the Yankees had yet to win a pennant or mount much of a challenge to the powerful Giants of the National League. That may have been the last bit of unfinished business left for his league in its long, drawn-out battle against the NL. That conflict, while outwardly peaceful, had lasted more than a decade and was still occasionally acrimonious. Johnson had tried several times to steer a pennant New York's way, including in 1904 when he tried to do so at Boston's expense. Jack Chesbro's ill-timed wild pitch had thwarted that effort, and in recent years New York's two corrupt co-owners, Frank Ferrell and William Devery, had squandered every advantage Johnson had steered their way. The role of Giant killer now fell to other American League franchises. The Athletics had successfully filled the role in 1911, and the more optimistic Red Sox fans in 1912 hoped it was now Boston's turn. But any talk of besting the Giants in the 1912 World's Series was as yet a premature and distant dream, one that had no reality whatsoever unless the Red Sox could first prove they were better than the Yankees, not to mention the Athletics, Tigers, and other AL powers.

They got a start on that on opening day at Hilltop Park. After watching patiently while New York went through with the usual opening day rituals, including the presentation of a loving cup to manager Harry Wolverton, Boston began the first inning as if they were executing a plan. Leadoff hitter Harry Hooper singled, stole second, went to third on an errant throw, and then walked home when Jake Stahl sent a deep drive to left. It was 1–0 and Joe Wood had yet to break a sweat.

Unfortunately, by the time he did New York led 2–1. In the bottom of the inning the Yankees jumped all over him, taking advantage of a walk to leadoff hitter Harry Wolters and then using a series of sacrifices, stolen bases, and daring base running to plate two runs while Boston threw the ball all over the lot. Only a strong peg from Duffy Lewis in left that cut down a run at home allowed Boston to escape the inning.

It might have been the best thing that could have happened to Joe Wood. In one short inning he demonstrated every trait that had made him so frustrating to watch in 1911—a bout of wildness coupled with an inability to hold runners on had combined to cost him a lead, underscoring every point Stahl had been trying to make to him all spring.

It finally began to click. Wood settled down after the first, and like his Yankees counterpart, Ray Caldwell, he held the opposition scoreless through the next seven innings. He may have been helped by the fact that in 1912 American League pitchers were allowed to make some warm-up tosses before each inning. In 1911, when the practice had been banned, Wood and every other pitcher in the league faced the first hitter of each inning stone-cold. For a hard-throwing youngster like Wood, the chance to take a few warm-up tosses could only help.

Still, the Sox entered the ninth trailing 2–1. Then Stahl started the inning with a walk. Playing to tie the score, Gardner sacrificed him to second, and Lewis made his manager look like a genius with a single to tie the game. Caldwell then made Stahl look even smarter as he came unglued. By the time he was pulled from the game, Joe Wood's two-run single had made the score 5–2. The Sox pitcher held on in the bottom of the inning, and the Sox won, 5–3. They beat New York the next two days behind Buck O'Brien and Charley Hall. Hall came on in relief of Casey Hageman, who in the first inning discovered that the Yankees were a bit harder to retire than the boys from Harvard.

His performance was such a disappointment that it virtually ended his Red Sox career. The first Red Sox pitcher to appear at Fenway Park—albeit in an exhibition—would make only one more appearance in a Boston uniform.

After the game the Sox took the train to Philadelphia to face the defending champions in a three-game series before returning home for the official opening of Fenway Park scheduled for April 18. By the time they took the field against the Athletics on the afternoon of April 15, newsboys on every corner were screaming out headlines from the local papers, letting everyone know about the deadly sinking of the RMS *Titanic*. An Olympic-class passenger liner owned by the White Star Line, a British shipping company, the ship had struck an iceberg and sank in the North Atlantic, killing 1,517 of the 2,223 people on board, one of the deadliest maritime disasters in history.

Many historians have subsequently claimed that opening day at Fenway Park was overshadowed by the disaster and have blamed it for the apparent lack of sufficient newspaper coverage of the event. Such an interpretation not only ignores the fact that the *Titanic* sank a full five days before the Red Sox actually opened Fenway Park but shows little understanding of baseball's role in society or of the journalism of the day.

In 2012, or at any other time in the last five or six decades, the opening of a new major league ballpark, a symbol of civic pride or urban renewal, has almost always spawned newspaper coverage ranging from the comprehensive to the excessive. Not so in 1912. Ballparks were seen as utilitarian structures symbolic of little more than the need to put more people in the seats. Few lasted more than a couple of decades, so the building of a new park was not a once-in-a-lifetime event that inspired much poetry. In the context of the era the opening of Fenway Park was simply not that big of a deal.

The size and scope of the coverage in the sports sections of the Boston papers was unaffected by the *Titanic* story—on Saturday, April 20, the day the park finally opened, the *Globe* sports section, for example, was its usual three pages, with a full page given over to the running of the Boston Marathon. Coverage of the opening of Fenway Park and the first Red Sox home game of the 1912 season appeared the next day in the expanded Sunday papers, where there was more than enough room to report on the game, the opening of Fenway Park, and the *Titanic* disaster. Most papers, including the *Globe*, still found room to begin their game story on page 1, sharing it with news of the disastrous accident, but none saw the need to go overboard with their coverage of the opening of the ballpark. Two years later the opening of Braves Field would be treated in the same matter-of-fact fashion. There is simply no evidence whatsoever that the sinking of the *Titanic* had any adverse or significant impact on the coverage of the opening of Fenway Park.

In Philadelphia, where the A's had already opened their season a few days before, the game went on without regard to the disaster and the players seemed unaffected. Boston pitchers continued to experience first-inning woes as the A's jumped on knuckleballer Eddie Cicotte for four runs and won going away, 4–1, but the next day the Sox bounced back to score four runs of their own in the first inning and stake Joe Wood to a 4–0 lead.

Once more, however, Wood exhibited first-inning jitters as the A's parlayed a couple of hits and a passed ball into a run. An exasperated Jake Stahl was about out of patience and had Buck O'Brien already warming up when Danny Murphy ripped a line drive down the third-base line. Larry Gardner left his feet, stretched out, and snared the ball. A's third baseman Frank Baker was already halfway to third when Gardner doubled him off second to end the inning and give Wood another chance.

He did not disappoint. Over the remainder of the game he found both the plate and his fastball, striking out eleven and giving up only one more run as the Sox gained some confidence with a decisive 9–2 win over the A's. So far they hadn't seen anything from either New York or Philadelphia that scared them. The final game of the series against Philadelphia, on April 17, was rained out. The Red Sox immediately caught a train north and made it to Back Bay Station just before 10:00 p.m. They scattered for their homes and hotels in anticipation of the official christening of Fenway Park the following afternoon, on April 18.

Although the *Titanic* did not affect the game, once again the weather did, as it had all spring long. The same system that caused the rainout in Philadelphia on April 17 was parked over Boston when the players awoke on the morning of April 18. Nevertheless, despite the gray skies and the fact that the forecast called for clearing the following day, Patriots' Day, the Sox prepared to play. Jake Stahl intimated that either Buck O'Brien or Charley Hall would be the starting pitcher for Boston.

Out at Fenway Park a great deal of activity had taken place since the exhibition game versus Harvard. All the grandstand seats were now in place, each one numbered in gold leaf, and the left-field wall was finished, reaching its full height. A few warm, sunny days had helped the field turn a bit greener, and Jerome Kelley's crew had handled the grounds with care. They were delighted that one of four sections of rubberized canvas designed to protect the infield from inclement weather arrived before the game. They would soon need it.

Workers had spent the previous day hanging bunting from the box seats at the base of the grandstand and clearing the park of construction debris and other signs of the work that had occupied hundreds of men from October until the last few hours. To the fans the park was, for all intents and purposes, finished. But there was still no one working behind the windows on the second floor of the Jersey Street building. Apart from the first-floor ticket office, the rest of the team's offices were still unfinished and incomplete, as was the players' clubhouse. For the time being they would continue to dress at the riding school and walk to the park.

The Sox planned to open Fenway with a bit of pomp and circumstance. The Letter Carriers' Band, a staple at big events at Huntington Avenue, was scheduled to be on hand and begin serenading the crowd at one o'clock, accompanied by a quartet. Section L of the grandstand was held in reserve for local luminaries, primarily politicians and members of the Church. In a longstanding tradition in Boston baseball circles—one that, to a degree, is still in effect and until recently was little changed—free tickets and passes for opening day were distributed to the most powerful denizens of City Hall, virtually all of whom took advantage of the perk. Cardinal William O'Connell, a close friend of contractor Charles Logue, had it even better. McAleer and Stahl had already presented him with a gold lifetime pass to the new park, and he was expected to take advantage of it. Logue himself also intended to attend, and presumably so did architect James McLaughlin.

McAleer and company expected a big crowd. The advance sale at Wright and Ditson's was enormous, and the Sox decided to hold back 7,500 tickets to sell on the day of the game so fans who arrived without a ticket would not be turned away, and, just as significantly, to keep the precious tickets out of the hands of speculators.

But rain that began as a fine mist turned into a drizzle. Just after noon, as the first fans began to show at the park, it became a deluge. McAleer had no choice but to cancel the game. Opening day was a washout.

McAleer then tried to make lemonade from the cancellation. As Paul Shannon put it in the *Post* the next morning, evoking the gods, "should J. Pluvius [Jupiter, god of sky and thunder and the sender of rain] conclude to hold the dipper out and sidetrack the downfall that threatened last night to make a swimming pool out of the new Red Sox park," McAleer had a contingency plan. Friday, April 19, was Patriots' Day in Massachusetts, a state holiday that commemorated the Revolutionary War battles of Lexington and Concord and was also the traditional date for the running of the Boston Marathon. The Sox were scheduled to play their second contest of the season that afternoon and had already sold thousands of tickets for the holiday event. Rather than turn that contest into a doubleheader, going head-to-head with the marathon and losing out on a full house, McAleer decided to play a morning/afternoon split doubleheader, the first game at 10:30 a.m. and the second contest at 3:15 p.m. That would allow fans from the first game to see the end of the marathon as runners trekked down nearby Commonwealth Avenue toward Copley Square, while the crowd that gathered for the marathon could watch the runners pass and then go to Fenway Park. While a Patriots' Day contest would not become an annual event for the Red Sox until 1959, purely by accident McAleer seemed poised to take advantage of the fortuitous circumstance that paired the holiday with a big crowd just outside Fenway Park. By splitting admission for the two games, he was guaranteed a windfall—if the weather held.

Tickets that had been bought in advance for the canceled contest the day before would be honored at the 10:30 game, and those who had bought tickets at the park could exchange them for any contest played over the course of the remainder of the season. Stahl announced that Charley Hall would have the honor of being the first Sox pitcher in an official game in their new home and that Buck O'Brien would work game 2.

Unfortunately, J. Pluvius dropped the dipper. As the sky brightened over Fenway Park on the morning of April 19, it was clear that even if it stopped raining immediately the floodwaters that covered Fenway Park were more appropriate for duck blinds than baseball watching. McAleer and McRoy canceled the morning contest, but McAleer held out hope that the club would get in the afternoon game. While his ball club napped and chewed the fat, wandering back and forth from underneath the stands to the dugout, McAleer paced the grandstand all morning long, looking back and forth from the sky to the field. The rain was intermittent, but the field was a mess. Had the rest of the tarpaulin arrived, the infield might have been playable, but with the one piece of canvas available Kelley could only cover the pitcher's plate and batter's box. Elsewhere, there were puddles and mud where there should have been grass or sand and crushed clay.

Finally, at 1:20 p.m., he made the call and canceled opening day for a second time. He told the assembled sportswriters that the club would try to play the opener the following afternoon, not a doubleheader but a single contest at 3:15 p.m., both to give the park a chance to dry out and because, with the holiday over, a morning contest no longer made sense, not even on a Saturday, which was still a partial working day for most Bostonians. The players raced back to the Park Riding School, changed out of their uniforms, and dashed to Kenmore Square to see marathon winner Michael Ryan jog by on his way to setting a new course record. Soon after he passed, hundreds of fans abandoned the course for the ballpark, unaware of the cancellation.

Nearly five thousand made their way to the park, only to find the flag atop the grandstand down and the gates locked. Well, most of the gates were locked. One had been inadvertently left open, and several dozen fans made their way inside and gave themselves a private tour.

The three cancellations had probably cost the club 60,000 admissions, no small number in an era when 500,000 fans for a season was considered enormous. It was perhaps the first sign that the franchise was not quite the cash cow McAleer had imagined it would be for him when he first purchased the club.

Finally, on the morning of April 20, dawn revealed baseball weather, the sun blazing and the sky a deep blue. The gates opened at noon, and as soon as they did fans began to fill the stands.

The Red Sox had been at the ballpark since earlier in the morning, taking batting practice as Stahl worried that after three days of waiting they had lost their batting eyes. As fans milled around the stands the players from both squads wandered the field, playing catch and loosening up according to baseball custom.

Apart from the bunting that still hung from the stands and the size of the crowd, there was nothing to distinguish the game from any other. The delays had led the team to cancel all inaugural ceremonies. The Letter Carriers' Band and the singing quartet were nowhere to be seen, and many baseball officials who had traveled to Boston for opening day, like Ban Johnson, had grown tired of waiting and returned home.

Still, the fans were impressed. After seeing so many contests at the Huntington Avenue Grounds or the South End Grounds, Fenway seemed huge to them. They stood pointing and craning their necks to take in as much of the park as possible, waving and hallooing, trying to get the attention of friends they spotted elsewhere in the immense grandstand. The official seating capacity was 24,400—11,400 in the grandstand, 8,000 in the pavilion, and 5,000 in the distant center-field bleachers—standing-room capacity was not included. From start to finish, the park had been built in four and a half months; construction officials calculated that poor winter weather had shut down most work on the park for the equivalent of two months. Seven thousand barrels of cement and 270 tons of structural steel had been used during construction, plus hundreds of thousands of board feet of lumber in the concrete formwork, the construction of the bleachers and pavilion, and the fences. All told, the cost was $600,000, a cost per capita of only $24 per seat, making the Fenway Park stands, on a cubic foot basis, some of the most lucrative real estate in the city of Boston. None of those seats, apart from a handful in the bleachers, can be occupied today for even a single game for what it originally cost to construct. Each has earned its cost back many, many, many times over and continues to do so eighty-one times each summer and at an increasing number of special events throughout the year.

As game time approached and each and every seat was occupied, the team kept selling tickets anyway, filling the promenade along the upper reaches of the grandstand with 2,500 fans willing to stand and watch the game while peering around columns and under the roofline. Then, with the center-field bleachers and the pavilion filled to sardine-can capacity and still more fans pushing their way in, the cramped and claustrophobic fled. First one and then another climbed over the railing and onto the field. Soon dozens and hundreds of fans were fleeing the stands, racing to secure spots on the field, first filling the incline in left field and then staking claim to the nether reaches of the outfield in front of the towering flagpole in the deepest portion of the playing field, on the western edge of the wedge of the bleachers in center field. The club sent ushers and police out to maintain order, and the crowd was hustled behind ropes that were hastily stretched from one foul line to another as fans stood in the outfield six or eight feet deep, just as they had for so many big games over the years at Huntington Avenue. Meanwhile both teams took infield and loosened up, taking time now and again to look around and take in the scene, amused, delighted, and amazed by it.

After the dull muted tones of winter, the bright blue sky, puffy white clouds, mostly green grass, and red-white-and-blue bunting made it seem as if spring had come on all at once. Atop the grandstand eight color-coded pennants snapped in the breeze, one representing each team, arranged in the order of the standings. On this day Boston's red-and-white flag led the pack.

Although Stahl had indicated earlier that Charley Hall would pitch the opener, the delay caused him to change his mind. Buck O'Brien and catcher Les Nunamaker started making their warm-up tosses in foul ground along the first-base line, while their New York counterparts, Ray Caldwell and Gabby Street, did the same along third. As game time approached, umpires Tommy Connolly and Eugene Hart strode onto the field, held a quick conference, and then waved Jake Stahl and New York manager Harry Wolverton to meet with them at home plate to exchange lineups and go over the ground rules. The umpires decided that owing to the close proximity of the overflow crowds there would be no possibility of home runs during the game. Any ball that reached the crowd, either on the ground or in the air, would be ruled a double. By definition that included any ball hit over the fence, but that possibility seemed so remote and unlikely that it was not even discussed.

The men dispersed, and the crowd, which was already cheering and chanting and singing the old songs just the way they had at Huntington Avenue, raised the volume another notch. As the Red Sox took their positions on the field, hardly anyone noticed or even saw Les Nunamaker trot over to the third-base line at the front of section J, where John "Honey Fitz" Fitzgerald, the mayor of Boston, threw him the first pitch.

Nunamaker caught the ball, and after a quick handshake and an encouraging word, Honey Fitz gave a wave to his constituents and Nunamaker trotted out to his place. O'Brien toed the rubber, raised his hand to his mouth to apply saliva to his fingertips, and made the first of several warm-up throws to his catcher. As he did, Jake Stahl rolled a few ground balls to his fielders—Steve Yerkes at second, Charlie Wagner at short, and Larry Gardner at third, while Harry Hooper in right, Tris Speaker in center, and Duffy Lewis in left all found their places only a few dozen feet from the overflow crowd.

SOX OPEN TO PACKED PARK

As O'Brien stood behind the rubber, ball in glove, Tommy Connolly held up his hand, then called out the words so many had been waiting so long to hear.

"Play ball!"

New York left fielder Guy Zinn, batting from the left side, stepped into the batter's box and waved his thick, dark bat in the air. O'Brien wound up, stepped toward the plate, and threw the first official pitch in the history of Fenway Park. Nunamaker reached for the pitch, and Connolly kept his right arm at his side, indicating a ball.

Up in the press box, a club employee manned the keyboard that communicated with the new, two-part, steel-framed "electronic" scoreboard that ran vertically up the full height of the left-field wall.

Nearly identical to a scoreboard at Detroit's new park, it was among the first of its kind. Each section of the scoreboard stood nearly twenty feet square and extended out from the wall a few inches. Although the club referred to the scoreboard as "electronic," that did not mean it was solely operated electronically or that it featured lights. While electrically operated scoreboards had been patented and Boston was the home of the Electric Score Board Company, fully operational electric scoreboards, which changed all numbers through the cumbersome use of pulleys and gears, were not yet viable. Instead, the "electronic" designation meant that the press box keyboard operator could communicate some information to the scoreboard operators electronically. Operators stationed on the scoreboard's backside scrambled up and down a network of ladders and steps and benches, out of view of the fans inside the park. While some information may have been conveyed through some kind of electronic device, most was communicated by hand.

The first of the two scoreboards, only twenty or thirty feet off the left-field line, provided the line score of not only the game currently under way but of other American League contests that day. The operator of this scoreboard probably received his information the old-fashioned way—by way of a runner from the press box who would periodically ferry out scores as they arrived at the park by telegraph.

The second scoreboard—identical to the scoreboard at Detroit's Navin Field—was located another seventy or eighty feet out toward center field, and had the same dimensions but was somewhat different. At the top were letters three feet high reading "BATTER." Below that word were two rows of slots filled with single digits representing the fielding position of each batter in the lineup, for the players themselves, as yet, did not wear uniform numbers on their jerseys. Already, a large "7" occupied the first slot, letting fans know that the first hitter was the left fielder, Zinn.

Below that area the scoreboard read "BALL" and "STRIKE," each word above three and two slots, respectively. Below those slots the word "OUT" was flanked by two slots, and below that was the word "UMPIRES," also flanked by a slot on each side, with the word "Plate" above one and "Field" above the other, each already filled with the unique number that represented each umpire in the league.

In the press box the keyboard operator watched Connolly closely. When he saw the umpire's right arm remain at his side and the scribes in the press box react by offering that the pitch had missed the plate, he reacted and pushed a button. A split second later, the scoreboard operator, sitting at a bench behind the left-center-field scoreboard, paid close attention to an electronic board activated by the keyboard operator in the press box.

In an instant he had decoded the meaning and slid a marker into a slot on the scoreboard.

In Fenway Park the eyes of nearly thirty thousand fans were not on the ball that Nunamaker was tossing back to O'Brien but turned toward left-center field. Beneath the word "BALL," they saw one of three dark square slots on the left-field side of the sign miraculously change as a round marker slid into place.

They roared at the majesty it represented, a feat of technology that almost seemed magical. Even patrons in the most distant reaches of the park could know with certainty that the first official pitch thrown in the new ballpark was a ball.

The game had begun. The 1912 season was under way.

Winter was over, and Fenway Park was open for business.

5

The Wall and the Cliff

From the ponderous horseshoe of the big grand stand the prairie
spreads out several miles, more or less, to the fences. There is room in
the playing field for a hit of any caliber, and so much room in the stands
that the crowd of yesterday rattled around like a squadron of lima
beans in a number 8 hat . . . Few of the fans who have been to Fenway
Park believed it possible to knock a ball over the left field fence.

—R. E. McMillen, *Boston Herald*

IT MAY HAVE been a simple case of nerves from pitching before
such a large crowd, the adjustment to throwing from the mound
at Fenway Park for the first time, or the number of friends and
family members who had made the trip up from Brockton. Then again
it may have been the fact that he had not pitched in eight days and felt
too strong or that his spitball was breaking too much. Or it may have
been that after a wet spring he found sunshine to be distracting, but
whatever the reason, Buck O'Brien couldn't find the plate.

The first four official pitches thrown in Fenway Park were all balls,
and Yankee left fielder Guy Zinn trotted down to first with the honor
of becoming the first official base runner.

Harry Wolter, batting second, took a half-swing and became the
first player to strike a ball at Fenway when he tapped it halfway to the
box. Both Stahl and O'Brien went for the ball. O'Brien got there first,
but there was no one covering first base. Steve Yerkes, for some reason, covered second. Hal Chase dropped a sacrifice to move both runners up a base, and then shortstop Roy Hartzell drove a ball between
third and short toward Duffy Lewis in left field. Zinn, one of the first

Jewish players in the major leagues, made it home easily, scoring the first official run in Fenway Park.

Just as the number "1" slid into place next to "New York" on the scoreboard, Bert Daniels hit a comebacker to O'Brien, but he didn't find it any easier to find the plate as a fielder than he did as a pitcher. He threw the ball past Nunamaker, scoring Wolter and forcing the scoreboard operator up out of his seat once more. The catcher recovered the ball in time to catch Hartzell at second, but O'Brien, as if determined to put a man on base by every way possible, then beaned Cozy Dolan. Earle Gardner singled to knock in New York's third run, and as Paul Shannon noted in the *Post*, New York catcher Gabby Street "ended the agony by fanning." It would not be the last time an inning at Fenway Park would seem like torture to devoted Boston fans.

But even on its first day this was Fenway Park, where no lead would ever, ever be safe. Harry Hooper led off for Boston against Ray Caldwell and tapped back to the pitcher for the first out, bringing up Steve Yerkes.

A graduate of the University of Pennsylvania, Yerkes had signed with the Red Sox in 1909, spent one year in the minors, and earned a starting job in 1911, playing shortstop while Wagner nursed his arm. A cerebral man who would later become a minor league manager and deliver impromptu lectures to his players on topics like Russian literature, Yerkes, although considered a solid if unspectacular fielder, was otherwise of limited ability. Nevertheless, his name would be on the lips of fans during both the first and last games of the 1912 season played at Fenway Park.

Yankee left fielder Guy Zinn and Yerkes would be the first two men to realize that Fenway Park was unlike any other ballpark in the major leagues. In his first official Fenway Park at-bat Yerkes hit one of the longest drives of his career, smacking the ball on a line to left, over the head of Zinn and just to the left of where the crowd standing behind the ropes in center merged into the crowd on the embankment. The outfielder tracked the ball back, and as he reached the fans standing shoulder to shoulder behind him, the mob parted slightly. Zinn, stepping up for the first time, stretched for the ball, then stumbled on the embankment as the ball landed just past his reach. The crowd scattered for a moment as some grabbed for the ball and others fled, and everyone had a hard time staying in place on the earthen slope, which was still wet and slippery from rain the day before.

If not for the crowd, Yerkes's drive probably would have skipped up the embankment, bounded off the wall, and rolled back down, sending Zinn scampering after it, and Yerkes might well have made a triple. Incredibly, Yerkes's drive had nearly made the wall and seemed to indicate that the left-field fence, which everyone had said was virtually unreachable, was perhaps a bit closer than it looked. Had the ball been hit just a bit harder, it would have struck the fence on the fly. It had taken all of one inning for the wall and the embankment to become Fenway Park's most distinguishing feature.

On the Boston bench Duffy Lewis, Boston's left fielder, watched the proceedings with special interest. That embankment would be looking over his shoulder all season.

By the time Yerkes reached first base umpire Eugene Hart was already waving his hand in the air and pointing toward second base. When Yerkes pulled into second the crowd was still buzzing with excitement. The first hit by a Boston player in Fenway Park was a ground-rule double.

So was the second. Tris Speaker smacked a pitch over Daniels's head into the crowd in center field for another two-base hit, knocking in Yerkes. On another day Speaker's hit might have rolled to the bleachers for a home run, even without the crowd, but the soft outfield ground, which in places collected footprints, may well have slowed it down and held Speaker to a triple. He pulled into second, and the crowd watched as the numeral "1" slipped into the slot beneath the "3" that represented New York's three first-inning runs. Boston was on the board.

Speaker was stranded, and a game that started sloppy continued that way as it soon became clear that neither club, nor the field itself, was in anything close to midseason form. Together the two teams would combine for ten errors and several other miscues. Ground balls collected mud and either stopped short or careened away, while drives that found the ground barely bounced at all, and fielders who pulled up short or had to cut quickly discovered the ground giving out beneath them. Steve Yerkes had a particularly tough time, collecting three errors for the day. Jake Stahl didn't help matters much by dropping nearly every chance he had that didn't arrive chest high, leading Fenway fans to jeer the man they had expected to welcome back with cheers. O'Brien gave up two more runs in the third, and when Boston loaded the bases in the fourth and the pitcher was due to bat, the manager decided he had seen enough. Stahl pinch-hit Olaf Henriksen for O'Brien and sent Charley Hall down the line to warm up. Henriksen walked to score a run, Hooper knocked in another with a force-out, and then Yerkes collected another hit to make the score 5–4.

It was a close game, and with Charley Hall on the mound it stayed that way. The burly Mexican American did what O'Brien could not, which was recognize the strike zone. He kept New York off the board, helping his own cause by leading off the sixth with a walk and coming around to score and tie the game. But in the eighth Hall threw away a pickoff attempt at second base, and when Hal Chase knocked the runner in from third the Yankees went up 6–5.

But Steve Yerkes was having the game of his life, at least at the plate, where his four hits thus far more or less offset his three errors. He led off the eighth belting another double and tied the game when Jake Stahl collected his first hit with a long drive to center, a certain home run if not for the crowd.

The game entered extra innings, and in the eleventh New York loaded the bases but did not score. The contest was already three hours old when Hall stepped in to lead off the Boston eleventh, and it was becoming hard to see. He struck out, and when Harry Hooper hit a foul pop-up for the second out it seemed likely that, unless the Sox scored, the game would soon be called. The first game at Fenway Park seemed destined to end in a tie.

But Yerkes was not finished. In his seventh at-bat of the game he rolled a slow one to third base. Cozy Dolan took the ball on the run and was still running when he threw the ball to first. So was Yerkes, and as the ball sailed over his head so was first baseman Hal Chase, who raced after the errant toss as Yerkes ran to second. Catcher Gabby Street then gave up a passed ball, sending Yerkes to third and bringing up Tris Speaker.

Fenway Park was still full, and everyone was on their feet screaming as Speaker stepped in against pitcher Hippo Vaughn. There was no other hitter in the lineup Sox fans and Speaker's teammates would have preferred to see at the plate.

It was at times like this that Speaker set himself apart from other players. Pressure situations did not bother him. In fact, he usually felt most comfortable when it was late in the game with runners on base. After all, the pitcher had to come to him or else risk putting him on with a base on balls, and then watch him dance down the line. Vaughn worked carefully, and Speaker ran the count full, growing more confident with each pitch. Then he sliced a scorcher toward third and took off.

Yerkes broke with the pitch, and though Dolan managed to block the ball, which skidded along the ground, he failed to field it cleanly.

That was all Speaker, one of the fastest runners in the game, needed. Once an infielder bobbled a ball hit by Speaker there was little chance he would be thrown out at first. Dolan fired the ball toward Chase, but as the first baseman reached for it Speaker was already crossing the bag, his legs a blur and a laugh ready to form on his lips. He turned in time to see Yerkes cross the plate and leap into the arms of his teammates in front of the dugout as fans tossed torn newspapers and other impromptu confetti into the air. As some cut across the field to the exits, the scoreboard in left field told the story: Boston 7, New York 6. It was the first of hundreds of games between the two clubs that would be waged on Fenway's diamond over the next hundred years.

FENWAY PARK IS FORMALLY
OPENED WITH RED SOX WIN
24,000 Boston Fans Go Wild With Delight

The park cleared, and McAleer, McRoy, and Taylor breathed a sigh of relief. That had been their last concern. McLaughlin had been confident that his ramp system would allow Fenway Park to empty quickly, but since so few fans had attended the exhibition with Harvard, there had been no way to test the arrangement before the game.

But after only five minutes the grandstand was virtually empty, and only a few stragglers remained in the park, most loitering on the field, to the consternation of Jerome Kelley. No one had stumbled down the ramps and been trampled, and no one had been crushed, but they were making a mess of the infield.

With a record of 5-1, the victory left the Red Sox in first place, one game ahead of Philadelphia. With no game the following day because of local blue laws—April 21 was a Sunday—the Sox looked next to a four-game series with McAleer's old club, the Washington Nationals, due in on Monday.

That provided just enough time for the rain to return. On Monday, April 22, McAleer waited as long as possible before calling the game off, ordering the center-field flag to be lowered at 2:45 p.m., just as larger groups of fans were beginning to show up and the players were warming up on the field, gingerly stepping over puddles. It was already the fifth rainout of the young season, and both McAleer and Stahl were becoming a bit concerned. McAleer fretted over the loss of lucrative dates, and Stahl worried not only that the Red Sox would lose their edge but that the doubleheader makeup games later in the season would wreak havoc on his pitching staff. And if he had a real concern so far it was his pitching staff. Hageman had been horrible, and O'Brien was not much better. Despite their 5-1 record, only Hall and Wood had pitched according to form.

That kind of assurance ended the next day. The rain stopped, but it was, as one newspaperman described it, "like a bleak cold day in November." The two clubs combined for nine errors on the bitterly cold day as Washington roughed up Wood for six runs and beat the Sox, 6–2. Wood had a hard time finding the plate and walked seven men, including the leadoff hitter in four separate innings. Casey Hageman had hardly looked that bad. As Paul Shannon observed, "When Joe is right he is well nigh invincible, but when Joe has a bad day no rookie in the majors has anything on him for wobbling, and Joe wobbled yesterday, early and often."

Walter Johnson—already considered the best pitcher in the league at age twenty-five, and heir to the title of the game's greatest pitcher now that Christy Mathewson was beginning to show his age—took the mound for Washington the next day. The contrast was undeniable—he was everything Joe Wood was not. A tall, lanky sidearmer, the mild-mannered Johnson threw harder than any man in baseball, with the possible exception of Wood. But Johnson had far better control and made his fastball even faster by mixing in a sweeping curve that froze right-handed hitters and a deceptive "slow ball," or changeup. On his start to perhaps the greatest season of his career, Johnson toyed with the Red Sox on his way to an easy 5–2 win, a defeat made even worse by the loss of Jake Stahl. During warm-ups before the game he slipped on the dugout steps while retrieving an errant throw and badly sprained his ankle. Hugh Bradley took over at first base.

The defeat concerned Stahl more than the pain in his ankle. While Washington was obviously an improved club, and Johnson was always a challenge, the "Senators," as some called them, were not one of the league's elite teams. Although the Red Sox club still had a winning record, they were not playing inspired baseball. Even the sportswriters noticed. Boston games were taking forever to play. The players, as if their blood had been thickened by the unceasing cold and rain, seemed barely able to drag themselves onto the field. Paul Shannon had observed that the Senators were playing as if something was at stake while the Red Sox played "as though they were so slowed by the cold that they had lost all ambition."

The one exception was moon-faced Duffy Lewis, a player who always seemed to have a half-smile on his face. He was hitting more than .300 and playing inspired defense. Born George Lewis in San Francisco on April 18, 1888, he shared a birthday, April 18, with the great San Francisco earthquake, which in 1906 he had survived. One of John I. Taylor's western discoveries, Lewis joined the Red Sox in 1910 after playing one year of college ball for St. Mary's, then spending one year in the California League and another in the Pacific Coast League before becoming a member of a Boston team that sportswriters of the day called "the Speedboys" in deference to their style of play.

Lewis didn't fit in, either by style or by temperament. Only twenty-one years old, the PCL graduate didn't defer to the club's veterans, who resented him for taking an outfield spot from veteran Harry Niles and not treating his elders with sufficient respect during bat-

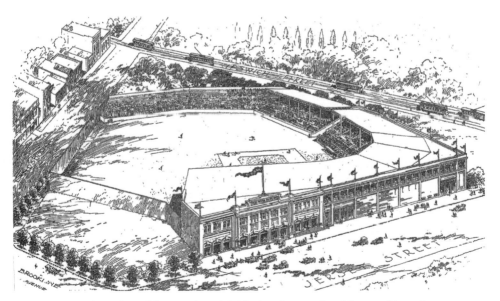

ILLUS. 1 When Fenway Park was first built, there was very little else in the neighborhood immediately surrounding the park. Van Ness Street did not yet exist. Prior to the building of Fenway Park, as the dotted lines indicate, there were tentative plans to put in streets perpendicular to Lansdowne, running through what is now the outfield and infield. *Courtesy of the Print Department, Boston Public Library*

ILLUS. 2 Drawing of Fenway (1911). This drawing, rendered from architect James E. McLaughlin's plans by illustrator J. C. Halden, was widely reprinted when Fenway Park was being built and was used as letterhead on team stationery in 1912 and for several years thereafter. However, the right-field bleachers shown in the drawing were not built until September 1912, part of the expansion made to accommodate the 1912 World's Series. *Collection of the author*

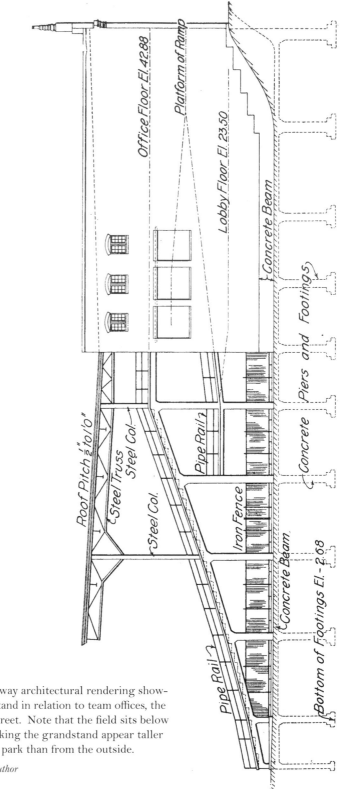

ILLUS. 3 Cutaway architectural rendering showing the grandstand in relation to team offices, the field, and the street. Note that the field sits below street level, making the grandstand appear taller from inside the park than from the outside.

Collection of the author

ILLUS. 4 Architectural rendering showing details of concrete reinforced beams
and columns supporting grandstand
seating deck (1912). Note that the floor
of the box seats is nearly four feet above
field grade. For the World's Series, additional box seats were built and extended
to field level. The four-foot gap between
the floor of the box seats and grade is the
area where fans, on at least one occasion,
watched the game.

Collection of the author

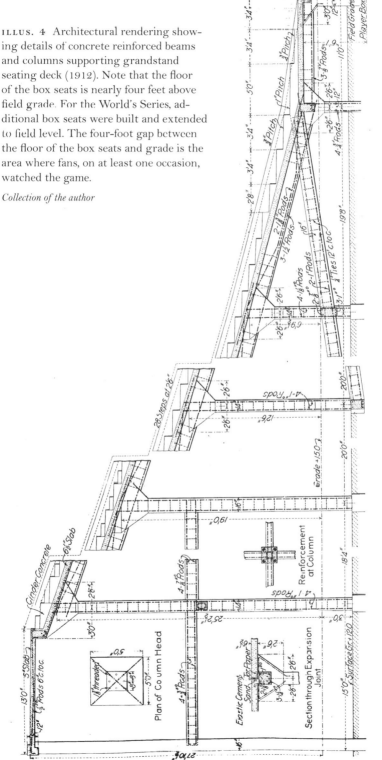

ILLUS. 5 Fenway Park third-base dug-out (1912). The original dugouts were only forty feet long. Virtually cut in half by a concrete column, they featured a slat-style bench similar to those once used in railroad stations. Note the square openings on the dugout wall, which apparently provided ventilation from beneath the stands.

Collection of the author

ILLUS. 6 Concrete reinforced columns and beams form a network of support beneath the grandstand deck. This style of construction was state of the art in 1912. Many fans today still reach their seats by walking up the ramp featured here. *Collection of the author*

ILLUS. 7 Contractor Charles Logue (1912). Charles Logue, a native of Ireland and father of sixteen, supervised the construction of Fenway Park. Logue is standing at the end of the grandstand, third-base side. Note the poor condition of the field after an extremely wet spring.

Courtesy of the Logue Family

ILLUS. 8 Fenway Park exterior (1914). Architect James McLaughlin's inspiration for the Fenway Park facade and team offices was rooted in Gustav Stickley's "Arts and Crafts" movement. Even two years after Fenway Park opened, the lot on Jersey Street opposite the ball-park remained undeveloped and horses and buggies were still familiar sights on Boston streets.

George Grantham Bain Collection, Library of Congress Prints and Photographs Division

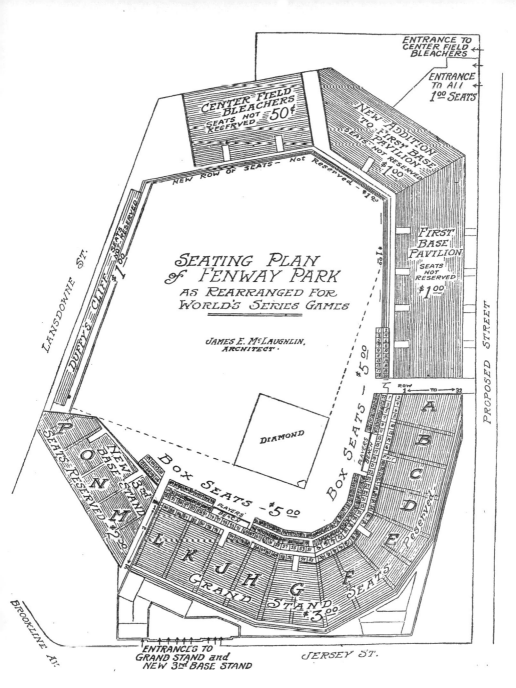

ILLUS. 9 "Seating Plan of Fenway Park as Rearranged for World's Series Games" (1912). In an effort to maximize profit during the World's Series, during a road trip in September the Red Sox added 11,600 seats to Fenway Park, significantly diminishing the size of the field of play, enclosing the field for the first time, and giving Fenway Park the same basic footprint still recognizable today. Actual construction varied slightly from these plans. *Collection of the author*

ILLUS. 10 Construction of the right-field bleachers (1912). Workers rushed to build the new all-wood bleachers section before the World's Series in the space between the pavilion in the foreground and the center-field bleachers. Unlike the pavilion or main grandstand, no steel or concrete columns were used to support the bleacher structure. Note the network of wooden scaffolding that supports the center-field bleachers.

George Grantham Bain Collection, Library of Congress Prints and Photographs Division

ILLUS. 11 In combination, these three photos, taken from right field, show the pavilion, the grandstand, the third-base stands and Duffy's Cliff bleachers, and the left-field wall. Together they provide the best photographic documentation of the interior of Fenway Park in preparation for the 1912 World's Series. Note how the new construction has diminished the size of the field of play and completely enclosed the playing field with stands. The press box has not yet been expanded, but the curious fence in right field, eighteen inches high and topped by a rail, is in place. Balls that bounced over or through the fence were home runs.

George Grantham Bain Collection, Library of Congress Prints and Photographs Division

ILLUS. 12 Fenway Park press box and grandstand roof (1914). Although this photograph dates from 1914, when the Boston Braves played and won the World's Series in Fenway Park, Fenway looked much the same for the 1912 World's Series. The original press box was removed in September 1912 and replaced by the much larger press box seen here.

George Grantham Bain Collection, Library of Congress Prints and Photographs Division

ting practice or in the clubhouse. He and Tris Speaker, who ran in separate circles on the club, never saw eye to eye, a fact that Lewis was surprisingly blunt about in his later years. He once said, "It's simply that we weren't intimate. I spent most of my leisure time with one group of mates. He went around with another group . . . I was friendliest with Bill Carrigan and Heinie Wagner and the other card players on the club. Each group went its own separate way." Lewis liked his drink and was a bit of a rake—the girls who didn't swoon over Joe Wood got giddy over Lewis. Every few months it seemed there was a report in the Boston newspapers that he was engaged to yet another young woman.

Compared to many of his teammates, Lewis also played a different style of ball. For one, he couldn't run—at least not enough to steal more than a dozen or so bases a season, which made him a relative tortoise on a team of hares. And unlike most players of the era, who were place hitters who went with the pitch, Lewis was, as he referred to himself, a "chronic pull hitter." Opposing infielders even shifted dramatically when he came to bat, a rarity in the era.

His one outstanding talent was his ability to track and catch fly balls, a skill he had learned as a youngster when he served as mascot for the Alamedas of the California League and shagged flies for hours as the team practiced. Lewis was not fast, but he got a good jump on the ball and rarely took a bad route. And while his arm was only average, it was accurate and he got rid of the ball quickly.

Joining an outfield that already included Tris Speaker in center and Harry Hooper in right, both of whom could run and throw, created the perfect situation for Lewis. Speaker ranged far and wide in center, giving Lewis somewhat less territory to cover than if he had been paired with another center fielder. And since opponents rarely took their chances with the arms of Hooper and Speaker, they ran on Lewis instead—but more often than not found out that the arm that looked weak when compared to his companions was not so weak after all.

Moving from the Huntington Avenue Grounds to Fenway Park was a boon for Lewis. Left field was enormous at Huntington Avenue—350 feet down the line before angling back sharply to 440 feet in left-center. There Lewis had been forced to play deep. If a ball got over his head, it was an almost certain home run.

In Fenway Park, however, Lewis felt as if he'd been set free. After playing only a few games, he realized that, with the embankment and the left-field wall behind him, any ball hit over his head wasn't going to go very far. He was the first to recognize, as Sox left fielder Carl Yastrzemski later noted, that "what we're playing out there is deep shortstop." The fence and embankment allowed Lewis to play much closer to the infield, a placement that not only helped his arm but helped out Boston pitchers. The number of his putouts would increase dramatically, from 203 in 1911 to 301 in 1912, as he caught flares over the infield that in previous years would have fallen for hits. This change in Lewis's play particularly helped a pitcher like Joe Wood, whose fastball tended to jam hitters, not unlike Yankee reliever Mariano Rivera today. When batters did make contact off Wood, they often fisted weak fly balls that barely made it to the out-field. Such drives that had fallen in for hits in the past were now outs.

On April 25, in the series finale against Washington, Lewis gave dramatic evidence of just how big an impact Fenway Park's left-field wall would have, not only on himself but on the Red Sox. Despite the fact that President William Howard Taft was in Boston to deliver a speech, the most memorable phrase stemming from the events of that day would be inspired not by world affairs but by Duffy Lewis.

With Charley Hall on the mound and two outs in the first inning, speedy outfielder Clyde Milan hit the ball to left-center, splitting the outfielders. In the Huntington Avenue Grounds such a hit would have been an automatic double for a hitter like Milan.

But Lewis was playing thirty or forty feet shallower than in the past. He raced after the ball, cut it off, then spun and threw like count-less Red Sox left fielders have done since after playing a ball off the wall. Milan's hit didn't make it that far, but Lewis's approach was the same. His throw beat a shocked Milan to second, and the inning was over.

Lewis made two nice running catches in the fourth and another in the seventh as Boston built a 4–1 lead. At the Huntington Avenue Grounds one or both of those balls would have dropped for a hit. Then, in the eighth, with two out, catcher John Henry of Washington drove the ball deep to left. Lewis turned and ran once more, and the long fly hung in the air, giving him a chance to catch up to the ball.

Running hard, Lewis was just beginning to slow and reach for the hit when he suddenly discovered the ground coming up to meet him.

It was the embankment. He had run into it at full stride, and the shock of his foot finding the earth a split second before he expected it sent him sprawling to the ground.

But Lewis didn't give up. Even as he fell he managed to keep his eye on the ball, twist back, reach up with his glove hand, and catch the ball, only inches from the ground, as he fell spread-eagled on his back on the embankment. Several thousand Red Sox fans whooped and hollered and came to their feet as Lewis lost his, then remained standing, cheering him, as he ran smiling back to the dugout.

Lewis, however, was not yet finished for the day. Leading off the bottom of the inning, Lewis showed Washington how it was done. He turned on a pitch from "Long Tom" Hughes and, true to form, pulled it to left-center. The ball hit on the embankment, skipped to the wall, and then rolled back down. Lewis made second easily, and when the throw went wide he took third base.

Boston held on to win, 4–1, and Lewis was the talk of the game. A *Globe* headline called it "the catch of the season and the throw of a lifetime." There simply wasn't enough room to mention the hit. But on that day Lewis took ownership of both the wall and the embankment. The need for a Boston left fielder to play both features well was underscored for all time as Lewis immediately dedicated himself to learning how to do it. "I'd go out to the ballpark mornings," he later told a sportswriter, "and have somebody hit the ball again and again out to the wall. I experimented with every angle of approach up the cliff until I learned to play the slope correctly." Although Lewis would still take the occasional tumble before he became completely adept at scaling the embankment, he was far better at it than opposing left fielders, providing the Red Sox with a real advantage. By midsummer the embankment was being called "Duffy's Cliff" in honor of Lewis's prowess, both with the glove and with the bat. And it retained that name until the wall was greatly scaled back after the 1924 season and finally removed entirely a decade later.

It was a good victory, and a necessary one, over the Senators. The Philadelphia Athletics followed Washington into Boston, and the Red Sox needed a bit of momentum before meeting the defending champions. Once again, Boston's unique left-field barrier would prove to be the most memorable component of the game.

Stahl was still scrambling to find a pitching rotation, and there was even speculation that Cy Young, who was at the park nearly every day, might be brought back. Before doing so, however, Stahl seemed determined to give every other man on the pitching staff a chance to earn a job. For the opener against Philadelphia on April 26 he selected Larry Pape. The Ohio native had been a valuable member of the pitching staff in 1911—starting nineteen games, pitching two shutouts, and winning eleven, he had tied Ray Collins and Eddie Cicotte for the second-highest total on the staff behind Joe Wood—but Stahl was not impressed. Pape was a nibbler, a pitcher whose success depended on his ability to hit his spots and who didn't have enough stuff to make mistakes.

Against Philadelphia he missed those spots, giving up two hits in the first inning, but he managed to escape without giving up a run. His reprieve would be brief.

Veteran Cy Morgan started the game for A's manager Connie Mack. After Harry Hooper struck out to start the game, Steve Yerkes walked and Tris Speaker reached on an error, bringing up Hugh Bradley.

The singing first baseman, a native of Grafton, Massachusetts, and a graduate of Holy Cross College, was the nephew of George "Foghorn" Bradley, who had pitched for Boston in 1876 and then umpired all over New England. His nephew was a fan favorite whose off-field talent as a singer had made him far better known than a backup first baseman had any right to be. After taking over at first base one day earlier he had impressed everyone with his glove work, but on this day fans would leave Fenway Park talking about his bat.

Bradley was known as a "free hitter," an aggressive batter who swung from his heels rather than trying to place the ball. He sometimes had a hard time making contact and was inconsistent, but when he did strike the ball he was capable of hitting it as far as any man on the team.

This time he did both, pulling the ball hard to left field on a line. Athletics left fielder Amos Strunk turned to chase after the hit, and a split second after the ball sailed past him it struck halfway up the wall with a loud crack and bounded back toward the field. Yerkes and Speaker scored easily, and Bradley pulled into second base with an easy double.

The hit sent fans chattering to one another and pointing toward the outfield. It was the first time in the brief history of Fenway Park that a batted ball had struck the left-field wall on the fly.

Outfield distances were not marked on the fences at the time—nor would they be at Fenway Park until after the 1933–34 renovation. If documents held by the Osborn Engineering Company are accurate, they indicate that when Fenway opened the distance down the left-field line was 320 feet, while the flagpole in center field stood 468 feet from home plate, just a few feet in front of the fence. The distance down the right-field line when Fenway Park opened is less certain—the extreme end of the pavilion jutted out into the field. But it was probably even less than 300 feet.

No one expected the left-field wall ever to be breached, but in only five games several balls had already landed on the embankment, and now one had reached the wall itself. While a blast over the wall still seemed remote, it no longer seemed completely impossible. Fans could not help but wonder what might have happened if Bradley had just gotten under the ball a bit more.

Larry Gardner knocked Bradley in with a single to score Boston's third run and stake Pape to a 3–0 lead, but after he recorded two quick outs he imploded and gave up three straight hits, including Amos Strunk's triple, which scored two. That was enough for Stahl, and Ed Cicotte came on to pitch the third as Lefty Russell, in relief of Morgan, shut down Boston. But Cicotte was no improvement. He gave up two runs in the third and single runs in both the fourth and the fifth to put the A's ahead 6–3. In desperation Stahl called on young Hugh Bedient for the first time all season to start the sixth.

After taking the lead, the A's had grown cocky and directed a steady stream of banter toward the Boston players. Tim Murnane later wrote that "I never heard or saw so much kicking . . . the Mackmen kept up a continual howl," complaining, for instance, that Bedient was balking and that the Red Sox had tried to slip an older, softer ball into play when the A's were at bat.

Pitching against the champions was a challenge for Bedient, but after some initial jitters, he shut the A's down. While he did not shut them up, his performance gave the Red Sox a chance.

In the seventh inning, with one out, Bedient helped his own cause and worked a walk from Russell. The pitcher then struck Hooper with a pitch, and after Yerkes flew out, Tris Speaker singled, scoring Bedient and sending Hooper to third.

The A's still led 6–4 when Hugh Bradley stepped into the batter's box. In theory, he was the go-ahead run, for a home run could give Boston the lead, but even after Bradley's first-inning blast off the wall the possibility of a home run was still so remote that no one dared think about it out loud. The Red Sox had hit only thirty-five home runs in 1911, twenty at the Huntington Avenue Grounds, and had none thus far in the 1912 season. In his brief career Bradley had collected only one major league home run, and in four seasons in the minors he had hit only eight. Expecting to hit a home run was like expecting to be hit by lightning.

Russell was known for his curveball, which he had used effectively since entering the game in relief, and he went with the pitch again. It dropped over the plate knee high as Bradley took his usual hard swing.

The ball left his bat in a blur, and left fielder Amos Strunk took off toward left-center field, as did Rube Oldring in center, tracking the ball in its flight. After only a few steps, Oldring, realizing he could not catch the deep drive, slowed and prepared to play the carom off the fence. But Strunk reached Duffy's Cliff in a full sprint and kept going, striding up the embankment until he reached the wall. Then, as if unable to believe what was happening, he pressed his body flat against it, his head tilted back and looking up.

Overhead, Bradley's hit just kept carrying. It cleared the top of the wall with plenty of room to spare and kept going, disappearing from sight.

The crowd, which had risen to its feet when Bradley first struck the ball, was stunned. A moment of silence was followed by whoops and yells and screams and hoots of delight. Some spectators threw their hats in the air, and others jumped up and down and slapped each other on the back with delight. They could not have been more surprised if Halley's comet had made an appearance. Bradley, meanwhile, raced around the bases, the notion of a "home run trot" completely foreign to him, as Bedient and Speaker crossed the plate ahead of him. Bradley raced after them toward the dugout, where his teammates, fully aware of what had just happened, bolted from their seats to meet him. Boston now led 7–6.

Bradley's home run was no popgun shot that just snuck over the wall, like Carlton Fisk's famous homer in game 6 of the 1975 World Series, or Bucky Dent's infamous home run during the 1978 playoff game versus the Yankees, but a bona fide blast. According to reporter R. E. McMillen of the *Herald*, it "not only cleared the barrier but the building across the street," the garage that remains there to this day. That may have been hyperbole, but if the ball cleared the wall it may well have landed on the roof of the garage and then bounded over it.

The hit took the air out of the A's, for, as Wallace Goldsmith later noted, the blast did not "seem human." The A's bench jockeying stopped, and Bedient didn't give up another hit as the Red Sox won, 7–6. Bedient's performance had just as much to do with the victory as the home run, but all anyone wanted to talk about was Bradley's drive. McMillen estimated that it had cleared the fence "seven feet from the upper rim." Paul Shannon, noting that the ball cleared the fence above an advertisement for a taxi company, wrote that "reports from the Athletic headquarters say that the sphere boarded a waiting taxicab." If the advertisement in question is the same one that was on display later during the 1912 World's Series, then Bradley's drive cleared the wall some fifty to seventy feet from the left-field line, to the right of the scoreboard that displayed the game's line score. In Fenway Park today that would be east of the light stanchion closest to the left-field line, approximately where the ladder on the left-field wall remains in place today.

BRADLEY'S TERRIFIC SMASH GOOD
FOR THREE RUNS AND GAME, 7–6
Mackmen Have 6–4 Lead When He Bangs Ball Over Fence

Bradley unquestionably hit the ball on the nose, but he may have had a bit of help. Several newspapers reported that the ball was helped by a stiff wind blowing out to left, and the A's, by intimating that Boston was substituting a used ball earlier in the game, may have led the umpire to introduce a brand-new ball into the game sometime later. A newer ball, one not yet softened by repeated contact with the bat, would certainly have traveled farther than an older one.

Yet despite the fact that in only the sixth game ever played at Fenway Park a player had one hit against the wall and another over it, home runs of any kind at Fenway Park did not become a regular occurrence. For part of the 1914 season and 1915 the Boston Braves played at Fenway while Braves Field was being built. On May 22, 1915, Heinie Zimmerman of the Cubs hit a home run over the left-field fence, and it was reported that his home run was only the sixth such home run ever hit. After Bradley's blast, according to the author of this report, Duffy Lewis and Jake Stahl had both managed to duplicate the feat for the Red Sox, as had Clarence Walker for the St. Louis Browns and Rube Oldring for the A's. Only after the lively ball was introduced in the 1920 season did home runs to left begin to become commonplace, and even then they were usually hit by Boston's opponents. Not until Jimmie Foxx joined the Red Sox in 1936—when twenty-one of his forty-one home runs were hit at Fenway Park, and most of those to left field—did the Red Sox lineup include a slugger who breached the wall with regularity.

It is important to note that no one anywhere was as yet referring to the left-field wall as "the Green Monster" or using any other such name for it. The only thing green about the wall in 1912 was the lumber used in its construction and some of the paint in the advertisements that covered nearly every square inch of it, save for the scoreboards.

Although the wall was first painted "Dartmouth green" in 1947 when Red Sox owner Tom Yawkey decided to remove all advertising from the left-field fence, the name "Green Monster" would not be used to describe the feature for a number of years. Even then, the name would not become commonplace until the late 1970s, when the Red Sox were regularly featured on national television broadcasts and a nationwide audience was introduced to what had been a rather obscure parochial nickname. Most baseball fans, both in Boston and elsewhere, simply referred to it as "the Wall."

The origins of the name "Green Monster" in reference to Fenway's left-field fence are somewhat murky, and likely to remain so, but the phrase itself was already familiar to sports fans before it was ever used to describe a feature at Fenway Park. The term had long been used to indicate something intimidating, which, as baseball evolved into a power game, is precisely what the left-field wall would prove to be for major league pitchers.

In 1951 golfer Ben Hogan won the U.S. Open at Oakland Hills in Michigan, his second consecutive U.S. Open victory, by firing a final round of 67 for a 7-over-par finish of 287. Course architect Robert Trent Jones had modified the course for the event, and par had been lowered from 72 to 70 for the week. Hogan's final-round 67 was one of only two under-par scores shot during the tournament. Afterward he said, "I am glad I brought this course, this monster, to its knees." In subsequent years sportswriters took their cue from Hogan and began referring to the course as "the green monster," a phrase used intermittently throughout the 1950s and 1960s, but only rarely today.

In 1952 two brothers from Ohio, Art and Walt Arfons, began building dragsters and competing on the drag racing circuit. Their first car, which the brothers painted with green tractor paint, was dubbed "the Green Monster" by track announcer Ed Paskey. The brothers then retained the name for each dragster they subsequently built together, becoming one of the sport's best-known teams. In 1962 Art Arfons, taking aim at the world land speed record, built a jet-powered car, which he also dubbed "the Green Monster," to race at the Bonneville Salt Flats. There was intense competition for the record in the mid-1960s, and his efforts received widespread press coverage. In 1964 and 1965 he set the record on three separate occasions in his "Green Monster." Any sports fan anywhere in the United States asked at the time to identify "the Green Monster" probably would have responded by citing Arfons's vehicle.

The name was not used as a nickname for the left-field wall at Fenway Park until the late 1950s at the earliest, and then probably only by the players and sportswriters who covered the team. The phrase appears sporadically in newspaper and magazine accounts during the early and mid-1960s, but players, fans, and sportswriters alike were still far more likely to refer to the left-field fence as simply "the Wall."

Significantly, the term does not appear in classic Boston baseball reportage of the era, such as John Updike's signature report on Ted Williams's retirement in *The New Yorker*, "Hub Bids Kid Adieu," or Ed Linn's similar portrait published in *Sport* magazine.

That began to change during the 1967 World Series. When the national press came to Boston it seemed as if the entire country discovered Fenway Park for the first time. Associated Press stories that previewed the Series and were carried by newspapers all around the country popularized the phrase, as did references to it during the broadcast of the Series, giving the expression a toehold in the national lexicon. Nevertheless, use of the term remained far from common. Roger Angell's account of the 1967 season in *The New Yorker*, "The Flowering and Deflowering of New England," makes no mention of it.

The same pattern was repeated during the 1975 World Series and was underscored by Fisk's famous home run to end game 6. Yet even then, fans and scribes alike were still more likely to refer to the left-field fence as "the Wall" rather than as "the Green Monster," as if "the Wall" were the proper name and "Green Monster" simply a nickname. In his famous account of Fisk's home run, esteemed *Boston Globe* baseball writer Peter Gammons still called it "the Wall." It was not until the mid to late 1980s that use of the phrase "Green Monster" became widespread.

Neither Hugh Bradley nor anyone else, of course, had any idea that his home run would still be talked about one hundred years later. Although the blast proved to be the winning margin in the game, and the victory over the A's was important, in terms of the 1912 season the home run was not even the most important occurrence that day. Mild-mannered Hugh Bedient, who pitched the final four innings to collect the win while giving up only one hit, got the attention of his manager. Stahl was beginning to realize that his team's biggest problem was not hitting the ball against or over the left-field wall themselves, but preventing the opposition from doing the same.

Bedient's relief performance appeared to be a small step in the right direction. Only Charley Hall and Joe Wood had come close to pitching as well as Stahl had hoped, and even Wood had been inconsistent. With Wood on the mound the following day, the Sox hoped to get on a roll.

Fat chance. The hardheaded Wood was rocked early, staking the A's to a 5–1 lead. Boston, led by Bradley again, stormed back to take the game, 6–5, but Stahl and everyone else knew that even though the Red Sox were winning, unless the pitching came around, they were not playing championship baseball. In the Dead Ball Era it was virtually impossible to win consistently without strong pitching. Offense—what there was of it—was built around steals, sacrifices, place hits, bunts, and stolen bases—what was referred to at the time as "scientific" or "inside" baseball. Even Hugh Bradley, who led Boston's comeback with a couple of hits, including another double, had been called upon to sacrifice with two on and none out in the eighth inning. The ploy had worked, and Boston went on to score three runs and take the game. Afterward one sportswriter noted that Fenway Park seemed uniquely predisposed to come-from-behind wins: "Nobody will think of leaving Fenway Park until the last out if we have any more of these hair-raising finishes." While the influence of the park on such finishes was as yet debatable, the observation contained a grain of truth—so far the Sox were a tough team to beat in their new ballpark.

O'Brien got the call for game 3 of the series, but he failed in the sixth, followed by Bushelman and Hageman, neither of whom was impressive, and the Sox fell, 7–1. Stahl's doghouse, which already included Hageman, Pape, and rookie Dutch Leonard, who hadn't even pitched, got a bit more crowded as Bushelman forced his way in the door, and O'Brien and Cicotte both seemed likely to follow him inside. Ray Collins, for the time being, had a deferment due to a sore knee, the result of an infection he suffered from a spike wound during spring training. Stahl's ankle was still in such bad shape that he had to use a cane to get around.

Charley Hall got the next start and seemed to be the answer as he nursed a 3–1 lead into the fourth. But with two on and two out, Hall took exception on a ball four call by umpire Silk O'Loughlin that loaded the bases and started to squawk. The arbiter, a former player, was supremely confident of his ability, having once said, "A man is always out or safe or it is a ball or a strike. The umpire, if he is a good man and knows his business, is always right. I am always right." O'Loughlin didn't like Hall telling him otherwise, and as the pitcher continued to stomp around on the mound the partisan crowd at Fenway Park unloaded on the umpire. Hall stepped up his antics and with a flourish finally tossed his glove to the ground.

When he did O'Loughlin stepped toward the pitcher and raised his arm in the air, tossing the bellowing Hall, whose nickname was "Sea Lion," from the game.

Now the crowd really cut loose, hissing at the umpire and tossing debris onto the field as Hall took his time following O'Loughlin's directions and the umpire stoically tried to wait out the crowd. Thinking fast, Stahl had Bedient throw some warm-up tosses on the side so he would not have to enter the game cold.

There was no bullpen at Fenway Park, not even a practice pitcher's mound. Technically, there was no need for one. Pitchers warmed up in the foul ground alongside the outfield. Even though most teams built up the ground around the rubber several inches, the practice was illegal, and new pitchers loosened up on flat ground. When Bedient entered the game he managed to escape the inning, and then he once again held the A's to a single hit the remainder of the game as the Sox went on to win, 6–1. Philadelphia's only highlight came when outfielder Bris Lord made like Duffy Lewis on his Cliff and snagged another drive by Bradley while lying on his back.

SILK THE ARBITRARY, NOT THE ARBITER,
Is Right Title For Umpire O'Loughlin

After the game the club left for a four-game series with Washington, joined by their owner, who was looking forward to crowing over his former cronies. To most observers, that seemed likely. The Sox appeared to be in fine shape. With a 9-4 record, they were in second place, just a half-game back of the surprising White Sox, and the club still looked down on the Senators. But not all the Red Sox made the trip. Stahl left behind three pitchers — Leonard, Pape, and Hageman — as well as catcher Hick Cady, and ordered the three to get some work in and be better prepared by the time the club returned to Boston for a long home stand on May 5.

They would not be alone, for as soon as the Red Sox left town groundskeeper Jerome Kelley and his men got going, working dawn to dusk in the team's absence. The poor weather had wreaked havoc on the field, and they needed the four days to roll it flat again and fill some bare spots with sod. It was coming along, but the players had been letting him have it over the condition of the field.

The trip to Washington was a disaster: Boston dropped three of four. Wood again pitched just well enough to lose as Bill Carrigan's failure to corral a pitch in the ninth cost him a win, and no other Boston pitcher threw well. Even Bedient took a step back when he was given a start and failed to make it to the third inning. The 9-4 second-place Sox left Washington in third place, 10-7, and looking worse than that. As A. H. C. Mitchell observed in *Sporting Life*:

> Now that the season is nearly a month old one can make some kind of fair criticism. It is yet doubtful if Wagner can come back to old-time form. He is there one day and not there the next. He makes one grand, old-time throw and then tosses one wild . . . Joe Wood has hardly shown his best form of last year. He insists on having Bill Carrigan catch for him and Bill cannot seem to hold him. There are usually a number of short passed balls when Bill is behind the bat for Joe. In Washington they were costly. Most of the pitchers want Bill, so the management puts him in most of the time

On the way back to Boston the club stopped by Baltimore for an exhibition and then headed toward New York to play a makeup game, but the contest was rained out.

There was little joy on the train trip back to Boston. The sour look on McAleer's face as he watched the proceedings from a box seat in Washington had told the story, and when he sat down with his manager for the journey back to Boston his mood had not improved. Unlike his predecessor, John I. Taylor, McAleer still thought of himself as a manager and was not shy about telling Stahl how to run his ball club. The Sox had thoroughly collapsed in Washington and made McAleer look bad in his old hometown. In addition to the problems cited by Mitchell, Bradley had stopped hitting, Lewis went hitless for the entire road trip, and Yerkes was out of the lineup with a minor injury. McAleer took Stahl to task over a few in-game decisions and his choice to pitch Buck O'Brien opposite Walter Johnson instead of sacrificing one of his rookie pitchers in what had been likely to be a losing cause. McAleer then made a public complaint to the press, saying bitterly, "We should have taken three games from Washington in a walk. Except for Speaker, we looked like a lot of bush leaguers."

Fortunately for the Red Sox, they were headed back home. Over the next three weeks they would play their longest home stand of the year. By the time the Red Sox took to the road again in June, they would know a lot more about themselves — and about Fenway Park.

Home Stand

There is a feeling among base ball men that I have talked with
that this is not going to be a big year. There doesn't seem to be the
enthusiasm that there ought to be . . . But still, there is no knowing what
a season will bring forth. Maybe with some warm weather, the base
ball fever will return. In late years the seasons in Boston have been
later. Time was when May was a warm month here. It isn't any more.
As yet we haven't had a really warm day and there is none in sight.

—A. H. C. Mitchell, *Sporting Life*

O NE MONTH INTO the season the reviews were all in. Despite the glowing reaction from the press on opening day,
by the time the Sox returned to Boston Fenway Park was
starting to lose some shine. After seeing Washington's brand-new
park, which had opened in 1911 but had had a second deck added for
the 1912 season, Boston's new park seemed a little lacking, somehow
unfinished, both too small in capacity and too spacious in the field.
A. H. C. Mitchell observed:

There has been considerable growling among the fans in regard to
the new grounds. The bleacher crowds say they are too far away
from the diamond, and the 50-centers say they are too far away
from first base. As a matter of fact, the Boston fans have always been
accustomed to small grounds . . . On the old Huntington Avenue
Grounds of the American League, the 50-cent seats were close to
first base on one side and close to third on the other. On the new Red

Sox grounds the grand stand extends way around to first and third bases and this, of course, throws the 50-cent Pavilion further away.

That was one reason, along with the weather, why crowds had thus far been disappointing. Compared to Huntington Avenue, the scale and layout of the park concentrated fans in three nearly separate locations—the lower reaches of the grandstand, the pavilion, and the center-field bleachers. That made the crowd look smaller than it sometimes was and made spectators feel cut off from one another and, for those in center field, cut off from the game. The team was drawing no better in Fenway Park than it had at Huntington Avenue.

These different areas of the stands soon developed their own character and reputation. The grandstand was for the swells and the well connected who could afford the pricier tickets. The most-sought-after spots were directly behind the plate, behind the Boston dugout, and in section L (section 27 today), where the Royal Rooters staked out their territory and walked around as if they owned the place, tooting their horns, beating their drums, and singing just as they had been doing at baseball games in Boston for two decades. In that sense the character of the crowd was not so different from Huntington Avenue.

But elsewhere in Fenway Park the average fan was squeezed out and exiled. The fifty-cent pavilion was farther down the line than comparable seats at Huntington Avenue, so they were less intimate. Also, the best seats were quickly taken over by a rabid contingent of gamblers who bet on absolutely everything imaginable, ranging from the eventual winner to numerous "do they or don't they" bets—wagers on the smallest elements of the game, such as ball and strike calls, or pop-ups versus ground balls, or the number of hits or runs each inning, or even such arcane issues as whether the wind would change direction. In this section of the stands along the first-base line the crowd sometimes behaved like the brokers on the floor of the stock exchange: men stood and waved dollar bills and screamed out odds and bets as if oblivious to the contest on the field, yet somehow they kept a running tally of winnings and losses. While many fans were unbothered by such activities, others not only felt uncomfortable but found the constant betting activity distracting. Yet they were too intimidated to complain. Even if they had, Red Sox management had neither the incentive nor the means to change fan behavior apart from banning gamblers from the ballpark, and they were loath to turn away paying customers of any kind.

Such activity in the ballpark was not just a Boston problem— though it may have been somewhat more pronounced in Boston than in other big league cities. Gambling and baseball had enjoyed a long-standing relationship and were not yet embarrassed to be seen to-gether. Gambling was as intertwined with professional baseball as the stitches used to hold the ball together, and it had been an integral part of the game from the very beginning.

For fans who either felt uncomfortable in the pavilion or could not afford a fifty-cent ticket, the twenty-five-cent bleachers were no bet-ter. While populated by far fewer gamblers, fans were also more than four hundred feet from home plate, too far to hear or even see most of the calls by the umpires, and for many the new scoreboard was out of view. With much of the game taking place more than a hundred yards away, viewing the game was akin to the experience of following the World's Series on one of the mechanical scoreboards the newspapers erected each October in front of their offices. Bleacher fans could tell what was happening, but little more.

The stands at Fenway Park were not segregated by race, nor had they ever been segregated at the South End Grounds or the Hunting-ton Avenue Grounds. Although ballparks throughout the South were routinely segregated—and would be until the 1960s—the only major league parks that were segregated in 1912 were in St. Louis. Black fans were rare in Fenway, and they may not have felt welcomed, but they were not banned.

There was also, as yet, no reason apart from Fenway Park to linger in the area, either before or after the game. When the Sox played at Huntington Avenue, several establishments with longstanding ties to Boston baseball had given some fans reason to arrive early and stay late. Nuf Ced McGreevey's Columbus Avenue saloon and other taverns in the area, such as the first-floor kitchen and tavern at the Putnam Hotel, had long been gathering places for fans on their way to or from both the Huntington Avenue Grounds and the South End Grounds to discuss the contest, most arriving and leaving along well-established routes that created a unique ambiance as one neared the park.

Amenities of this kind had yet to spring up around Fenway Park. There were few nearby buildings and virtually no taverns or restaurants in the immediate area. Apart from the Buckminster Hotel, built in 1897 as a lone outpost on Boston's western fringe, there were no nearby hotels. Development in Kenmore Square—officially known as Governor's Square until 1932—and the Fenway neighborhood was in its infancy and would not take off until the subway opened in 1914, sparking a building boom around Fenway Park. By 1920 the park would be surrounded by structures as garages, warehouses, and other businesses sprang up around it on Lansdowne Street, Ipswich Street, Van Ness Street, and Jersey Street. In 1912 fans seemed to arrive at the park from all directions and dispersed so quickly that unless the crowd was unusually large, within fifteen minutes of the finish of a game there was little sign that anyone had been in attendance. Some Roxbury fans still made the trek back down to McGreevey's afterward to retain some of the familiar conviviality, but it was not quite the same.

McAleer and company hoped that those feelings might change during the long home stand that would keep the team in Boston for the remainder of May. The Sox would host every team in the league except the Yankees, and if they played well they could end the month fighting for first place. Then, as now, in order to compete for the pennant the Red Sox knew they had to win at home, and in order for McAleer to survive financially he needed the turnstiles at Fenway Park to start spinning. By June he would know what kind of team the 1912 Red Sox were and just how much of a help—or hindrance—Fenway Park would be to their cause.

It helped that the players were finally able to use the new clubhouse and stop using the riding school to dress before games. The clubhouse accommodations, though much more spacious than they had been at the Huntington Avenue Grounds, were still spartan compared to facilities at most of the other new parks, some of which provided separate player lounges and even billiard rooms. Boston's clubhouse was a dressing room with an open shower bath and little else. Still, compared to the riding school the accommodations were absolutely sumptuous. The team offices in the building on Jersey Street—where the first floor was used for ticket sales and McAleer, McRoy, and other team officials had offices on the second floor—were complete as well, or at least close enough to being finished that they could finally close up shop on Huntington Avenue and move in.

The Detroit Tigers, who had finished second in 1911 but would struggle to play .500 baseball in 1912, opened the home stand in Boston. As far as McAleer was concerned, the Tigers were a welcome sight. Not that they were pushovers, but outfielder Ty Cobb was one of the biggest draws in the league. The twenty-five-year-old Tiger outfielder was at his peak, playing with a devastating and intimidating combination of speed, daring, and—for the Dead Ball Era—power. In 1911 he had hit .420 and led the league in both average and slugging, and he would do the same in 1912, hitting .409.

No one was quite aware of it yet, but Cobb had a challenger. Tris Speaker, coming off a season in which he had hit .334 and slugged .502, was about to make a claim that perhaps he, not Cobb, was the greatest player in the game. For just as Fenway Park would prove a boon to the career of Duffy Lewis, so too would Fenway Park work to Tris Speaker's advantage.

In his first few seasons in the league Speaker had impressed everyone with his all-around play, but entering the 1912 season, although the outfielder was considered a dangerous hitter, his defensive reputation still outstripped his offensive record. His arm, in particular, stood out. During his first full season, in 1909, the former high school pitcher threw out thirty-five base runners from center field. Although that number dropped over the next two seasons as runners became a bit more cautious about running on balls hit his direction, Speaker still managed to throw out twenty or more base runners each year.

The number probably would have been even higher if Speaker, like other Boston outfielders, had not had to play so deep, owing to the vast dimensions of the Huntington Avenue Grounds. If a ball made it over his head or between outfielders, it was a certain extra-base hit. And though Speaker was one of the fastest runners in the league and could go get the ball with the best of them, shallow flares hit to center field that would have been outs elsewhere sometimes fell for hits at Huntington Avenue.

No one was more familiar with the old park than pitcher Cy Young, who had taken the rookie Speaker under his wing in 1908. Young recognized that Speaker, because of his speed and instincts, was uniquely equipped to diminish the park's effect, something that was clearly in Young's interest. As Speaker later told a writer, "When I was a rookie, Cy Young used to hit me flies to sharpen my abilities to judge in advance the direction and distance of an outfield-hit ball."

All that extra work underscored something Speaker already sensed. "I know it's easier, basically, to come in on a ball than go back," Speaker said years later.

> But so many more balls are hit in front of an outfielder . . . it's a matter of percentage to be able to play in close enough to cut off those low ones or cheap ones in front of him. I still see more games lost by singles that drop just over the infield than a triple over the outfielder's head. I learned early that I could save more games by cutting off some of those singles than I would lose by having an occasional extra-base hit go over my head.

But it was not until he began playing at Fenway Park that Speaker was able to demonstrate his remarkable ability to play shallow enough to cut off flares over the infield while still managing to catch most balls hit over his head. In fact, on at least six occasions during his career he turned an unassisted double play at second base, racing in to catch a ball on the fly and then outrunning the base runner to second base, doubling him up. Significantly, however, Speaker performed that feat for the first time at Fenway in 1912, having never executed the play at Huntington Avenue or in other spacious Dead Ball Era parks. For just as the left-field wall allowed Duffy Lewis to play shallower than at Huntington Avenue, the presence of the center-field bleachers in Fenway Park allowed Speaker to play shallower as well. Unless a ball hit over his head was aimed directly at the flagpole, where Fenway's back fence was nearly five hundred feet from home, the center-field bleachers, more than four hundred feet away from home at their nearest point, still gave Speaker some cover and allowed him to play closer than at the Huntington Avenue Grounds.

Although observers would occasionally estimate that Speaker

played as close as forty feet from second base, that is likely to have been either hyperbole or a description of his play under special circumstances, such as late in a game with the winning run on third and less than two outs, a situation in which anything more than a short fly ball would be certain to score a run. Most outfielders have an effective range of about 125 feet when pursuing high fly balls, which rarely stay in the air more than five seconds. During the Dead Ball Era a long drive was one that traveled between 325 and 350 feet in the air, and anything longer was an anomaly—so rare as to not be worth worrying about. In all likelihood Speaker generally played two hundred feet or so from home plate, or about seventy-five to one hundred feet behind second base, but still some seventy-five to one hundred feet shallower than the average center fielder does today.

Speaker was suited to the position not only physically but temperamentally, once saying, "I was raised to it. I feel better in the outfield, in center field, with room to swing my elbows. I think maybe the feeling was born down in me down in Texas. I got used to the idea of space all around me."

At the same time—and for an entirely different reason—Fenway Park also served Speaker as a hitter. Like Lewis, Speaker was a pull hitter, but as a left-handed batter he favored right field. Speaker himself once noted that "I cut my drives between the first baseman and the line, and that is my favorite alley for my doubles." Relatively speaking, right field is much larger than left field in Fenway Park, a fact that was even truer in 1912 than it is today, since the construction of the bullpen, among other reconfigurations, has diminished the size of the outfield. And while conventional wisdom has always held that the left-field wall is helpful to right-handed power hitters—particularly home run hitters—the relatively small size of the outfield in left can hold down batting averages. In right field, while home run power is suppressed, there is simply more room for hits to fall in. That is the major reason why most left-handed hitters in Fenway Park have tended to hit for a higher average. Ted Williams, for example, hit twenty-five points higher in Fenway than elsewhere, Wade Boggs hit .328 for his career but .369 in Boston, and through 2010 David Ortiz, a career .281 hitter, had batted .306 in Fenway Park.

During the three-game series against Detroit that began Boston's home stand, Fenway Park continued, like a curtain slowly rising, to unveil both its offensive and defensive impact on the game. In the opener, on yet another cold and damp day, Joe Wood took the mound opposite Tiger ace George Mullin. In the first inning Ty Cobb sent a line drive to center field that in another ballpark might have fallen in for a hit, but Speaker, playing shallower in Fenway Park, was able to snag the drive. Although the Tigers hit Wood rather freely, Boston rode a four-run sixth-inning outburst to a 5–4 win.

The two teams were rained out the following day, and players from both clubs were feted at a banquet by 1,500 members of the local Elks Club, an evening that, among other things, featured the singing of Buck O'Brien. But the most interesting exchange took place when Major P. F. O'Keefe, the exalted ruler of the Boston Lodge, introduced Ty Cobb and Tris Speaker together, as if the two were equals.

Cobb played the southern gentleman to the hilt, but as the *Globe* noted, "he sent some hot ones in the direction of Tris," each barb delivered with a disingenuous smile frozen on his lips. He concluded by damning Speaker with faint praise, saying that "I am not much of a talker, but as there is the greatest 'Speaker' of all to follow me, I waive the privilege of taking any more of your time." Speaker spoke only briefly and failed to respond in kind, but on the field the next day Speaker stood his ground as he and Cobb waged a bit of a private battle against one another.

GEORGIA PEACH SPECKED BY BRADLEY BLIGHT AND NIPPED BY SPEAKER FROST

Boston won 7–4 behind Hall in a steady rain, but the final score was perhaps the least important part of the contest. In the third inning, with Boston nursing a 3–2 lead, Cobb cracked a double to the gap. Sam Crawford followed with a fly ball to center field, which Speaker caught with little effort.

Nevertheless Cobb tagged up after the catch and lit out for third. It made little sense strategically, for Cobb was already in scoring position, but the volatile outfielder was always playing for something more than the score. In this instance he was looking for an opportunity to assert his dominance over Speaker.

Speaker was not playing as deep as the Tiger star was accustomed to, and his throw to Larry Gardner beat Cobb to the base, where despite Cobb's usual hard slide Gardner's tag put him out. In the fifth inning, however, Cobb was able to extract a measure of revenge. With one man on, Charley Hall threw Cobb a low curve. He golfed the ball high down the right-field line.

As Cobb raced toward first base and Harry Hooper chased after the ball, both catcher Bill Carrigan and umpire Billy Evans lined up behind home plate, watching as the ball curved toward the short pole, perhaps twenty feet tall, that marked where the foul line met the stands. As the ball came down it curved toward the line, then plopped over the four-foot-high barrier and into the seats where the extreme end of the pavilion jutted into fair territory, just out of the reach of Harry Hooper. Had the ball been hit a few more feet fair, it would have been far short of the fence and an easy out.

Evans waved his hand toward fair territory, and Cobb fairly chortled as he toured the bases with the second over-the-fence home run in the history of Fenway Park, one that barely traveled three hundred feet in the air. Cobb's home run was also the first down the right-field line and around the much shorter genetic ancestor of the now famous "Pesky Pole," the name that pitcher Mel Parnell gave the right-field foul pole after Red Sox infielder Johnny Pesky hit a similar home run a generation later. Bill Carrigan put up a mild protest, but Evans was certain of his call. Speaker may have made Cobb look bad on the bases, but the home run put the Tigers up by a run.

Fortunately the Red Sox, behind Bedient in relief, stormed back to win. The Tigers then avoided a sweep in the finale by scoring three ninth-inning runs and holding on as the Red Sox fell short and lost 6–5. Once again Fenway Park played a part in determining the winner.

It was sunny for a change, which must have brought a smile to Jerome Kelley's face. Because of the weather, the infield at Fenway Park was still a mess. The *Post* referred to the ground around second base as being in "frightful condition," featuring a "glaring hole" filled with quicksand, and blamed the field conditions for the pathetic fielding performance by Clyde Engle, who was still filling in for the injured Yerkes at second base. The husky infielder, who had little range to begin with, made two blatant errors and failed to reach several other balls as he trudged after them through the mud.

Even the sun was a mixed blessing. Although the players much preferred sunshine to rain, since the game started at 3:15 p.m., toward the later innings, when the sun hung low in the western sky, it shone directly into the eyes of the right fielder.

With Detroit nursing a one-run lead in the top of the ninth, the Tigers' Ossie Vitt looped one to right field. Hooper, with little but open space behind him, was playing deep, and Clyde Engle, lumbering out from second, couldn't come close to the ball, which fell for a hit. Cobb followed with a hit through the hole between second and first, bringing up Sam Crawford.

The Tiger outfielder hit the ball on the nose, right at Hooper but over his head. The outfielder looked up but saw only the sun and did not even turn around until Speaker, closing hard from center field, yelled that the ball had landed behind him and was now rolling unimpeded in no-man's-land. By the time Hooper ran it down all three men had scored, and Crawford received credit for a home run.

That would not be the last time a right fielder at Fenway Park had a hard time seeing the ball in the late afternoon sun — none more famously perhaps than the Yankees' Lou Piniella, who lost Jerry Remy's ninth-inning fly ball during the 1978 playoff game between Boston and New York and avoided the goat horns only by making a blind stab to catch the ball on the hop. That is one reason why outfielders today are glad that the day games generally start several hours earlier. The game is generally over by the time the sun is low enough on the horizon to cause a problem, and modifications to Fenway Park have increased the height of the grandstand, which now starts blocking the sun when it is somewhat higher in the sky.

When St. Louis followed the Tigers into Boston, the Sox hoped to gain some ground in the pennant race by beating up the lowly Browns. While the Red Sox were alone in second place, the Chicago White Sox, to everyone's surprise, had sprinted into first place. With a record of 18-5, they were threatening to run away with the pennant.

No one in the game thought the White Sox could sustain that pace, but then again, no one had thought they could get off to such a good start either. They had last won a pennant in 1906 with a squad the press had dubbed "the Hitless Wonders." The White Sox still found crossing home plate a challenge. On offense they were a rather nondescript group that lacked a bona fide star, and the pitching staff, by and large, was not much more impressive. The exception was spitball ace Ed Walsh.

In the early days of the season Walsh was almost unhittable. As Sam Crawford once told author Lawrence Ritter, when Walsh threw his spitter, "I think that ball disintegrated on the way to the plate, and the catcher put it back together again. I swear, when it went past the plate, it was just the spit went by." The White Sox were riding Walsh hard: he was pitching every third or fourth game and also appearing in relief, a breakneck pace that no other pitcher could maintain. With the White Sox due to follow the Browns into Boston, the Red Sox needed both to beat up on the last-place club and to get into a groove before they faced the White Sox, who were gaining more confidence every day.

BROWNS ALWAYS AT WOOD'S MERCY

They needn't have worried, as the Browns were compliant in both areas. Joe Wood won the first and last games of the series, striking out a total of sixteen and nearly throwing a no-hitter as the Red Sox won in every way possible—scoring big, scoring late, coming back, and hanging on—to sweep all four contests. Nearly every Red Sox player came out of the series on fire and brimming with confidence. Speaker, in particular, feasted off St. Louis pitching and lifted his average to nearly .400.

The big story that day, however, was not Boston's victory but what had taken place in New York, where the Yankees were playing host to the Tigers. A fan named Clyde Leuker heckled Ty Cobb for most of the game, and when he called the southern slugger a "half nigger," Cobb lost it. In a rage he ran into the stands, climbed over other spectators until he reached Leuker, then proceeded to beat him senseless as hundreds watched in horror. When some fans told Cobb that Leuker, who had been in an industrial accident several years before, had no hands and was essentially defenseless, Cobb responded, "I don't care if he doesn't have any feet," and continued to pummel the heckler.

Ban Johnson, who was in the stands and witnessed the altercation, immediately suspended Cobb indefinitely. Cobb's teammates, seeing their chance for a pennant slipping away, backed their star and howled. They went on strike to protest the suspension. Not until the Tigers took the field a few days later with a replacement squad of amateurs and lost 24–2, making a travesty of the game, did Johnson back down. He cut Cobb's suspension to ten games, and the real Tigers returned to the field. Although Cobb was unaffected upon his return, the Tigers never got back on track as a team, and the Red Sox had one less contender to worry about.

Boston's four-game winning streak ran their record to a stellar 16-8, but they were still three and a half games behind Chicago, which led the league with a 21-6 mark. The opening game of the series, scheduled for May 16, was also "Dedication Day" at Fenway Park, McAleer's final attempt to use the new park to drum up a big crowd.

VIPs were sent engraved invitations that featured the 1910 drawing of the park, which was also reproduced on the header of the club's new official stationery. Apart from including a few design elements, like the right-field bleachers, that did not exist, the drawing lacked what was thus far Fenway Park's most distinguishing characteristic—rain clouds. Dedication Day was no exception. It poured all day, which not only left huge puddles on the field but, according to Paul Shannon, "cost the Red Sox many thousands of dollars" when the contest was postponed for a day. Nevertheless McAleer entertained the distinguished guests and VIPs at the ballpark, crammed into the team's offices for drinks and a catered meal.

The sun came out the next morning, and Jerome Kelley's men once again tried to whip the park into shape. Apart from sweeping the field of water, his staff had strung bunting along the grandstand and placed potted plants along the sidewalk outside and the walkways inside the park. Most of the luminaries who had tried to attend opening day were now on hand for the dedication, including Charles Comiskey, Ban Johnson, Charles Logue, and James M. McLaughlin. The latter two men finally had an opportunity to see the park not only nearly full—seventeen thousand fans turned out for the game—but bathed in sunshine. For the first time all season Fenway Park looked and felt warm and welcoming. The players paraded before the game to center

field, where the largest American flag ever seen in the city of Boston
was raised on the flagpole as the Letter Carriers' Band played "The
Star-Spangled Banner."

But when Jake Stahl learned that the White Sox planned to pitch
Ed Walsh in what was already his eighth start of the year, he chose
to back off, Dedication Day or not. Joe Wood, with only one day of
rest since facing St. Louis, was unavailable, but everyone else on the
pitching staff was ready to go, including Buck O'Brien, Charley Hall,
and Hugh Bedient. Rather than risk wasting one of his better pitchers against Walsh, however, Stahl all but gave up on the game and
selected Larry Pape to make only his second start of the season. In
the Boston clubhouse eyes rolled.

It would not be the first time Stahl's choice of a hurler caused observers to scratch their heads, but for the first eight and two-thirds
innings Pape made Stahl look like a genius as he scattered twelve hits
yet somehow managed to give up only one run. Although the Sox
scratched out two first-inning runs off Walsh, after that the pitcher
was his usual magnificent self.

When Walsh came to bat in the ninth, Pape was one out away from
a win, and when Walsh tapped the ball back to the box, Pape was only
one soft toss to first base away from a victory.

But there was a reason Pape had barely pitched all season long. He
botched the ground ball for an error, and Walsh reached first base.

The end came fast as Pape then gave up a double, a walk, and a hit
batsman before another error by Clyde Engle and a single gave the
game to Chicago, 5–2, and let all the air out of Boston's balloon.

The club stayed deflated the next day as the White Sox outhustled
them to a 3–1 win, beating Bedient and stretching their lead over
the Red Sox to five and a half games. "What has become," wondered
Tim Murnane aloud in the *Globe*, "of the star pitchers whom fans are
looking to land the money this year?" Boston players were asking
the same question as the fractures between the club's two factions
increased each day.

Stahl quieted the dissension in the series finale by selecting Wood
to square off against Walsh, and his teammates responded by playing
airtight baseball on a day in which a stiff north wind made hitting in
Fenway Park difficult. With no surrounding buildings to block the

breeze, hitters faced a virtual gale that knocked down any ball hit into the air. Boston scratched out two runs in the second inning on only one hit, and Wood, with help from Larry Gardner, Hugh Bradley, and Steve Yerkes, who finally returned to the lineup, made it stand up with some stellar defensive play as the Red Sox dumped Chicago 2–0. The Red Sox had lost the series and lost ground to the White Sox, but the victory in the final game provided some comfort. The club believed that if Stahl had made some better decisions about who to pitch—or if Pape had simply fielded a routine ground ball—they would have taken two of three from Chicago. The White Sox left Boston still in first place, but just as Boston's first series with the Athletics had told them they were a better team than the A's, the series against Chicago told them that the White Sox were beatable. Each team in the league played the others eighteen times, so with fifteen games remaining against the White Sox, a four-and-a-half-game lead was not insurmountable.

The Sox began chipping away at Chicago's lead in their next three games against Cleveland, sweeping them behind O'Brien, Hall, and Cicotte. All of a sudden Boston was riding a four-game winning streak. Connie Mack's Philadelphia Athletics followed Cleveland into Fenway, and the Red Sox were eager to take advantage of the struggling A's, who were still under .500. Despite their so-so record, there was no dramatic difference in the champions from the previous season. Most observers felt that they simply had not yet hit their stride.

To that end McAleer, dissatisfied with Hugh Bradley's play and uncertain if Jake Stahl's ankle would hold up, began to cast about for a replacement. He settled on New York first baseman Hal Chase. The Yankees had offered him to Boston when Stahl was first injured, only to be rebuffed when they asked for Tris Speaker in exchange. Now, apparently, the price had dropped.

Among his peers, the flamboyant, twenty-eight-year-old Chase was considered one of the best players in baseball. The greatest fielding first baseman the game had ever known, Chase played first base as if he were a shortstop, ranging all over the diamond and often taking throws at first while on the run. He was somewhat less impressive at bat, but was a savvy hitter who knew how to play inside baseball and was coming off the best season of his career, hitting .315 for New York in 1911.

But Chase, a ladies' man and bon vivant known far and wide as "Prince Hal," was also baseball's greatest prima donna and would soon earn a reputation as perhaps one of the most corrupt players in baseball history. New York manager George Stallings had already accused Chase of "laying down"—throwing games—during the 1910 season. With New York going nowhere, Chase, who earned a pretty salary, was available. All the Yankees wanted now was Hugh Bradley and backup outfielder Olaf Henriksen in return.

The deal was tempting, but acquiring Chase risked alienating Stahl and possibly creating yet another rift on a team that already had its problems off the field. McAleer was tempted, yet in the end he turned the Yankees down. The Red Sox would win—or lose—with what they had.

The ballpark—finally—was rounding into shape. A stretch of relatively warm and dry weather finally gave Jerome Kelley a chance to do some real work on the field, and for the first time all year infielders and outfielders alike began to feel more secure chasing down batted balls without worrying whether they would end up either slipping or stuck in the mud. Moreover, the Red Sox, their opponents, and their fans were becoming more accustomed to the vagaries of Fenway Park. Fly balls to Duffy's Cliff were no longer the subject of amazement but were becoming an expected part of the Fenway Park experience.

That was on display in the first inning against Philadelphia. Facing Hugh Bedient, who had dominated the A's in two appearances earlier in the year, Frank Baker doubled off Duffy's Cliff with one man to give the A's a quick 1–0 lead. But with one out in the bottom of the inning, Steve Yerkes also hit one to the bank, the ball skipping up and then off the scoreboard. After another hit and walk, Connie Mack was in a panic. He pulled pitcher Lefty Russell so quickly, as Paul Shannon noted, "that many of the fans never saw him go out." The Sox ended up scoring twice to take a 2–1 lead.

The two clubs traded the lead back and forth, and with the score tied in the fifth inning, Rube Oldring, the A's center fielder, lofted one to left field.

This time it was Duffy Lewis's turn to run to the wall and look up in wonder as Oldring's drive cleared the left-field wall for a home run. The blast caused the usual buzz among the fans, but not at the same level as the first time it happened. Oldring's home run wasn't hit quite as well as Hugh Bradley's—it cleared the fence, and then just barely, somewhat closer to the line—but in only twenty-two games the wall had now been breached twice.

Bedient, however, was unbothered. His cool under pressure would serve him well on the mound. He shut the A's down the rest of the way and helped his own cause with a run-scoring single in the seventh. Speaker then knocked in the winning run, and the Red Sox won their fifth in a row. With Wood and O'Brien scheduled to pitch next, the Sox seemed poised to make a run at the White Sox, who had stumbled since leaving Boston and now led by only three.

But Joe Wood and Buck O'Brien were still both maddeningly inconsistent. With each pitcher coming off his best start of the year, each followed up with his worst start of the young season. Wood had no control, walking five and hitting another as the A's beat him 8–2, and O'Brien made the case that he might have been better off back at the boot factory when he lost 12–6. Fortunately for the Red Sox, Connie Mack inexplicably chose the series finale to "try out" a series of youngsters on the mound, including eighteen-year-old Herb Pennock. While Pennock would one day earn admission to the Hall of Fame, on this day neither he nor anyone else Mack chose to throw even earned their way into the ballpark as the Sox salvaged a series tie on the first hot and muggy day of the year with a 7–3 win.

Now that the rain that fell for so much of the spring had finally abated, the Sox had to pay for the effects of the earlier deluge and make up a rained-out contest with Washington by playing a doubleheader on May 29, one day before a previously scheduled Memorial Day doubleheader on May 30. It was just the kind of thing that had worried Stahl when the games had first been canceled. Boston felt that they were a better team than Washington, but playing four games in two days would test a pitching staff that was still unproven.

It would also test Boston's offense, for while the Sox had come up with the occasional explosion of runs, they were also struggling to score on a consistent basis. Speaker was the only regular on the team hitting over .300. Both Duffy Lewis and Harry Hooper, though showing some power, were hitting only around .250. Hugh Bradley, still filling in at first for Stahl, had not hit at all since going over the left-field wall. Steve Yerkes hadn't had a dozen hits since opening day, and behind the plate Bill Carrigan and Les Nunamaker were barely hitting their weight.

Fortunately for the Red Sox, the weather had turned at precisely the right time. It was not quite as warm for the first doubleheader against Washington as it had been the previous day, but there was still a stiff wind blowing from the southwest. Both clubs would soon learn that when the weather is warm and the wind is blowing out at Fenway Park, hitting there is quite a different experience.

After two scoreless innings Washington scored a single run in the second before Boston rallied, stringing together walks, hits, and errors to plate three runs, then adding three more when Charlie Wagner got a ball in the air. Riding the wind, it soared over Clyde Milan's head in center field, hit the ground, and then kept going as Wagner toured the bases for a home run. The rout—and the record-setting—was on.

Fenway fans and pitchers both got stiff necks watching balls fly around Fenway for the rest of the day as every ball every pitcher threw seemed to get hit hard and every ball hit hard in the air seemed to fly over an outfielder's head. At least six balls either found Duffy's Cliff or ricocheted off the left-field fence, and both right fielders spent most of the day with their backs to the infield, chasing down drives. When game 2 was called because of darkness after only seven and a half innings the two teams had combined that afternoon for seventy-seven total bases, fifty-six hits, fourteen errors, thirteen doubles, eleven walks, six stolen bases, one triple, and one home run, scoring a combined total of fifty-two runs, with another twenty-four base runners left stranded and exhausted on base. According to the *Globe*, which speculated that the official scorer "might have lost a run or two in the excitement," players who scored a run in the game "ran an aggregate distance of 3 6/11 miles."

Somehow the Sox had managed to win both contests during the five-hour marathon, taking game 1 behind Wood, 21–8, as he threw a million pitches and hurled a complete game, and winning the second game 12–11 despite falling behind 6–0 in the first inning when Eddie Cicotte failed to retire a hitter. The victories were even sweeter due to the fact that the White Sox also dropped a doubleheader, allowing the Red Sox to pull to within two games of first place.

The next day, with the wind calm and the day cool, both teams played as if still recovering from the merry-go-round of the day before. They split the holiday doubleheader: the Sox won the first game 3–2 behind Bedient and then fell in the finale, 5–0, as Walter Johnson struck out thirteen. As soon as the game ended the Red Sox hustled over to South Station and caught a train for Cleveland. Now that their longest home stand of the season had ended, it was time for their longest road trip of the year—twenty-seven long days that would take them everywhere in the league but Philadelphia.

By this time they knew that they would miss Fenway Park. Over the course of the last month they had adjusted to their home field and seemed to have figured out how to use the park to their advantage, going 16-9 for the month, including winning nine of their last thirteen. While they still trailed the White Sox by two games, there was a certain optimism surrounding the club, and several lesser Boston newspapers that generally did not send reporters to cover the team hurriedly made arrangements to send a correspondent to follow the Red Sox on their month-long excursion.

On the roof of the Fenway Park grandstand, the red flag representing the Red Sox fluttered in the breeze, sandwiched between the flags that represented the third-place Athletics and the first-place White Sox. By the time the Red Sox would see them again, they were hopeful those flags would be unfurled in a different order.

✦ 7 ✦

The Big Trip

Some of the most exciting early games I saw were in 1912 . . . Smoky Joe
Wood, who belongs in the Hall of Fame, won 34 and lost 5 that year . . .
With the shadows pushing over the ballpark he would stand out there on
the pitching mound with his red trimmed gray road uniform, hitch up his
pants and throw. To this day I have a recollection of a strange sensation
as if my head had emptied when he fired the ball in the shadowy park.

—James T. Farrell, *My Baseball Diary*

IDWAY THROUGH THE 1912 season editor F. C. Lane of
Baseball magazine penned an article that tried to answer
the question of who was the greatest pitcher in baseball.
The author spent considerable time pondering the relative merits of
pitchers such as Christy Mathewson and Rube Marquard of the Giants and Ed Walsh of the White Sox before finally concluding with
certainty that "Walter Johnson is the greatest pitcher of the present
day." Oh, Joe Wood was in the conversation, but only ever so briefly.
Although Lane admitted that because of Wood's performance in 1911,
when he twirled a no-hitter and in another game struck out fifteen,
one shy of the record at the time, the pitcher "deserves admittance
into the front ranks," he concluded that "there are few people who
would not pick some other pitcher in preference to the star of Jake
Stahl's club."

There were reasons for that, and as Boston's train rumbled
through the night toward Cleveland, where the club would begin the
long road trip that could make or break their season, Joe Wood could
not have been satisfied with such an assessment. The prevailing view

throughout baseball was that Wood, while talented, was not all that he could be as a pitcher. Lane, in fact, was being kind, because thus far in 1912 Joe Wood had been plain rank nearly as often as he had been in the front ranks. And unless he did better, and soon, the 1912 season would be one that Sox fans would soon forget. The opening of Fenway Park would be a mere footnote to an otherwise desultory campaign.

After beating Washington 21–8 on May 28, Wood's record for the 1912 season stood at 9-3, 8-3 as a starting pitcher. In an era that valued statistical victories above all other measures, Charley Hall, at 7-0, was considered Boston's most successful pitcher of the first two months of the season. Wood's nine wins, while outwardly impressive, were also misleading. He was in fact barely scraping by. His best two starts by far had come against the dismal St. Louis Browns, the worst team in baseball, winners of only twelve games through May. In four of his starts Wood had given up five or more runs, and in his last two efforts he had given up nearly a run an inning and allowed twenty-five base runners in only seventeen innings of work. On at least three other occasions he had pitched indifferently but been saved by his offense. Thus far, Wood was much closer to being 6-6—or worse—than 12-0.

For all his vaunted speed, the man Paul Shannon would later dub "Smoky Joe" Wood, owing to the speed of his fastball, was a disappointment. An earlier nickname, "Ozone" Wood, was still more appropriate, for Wood sometimes pitched as if his head was in the clouds. His good fastball had been on display only intermittently, and he had been plagued by inexplicable bouts of wildness. The word "potential" hung around Wood's neck like a noose. Like that of the 1912 Red Sox, his season—and perhaps his career—was at a crossroads.

It was going to be good, perhaps, for Wood to escape Boston for a while so he could focus on the task at hand, for there was some cause to blame the city for his troubles. For one, he had little anonymity in the Hub, and his popularity sometimes proved distracting. At the house he shared with Tris Speaker on Circuit Street in Winthrop, Massachusetts, Wood and Speaker sometimes came home after a game and found their front porch crowded with boys and girls—and young women. The address of the seaside cottage had appeared in the newspapers, and Wood's mailbox filled to overflowing each day with "mash notes" and more. As Wood once admitted in regard to the 1912 season, these were "wild days . . . there were a lot of girls. They didn't stay home as much as they do nowadays." Rumors that Wood was about to marry seemed to hit the papers every few weeks—rarely with the same name attached. He was already juggling two fiancées— Laura O'Shea, his longtime girlfriend from Kansas City, whom he would eventually marry, and May Perry, a Boston girl who had spent the off-season in Philadelphia to be closer to Joe.

Although Wood did not drink anything harder than beer and even avoided coffee and tea during the season, he was adept with a cue stick and very much a man's man. The temptations that confronted a ballplayer in 1912 were little different from those that confront the professional athlete in 2012. Indeed, only a few years before, Red Sox player-manager Chick Stahl had committed suicide largely because of a complicated personal life—after he had married, a previous conquest informed him she was pregnant. Even though the same temptations existed on the road as in Boston, at least when he was away from Boston Wood could walk down the street and not be recognized.

But there was more to Wood's troubles than scented envelopes and blushing babes. The problem came down to Wood's fastball—his command of the pitch and his faith in it. Unless he found both, and soon, both his season and Boston's would slip away. During the road trip Wood was somehow going to have to find a way to harness his ability.

Pitchers are creatures of habit, and some of Wood's difficulty so far in the 1912 season seemed to stem from his inability to get into a rhythm, a comfortable routine on the mound that would allow him to block out everything but throwing to the glove. The weather had made it difficult to get in work on a regular basis, and pitching in Fenway Park had proven to be a challenge. As Wood's last two outings had demonstrated, Fenway could be a dangerous place for a pitcher to work, particularly on warm days with a southerly wind, which seemed to push every fly ball hit to left field up onto Duffy's Cliff. He was also adapting to the change in his motion with men on base that

Stahl had forced him to implement in spring training. When he took the mound he was often thinking about everything but getting the batter out, and he found it difficult to stay in a groove.

Even the mound was a distraction. At the time the rules stated only that the pitching rubber, then called the "plate," "shall not be more than 15 inches higher than the base lines or home plate." That left plenty of room for interpretation, and each pitcher had his preference. Wood had become as accustomed to the mound at Huntington Avenue as if it were an old shoe, but in Fenway Park, although the sod had been transferred from the old park, the soil was different. For most of the month of May Red Sox pitchers had consulted almost daily with Jerome Kelley and his crew, some of them preferring the mound to be low and flat while others asked for it to be higher and steeper. Kelley was accommodating to a point, but the weather had made his job even more difficult: after each game played in a downpour the mound had to be rebuilt.

The mound was important to Wood because it affected his ability to throw and control his best pitch, the fastball. Baseball writers of the era noted that Wood threw what they called a "jump ball"—an overhand, rising fastball that on good days had a "jump" or "hop" at the end of it. Although the phenomenon is an illusion—no ball thrown overhand truly rises on its way to the plate—a hard, high fastball like Wood's dropped less than hitters were accustomed to seeing and therefore appeared to rise as it reached the plate. When Wood was on his game, hitters could not resist swinging at a pitch that appeared to be coming in just above the belt. Yet as they whiffed they often discovered that they had actually offered at a pitch that crossed the plate at the letters. A higher mound helped Wood get on top of the ball and increase the downward angle of the pitch, which gave him more leverage and increased the illusion.

Like Pedro Martinez many years later, Wood had unusually long fingers that he used to impart terrific backspin on the pitch to help it move, and he delivered the ball with a unique and pronounced snap of the wrist that drew comment from everyone who saw him throw. "The wrist comes down and the ball leaves my finger quickly," Wood once explained, "thereby giving the ball the extra speed they say I have." He also threw each pitch, as he once said, "with all the energy I have," a habit that caused old-timers to shake their heads and wonder what was keeping his arm from falling off. Wood complemented his fastball with a so-called 12-6 curveball that did not curve so much as drop straight down, from twelve o'clock to six o'clock, a pitch that he could throw at various speeds. Wood occasionally claimed that he never threw what was then called a "slow ball" or a changeup, but that was a ruse. Smart hitters knew better.

Yet unless Wood could command his fastball, his other pitches were ineffective, and he knew it. His pitching philosophy was uncomplicated and direct and built around his best pitch. "When you stop to think of it, good pitching is only the knack of throwing the ball accurately so it will pass the batsman in a way that queers the sure eye," Wood once said. "That's why I believe in the fastball." It was that simple. In order to succeed Wood needed confidence in his ability to throw the fastball whenever and wherever he wanted.

That was what made Wood's catcher so important him. Despite the earlier report indicating that Wood had asked to pitch to Carrigan, as the season continued the two men, who were not close anyway, did not see eye to eye. Yet Wood's growing discontent with Carrigan as a receiver went beyond any personal animosity. Before breaking his leg in 1911, Carrigan had been one of the quicker and more active backstops in the game. But the broken leg had slowed him down. He did not move as well behind the plate anymore, either receiving the ball or throwing it. That affected Wood more so than Boston's other pitchers. Not only did Carrigan have a bit of trouble handling Wood's fastball—particularly when Wood missed location and Carrigan had to react quickly—but Wood, who still struggled to hold runners on base despite throwing from the stretch, needed a good-throwing catcher to keep base runners close and allow him to concentrate on pitching. The problem was that no matter how close Wood held runners to first base, Carrigan could no longer get rid of the ball fast enough to prevent most players from stealing. As a result Wood was forced to pay more attention to men on base and to pitch differently to hitters, both to keep them off base in the first place and then to hold runners close when they did reach first.

Earlier in the season Wood had successfully lobbied Jake Stahl to have Les Nunamaker catch on the days he pitched, but in truth Nunamaker wasn't a dramatic improvement over Carrigan. The two other catchers on the team, Hick Cady and Pinch Thomas, were on the roster primarily to keep them from playing for anyone else. Neither had major league experience, Stahl had no faith in either man, and they had hardly played.

Wood was not the only Boston pitcher struggling. Although Hall was pitching well and Bedient was gaining confidence, Eddie Cicotte remained awful, and Buck O'Brien was maddeningly inconsistent. Perhaps they all needed some time away from Boston.

Unfortunately, Cleveland was not the cure. Although the Indians were only playing .500 baseball, they took three of four from Boston, giving Hall his first defeat of the season and also beating Bedient and O'Brien. Wood won his eleventh game, but still gave up four runs and had to pitch ten innings to earn the victory. The only good things that happened in Cleveland were that lefty Ray Collins of Vermont, a stalwart of the staff in 1911, made his first appearance in relief and, after weeks of inactivity, Jake Stahl finally made a brief appearance. He had been out for so long with the bad ankle that some had questioned his fortitude. Indeed, according to some baseball historians, the phrase "jaking it," which refers to an injured player milking his recovery, was first used in reference to Stahl. He knocked in three runs in one game against Cleveland before returning to the bench, having turned a sure home run into a triple because he still couldn't run. Still, he would soon return to the lineup full-time and send Hugh Bradley and his anemic bat back to the bench. With each passing day Bradley's blast over the left-field wall seemed more and more an anomaly. In fact, a little more than a month after the Yankees had wanted Bradley as part of a deal for Hal Chase, the Red Sox put Bradley on waivers and found no takers. The Sox left Cleveland for Detroit down another game to the White Sox.

When they arrived in Detroit on June 5 they got their first look at Detroit's new ballpark, Navin Field, named after Frank Navin, who owned half the club. The other half was owned by Bill Yawkey, who inherited his money from his father, who had made his fortune in the logging and deforestation of Michigan's great north woods. When Bill Yawkey's sister's husband passed away, he would eventually adopt his nephew, Tom Austin. Bill Yawkey would give young Tom both the Yawkey name and, eventually, the Yawkey fortune, which in 1933 Thomas Austin Yawkey would use to purchase Fenway Park and the Red Sox. Although Yawkey was as responsible for the new park as Navin and could have had his name attached to it had he wanted, he deferred to his partner. He liked owning the Tigers because he liked palling around with ballplayers and was uninterested in leaving behind a monument bearing his name.

Because of the rain that had delayed the opening of Fenway Park, Navin Field had opened for business on the same day. Built on the same site as its precursor, Bennett Park, Navin Field was in many ways Fenway Park's spiritual and architectural cousin, albeit a bit more spacious. That was no accident, for both clubs utilized the services of Osborn Engineering in Cleveland in the building of their parks. Like Fenway, the concrete-and-steel ballpark in Detroit featured a single-deck grandstand with a similar configuration and pavilions that stretched down not just the first-base line, as in Fenway, but down the third-base line as well. And just like Fenway, center field was occupied by a section of bleachers. The twin scoreboard on the left-field fence was identical to that at Fenway Park and had been built by the same manufacturer. The field even mimicked Fenway Park's orientation to the sun. In 1926, however, a second deck would be added to the original single-deck structure, and any similarity to Fenway Park would be obliterated.

The construction of so many concrete-and-steel ballparks in such a brief time period provided evidence of just how deeply the game of baseball had become ingrained into the fabric of American life and how important it had become. Prior to the concrete-and-steel era ballparks had been less permanent, wooden structures that after only a few years were destined to decay. Although investments in concrete-and-steel structures were made primarily because of insurance and safety concerns, the decision to invest in such a durable structure was also emblematic of baseball's permanence. Baseball franchises like the Red Sox had come to represent the character of their city and were now worthy of homes that reflected their place in the hearts and minds of their people. The concrete-and-steel ballpark era provided evidence that baseball was a lasting part of the culture. Like public buildings, they were built to last. The game was here to stay and so, presumably, were its structures. These ballparks became homes for the aspirations of the game, and they would evolve to fit their cities and grow in importance to the fabric of the surrounding communities.

The Sox were impressed. Navin Field was much like Fenway, only bigger in scale, including a 125-foot flagpole in deep center field and a few other interesting features, such as a dark green backdrop in center field for the benefit of hitters, which batters loved but pitchers detested. That feeling became even more pronounced among Boston pitchers after the Red Sox dropped two of the first three contests to the Tigers. Since beating Washington in the first game of a double-header on Memorial Day, the Sox had now lost five of eight.

Yet there was still some reason for optimism. Although Hall lost again, Buck O'Brien pitched well to earn a win, and in his first start of the season Ray Collins, his bum knee finally healed, pitched relatively well in defeat as he replaced Eddie Cicotte in the rotation. And fortunately for the Red Sox, the first-place White Sox had gone into a tailspin. Instead of falling further behind in the race, the Red Sox remained only two games behind Chicago, although Washington, which had not lost since that same Memorial Day doubleheader against Boston, was closing fast.

Wood pitched the series finale, and after the Sox erupted for four runs in the top of the first, he made it stand up and salvaged a split for Boston with an 8–3 win. He still wasn't the best pitcher in baseball, but he had been able to get outs when he needed them. Tim Murnane noted that "Wood never worked more earnestly in a game. Several times Ty Cobb was in position to make trouble with a safe drive, but the Kansas Cyclone cut the Georgia Peach off without the semblance of a hit." Chicago lost again, and with their next stop St. Louis, Boston now trailed by only a game.

The Red Sox arrived in St. Louis knowing there was nothing like a series against the Browns to cure the ills of a flailing ball club. Boston's batters relished the opportunity to feast on the Browns' pitching staff, and Boston's hurlers looked forward to throwing in the steamy heat of the old river town, which made the arm feel loose and free. Even better, the Browns had gotten off to a slow start and were now lurching to a complete halt. About the only thing about the club that did not reek of ruin and decay was their ballpark, Sportsman's Park. An earlier wood structure had been rebuilt in steel and concrete in 1909, the third such park in the majors. It was, in a way, the kind of park Fenway was first intended to be: the grandstand featured a double deck with single-deck wings extending down each line. But of all the concrete-and-steel ballparks of the era, Sportsman's Park, like the Browns themselves, was rather dull and uninteresting. Although later renovations would give the park some charm, as first constructed it was as colorless as the team that called it home.

St. Louis fans were accustomed to watching the Browns lose, and they were not disappointed when Boston came to town. In the first game things got so bad that St. Louis fans spent most of the game cheering Tris Speaker, and with good reason. He hit for the cycle, and Duffy Lewis also chipped in with a home run as Bedient scattered ten hits in a 9–2 win. But the big news was in Chicago, where the White Sox, playing at home, were falling apart. All of a sudden Boston was closing on Chicago.

They could smell it, and the next day, for perhaps the first time all year, the Red Sox came alive and through pure effort won a game they should have lost. Trailing the Browns 2–1 behind O'Brien, Boston tied the game in the eighth when Carrigan knocked in Larry Gardner. Then, in the ninth, Steve Yerkes singled. After Speaker made an out, Stahl called for the hit-and-run play. Yerkes broke for second base, and Duffy Lewis complied by bouncing a slow ground ball to Browns third baseman Jimmy Austin. He fielded the ball cleanly and threw to first as Lewis gamely raced down the line.

But Lewis's hard run caused Austin to make what Paul Shannon described as a "lurid throw" that sailed high and careened against the stands. In Fenway Park, where the pavilion was angled toward the field, such overthrows usually bounced back at a sharp angle toward the field of play, making it difficult to advance more than one extra base. But in St. Louis the pavilion was parallel to the foul line, and the ball bounded along the barrier into foul territory far down the right-field line. As Steve Yerkes, hardly a speed demon, rounded second base he saw manager Jake Stahl waving madly in the coach's box. Yerkes kept running, and when Stahl sent him around third base, he headed home and barely beat the throw to the plate. When Yerkes made it to the dugout he was swept up in the arms of his teammates, a rare expression of public camaraderie on a team that still struggled to pull together as one. Meanwhile the White Sox were losing again, and when Duffy Lewis gathered in a fly ball at the base of the left-field bleachers for the final out of the game, the Red Sox were in first place in the American League for the first time since April 23.

Winning made everything easier, but it was not a time for gloating. The Red Sox realized, as one Boston writer noted, that their spot in first place "was accomplished not so much by the superior playing of Boston as by the unlooked for slump of the Chicago team." Besides, Washington still had not lost since Memorial Day, and truth be told, Boston worried more about the Athletics, a sleeping giant lurking in fourth place, than about either Washington or the White Sox.

A's manager Connie Mack thought his 1912 team was the most talented he had ever managed, but after winning two pennants the A's were both overconfident and wracked by dissension. Much of that was due to a series of articles that A's second baseman Eddie Collins authored in *American* magazine during the off-season. In one, he revealed how opposing pitchers tipped their pitches. Collins's teammates were incensed that he revealed such critical information for his own personal gain at their expense. The A's clubhouse began to fracture and slowly split apart.

The next day the news got better for Boston by getting worse. Charley Hall, using what the *Post* called "a variety of benders and shoots that had the Browns ducking and backing away," was working on a 4–0 shutout. Then, with one out in the third inning, St. Louis shortstop Bobby Wallace took a cut and fouled a pitch straight back. Boston catcher Les Nunamaker didn't have a chance. A week before, in Cleveland, he'd taken a pitch off his bare hand, and it was still sore and swollen. Now the ball split the skin between his thumb and forefinger. He bent over double as blood spurted to the ground like a fountain. He was rushed to the hospital for stitches, and Bill Carrigan came into the game.

George Ellard, catcher for the old Red Stockings in 1869, once captured the catcher's plight in verse:

> *We wore no mattress on our hands*
> *No cage upon our face*
> *We stood right up and caught the ball,*
> *With courage and with grace.*

Nunamaker and other catchers of his era had benefited from some improvement to the equipment, such as a padded glove, a thin chest protector, a wire face mask, and rudimentary leather shin guards, but compared to today's catchers, decked out in high-tech armor, they were almost defenseless. Few catchers at the major league level had all their teeth, most had had their nose broken multiple times, and their fingers were usually contorted and misshapen from repeated breaks.

Nunamaker's bad break, however, proved fortuitous to the Red Sox. Boston was due to play in Chicago next, and there was some speculation that Stahl would hold Joe Wood back a day to pitch the opener. But with the White Sox on the skids, he once again chose to avoid wasting Wood opposite Ed Walsh, and Wood got the call to pitch the series finale against St. Louis.

Despite the injury to Nunamaker, his catcher would not, however, be Bill Carrigan. Forrest "Hick" Cady, Boston's third-string catcher, drew the surprise assignment.

The hulking, twenty-six-year-old rookie from Illinois—whose nickname was an abbreviated version of his childhood nickname, "Hollick," though it could have described his rural upbringing and naïveté—had been a professional since 1906. He was so raw when he started his pro career that he later liked to tell a story about the time his minor league manager ordered him to call for a pitchout. He did not, and when his manager asked why, Cady explained that he didn't think it was in his pitcher's repertoire. The catcher himself had not known what a pitchout was. Nevertheless Cady learned fast, and in 1911 he had benefited from catching the aging veteran and former Giants great "Iron Joe" McGinnity for Eastern League Newark, impressing Boston scouts. After the season the Sox, worried about the condition of Bill Carrigan's broken leg, acquired Cady in exchange for $6,000 and two players.

He impressed observers from the outset, particularly with his arm. Tim Murnane noted that Cady threw "dead to the mark all the time." Even though the Sox did not really need him after Carrigan proved relatively sound, in the spring of 1912 Cady made the roster to keep him from being grabbed by another club. Yet he hardly ever played. An ankle injury early in the year had slowed him down, and with Carrigan and Nunamaker on the roster he was still, at best, Stahl's third choice behind the plate. He spent most of his time warming up the pitchers Stahl tried not to use.

Cady was a large player for the era, standing 6'2", and although not very fast, he was quick and agile. For the rest of the season—and for one season only—he was the answer behind the plate for Boston, just as veteran catcher Elston Howard would be for the Red Sox in 1967 after being acquired in midseason. As A. H. C. Mitchell accurately observed later in *Sporting Life*, "Wood has more confidence with him [Cady] behind the bat." He wasn't alone. From the time he entered the lineup virtually every Boston pitcher threw the ball better with Cady behind the plate, and the rookie also hit better than any other Boston backstop. If there was one change that made a difference for the Red Sox during the course of the 1912 season, it was when Hick Cady entered the lineup. He helped make Joe Wood a star.

As Carrigan and Nunamaker looked on the next day Wood pitched to Cady for the first time in competition since spring training. At the start of the game Nunamaker, Cady's roommate, called for him to "keep up the reputation of the room!" Cady, normally soft-spoken, took that as a challenge. He turned to the bench and called out, "If they give me the chance, they'll never miss you." The remark raised some eyebrows, but Cady was correct. Although he and Wood were not yet on the same page—Cady did not know the strengths and mostly weaknesses of the Browns hitters, and Wood shook him off repeatedly, in essence calling his own game—that was probably for the best. That gave Cady a chance to see how Wood liked to work, and for the first time all year Wood got to throw exactly what he wanted, when he wanted.

It worked. Wood dispatched the Browns 5–3 as Cady chipped in with a hit and a sacrifice, and Wood blasted a home run to help his own cause, although he gave it back when a base runner took advantage of his slow wind-up and stole home. Still, it was a nice start for what would soon become Boston's best battery. And in a superstitious age Wood's victory with Cady behind the plate gave Jake Stahl a great excuse to continue to have Cady catch Wood instead of Carrigan—it was considered bad luck to break up a winning combination. As Cady predicted, Nunamaker was not missed and barely played the rest of the year. Wood was now 12-3 and finally starting to pitch up to his record.

A happy ball club boarded the train that night for Chicago, eager to face the White Sox. The Red Sox led by a game and were winners of six of their last seven, including five straight. If the Red Sox could stay hot against the White Sox and take the series, they could take command of the pennant race.

In the National League there was no race at all, except for the record book. The New York Giants, 36-8, led the second-place Cincinnati Reds by eleven and a half games. The Giants had already run off two winning streaks of nine games each and another of ten, and they were about to take off on a record nineteen straight victories. New York baseball writers were already arguing over who should start in the World's Series, Christy Mathewson, Rube Marquard—who thus far was undefeated for the season—or rookie Jeff Tesreau. Manager John McGraw's biggest worry was staying awake as he watched his team club the opposition senseless, for so far the Giants had outscored their opponents by nearly a two-to-one margin.

In an effort to boost the gate White Sox owner Charlie Comiskey declared that Flag Day, June 13, the first game of the series against the Red Sox, would also be "Boston Day." The weather cooperated and provided Boston weather—rain—for most of the contest as the umpires didn't even allow players to warm up in an attempt to keep the field playable. As both Ban Johnson and Comiskey looked on, the White Sox tried to kill the Red Sox with kindness before the game. James McAleer was presented with a silver case, Robert McRoy received a gold watch, and Jake Stahl limped off with several enormous floral arrangements.

Instead, Boston should have just asked the White Sox to pitch anyone but Ed Walsh. He scattered three hits and beat Ray Collins 3–2. The victory pulled the White Sox back into a tie for first place. When game 2 of the series was rained out, manager Jimmy Callahan of the White Sox turned to Walsh once more, starting him for the fourth time in five games against Boston for the season.

Comiskey Park was nearly overflowing as twenty thousand Chicago fans turned out for the contest, most of them hoping to see the White Sox regain their lead. The concrete-and-steel park had opened in 1910 and featured a double-decked grandstand flanked by two pavilions. The symmetrical field was among the more spacious parks of the day—362 feet down each line and 420 feet to center field. This time Jake Stahl was given a silver case before the game by his hometown admirers and the crowd was serenaded by a band as Chicago, with Walsh on the mound opposite O'Brien, seemed prepared to celebrate. As the big pitcher took the mound to start the game exuberant fans spontaneously broke out in song, singing "For He's a Jolly Good Fellow."

The Red Sox thought he was jolly good as well. They finally solved the spitballer, boxing him around for three runs in the first and driving him from the game after only two innings, then hanging on as O'Brien won his third straight with a 4–3 win, leading Jimmy McAleer to predict that, "if Buck makes good on last year's record with Boston the Red Sox will win the championship." The win pulled them back into first place, but also cost them the services of Bill Carrigan.

In the fourth inning Carrigan came to bat against Chicago relief pitcher Joe Benz and took an "inshoot," a running fastball, off the side of his head. Carrigan dropped to the ground, almost knocked out, but eventually he sat up, then stood and tried to continue, walking like he was on the deck of the *Titanic* as it was going down. Stahl wisely pulled him from the game and sent Cady in to catch.

It was the best thing that could have happened. Cady made a diving catch of a foul ball that Carrigan would not have come close to. Then, in the ninth, with two outs and Boston nursing a one-run lead, Cady gunned out Rollie Zeider trying to steal second base to end the game.

Cady was behind the plate the next day as well, again catching

Joe Wood. He made good once more, making two perfect throws to second to shut down Chicago's running game, blocking a runner off the plate on a play at home, and knocking out a hit to spark the winning rally. And that wasn't the half of it. Wood won again, 6–4, but pitched better than the score: with one bad error and two dropped throws, shortstop Charlie Wagner was responsible for most of Chicago's runs. Wood gave up only five hits, and Tim Murnane noted that over the course of the game, as the pitcher became more comfortable with his catcher, he threw more and more fastballs. Cady clearly had no trouble handling Wood's best pitch. No one realized it yet, but everything was now in place. For the remainder of the season the 1912 Red Sox would play as well as any team in Red Sox history, and Joe Wood was almost unbeatable.

The White Sox tried Walsh again in the finale, but Boston had broken his spell and knocked him around for thirteen hits in their 4–1 win behind Charley Hall. Hick Cady had two more hits, threw out another base runner trying to steal, and made another spectacular, sprawling catch of a foul ball. The Sox didn't miss Carrigan, who stayed in the game by coaching first, or Charlie Wagner, who had been suspended for three games the day before after dressing down umpire Jack Sheridan in language that left the umpire flushed with anger.

The Red Sox left the ballpark only ten minutes after the victory and rushed to the station to make their train for New York. They could not wait to play the Yankees. Three wins against the White Sox had left them two games up on their rivals. The Senators, after winning sixteen in a row, had finally lost, giving the Sox even more confidence going into New York, where the Yankees, at 17–36, were doing a fair imitation of the Browns. After New York the Sox would visit Washington, where they hoped to discard the surprising Senators like something on their shoe before returning to Fenway Park to start a home stand with another series against New York. If everything broke right, it was not unthinkable that the Red Sox might open up a double-digit lead on the rest of the league.

Pitching, which had been the issue when they left Boston three weeks before, was now the least of Boston's concerns. With Cady manning the plate almost every game, it had been two weeks since

anyone had scored more than four runs in a game off Boston pitching.
The Red Sox suddenly felt so secure that the club worked out a deal
to trade Eddie Cicotte to Cincinnati and put him on waivers, hoping
he'd clear the league so they could make the transaction and fill a
hole. Reserve infielder Marty Krug was hurt, and the Sox needed an
experienced man to back up Wagner, Yerkes, and Gardner. But the
White Sox, now desperate for a pitcher to take the load off Walsh,
put in a claim and blocked the deal. Cicotte remained with Boston,
but his status was in limbo. He wasn't needed, not even to mop up.
Jake Stahl, like other managers at the time, rarely pulled an effective
starting pitcher no matter what the score.

Over the next five days, as if apologizing for allowing the pitching
staff to carry the load on the road trip, the Red Sox offense exploded.
After Hugh Bedient won the first game of the series 5–2, Boston
made the Yankees look like a semipro club and battered them in the
next four games, winning 15–8, 11–3, 13–2, and 10–3 as O'Brien, Hall,
Wood, and Collins all collected victories. Cady continued to prove
to be a revelation, both at the plate and behind it, and even the loss
of Harry Hooper for a few games to a minor injury seemed not to
matter to Boston. Although Bill Carrigan was healthy again, Cady
was Wood's full-time catcher and split the other duties with Carrigan, who now found himself coaching first base almost as often as
he caught. Over time the role of each catcher would become more
clearly defined. Just as Cady became Wood's personal catcher, Bill
Carrigan would generally catch O'Brien. Boston arrived in Washington with a record of 40-19, the winners of eight straight, and with a
four-and-a-half-game lead on the White Sox and a five-game lead on
the Senators.

Jimmy McAleer's former club, which had finished in seventh place
in 1911 with McAleer at the helm, had been remade in the off-season,
getting younger, faster, and considerably more athletic. Outfielder
Clyde Milan was blossoming into a full-fledged star, in the same conversation with Speaker and Cobb, but the real difference was Walter
Johnson. In 1911, at age twenty-three, he had won twenty-five games.
But he was even better in 1912. He was everything Joe Wood aspired
to be.

Although Johnson, like Wood, was a fastball pitcher, he shared little

else with his Boston counterpart. Where Wood was cocksure and ar-
rogant and occasionally even cruel, Johnson was even-tempered and
polite. Wood later called him, without any irony whatsoever, "a prince
among men," a characterization virtually everyone agreed with. Unlike Wood, the right-handed Johnson threw sidearm, a buggy-whip
action that was particularly hard on right-handed hitters.

Yet hitters did not fear Johnson—Johnson feared them, for he
knew full well how hard he threw and worried that he might one day
hit a batter and kill him. When asked once why he didn't brush hitters off the plate, Johnson replied with uncharacteristic anger: "The
beanball is one of the meanest things on Earth and no decent fellow
would use it. The beanball is a potential murderer. If I were a batter
and thought the pitcher really tried to bean me, I'd be inclined to wait
for him outside the park with a baseball bat."

As a result Johnson rarely pitched inside, preferring to stay away
from hitters. Had he been more aggressive, batters would have had no
chance. As it was, their chances were still somewhere between slim
and none. All by himself he made the Senators, who otherwise were a
.500 team at best, a bona fide contender.

His only other weakness was that he could not pitch every game,
something every team in baseball knew when they faced the Senators. Just as Jake Stahl had maneuvered his pitching rotation to avoid
putting an ace opposite Ed Walsh, many Washington opponents took
the same approach in regard to Johnson. Stahl, in fact, planned to do
just that, particularly after Bedient beat the Senators in the first game
of the series to give Boston its fourteenth win out of the last fifteen.
Rather than pitch Wood opposite Johnson, he opted for O'Brien. The
defeat took some air out of both the Senators and their fans, who had
turned out in force and were finally starting to believe in their ball
club. But while the Washington crowd had the upper hand at the
start, by the end of the game the big noise in the ballpark was being
made by a contingent of nearly one hundred Royal Rooters who had
made the trip from Boston.

The rabid bunch of fans had been leading the way back in Boston
while the Red Sox mopped up on the road, and they simply couldn't
wait for the team to come home. Dozens had boarded trains for
Washington, where they hoped not only to see the Sox dispatch the

Nationals but also to take some money from overly optimistic Washington fans.

The Red Sox players welcomed their arrival. After spending weeks together in hotels and trains with only each other for company, it was nice to see a few familiar faces. Besides, the Rooters were always good for a free meal and a few drinks when they were in town.

Unfortunately, the Rooters were disappointed in game 2. Walter Johnson and Buck O'Brien were scheduled to square off, but Johnson had a touch of tonsillitis, and when Washington manager Clark Griffith saw that it was raining, he called the game off, causing a doubleheader to be scheduled for the following afternoon. Jake Stahl was out with indigestion, leaving management of the club to Charlie Wagner and Bill Carrigan, whom the press had dubbed Boston's "Board of Strategy." Now that Wood and Johnson were going to pitch on the same day anyway, they saw no reason to hold Wood back from pitching opposite Johnson. He did not need to be coddled. Besides, with a six-game lead over the Senators, Boston was going for the throat.

The Senators felt the same way. Before the game Washington owner Griffith offered the opinion that Johnson was pitching so well that he did not think his ace would lose another game all season. So far it had been a season of streaks, for apart from the Senators' own recent winning streak and those of the Giants, New York pitcher Rube Marquard, at 17-0, had not lost all year.

In the meantime the Red Sox made a move. With Marty Krug still laid up, the club purchased infielder Neal Ball from Cleveland. Considered a fine fielder, Ball was beginning to show his age and had become expendable when he lost the shortstop job to young Roger Peckinpaugh. Ball was best known for turning a line drive by Charlie Wagner into an unassisted triple play three years earlier. But the Sox weren't asking him to repeat that miracle. They just hoped he could give Wagner and Gardner the occasional rest and provide some insurance against injury, but the deal was telling. It was the kind of move made by a good team beginning to look forward, trying to anticipate a need before it became apparent and picking up a veteran who could be counted on during a pennant race—or in the World's Series.

When the players awoke on the morning of June 26, the rain that had washed out the game the day before was gone and it was already hot, with the kind of humidity that made the act of breathing akin to chewing the air. By the time the ballplayers reached the ballpark the temperature was above ninety degrees and rising, but there was still a crowd of more than twelve thousand. All through the stands fans loosened their collars and fanned each other with hats, while the players dabbed their foreheads with ammonia water and tucked cabbage leaves under their caps to keep cool. Washington's season was on the line. The club simply could not afford to be swept by Boston.

Buck O'Brien, who looked haggard on a good day, took the mound in game 1 opposite Washington's Buddy Groom. By the end of the game he looked completely wilted as the home crowd got what it wanted. With the score tied 2–2 in the bottom of the tenth, O'Brien, his wool uniform heavy and sagging with sweat, opened the inning by giving up a base on balls to Tilly Walker, his eighth free pass of the game. Eddie Forster then stepped in and smacked the first pitch he saw hard to left.

Duffy Lewis moved in on the ball. The layout of Washington's ballpark, later known as Griffith Stadium but in 1912 simply known as American League Park, was nearly the mirror image of Fenway Park. The right-field fence was only 280 feet from home down the line, but in left it was more than 400 feet to the wall. As a result Lewis was playing much deeper than in Fenway Park. He had to because in Washington, with no Duffy's Cliff or fence close behind, any ball that got past him was an extra-base hit.

When the drive hit the ground and skipped toward him, Lewis bent and reached down to field the fast grounder . . . then watched it bound between his legs. Walker was already tearing around second. Lewis spun and began to run after the ball but stopped after a few futile steps, saving what energy he had left for the next game. Walker raced across the plate as the Washington crowd roared in approval. They had barely let up when they started roaring again as Walter Johnson strolled out of the dugout to begin warming up for game 2. As Joe Wood soon followed him onto the field Washington fans began to dream of a sweep.

The game was important to Wood, and he knew it. His ball club was in first place, but it went far beyond that. Johnson had the respect of every man in the league and every fan in the game. That was the kind of recognition Wood wanted for himself. As Tim Murnane commented later, "Wood was hungry for a little glory and the scalp of one of the big guns." Johnson was the biggest gun of all, and a victory over baseball's best pitcher could give Wood the boost he sorely needed.

Only ten minutes after the end of the first game umpire Fred Westervelt called out, "Play ball," and game 2 began as Johnson, his uniform already dark with perspiration, poured the first pitch over the plate. Even for himself, Johnson was in rare form from the start, his fastball a blur and his sweeping curve a knee buckler. But so was Joe Wood. As the *Washington Post* noted the next day, "Walter Johnson and Joe Wood hadn't gone more than an inning each in the second game before it was apparent that the winner wouldn't need more than a run or two, and probably that some break in the luck of the game would decide it."

Johnson retired the first nine Boston hitters in order, and Wood nearly matched him. But with two out in the third, Johnson, like Wood a fine hitter, hit a fly to right that Harry Hooper misplayed into a double. Wood then escaped without further damage.

Boston didn't even have a hit through the first four innings. But with one out in the fifth, Gardner singled to right field. Now came that "break in the luck of the game." It was Washington right fielder Tilly Walker's turn to make a mistake, and he overran the ball. Gardner kept running, and when the throw to third was high and wild he lit out for home. The throw beat him there, but catcher Eddie Ainsmith dropped the ball. Boston scored a run it did not earn but was glad to accept nonetheless.

On the mound, Johnson's expression did not change. He never showed up his own players by expressing displeasure at their mistakes. He knew that even he was not infallible, and in the sixth inning he proved it.

Hick Cady was facing Johnson that day for the first time in his career. Johnson should have had the advantage, but Cady, overmatched like almost every other hitter in the league, did the wise thing in his second appearance. He kept his bat on his shoulder and managed to draw a walk. Wood then swung through three straight pitches to strike out, but Hooper singled to left, and Yerkes flied out to center, bringing up Speaker.

Speaker was the exception. He was not overmatched by either Johnson or anyone else. Knowing that Johnson would not pitch inside against him, he gave up all thought of pulling the ball and instead looked up the middle and to left. In a later era Johnson might have chosen to pitch around Speaker, who was batting nearly .400, or even intentionally walk him to face Larry Gardner, a good hitter but no Tris Speaker. But that strategy was considered a sign of cowardice and rarely used. Baseball's best pitcher went after baseball's best hitter without a moment's hesitation.

There was no mystery when a hitter faced Johnson, particularly a good hitter. It was simply Johnson's fastball against the batter's reflexes, the speed of the ball and the speed of the bat. This time Speaker won the battle, squaring up a fastball and driving it deep to left-center, splitting the outfielders and bounding up against the fence. Cady and Hooper both scored as Speaker, who loved playing in the hot weather, which reminded him of home, raced to third base with a triple. Now Boston led 3–0.

Wood, with a lead, and Johnson, trailing, both stiffened, and over the next three innings only two men reached base, one for each club, as hitter after hitter went back to the bench dragging his bat behind. Boston—and Wood—won, 3–0, as Johnson gave up four hits and Wood only three, Wood walked one man and Johnson two, and Wood struck out nine and Johnson ten. There was only a hair's breadth of difference between the two pitchers, but that difference—and the relative difference in the strength of the lineup each man faced—was just enough to tilt the game in Wood's direction. In the context of the 1912 season, both men would see the game as something special. For Wood the game affirmed that he could be what he wanted to be— the best—and it gave him confidence. Johnson, on the other hand, seemed to realize that he could not afford a letup of any kind. He had to be perfect. Over the next two months each man would be almost unbeatable.

JOE WOOD OUTPITCHES WALTER THE
GREAT AND SCORE IS 3–0

But the significance of the win went beyond that. By ensuring at least a split of the series, Boston's win had stopped Washington's surge. Washington had lost its best chance to close the gap on Boston, and the two clubs would not meet again until September. Their destinies would be controlled by others.

On the last day of the road trip the Senators salvaged the split with an 8–4 win in a game cut short so the Red Sox could make their train back to Boston. They dashed to the station, piled into the dining car for supper, and then collapsed in their berths, happy and exhausted, dreaming of sleeping again in their own beds. But apart from the fitful sleep they gained aboard the sleeping car, there would be little rest for Boston. Because of the rainouts earlier in the season, over the next two days they were scheduled to play back-to-back doubleheaders against New York.

Nevertheless the club that had left Boston four weeks before in second place and in disarray was returning home to Fenway Park full of confidence, knowing that they could win both at home and on the road and that they had a pitcher, Joe Wood, who now seemed the equal of the great Walter Johnson.

◆ 8 ◆

Home Safe

The Red Sox, under the able leadership of "Come Back" Stahl, are
cutting a wide swath in the American League pennant race this season.
In fact, they are creating quite a bit of a stir . . . and the critics around
the circuit are wondering who will pull them down from their lofty
perch at the top of the ladder. The Red Sox are a well balanced club
with good pitchers and catchers, the best all around outfield in either
league and an infield that is as good as the average. They have the
pennant bee buzzing in their bonnet, too, and that is half the battle.

—*Atlanta Journal Constitution*

Jake Stahl's Crimson handled speed boys have taken the whip
hand in the American Committee meet and are steamrolling
the competition at a fearful rate. By seating only their own
delegates the Red Sox are having everything their own way in
the new organization and are carrying the day in full sway.

—*Lima* (Ohio) *Daily News*

AFTER TRAVELING MOST of the night from Washington
and then passing out in their beds, the groggy Red Sox
squad made their way late on the morning of June 28 to Fenway Park, where they saw the sight they had hoped to see when they
left Boston four weeks earlier. Atop the Fenway Park grandstand, the
red-and-white pennant that represented the franchise flapped gently
in the warm breeze. Like that pennant, the Red Sox were flying above
all others. Later that day, for the first time since their first game in
Fenway Park, the Red Sox would take the field alone in first place.

Boston was starting to believe, and baseball fans all around the country were starting to notice. The Red Sox were a championship-caliber team worthy of facing the mighty Giants in the World's Series. And now, after a spring marred by rain and mud and inconsistency that had held attendance down to an average of only about seven thousand fans a game, the change in the weather and the first-place team were getting everyone's attention. It was summer, the Red Sox were suddenly in every conversation, and Fenway Park was as popular a destination as the sands of nearby Revere Beach. Pennant fever was sweeping the Hub.

As game time approached fans poured toward Fenway Park in a flood. Nearly filling the place, a crowd of fifteen thousand fans — the largest of the year apart from special events and holidays — had found reason to skip work and spend the afternoon in the warm sunshine of Fenway Park.

For once, the park looked the way a baseball park was supposed to look, the stands filled almost to overflowing and the grass lush and green. A month in the sun without ballplayers running back and forth over the turf had helped the field immeasurably, while the sight of a full grandstand gave the tired Sox a much-needed jolt of adrenaline. Over the next four weeks the club would play the Athletics six times and the White Sox nine. If the Red Sox could maintain their momentum, the pennant was theirs for the taking.

Fenway proved friendly for Boston. On June 28 and 29 the Red Sox swept New York in back-to-back doubleheaders. In the second twin bill, this time in front of twenty thousand, Boston battered New York, pitching for thirty-one hits and nineteen runs, winning the first game 13–6 and the second 6–0 in seven innings as Wood gave up only one hit in a game cut short by darkness and the utter inability of the Yankees to beat the Red Sox. A 4–1 win the next day gave the Sox their twenty-second win in the last twenty-five games, a pace that even the mighty Giants would have a hard time matching.

What made Boston's streak even more amazing was the fact that they were winning without much of a contribution at all from right fielder and leadoff hitter Harry Hooper. While his teammates were flying high, the horse-faced outfielder was moping and walking around like his dog had just died. In the two doubleheader sweeps

Hooper had managed only one hit, and his batting average was lingering below .250. If there was a weakness in the Boston lineup, and a place for a statistically astute critic to question Jake Stahl's acumen, it would have been the decision to bat Hooper leadoff and leave him there all season. Although no one was keeping track of stats like OBP (on base percentage) and OPS (on base percentage plus slugging percentage), Hooper's, like his batting average, were near the worst among Boston regulars. Putting Hooper in the leadoff slot was akin to having an Orlando Cabrera bat leadoff rather than someone like a Johnny Damon.

In 1911, at age twenty-three, he had hit .311 and led the team with thirty-eight stolen bases and ninety-three runs scored. Although those numbers did not put him quite in the same class as Tris Speaker, the Red Sox had every right to expect continued improvement. Unfortunately, the 1912 regular season, in many ways, was the worst of Hooper's career.

Thus far in 1912 his contributions had been primarily on defense. A decade later Giants manager John McGraw would include Hooper, along with Cobb and Speaker, in his all-time best American League outfield. A number of Hooper's contemporaries, among them Babe Ruth, would come to a similar conclusion, and of Boston's three outfielders, Bill Carrigan believed that Hooper, not Speaker, was the best fielder.

In Fenway Park, where there were as yet no bleachers or bullpens in right field, Hooper had to cover nearly as much ground as the center fielder, and he was every bit his teammates' defensive equal, save for Speaker's signature ability to go back on the baseball. Hooper, in the words of Tim Murnane, "covers the ground like a shadow, but with a speed that is phenomenal, though not showy." Of all the Boston outfielders, Hooper made the fewest errors, had the strongest arm, got rid of the ball the quickest, and was the most accurate and perhaps the smartest. He pioneered the use of sunglasses in 1911 to aid him in catching the ball, and he was a master at luring hitters into trying to take an extra base only to gun them down.

At the plate, however, Hooper struggled, particularly in 1912. A natural right-handed hitter when he entered St. Mary's College in California, Hooper had experimented with switch-hitting before finally choosing to bat left-handed full-time. It was the Dead Ball Era, and he figured that being a step or two closer to first base would serve him well. It did, but the move to Fenway Park in 1912 hurt Hooper's offense. Although he would later develop a reputation as something of a pull hitter, in 1912 he was still more accustomed to slapping the ball the other way. When he did that at the Huntington Avenue Grounds the flares he hit over the infield to left tended to fall in. That was not the case at Fenway Park.

Yet there was no call for Hooper to be dropped in the batting order, either from the fans or from his teammates. Hooper was a crowd favorite, and he enjoyed a reputation as a hitter who hit when it mattered. "If there was any one characteristic of Harry Hooper's," said Joe Wood once, "it was that he was a clutch player. When the chips were down that guy played like wildfire."

The other reason for Hooper's offensive struggles in 1911 probably stemmed from his personal life. He spent much of the 1912 season pining for his girlfriend, Esther Henchy, whom he had left behind in California. The two would marry in November 1912, and if the endearing letters he wrote to his young wife in 1913 are any indication, in 1912 Hooper felt like a lovesick puppy. He wasn't the only Red Sox player contemplating marriage either. When the Red Sox returned to Boston from the road trip Hugh Bedient, who had been lobbying Stahl for a few days off for, as a local newspaper reported, "some mysterious purpose," got tired of waiting around. He had his fiancée come to Boston, and after one of the New York games they married.

The newly married Bedient, perhaps still in the thrall of his abbreviated honeymoon, failed to perform as well as he had as a bachelor. Boston was caught looking ahead to their series with the A's as New York took the final game of the series, 9–7, Boston's first loss all year to either the Yankees or the Browns. But in a rarity, the Red Sox, who hit only twenty-nine home runs for the season, cracked three in a losing cause. Larry Gardner hit two, the first striking the fence in center field on the fly as he nearly became the first player to clear the center-field fence, and his second rolled into no-man's-land in deep right. Boston's other home run, by Duffy Lewis, was the third in the short history of Fenway to clear the left-field wall, reportedly "a longer hit than the first of the year made over the same boundary by Hugh Bradley." The crowd was not quite oblivious when the ball went over the wall, but the feat was no longer worthy of a headline, or even more than a few lines, in the game stories in the newspapers the next day.

When the Red Sox boarded the train to Philadelphia after the game no one was more anxious to reach Philadelphia than pitcher Buck O'Brien. Earlier in the year he had made the acquaintance of Marguerite Mack, Philadelphia manager Connie Mack's nineteen-year-old daughter. She spent most of her summers in Massachusetts with her cousins and was a frequent visitor to Fenway Park. Although her father had forbidden all his daughters to date ballplayers, O'Brien—older, silver-tongued, and quick-witted—had swept her off her feet, quite an accomplishment for the former factory worker. Connie Mack had yet to get wind of the romance, but when he did there was no question that the suitor was in for a rough time. Although Mack was outwardly gracious and mild-mannered, he wielded an enormous amount of power in the game. Getting on his bad side was something no player wanted to do.

The A's, however, were looking forward to playing the Red Sox. For the first time all year they were playing like a championship club, going 11-4 over the last two weeks and winning eight of ten from the Senators to push their way into second place, six games behind Boston. With a six-game series against Boston in Shibe Park, the A's had a chance to leapfrog into first place. After all, no one yet knew how the youthful Sox would respond to the pressures of leading the league. Even if the Athletics did not sweep the Red Sox, they hoped to give Boston something to think about.

They made that clear before the first game. With twelve thousand fans on hand, the A's chose the date to raise their 1911 championship banner. They paraded onto the field behind a brass band and a one-hundred-member chorus, then celebrated the flag-raising with the launch of hundreds of helium-filled balloons. Every man on the field had to stop and watch except for the pitchers, who were beginning to warm up to start the game.

It had been a foregone conclusion that Joe Wood would pitch the first game of the important series for Boston—and Stahl did send him out to warm up. But he also sent out Ray Collins. When Stahl saw that Mack had selected his pitching ace, Jack Coombs, to start the game, Stahl pulled a switch and substituted Ray Collins for Wood.

It was a risk, for if Collins faltered and then Wood did the same the next day, Stahl would be left wide open to criticism. But it was a risk that Boston, leading by six games, could afford to take. It worked to perfection as Collins solidified his spot in the rotation and the Red Sox knocked Coombs around before emerging with a 7–2 win.

IT'S ALL RED SOX IN FIRST BIG MIX — ATHLETICS CLEARLY OUTPOINTED AT EVERY STAGE, IN EVERY WAY

In a split-admission doubleheader the next day fifty-five thousand fans shoved their way into Shibe Park, hoping to see the A's push back against Boston, only to be disappointed. In the first game Joe Wood took a no-hitter into the fifth, but then got knocked around and lost, 4–3. In game 2, however, Charley Hall, in relief of the bridegroom Hugh Bedient, stopped the early bleeding, and the Sox salvaged a split, winning the second game 6–5.

The A's were spinning their wheels, and they knew it. O'Brien lost the fourth game of the series, 3–2, in front of his potential father-in-law, but Collins won game 5. Then, in the finale, even the forgotten man, Eddie Cicotte, got into the act, coming away with a sloppy victory. Boston took the series four games to two as the Athletics' pennant dreams evaporated before reality. In a story in the *Philadelphia Inquirer* the anonymous author noted after the final contest that "there was no particular play or psychological period of the finale that can be pointed out as the pivotal point of the contest on which to place some 'might have been,' it was just a general breaking up of the whole bulk that started amidships on the hurling deck and spread from stem to stern." The A's trailed Boston by eight games and would never get closer.

As the Sox returned to Boston for a twenty-game home stand their lead in the American League was beginning to look safe. The Senators had snuck back into second place, but the only other team above .500 was the White Sox. The remainder of the schedule was tilted heavily in Boston's favor. The Red Sox had only six more games remaining with the A's and seven with the Senators, while they still had fourteen games remaining with the last-place Browns.

No one was more aware of that than Joe Wood. Much of his reputation to date had been earned while dominating the Browns—his 1911 no-hitter had come against St. Louis—and there was no team in baseball he liked pitching against more. He was on the mound for the first game of the series against St. Louis on July 8 and did not disappoint.

He was getting to know Cady, and Cady was getting to know Wood. Together the two decided to change things up against the Browns. Instead of wasting his good fastball against a ball club that would have had a hard time hitting even if the ball was placed on a tee, Wood and Cady chose to save Joe's arm by having him "feed the Western men on stew made of slow drops and steamy curves," as the *Globe* put it. The Browns missed not only most of the pitches thrown by Wood but also a fair number of those hit by the Red Sox: the Browns made seven errors, and Boston won, 5–1, without even trying. Wood was now 17-4. Since Cady had taken over behind the plate, he had lost once and given up as many as four runs only twice. And he was just getting started. Although little about his victory over St. Louis was notable, apart from his dependence on the breaking ball, in retrospect the game would grow in significance.

On that same day in Chicago the undefeated Rube Marquard took the mound for the New York Giants, his 19-0 record the best start in baseball history. But on this day his luck—and his control—ran out: he gave up eight hits and seven walks against the Cubs. He was pulled in the sixth inning, trailing 6–2, and took the loss. It hardly mattered to the Giants—at 56-14, they had a fourteen-game lead in the National League pennant race—but it did break a rather remarkable spell. Their performance so far in 1912 had been absolutely otherworldly. With a winning percentage of .800, they were on pace to finish the season an ungodly 123-29.

But all was not as brilliant as it looked. Only a few weeks after the end of the 1911 World's Series the Giants had traveled to Cuba and spent a month playing exhibitions, making an already long season even longer. They were exhausted, and for the remainder of the 1912 season they would appear more out of breath than invincible, as if the rarefied air of their historic pace had finally starved them of oxygen.

Although few would notice or give it much credence, for the rest of the season the mighty Giants played like mere mortals. Oh, they would still win the pennant without really breaking a sweat, but they would go "only" 47-34 for the remainder of the season—.580 baseball. And Marquard, who for three months had seemed possessed of supernatural powers, would lose his magic almost entirely and over the remainder of the season lose more games than he would win.

Marquard's magic, in fact, suddenly seemed to reside elsewhere, for as his pitching streak came to an end, two others, nearly as remarkable, began. Five days earlier, on July 3, as Marquard won his nineteenth and final game of the streak, Walter Johnson picked up a victory, and now, on the day Marquard's string of victories came to an end, Wood won. For the next two months both Walter Johnson and Joe Wood pursued Marquard's record with streaks of pitching excellence that, in the end, would leave the Giant pitcher's performance almost forgotten in the annals of baseball history. The only race in the American League that anyone would really care about would be the one between Joe Wood and Walter Johnson. The two pitchers were on a collision course, one that Fenway Park would soon frame as its first great contest.

The Red Sox were feeling so confident after Wood's win over the Browns that they made a deal with the club that until only a few weeks earlier had been playing rabbit to Boston's tortoise—the White Sox. For months Boston had been trying to get Eddie Cicotte through waivers and trade him out of the league, where it would be impossible for him to come back and haunt them. Yet each time they placed him on the procedural list the White Sox claimed him. Unwilling to give another contender a starting pitcher, Boston would pull Cicotte back off waivers and try again a few days later, only to have Chicago claim him once more.

Now Boston no longer considered the White Sox a threat. At the beginning of the 1912 season Cicotte had seemed to be a stalwart of the rotation, but he had never gotten untracked, and first Hall, then Bedient, then O'Brien, and now Ray Collins had pushed past him. He became a spare part the Red Sox did not need, and now they offered him to Chicago in a straight sale.

It was a smart move. The White Sox, eight and a half games behind

Boston, were only nominally in the pennant race, and even though Boston was still due to play them another eleven times, including immediately after the St. Louis series, the Red Sox were still more worried about the A's and the Senators. A quick look at the schedule told them that the White Sox had thirteen games left to play with Washington and fourteen with Philadelphia. If Cicotte could turn his season around and collect a few victories against either of those clubs down the stretch, it would only help Boston's cause. In fact, over the remainder of the year, even though the White Sox would stumble to the finish, Cicotte would thrive on regular work and be their second-best pitcher after Walsh, beating the A's and Senators three times. The trade would rejuvenate his career, and Cicotte would go on to become one of the most effective pitchers in the American League for the remainder of the decade before getting caught up in the Black Sox scandal and being banned from baseball for life.

Even though Cicotte did not instigate the throwing of the 1919 World's Series, he was certainly acquainted with one of the principals, Boston gambler Joseph J. "Sport" Sullivan, from his time in Boston. Sullivan was a regular in the hotel lobbies and taverns frequented by the team and was familiar to all the Boston players. Loosely aligned with the Royal Rooters, it was not at all uncommon for Sullivan to follow the Red Sox on the road and even stay in the same hotel, albeit in more sumptuous surroundings than the players, who bunked two to a room. Sullivan stayed in a suite. And Sullivan, like most other Boston gamblers, was already whetting his appetite in anticipation of the World's Series.

After doing away with the Browns by taking two of three, the Red Sox welcomed Detroit's Tigers, the next ball club to encounter the buzz saw that Fenway Park was becoming. Over the remainder of the regular season the Red Sox would lose there only nine times. Every-one—pitchers, fielders, hitters—had adjusted, and so too, finally, had the fans.

Championship clubs create their own generation of supporters. Over the course of a season championship teams draw new follow-ers who slowly fall in love, an April-to-October romance that builds slowly and finally blazes into passion just as the fall leaves explode into color.

Since coming into existence the Red Sox fan base had barely changed. At the beginning it consisted primarily of the Royal Rooters, who had transferred their allegiance from Boston's National League club, and the residents of Roxbury, the neighborhood that surrounded the park. But now, in 1912, a new constituency was finally beginning to discover the Red Sox—and Fenway Park. While the new park was somewhat less convenient for many of their older fans, new fans and residents of other Boston neighborhoods, like the Back Bay, found Fenway Park somewhat more convenient—and more comfortable than the old Huntington Avenue Grounds. Over the course of the season, as the Red Sox slowly built momentum with each victory, these new fans, who might have attended their first game on a lark or out of curiosity over Fenway Park, were now returning. Watching the Red Sox win was fun, and for these fans the old Huntington Avenue Grounds held no nostalgia. The feeling of separation that left some longtime fans pining for the old ballpark was not an issue for them.

Boston's population was exploding. With more than 100,000 residents added since the Red Sox played their first season in 1901, the population had swelled to nearly 700,000 citizens, and Boston now battled St. Louis for bragging rights as the fifth-biggest city in the country. And after a series of recessions in the early 1900s that made money tight, the economy by 1912 was in the midst of a long, sustained boom. Bostonians had money. The fans turning out at Fenway Park were suddenly younger, more enthusiastic—and more female. The newspapers published pictures of the players every day, and a young player like Joe Wood was much more than a name in the paper—he was now a picture on the wall and a page in a scrapbook. Fenway Park was not just a place where the Red Sox played baseball but, like a dance hall, a place to meet friends, spend time together, socialize, and share an experience. It was even possible to eat at Fenway Park, for the new park featured more concessions than had been offered at Huntington Avenue, where most fans brought their own snacks because only simple sandwiches and peanuts were available. At Fenway Park one could buy not only these items but also soda, popcorn, candy, cigars, and other items from vendors, usually young boys, sometimes unauthorized, who moved through the crowd hawking their wares. As yet, there were no concession stands per se, a feature that would first appear in major league baseball at Wrigley Field in 1914. Neither was there, apparently, liquor or beer, apart from what a patron could carry into the park by way of a flask, bottle, or bucket. Still, for a whole new generation Fenway Park was becoming the place to be and, just as significantly, also a place to be seen.

SOX GET TWO TIGER PELTS — COLLINS AND WOOD PITCH GILT-EDGED BALL FOR BOSTON

Bankers, brokers, office clerks, tradesmen, and housemaids all over Boston called in sick or begged off work on Friday, July 12, for the doubleheader against Detroit. Ty Cobb, a player the crowd loved to hate, was one reason for the turnout of fifteen thousand—a remarkable number for a workday—but the main attraction was Joe Wood. He was scheduled to pitch game 2. Even the casual Boston baseball fan was beginning to realize that when Wood pitched Boston was almost guaranteed to win. Ray Collins set the stage in the first game in a tidy one hour and forty-five minutes, holding Detroit to only four hits as the Sox won 4–1, the telling blow coming on a Duffy Lewis double off his left-field namesake.

The second game was the kind that would keep fans talking for weeks, the rare contest in which every pitch and swing was capable of changing the game. Wood and his Detroit counterpart, the capable Ed Willet, walked a high wire with no margin for error as fans oohed and aahed in astonishment each time one of the pitchers left the opposition stranded short of home plate. In the first inning, after Cobb singled and went to second on an errant throw, Wood, now more comfortable pitching from the stretch, picked Cobb off. In the second inning, with two on and no out, Wood reared back and struck out the side, and he again stranded runners in scoring position in the fifth and the sixth. In the ninth Jim Delahanty doubled, but Cady, in a great play, threw behind him on a pickoff play to put him out.

Boston went out in similar fashion, and as long shadows began to stretch over the field it began to look as if the game might end in a draw. Then Fenway Park—and Tris Speaker, looking to prove himself before Cobb once again—got into the act.

With two out in the eleventh inning, fans who had played hooky were getting antsy and thinking about heading home before anyone figured out they had gone to the ballpark when Tris Speaker stepped to the plate. Thus far he and Cobb had played each other even, Cobb collecting two hits, including a double, and being picked off, while Speaker had a double of his own. Yet Speaker hadn't fielded a ball in the air in center field all day as Wood, his fastball at its blazing best, struck out ten.

Boston had a friend in left field in the name of Duffy's Cliff, however, and that would make the difference. Speaker drove a ball deep to left-center field, where it skipped up the bank and then careened toward center. Speaker read the carom perfectly and chugged his way to third while Ty Cobb gathered the ball in too late to catch him. Duffy Lewis followed with a sharp single past second, and the ball game was Boston's. Wood was 18-4, and the Red Sox were two games closer to the World's Series.

The Sox took two of the next three from the Tigers as O'Brien followed Wood's shutout with one of his own, and Hooper finally showed some signs of life at the plate with three hits—while remaining a genius in the field, something Cobb could attest to.

With the Tiger outfielder on first, Sam Crawford hit a fly to Hooper. Cobb held at first, but as the ball started down toward Hooper's mitt, he appeared to lose the ball. Seeing that, Cobb jogged toward second, smugly certain that second base was his.

Only Hooper had not lost the ball. He fielded it on the short hop as it touched the ground, then gunned to second, high, where Wagner, acting nonchalant, suddenly jumped up and stabbed the ball out of the air with one hand and slapped a tag on the startled, sliding Cobb before he knew what was happening. Together, Hooper and Wagner had taken what might have been a small mistake and turned it to their advantage—still getting an out but exchanging Cobb, a maniac on the bases, for the more sedate Sam Crawford.

The play was a perfect demonstration of Boston's best-kept secret: their defense and mental alertness. Although everyone knew about the outfield play of Lewis, Speaker, and Hooper, the club's other defenders, while less spectacular, almost went unnoticed outside of Boston and caught the opposition sleeping all year long. Only Yerkes, at second, was a below-average fielder. Stahl was at least adequate at first base, while Larry Gardner and Charlie Wagner sealed off the left side of the diamond as well as any combo in the league.

Their performance was, of course, relative, for in an era in which gloves were little more than leather pads and field conditions were often poor, errors were far more prevalent than they are today. Wagner and Gardner combined for ninety-six errors in 1912 — sixty-one by Wagner. By today's standards those totals would probably lead to the outright release of both players, but in 1912 they were better than average, and each infielder also had more than adequate range and was known for a powerful throwing arm. As a team, the Red Sox did not often beat themselves in the field, or at least not as often as other clubs.

Part of the reason was the improved infield surface at Fenway Park compared to Huntington Avenue, particularly after the work that had been done on the field during the long road trip. While fielding is notoriously hard to judge through the few statistics available from this era, Boston's errors in 1912 dropped by 18 percent from the year before, and the team would end the season with the second-highest fielding percentage and the second-lowest number of errors of any team in the league. As a result, as later statistical analyses would reveal, they gave up nearly one hundred fewer unearned runs than the league average, a strong indication of the quality of Boston's defensive play.

To writers like Murnane, Shannon, Walter Barnes, and other veteran members of the Boston press corps, however, the defensive contribution of Boston's infielders did not go unnoticed. Murnane, for instance, called the play on Cobb a "remarkable play by a wonderful performer." The Boston writers lavished praise on Wagner in particular, for both his infield play and his baseball acumen. Over the course of the season Wagner's fielding seemed to be mentioned in nearly every game story that appeared.

Wagner, who was born and raised in New York City, first made it to the big leagues as a member of John McGraw's Giants in 1902, but after he failed to hit in a brief tryout, he was released. He spent the next five years playing for Newark in the Eastern League — earning a reputation as a good fielder and a smart, scrappy player who struggled at the plate—before being drafted by the Red Sox in 1906. Dubbed "Heinie" because of his German heritage, his glove got him back to the major leagues. Then, rather remarkably and without explanation, he found major league pitching easier to hit than that of the Eastern League, and in 1908 Wagner, at age twenty-seven, finally became Boston's regular shortstop. A Catholic, Wagner fell in with the other KCs, becoming particularly close to Bill Carrigan, who would be his roommate. Together the two men became the leaders of that faction of the club.

While not a spectacular fielder, Wagner was the kind of shortstop pitchers like pitching in front of—dependable and steady, he made routine plays routine. In an era when few players could catch the ball and hold on with one hand, Wagner was particularly adept at doing so, and as he had demonstrated against Cobb, he managed to hold on to the ball when applying tags. He always seemed to be in the right place, anticipating plays before the base runners and, like Derek Jeter in a later era, sometimes catching the opposition off guard. Inside baseball was his forte. At the plate Wagner was particularly adept at the bunt, the hit-and-run, working pitchers for walks, and coming through in the clutch.

Wagner once admitted that "I would like to be as good a pitcher as Walter Johnson," but at 5'9", that was never more than a dream. Yet apart from the club's pitchers, he and Harry Hooper had the best arms on the team. On an almost daily basis he made plays that few other shortstops in the league could match. His sore arm in 1911 had played a part in Boston's poor performance, and his recovery in 1912 was like adding an experienced player to the team.

Although his arm made him stand out, it was Wagner's brain that made him even more valuable. The play he worked with Hooper was no accident. Nearly every day Wagner and Bill Carrigan met—sometimes with Stahl—and talked strategy. Once the team was on the field it was Wagner—and Carrigan when he was catching—who ran the defense, positioning the outfielders, deciding whether to play the infield in or out, and making other defensive calls. Yet Wagner's defensive leadership went beyond that. As the play on Cobb demonstrated, Wagner knew to be waiting at second for a throw because he had probably discussed with Hooper ways to use Cobb's legendary aggressiveness and baseball savvy against him. Another player might have gone halfway to second and waited to see if the ball dropped before committing to run, but Cobb, ultra-confident, had read the play and taken off, so certain that Hooper had lost the ball and could not make a throw that he did not bother to run hard. Only Wagner had not been surprised. He had been expecting the play, and even though the end result was subtle—the exchange of base runners—it was the kind of small play that sometimes changed the course of a ball game.

If some fans and writers around the league did not give Wagner his due, Boston's opponents did. A's second baseman Eddie Collins, who was still earning extra money by writing a syndicated column, wrote at about this time that Wagner "has been overlooked by those who only scratch the surface of baseball. He has held the infield together . . . and next to Tris Speaker, I would say that he is the most dangerous hitter on the club." His only problem, noted Collins, was that he shared a surname with his contemporary, Pittsburgh's Honus Wagner, still considered one of the best shortstops in the history of the game. "If his name were Krause or Keller or some other of the common names of German extraction, he would be very much better off as far as publicity goes," wrote Collins.

The White Sox followed Detroit into Boston for five games trailing the Red Sox by eleven and a half games, knowing this would be their last chance to get back into the pennant race. Four days later they left Boston thoroughly demoralized, knowing that for the remainder of the 1912 season they would do nothing more than play out the string. Ed Walsh—again—had won the first game of the series, beating Buck O'Brien 1–0, but after that it was all Boston as Wood took the second game of the doubleheader 7–3 before a crowd of twenty-one thousand. The White Sox chose to start Eddie Cicotte in the third game of the set on July 18, and the Red Sox battered their old teammate for ten runs in the first inning—only to have the skies open up and have the game called. In the series-ending doubleheader the next day Boston swept the Sox behind Collins and Bedient, then buried Chicago and got revenge on Walsh by beating him in the finale, 3–2, before a packed house of twenty-two thousand. The game was marked by Jake Stahl's home run over the left-field wall and Bill Carrigan's game-winning hit to center in the bottom of the ninth, as well as by what Tim Murnane described as "hair raising situations that were thicker than broken bottles along Revere Beach after a holiday." Cady was still getting his share of work behind the plate, and since he had bulled his way into the lineup, Carrigan had awoken and over the last month had made the most of his opportunities. Although Cady was often still the better choice behind the plate, Boston now had two catchers playing as well as any in the league.

OUR SOX GOING GOOD FOR THAT PENNANT GOAL

The Sox split the final four-game series of the home stand with Cleveland, as Wood upped his record to 20-4, and now had seven games on Washington and ten on Philadelphia. With Boston at 63-29, however, the pennant "race" was effectively over, Boston winning in a walk as neither challenger showed signs of gaining any traction. A few days earlier, in the *Post*, Paul Shannon, who was usually a bit stingy with praise, admitted that "the Red Sox are going at a whirlwind gait, dropping a game now and then [only] as a sort of 'rester' for the next series." In the *Globe*, Murnane furnished a kind of midseason report card, noting that Boston's lead was not "the result of a sudden spurt through a loose field, but a consistent gain," adding that "the Red Sox are now even money or better against the field." He lavished praise on most Boston players but gave most credit for the club's performance, not to Wood (although he admitted that Walter Johnson had "nothing in particular on him"), or to Speaker ("who has been hitting like a fiend all season"), but to Jake Stahl—for his play, his "knowledge of the inside of inside baseball," and his ability to fertilize the "soil of fellowship" among the players.

But if the team had one cause for worry it was Murnane's tribute to the "Board of Strategy," Wagner and Carrigan, which included the kind of praise usually reserved for the manager. There was, wrote Murnane, no one "more capable of working out a scheme for playing a whole game than this same board of strategy." But of the man who signed the checks and put together the roster, owner James McAleer, Murnane uttered not a single word. To be fair, it was not yet October, and the championship had yet to be won, but for the remainder of the season the question of who should receive credit for Boston's performance—or the blame—would fester until it finally burst into the open. Despite Murnane's propaganda about the winning ball club's "espirit d'corp," there were fault lines in the makeup of the roster that even winning could not quite mask.

Oddly, the impact of Fenway Park on Boston's pennant run garnered not a mention in the press from Murnane, Shannon, or anyone else at the time. Apart from the benefits of playing in front of a supportive crowd, the notion that a ballpark would or even could affect performance was an alien notion. Not until the Phillies' Gavvy Cravath took advantage of the addition of a section of bleachers in left field at Shibe Park to hit a record twenty-four home runs in 1915 did it become obvious that a ballpark could have a dramatic influence on the outcome of a game. But it would take a few more years—until Babe Ruth started hitting the ball out of the Polo Grounds with astounding regularity in his inaugural season with the Yankees in 1920—before the notion really took hold. The Yankees took note, and when Yankee Stadium opened in 1923, it was not so much "The House That Ruth Built" as "The House Built for Ruth." The Yankees were the first team to build a ballpark specifically tailored for its players, and it gave the club a tremendous advantage. In contrast, little mention would be made of Fenway's impact on the game until 1931, when Earl Webb tattooed the left-field wall on his way to a major league record sixty-seven doubles. Only then would it be widely recognized that Fenway Park had its own unique influence on the game. It was no accident that soon afterward the Red Sox began to seek out right-handed power hitters to take advantage of the wall.

After the Cleveland series the Sox and Naps, who became known as the Indians in 1915, both boarded the same train and headed west, the Red Sox heading to Chicago and Cleveland returning home. In Albany a car carrying the White Sox joined the train as well, and all three clubs traveled together through the night. Members of all three teams reportedly spent the evening "playing the national indoor game," which presumably referred to playing cards and drinking.

If anyone was expecting the Red Sox to collapse on the road trip, they were sorely disappointed. Boston won series in both Chicago and Detroit at the start and the end of the trip and split series in St. Louis and Cleveland in the middle before returning to Boston on

August 12 with a comfortable lead. Happy Sox fans all but ignored the impending U.S. invasion of Nicaragua. They were obsessed with baseball, not politics. Had a conquering army landed on the beaches of South Boston, few would have paid attention, at least not until after the game.

There was, however, some cause for concern. On July 28 against Chicago, Joe Wood cruised through the first four innings. But in the fifth, with one out, he hit a batter, then gave up a hit, then fielded a bunt and threw wild to first base. After a fly-out he then walked a man and gave up another hit, giving Chicago four runs and causing Jake Stahl to pull him from the game in favor of Bedient. It was Wood's worst performance since Cady had become his personal catcher.

The breakdown was inexplicable—at first. But a few days later there were whispers in the papers that Joe Wood, who had already started twenty-four games and made three relief appearances for the season, had a sore arm. Nevertheless, although it may have been wiser to give him some rest, on August 2 in St. Louis, Wood started against the Browns and seemed to alleviate concerns by tossing a three-hit shutout. Wood, wrote Murnane, "was in fine fettle . . . [with] remarkable speed, perfect control of his drop and curve, and was handled in superb style by Forrest Cady, a great catcher." But a few days later Wood was complaining again, this time about a sore wrist, an injury that might have occurred in an attempt to take the strain off his elbow or shoulder.

Although Wood would later sometimes claim that he never had serious arm troubles before 1913—when he apparently injured his arm after returning to the mound too quickly after breaking his thumb—the facts tell a different story. According to the papers, he was plagued by arm trouble over most of the second half of the 1912 season. Although Wood, who once said, "I threw so hard I thought my arm would fly right off my body," was still able to pitch, his chronic soreness may well have been a sign that his arm was already going bad. Somewhere inside his right arm the magic musculature that allowed him to throw the ball nearly one hundred miles per hour was starting to fray.

Today a pitcher with Wood's ability would be placed on the disabled list and treated like a fragile piece of crystal. But in 1912 it was frowned upon to "coddle" pitchers, even those with a sore arm. Once a pitcher lost the ability to take the ball every third or fourth day, he was considered damaged goods, a so-called Sunday pitcher who lacked the mental and emotional strength to appear more regularly. And besides, if a pitcher was hurt and could not pitch, he did not get paid. As a result, many sore-armed pitchers threw until, literally, they could not lift their arms and the damage was so severe that there was no chance of recovery. The road to the Hall of Fame has been littered with hundreds of pitchers who enjoyed brief, blazing success before becoming injured and then being discarded like an old appliance.

After his injury in 1913 Wood became just such a Sunday pitcher, a hurler who could pitch one or perhaps two or three games in a regular rotation but then would have to rest. Even though he remained effective, he would never again be the same. As he told Lawrence Ritter, following the injury, "I never again pitched without a terrific amount of pain in my right shoulder . . . After each game I pitched I'd have to lay off for a couple of weeks before I could even lift my arm up." The description of the malady correlates almost certainly with a tear of the rotator cuff, an injury that, while sometimes treatable today through surgery, is still perhaps the most debilitating injury a pitcher can have. Decades after he retired from baseball Wood's shoulder still gave him pain and restricted his movements.

With Wood ailing, it was even more strange that in the midst of the road trip Stahl removed Charley Hall from the pitching rotation. While Hall was not pitching quite as well as he had earlier in the year and had been battling a pulled muscle in his side, he was still effective and still taking a regular turn as a starting pitcher. Since the beginning of the season, the Red Sox, like most teams of the era, had loosely used a five-man pitching rotation, albeit one that occasionally skipped over a starter or shuffled the order, according to the whims of Stahl and whether or not a starting pitcher had been pressed to serve in relief. The Red Sox, as was more or less customary at the time, did not have a true relief pitcher on the staff. On rare occasions Larry Pape would be called on to mop up in a lost cause, but Stahl usually called on one of his stalwarts to step in and stanch the bleeding as needed.

Wood, Hall, and O'Brien had been in the rotation from the start, then Bedient and Collins had stepped in when Cicotte went to the woodshed. Yet suddenly Stahl chose to depend on four starting pitchers almost exclusively while relegating Hall to the bullpen. To a degree, the move made sense. Hall had been remarkably effective in limited relief duty. Eddie Collins once wrote that while Hall never had much success against the A's as a starter, "let him relieve … and invariably he would have the upper hand." But sending Hall to the bullpen without replacing him in the rotation risked creating more problems than it solved. Since getting married, Bedient had not pitched particularly well, now Wood's health was in question, and every starting pitcher's workload was due to increase.

The logic behind Stahl's thinking may have resided in New York, where the Giants, after tearing the league apart for the first half of the season behind Marquard, were suddenly slumping. Stahl's club, now that the pennant was wrapped up, was in the same position the Giants had been in a month earlier—far ahead and being pushed by no other team. He may have turned to a four-man rotation in an effort to avoid the kind of sag that had since plagued the Giants, the baseball equivalent of a jockey going to the whip hand long before the stretch. But it also guaranteed that his best pitchers would get additional work over the remainder of the season—Wood, after starting only five games in July, would start seven games in August and make two additional appearances in relief. In theory that would make a slump less likely, but it also threatened to gas the staff. Wood was already hurting, and although Hall was now in the bullpen, he would not be used to give pitchers a rest after five or six innings but would pitch only when a starter fared poorly, leading the *Boston Post* to call him a "rescue pitcher." Any way one looked at it, the change was a high-risk move. If any of the remaining four starters faltered or were injured because of the increased workload—particularly Wood—Boston's chances in the postseason would almost certainly suffer.

That seemed even more likely after Joe Wood pitched eleven long innings in his next start against Cleveland on August 6. He won, 5–4, but wasn't right, giving up thirteen hits, matching his season high, and striking out only five. Nevertheless the victory, number twenty-three, was his eighth win in a row. No one was making much of that yet, because Walter Johnson of the Senators was the winner of eleven straight, sparking speculation that in this season of streaks Johnson just might be able to break Jack Chesbro's American League record of fourteen consecutive wins. If he got lucky, he might even better the major league mark that Rube Marquard had set one month before. Although the Senators had little chance of heading off Boston in the pennant race—they were about to lose five of six, with the lone victory by Johnson—Walter Johnson and Joe Wood were on a collision course.

It was destiny. The two hottest pitchers in baseball would soon meet in Boston in what is still one of the most memorable regular-season games in Red Sox history.

They would change the ballpark forever. Fenway Park would never be the same.

Heavyweights

From all parts of New England came the fans to witness this
encounter, for the fame of the scheduled pitching duel had aroused
the attention of the country, and every train reaching Boston
before noon carried its quotient of fans bound for Fenway Park.

—Paul Shannon, *Boston Post*

A S THE DOG days of August settled in over Boston, enveloping the city in sweat, Sox fans seeking a respite from the heat and humidity still gathered before and after the games in the dark, wood-paneled confines of Nuf Ced McGreevey's Columbus Avenue tavern, Third Base. Despite the fact that the ball club had moved operations to Fenway Park, the stuffed mannequin known as "the Baseball Man" still adorned the front door, the lightbulbs shaped like baseballs still hung from the ceiling, and photographs of ballplayers still covered the walls. McGreevey's remained the passionate center of the baseball world for the Royal Rooters and other Boston baseball fans. As the cranks gathered to talk and quaff mugs of beer and shots of rye, with the pennant races in both leagues all but over and the World's Series still too far into the future to be the subject of much meaningful debate, there was really only one question that dominated the conversation. Who, one man would ask of another, is the better pitcher: Boston's young ace, twenty-three-year-old Joe Wood, or Washington's veteran star, Walter Johnson?

That was all it took to spark an argument. Thus far in the 1912 season there had been barely a dime's worth of difference between the two, and Johnson, even in Boston, had his defenders among the Royal

Rooters. Some old-timers in the group still argued that the real "King of Pitchers" was Amos Rusie, the Giants' star pitcher in the 1890s, or the Boston Nationals' Kid Nichols from the same era. Others scoffed and offered up the recently retired Cy Young, or the Giants' Christy Mathewson. But now most admitted that the crown was up for grabs between only Wood and Johnson.

As photographs of Wood and Johnson and other baseball luminaries silently gazed down upon the combatants from the tavern's walls, the diminutive McGreevey, rushing back and forth between the cash register and the bar, would listen closely. He would let such conversations continue, occasionally chiming in with his own ten cents' worth of wisdom and even egging each man on until the voices of the sparring parties, fueled by alcohol, began to grow loud, the conversations turned circular, and each party began to repeat the same arguments they had made only a few minutes before, only louder and with personal insults attached that would begin to be uttered with a sly smile but then begin to stick and sting. And then, when McGreevey saw the faces turn red and begin to flush with anger, he knew it was time to rein the participants back in toward civility. Slamming an empty beer mug or his palm on top of the bar, he would yell out loud enough for everyone to hear, "Nuf ced!" All recognized that as a sign that the argument was over and it was time for the debaters to lower their voices and back off.

However the Wood-versus-Johnson argument began, it tended to follow the same well-worn paths—a comparison of Wood's youth, toughness, athleticism, and relative exuberance with Johnson's experience, control, brains, and poise. But no matter how the conversation started, before long it generally boiled down to a single question— *Who threw harder?*

And now with each passing day it seemed ever more likely that the question might soon be answered. Like two fastballs thrown from opposite ends of the diamond that were destined to meet and explode over the pitcher's mound, Wood and Johnson, two unstoppable forces, rocketed toward one another. Each man was in the midst of an undefeated pitching streak that would soon threaten the record books.

They had already met once before in 1912, Wood defeating his counterpart, but that only provided more fuel for the argument. Johnson in fact had already faced Boston four times in 1912 and lost each time, falling once to Cicotte in April, losing twice to O'Brien—once by shutout—and being beaten by Wood, 3–0, on June 26. But instead of ending the debate, those earlier games only gave the arbiters more oxygen. In Johnson's first three games against Boston, one could argue, Wood had been available to throw, but Jake Stahl, fearful of Johnson, had chosen to avoid pitching him opposite the Washington star, just as he had done when Wood had the opportunity to pitch opposite Ed Walsh. And even though their meeting on June 26 had gone Wood's way, Johnson had been victimized by some poor defensive play and struck out ten while giving up only four hits, while Wood had struck out nine and given up three hits. The game had really decided nothing beyond cementing Wood's status as Johnson's foremost challenger. The sporting men in the crowd—and they were all sporting men when the odds were right—relished the opportunity for a rematch.

Johnson was the established veteran, the star, and as F. C. Lane's article in *Baseball* magazine had concluded, "the King of the Pitchers," a title that, over the last two and a half seasons, Johnson had wrested from Mathewson. In that time period he had won seventy-five games, and in an era in which hitters still considered striking out something to be ashamed of, Johnson had sent more than six hundred humiliated victims back to the bench.

While Johnson's six years in the league gave him the aura of a veteran, he was, at age twenty-four, only a year older than Wood. Already the winner of more than one hundred games, it seemed as if he had been in the league much longer. A rangy 6'1", with long arms and fingers, the soft-spoken Kansan had been a star from the start, even as he initially struggled to win with Washington's anemic offensive support. Everyone recognized that if he had played for a better team—the Senators were routinely one of the worst teams in baseball—his record would have been even more impressive. In fact, with better support, Johnson, not Cy Young, might very well hold the all-time record for most major league victories and baseball's annual award given to the best pitcher might bear his name, not Young's. As it was, despite rarely receiving any help from his offensively challenged teammates—he would lose 26 games by the score of 1–0 over the course of his career—Johnson would eventually retire with 417 wins over twenty-one seasons. By any estimation, even given his recent struggles against Boston and the fact that Boston had all but wrapped up the pennant race, Johnson was "the Champion."

Wood, on the other hand, was seen as the scrappy, youthful "Challenger." Despite pitching for the Red Sox, a team much better than the Senators, his record entering the 1912 season was barely above .500. Only recently had Wood's performance brought him into the same conversation with Johnson.

And that was because of Wood's fastball. His overhand pitch, while different from Johnson's sidearm whip, was just as devastating to batters, hopping at the end while Johnson's tended to dart and run. Each pitch made an audible sound, a hiss as the seams of the baseball cut through the air when the ball passed by the plate. Wood's motion was violent and quick, while Johnson's was easy and deceptive. In 1912 hitters found it equally difficult to square up the pitch from either man. In just over 1,400 innings Wood would give up only twelve home runs in his career, while Johnson, who would end the 1912 season with more than 1,700 career innings, would give up only thirteen to that point in his career. Hitters who did make contact against Wood often were jammed or popped the ball up. Against Johnson they took defensive swings and often beat the ball into the ground. In contemporary terms, Johnson's motion can perhaps best be described as combining Mariano Rivera's quiet delivery with an arm angle more like that of Randy Johnson (albeit from the right side), while Wood's would be more akin to the all-out effort of a Jonathan Papelbon or Tim Lincecum.

Both men, perhaps because of their shared western upbringing, were utterly respectful of the other. Johnson once said famously that "nobody can throw harder than Joe Wood," while Wood, who rarely praised opposing pitchers, once told Roger Angell, "I don't think anybody was faster than Walter Johnson." In the mind of each man the question of who was faster—and better—was best left for others to decide based on their records. The consensus seemed to be that while Wood may have been able to throw the occasional pitch faster than Johnson, he could not sustain his speed, something even Johnson had sensed. Earlier in the year he cautioned that Wood "has tremendous speed. But he acquired that speed in such a way that he can't stand it long." Citing Wood's use of the "deadly 'snap ball,'" Johnson offered that "I am afraid he will soon cease to be as effective as he is now, if he doesn't have to retire altogether," and he hoped Wood would "change his pace and extend his career." While Johnson's words would prove prophetic, for the 1912 season Wood's Faustian bargain with his right arm would pay dividends.

RED SOX RUN EASY — CHOCK FULL OF CONFIDENCE AND NOTHING TO WORRY

As August unfolded and the Red Sox slowly and inexorably increased their lead over the Senators—stretching it to six, then seven, then eight games—the Senators, apart from Johnson, slowly ran out of steam, and any dreams Washington had in regard to the pennant slowly evaporated. Washington fans—indeed, fans of any American League team but Boston—had little to look forward to other than Johnson's march toward the record book.

His effort was immense—Johnson almost kept the Senators alive through his own force and will, starting and relieving without regard to his health. On August 15 he won his thirteenth game in a row with a win in relief against Chicago, then started and beat the White Sox the next day for his fourteenth consecutive victory, facing only twenty-nine batters and twirling a one-hitter. Four days later, on August 20, he entered a game in relief with only one out in the first inning against Cleveland and pitched a shutout the rest of the way, emerging with yet another victory, number fifteen in a row. And then, on August 23, he toppled Chesbro in the record books with his sixteenth straight win by beating the Tigers to run his record to 29-7.

In the meantime Joe Wood played the snake in the grass. While the attention of the baseball world was increasingly focused on Johnson, Wood just kept winning.

On August 10 in Detroit, with Ty Cobb under the weather and out of the lineup, Wood beat the Tigers 4–1 in the rain, scattering seven hits and striking out ten. But after the game Wood said his right arm felt "a little lame," and the *Globe* reported that "Joe Wood was complaining of a very sore arm yesterday." The paper noted that Wood would not pitch again until August 15 or 16. Once again, the wise move for Stahl might well have been to give Wood even more rest and possibly skip a start or two to make sure he was strong for the postseason, but that kind of progressive thinking was not yet in vogue.

Besides, there were other elements at play. The Red Sox, beginning to admit to themselves that an appearance in the World's Series was in the offing, cautioned fans to "hang on to their rain checks" so that they would have "indisputable evidence that they are general fans and regular attendants at the games, and thus gain special consideration in the award of tickets." Fans were beginning to look ahead as well, and a near-capacity crowd of eighteen thousand turned out for the doubleheader against St. Louis on August 14. Finally, with the weather no longer a concern and the Red Sox riding a wave, McAleer's club was beginning to fill Fenway Park on a regular basis. The owner was eager to maximize the gate, and Joe Wood put fans in the seats.

When the Sox arrived at Fenway Park to face the Browns, they were surprised to find brand-new home uniforms hanging in each locker, as well as new, garish, double-breasted crimson coats, each with six big white buttons, white trim on the collar and the pockets, and the name "BOSTON" and a "B" emblazoned over the left breast. Their old uniforms had been a creamy white with the name "RED SOX" across the chest in plain block letters, a plain white hat, and socks with a broad horizontal red stripe. The new uniforms were white with red pinstripes, but otherwise unadorned. They would also soon unveil new, pinstriped road uniforms that were similar to the new home uniforms in every way except for being gray and having the "RED SOX" name in block letters across the breast.

Whether it was because of pressure to appear before a big crowd, because his arm felt better, or because Wood was already thinking about his winning streak and didn't want to miss an opportunity to beat the worst team in the league, after Charley Hall won, 8–2, in a spot start in game 1, Wood took the mound in game 2. He was magnificent, shutting out the Browns, striking out nine, and adding two hits. But all might not have been well. Although one reporter observed that "Joe Wood's arm looked mighty good for a lame one," it was noted that "he lobbed 'em up a lot and altogether had an easy day's work."

RED SOX CELEBRATE WITH A DOUBLE WIN — HALL AND WOOD IN THE BOX — LATTER WINS FOR 25TH TIME IN 29 GAMES

Even then, he got little rest. Two days later Buck O'Brien and the Red Sox trailed the Browns 3–2 after seven innings. To start the eighth Stahl called upon Wood—who didn't give up a run and struck out the side in the ninth—but the Red Sox failed to score and still lost, 3–2. The next day, Saturday, Detroit came into Boston, and Red Sox fans turned out in droves. "Long before the game started," wrote Tim Murnane, "every seat was filled. The crowd kept on coming, filling the back walks of the grandstand and finally bursting out on to the field back of third base taking advantage of every spot where a view could be had of the players."

"Back of third base" referred to the empty space in foul ground between the end of the grandstand and the fence that marked the park's northern border. There was nothing so strange about that— overflow crowds had sometimes spilled over into that area before. But Murnane also noted that "many were forced to look through the wire screen at the foot of the grandstand, yet no one kicked."

Murnane was referring to a place where no fans had ever been before and have probably never been since: squeezed into the narrow space that once existed beneath the concrete slab that formed the floor of the box seats at the foot of the grandstand and the ground. Since the stand was not faced with solid concrete all the way to the ground but was supported by only the occasional column, the effect created a narrow "overhang" about two feet high and eleven feet deep that ran beneath the box seats. To prevent stray balls from rolling beneath the stands, the gap was covered with a wire grate. The club never envisioned that anyone would try to watch a game from that perspective and had not bothered to barricade access to the area un- derneath the stands. But on this day desperate spectators crawled into the ersatz cavern on their bellies, sharing the space with rats, and watched the game while lying prone on the ground, their faces pressed against the screen, only inches above the field. These were not standing-room seats, or seats of any kind at all. More accurately, they were "lying-down" seats. Boston fans were never more enterprising and insistent than when the stands at Fenway Park were full and they wanted to see the game in person.

They all got their money's worth and more. The game had to be stopped several times and the crowd pushed back behind ropes. Even Boston players lent a hand. Jerome Kelley's crew was overwhelmed by the task, and Paul Shannon reported that "Red Sox players drove home the posts that held the crowd in check," using bats as hammers. Boston fought back from a 3–0 deficit with five runs in the seventh inning to take the lead. In Washington, where the game between the Naps and Senators had already ended, eight thousand fans still desperately hoping for a Boston collapse stayed inside the park to watch the result on the scoreboard. When the five-spot went up in Boston's half, "a chorus of groans" reportedly echoed through the Washington park.

But Boston's rally extracted a price. Jake Stahl, perhaps because of the size of the crowd, decided to do all he could to squeak out a win and in the seventh inning had Olaf Henriksen pinch-hit for Ray Collins. The move worked, but now he needed a pitcher.

Stahl, apparently concluding that even if Wood's arm was too sore for him to start he could still relieve, sent him out to the mound to pitch the eighth. The crowd roared with approval as their hero strode onto the field and toed the rubber. He retired the side in order in the eighth, but in the ninth, leading 6–3 with two outs, he began to falter. Catcher Oscar Stanage tripled, and pitcher George Mullin singled to make the score 6–4 and bring up leadoff hitter Davy Jones, the tying run. Fortunately for the Red Sox, Wood had one more good fastball left in his right arm, and he jammed Jones, who lifted a weak infield fly to end the game.

Sunday was an off day, but after Bedient beat the Tigers on Monday, Wood, despite his obvious fatigue, got the ball on Tuesday to pitch the series' finale. He still wasn't right, as it was reported that he depended on a "rare assortment of curves" to tame the Tigers. But he was nevertheless effective, winning 6–2 and, according to Murnane, "working Ty Cobb as a mother would a rich mine owner for her daughter," teasing him with curves and slow balls, holding the Tiger star to one hit and collecting his twenty-sixth win. The victory was his third in the last ten days over five appearances and his eleventh in a row.

Rest was not part of Stahl's plan for his ace pitcher. Wood took his regular turn against Cleveland just four days later, on Saturday, August 24. Once again Fenway Park was packed to the rafters to see Wood and the Sox erupt for an early 6–0 lead. After getting the lead, Wood reportedly took things easy again, using his breaking ball and changeup more often than usual. He won, 8–4, but gave up runs in three of the last four innings.

Sunday gave all of Boston a chance to take a break from the day-to-day drama of the season and assess the state of the Red Sox. Apart from a complete and utter collapse of historic proportions, the Red Sox were on course to win the pennant by double digits—if Wood's arm held up. Tris Speaker was hitting .401, Larry Gardner .311, and Hick Cady a robust .295 since seeing regular playing time, while Wagner and Duffy Lewis were both enjoying perhaps the best season of their careers. Together they made Boston's offense the most potent in the league.

Wood, however, was still the big story, and now the writers and fans began looking ahead. The press noted that in another ten days or so Wood and Johnson, whose winning streak now stood at sixteen games, might just meet up. The specter of Johnson, who by then might be going after Marquard's mark, facing Wood, hot on the heels of the same record, was absolutely delicious, particularly for the sporting men in the crowd. Such a contest would draw heavy betting action not just in Boston and Washington but over the entire country.

Washington manager Clark Griffith was no more cautious with Johnson than Stahl was with Wood, and even though the Senators trailed Boston by nearly ten games, he was still pushing hard for every victory. On August 26, with Washington and the Browns tied 2–2 in the seventh inning, men on first and second, and one out, Griffith called on Johnson to pitch in relief of Tom Hughes, one of thirteen such appearances he would make over the course of the season. Johnson struck out the first hitter he faced, but then gave up an uncharacteristic wild pitch, followed by a base hit, to give up two runs. Washington then went on to lose the game, 4–3.

Under today's scoring rules, Johnson would not have been credited with the loss. The two runners on base when he entered the game would be considered the responsibility of the pitcher who was on the mound when they reached base. But scoring rules in 1912 were much less clear, and a consistent scoring system would not be put in place until after the 1912 season. Had the game taken place in the National League, Hughes, not Johnson, would have been given the loss, but in the American League it was up to the official scorer to assign credit for the loss. Given Johnson's streak, however, scorekeeper Joe Jackson of the *Washington Post* was uncomfortable making such a ruling. He wired Ban Johnson, whom sportswriters referred to as "the custodian of the last guess" in such situations, to render a decision. Johnson responded that since Walter Johnson was on the mound when the winning run scored, he should be given the loss. He later explained: "[Johnson] had a chance to win the game by saving it. He failed. Therefore he is entitled to shoulder the blame. . . . I will not stand for any 'padding.'" The loss halted Johnson's streak at sixteen games and dropped his record to 29-8.

All of Washington howled at the ruling, which they felt was unfair. But Johnson, true to form, was magnanimous in defeat, saying, "It would be unfair to charge Tom Hughes with a defeat just to keep my record clean . . . I lost the game."

However, there may also have been a bit more to it than that.

The Giants, who had been virtually unbeatable over the first half of the season, now seemed out of steam. The NL pennant was still a certainty, but the question of the world championship remained open. Based on recent developments, not only did it seem likely that the Red Sox would win the pennant, but if they maintained their current level of play, the Sox seemed likely to beat the Giants in the Series. That was an outcome that Ban Johnson relished, for there was still considerable enmity between the two leagues and between Johnson and Giants manager John McGraw, who detested one another.

A decade before, McGraw, like James McAleer, had been one of Johnson's favorites when he was the player-manager of the American League's Baltimore franchise. But to John McGraw a baseball game was a battle to be fought every second and victory an outcome sought by any means necessary. After McGraw had incited a crowd to attack an umpire, Johnson suspended him, and the relationship between the two men began to sour. McGraw became increasingly belligerent and later that year got into a series of rows with umpires. Johnson had little choice but to suspend him indefinitely.

McGraw was both outraged . . . and delighted. He was being courted by the New York Giants of the National League, and in his mind the suspension set him free. Sure enough, McGraw signed with the Giants, a treasonous act in the eyes of Ban Johnson, who was best described as a man who "always remembers a friend and never forgets an enemy." Ever since that time there was little that Johnson liked better than sticking it to McGraw in ways both large and small, and the World's Series of 1912 seemed likely to present another opportunity to do just that.

On August 24—two days before Johnson's streak came to an end— Ban Johnson and Boston owner James McAleer were in Washington. Johnson asked McAleer to meet him for dinner, and the Boston owner agreed. McAleer knew full well that when Johnson asked him to jump, it was time to leave his feet. After all, Johnson had much more money invested in the Boston club than McAleer, liked to keep tabs on his investment, and as league president apparently had a plan to increase the value of that investment. Washington club president Tom Noyes had just passed away, leaving Washington manager Griffith, whose 10 percent stake in the club made him the largest shareholder, temporarily in charge. With McAleer acting as his willing frontman, the two men asked Griffith to join them for dinner at a private club.

The three men extended their condolences, talked baseball, and chatted about league affairs over drinks and a multi-course dinner, and then, to no one's surprise, the dinner conversation eventually turned to Walter Johnson and his remarkable streak. As Griffith extolled the virtues of the game's best pitcher, McAleer and Johnson nodded in agreement. Then, during a brief lull in the conversation, McAleer turned to Griffith and dropped a bomb.

"I'll give you fifty thousand dollars for Johnson and you turn him over to me tomorrow. Here's a thousand dollars right here to bind the agreement."

Griffith was stunned. Raising an eyebrow and scanning the faces of both men, he asked, "Are you kidding me?"

"No, I'm not kidding," deadpanned McAleer as Johnson looked on silently. "Here's the thousand here on the table." With that, McAleer reached into his pocket, withdrew a fat roll of bills, and began counting out the money, stacking it on the table in front of Griffith. The cash had almost certainly been supplied by Johnson. McAleer neither had such resources himself nor could have made such a bold and expensive proposal without Johnson's input.

As the pile rose higher Griffith, processing the scene before him, slowly began shaking his head. "Nothing doing," he said. "You couldn't even buy him for one hundred thousand dollars." But McAleer left the money on the table. He maintained that he was serious in his offer and appealed to Griffith's allegiance to the American League, explaining that Johnson "would win the coming World's Series for my club alternating with Joe Wood."

From the perspective of Boston—and Ban Johnson—the tandem of Wood and Johnson pitching for the same team in the World's Series was absolutely delicious, as close to an unbeatable combination as it was humanly possible to create. Never again in the history of baseball, in fact, would two pitchers perform at such a high level during the same season in the same league. Together, not only is it likely that Johnson and Wood would have routed the Giants in the 1912 World's Series, but the deal could conceivably have tilted the balance toward Boston for a generation or more. Both pitchers were still young and presumably looking forward to another decade or more of success. The result might have been a dynasty to rival any in the game, for at some point, all at the same time, the Red Sox roster might well have included Wood, Walter Johnson, Tris Speaker, and Babe Ruth.

But Griffith, whose nickname "the Old Fox" spoke to his acumen, would not be dissuaded. Although he was a supporter of Ban Johnson's league, he had had his own share of run-ins with the league president. In fact, when Griffith had first bought into the Washington club the previous fall, Johnson had reneged on a promise to loan him some money. And while the $50,000 offer was tempting—no player had ever commanded such a sale price—Walter Johnson was one of a kind, absolutely irreplaceable. Without Johnson, Griffith's stake in the team was worth considerably less than he had paid for it. Besides, Griffith knew that Washington fans would never forgive him if he sold the greatest player the city had ever seen. Washington was on pace to draw more than one hundred thousand more fans than in 1911, and Walter Johnson was the reason.

McAleer kept finding new ways to ask, but Griffith kept saying no as Johnson looked on and saw his great idea evaporate. McAleer finally stuffed the money back into his pocket and the conversation, now forced, turned to other matters.

Johnson did not forget. The league president was accustomed to getting his own way, and Griffith's refusal to sell his star may well have influenced Johnson's scoring decision a few days later. Now that the pennant race was over, Washington fans had little incentive apart from Johnson's streak to go to the ballpark for the remainder of the season. And now that Ban Johnson had put an end to it, they had even less of a reason to attend. Take *that*.

Although the end of Johnson's winning streak stripped the potential matchup between Wood and Johnson of some national interest, in Boston, if anything, it only increased the contest's significance. Now it was Wood and only Wood who still had a shot at Marquard's mark. That is, if he remained undefeated.

There was still a long way to go until that would be known, for Wood had at least two more starts before he could even entertain the possibility of pitching opposite Johnson. Meanwhile it seemed that Fenway Park was still the site of something new almost every day. The White Sox, after their wonderful start, were playing lousy ball, and it was beginning to show in their ill temper toward each other, the opposition, and even the umpires. On August 27 the Red Sox and their Chicago counterparts met in Fenway Park to play what might be considered the first night game in the history of Fenway Park.

NO MORE MOONLIGHT BASEBALL, SILK

It was a sloppy, back-and-forth game that spoke to Chicago's desperation in the face of a deteriorating season. Boston took command early, taking a 6–2 lead, but in the sixth the White Sox routed Bedient and scored five runs to surge ahead. Then Bill Carrigan's single in the seventh chased Eddie Cicotte, and Ed Walsh came on in relief for what seemed like his one hundredth appearance of the season. Charley Hall singled to center field, scoring a run and sending Carrigan on around second base.

That was when everything got weird. Carrigan took a wide turn at second, and Chicago center fielder Jimmie Callahan threw behind him, catching the Boston catcher between bases. A rundown ensued that eventually involved the entire Chicago infield as Carrigan darted this way and dashed that way, back and forth, racing away from the ball in great loops and skirting the outfield grass like a Little Leaguer who didn't know the rules. Finally, somehow, he dove back safe to second base.

As soon as he did several Chicago players stopped chasing Carrigan and started charging after umpires Silk O'Loughlin and Fred Westervelt, arguing that, while avoiding being tagged, Carrigan had run outside the baseline. But whether that was a violation of the rules was not exactly clear. Even the *Boston Globe* wondered "if there is any line drawn for such a play."

Within a few moments O'Loughlin was surrounded by virtually the entire Chicago team, half of them screaming and the others dramatically throwing their gloves in the air and waving their arms. He listened for a remarkably long time before finally walking away as Fred Westervelt made a show of taking out his pocket watch to move things along. But each time O'Loughlin returned to his place, the White Sox resumed the argument. The crowd got restless and booed the White Sox unmercifully, but even they grew tired. Over the next twenty minutes, as the White Sox continued to hound the umpires and Bill Carrigan stood patiently on second base, hundreds, if not thousands, of fans grew impatient and left Fenway Park. It was more than twenty long minutes before the game was able to resume.

After nine innings the game was tied, 8–8. The tenth inning was played in twilight, and with the game still tied, most observers expected it to be called because of darkness.

But now the umpires got their revenge on the White Sox. As reporters in the press box and fans at the top of the stands could clearly see, outside the park automobile drivers had turned on their headlights, the gas street lamps had begun to flicker on, and the electric streetcars were illuminated. But O'Loughlin and Westervelt, giving Boston every opportunity to win, refused to call the game. By the twelfth inning it was so dark that it was hard for those in the press box to see the outfielders, much less their scorebook. The players were becoming impatient too, and in the top of the inning Harry Hooper struck out on a pitch that observers thought might have been outside, but it was so dark they could not be sure. Finally, when Tris Speaker made the third out of the twelfth inning by trying to make second base from home after a dropped third strike—essentially trying to end the charade by getting himself called out on purpose—the umpires relented and called the contest. It was nearly 7:00 p.m., almost three and a half hours after the game began, and twenty minutes after the sun had dropped below the horizon in those days before Daylight Savings Time. Only a few minutes after the end of the game Fenway was bathed in darkness. Not until 1947 would lights be installed at Fenway Park and enable night baseball to be played.

A doubleheader was scheduled for the following day to make up for the tie, but most fans were far more excited by the announcement that it was finally possible to reserve World's Series tickets. In a press release the club instructed fans who had collected ten or more rain checks for grandstand tickets to send them in by mail to the Red Sox. Then, "if the Red Sox win the pennant," read the press release, "you will be advised what reservation has been made for you." The team was already worried about scalpers and hoped that by asking for rain checks speculators could be prevented from scooping up all the tickets.

The Red Sox swept the doubleheader before twenty thousand fans. Wood threw a shutout in game 2 to win his twelfth in a row as the White Sox, still smarting from the day before, played as if they could not wait to leave Boston. And once again, fans in Fenway found yet another new and novel place from which to watch the ball game. Deep in the left-field corner stood a portable ladder more than thirty feet high that Jerome Kelley's crew used to maintain the advertising signs on the left-field wall, propped against the fence in foul ground. On this day enterprising fans climbed the ladder and watched the game from that vantage point—including one, at the very top, who was dressed in a Red Sox uniform. In his cartoon account of the game,

Wallace Goldsmith took note and speculated that the scene had "a prophetic meaning"—Boston on top.

The A's followed the White Sox into Fenway for three contests, needing a miracle to pull back into the pennant race, but it didn't happen as the Sox swept the series before crowds that were becoming more frenzied each day. For the finale, the *Globe* estimated, thirty thousand fans packed Fenway Park, though the *Post* put the figure at thirty-three thousand, including some six thousand who ringed the field, standing behind ropes. Fans even sat atop the left-field wall, and one picture in the newspaper showed a woman standing on the aforementioned ladder captioned "Watching the Game from the Perch in Lewisville," now the occasional name for left field. In the last week nearly ninety thousand fans had packed Fenway Park. The World's Series was a month away, and Boston was already in a lather.

Before the Washington series the Sox gave everyone a break by traveling to New York for a Labor Day doubleheader. The city had been nothing but kind to the Red Sox in 1912, for they had yet to lose a game there, going undefeated at the Yankees' Hilltop Park. For this series, however, they would not be playing at Hilltop Park. In April and May 1911, after much of the Polo Grounds was destroyed by a fire, the Yankees had allowed the Giants to use their park while the Polo Grounds—also known as Brush Stadium, after Giants owner John Brush—was rebuilt in concrete and steel. The Giants now returned the favor and allowed the Yankees to use the Polo Grounds for their series against the Red Sox, including the big Labor Day doubleheader to take advantage of its larger stadium capacity. In fact, in 1913 the Yankees would abandon their own park completely and play at the Polo Grounds until Yankee Stadium opened in 1923.

Boston players and fans, daydreaming about the World's Series, looked forward to the opportunity to become familiar with the Giants' home field. That prospect, along with the opportunity for Boston rooters to make contact with their New York counterparts and prime the pump for the frenzied gambling that was certain to take place during the World's Series, was too tempting to ignore. The Royal Rooters telegrammed Boston club secretary Bob McRoy and asked him to secure 250 seats in New York behind the visitors' bench so they could scope out the prospects that awaited them in October.

Those who stayed behind in Boston, however, were not without entertainment. The Giants themselves were playing in the Hub.

The Polo Grounds, with its lofty, horseshoe-shaped, double-decked grandstand backed by the rock escarpment known as "Coogan's Bluff," made Fenway Park seem small and quaint, a diminutive outdoor stage compared to the Globe Theater that was the Polo Grounds. While Polo Grounds architect Henry Herts would describe his design as "utilitarian," it was anything but. The grandstand, nearly twice as high as its Fenway Park counterpart, towered over the infield. The upper deck was faced with a decorative frieze, and the facade of the roof was adorned with the coats of arms of all the National League teams. Ornate carved eagles perched along the top of the upper deck, easily the most decorative and distinctive element of interior ballpark design for the era, and the box seats were modeled after the royal boxes of the Coliseum in Rome. Although, like Fenway Park, the grandstand surrounded only the infield, when full it made for a raucous, intimidating arena, a place where the passion of the fans matched that of McGraw and his Giants and made life absolutely miserable for the opposition.

That is why the Red Sox were so happy to be playing the Yankees instead, who had none of the qualities that distinguished the Giants. Although a number of Boston players had played in the previous incarnation of the Polo Grounds, many of them in the postseason series between the Giants and Red Sox two years before, none had played in the new facility. And a number of key players, like Hugh Bedient, Buck O'Brien, Hick Cady, and Larry Gardner, had never laid eyes on the place.

The Yankees were compliant before a crowd of twenty-five thousand — many of whom cheered Boston — and played the Red Sox hard. Nevertheless, New York fell twice, 2–1 to Bedient, who nearly threw a no-hitter in the best performance of his career, and 1–0 to Wood. After being staked to a lead in the first inning, Wood had walked a tightrope the rest of the way, bending time and time again before finally securing his shutout, his twenty-ninth victory, and his fourteenth in a row by striking out pitcher George McConnell with the bases loaded and two outs in the final inning. The victory upped Boston's lead to thirteen games, much larger than the margin enjoyed by the Giants. After leading by as many as sixteen games earlier in the season, the defending NL champions had slept like a hare for two months until recently being jolted awake by the discovery that the Chicago Cubs were closing like a tortoise. The Giants responded with a sprint, and now, for the first time all season, the Red Sox players openly began to talk about playing their National League counterparts in the World's Series.

The game was rained out the next day, and it was a happy ball club that boarded the train back to Boston, for the Red Sox were beginning to look forward to clinching the pennant officially. Joe Wood's mother and little sister Zoe were aboard, making their first visit to Boston, and they were joined by Tris Speaker's mother and Jake Stahl's wife. The players had a bit of a party on the train ride back and took particular joy in stealing Tim Murnane's straw summer hat and returning it to him with the top punched out.

When Washington arrived for a three-game set with the Red Sox, Clark Griffith, still smarting over the decision that robbed Johnson of his chance to match Marquard's record, threw down the gauntlet. He announced that he was holding Walter Johnson back until Boston decided to pitch Wood. That way Johnson himself would have the opportunity to prevent Wood from matching his American League record of sixteen straight wins. "I want to give the fans a chance to see those pitchers hitched up and feel sure my man can win the honors," said Griffith. "Johnson's record this season was against all comers, and I want to see Joe Wood tied up with our man." Then Griffith made the challenge a little more personal. "Tell Wood," he sneered, "that we will consider him a coward if he doesn't pitch against Johnson."

To claim publicly that someone was a coward was an insult of the highest order, one that Griffith knew full well could not be ignored. And it was not. As soon as Jake Stahl got wind of it, he didn't waste any time in responding. "All right," he told the press. "Wood will pitch Friday. I had him down for Saturday, but to accommodate Griff we'll make the change and intend to defeat the Senators with Johnson pitching for them." The game was on.

Griffith hadn't announced just when he intended to pitch Johnson, who, like Wood, had last appeared on September 2. All he had said was that he would hold him until Stahl made a decision. Whether the two faced each other on Friday or Saturday did not much matter.

But it did to Boston. A Saturday game was certain to draw a crowd of more than twenty thousand no matter who pitched. It was, as Washington sportswriter Joe Jackson commented in the *Post,* "better business policy" to play the two pitchers Friday and ensure a good crowd on that day as well. Profit, and not necessarily the health of Joe Wood's golden arm, was still paramount.

Boston won the first two games of the series on Wednesday and Thursday, September 4 and 5, 6–2 and 4–3, behind Collins and O'Brien before a combined total of more than thirty thousand Boston fans taking advantage of their team's next-to-last home stand. After the Saturday finale the Sox would head west on a road trip, and play only one more regular-season series in Boston.

Not that anyone paid much attention to the outcome of the two contests, for as September 6 approached the buildup to the matchup between Wood and Johnson grew in intensity.

WOOD AND JOHNSON IN PITCHING DUEL TODAY —

One Of Greatest Battles Of Boxmen In Years
To Be Fought At Fenway Park

All the Boston papers touted the contest like no other played that year. Although Joe Wood would later rather famously claim that "the newspapers publicized us like prizefighters" and some newspapers did go overboard with their hyperbole over the matchup, that was not true everywhere. Joe Jackson referred to the game more accurately as "like a circus." But it was the biggest story of the day—and the season—thus far.

On the morning of Friday, September 6, the sun revealed a near-perfect early autumn day. The air was crisp, and a few puffy clouds floated overhead. The forecast was for light winds and temperatures in the low seventies—neither too hot nor too cold, an absolutely perfect day for baseball.

As Boston woke and people scurried to work, the buzz on the street was palpable. Over the summer storeowners had realized that baseball was good for business, and many downtown shops sported Red Sox pennants and other baseball paraphernalia in their windows. In recent weeks the players had been overwhelmed with endorsement offers and other commercial opportunities. Everyone wanted a piece of the Red Sox.

The Royal Rooters had always worn their allegiance on their sleeves and on their chests in the form of buttons and charms and banners and pennants, but now their passion seemed to spread over the entire city. For the first time ever in the history of Boston baseball, the souvenir business was booming. Anticipating a big crowd, vendors were already setting out their wares on the streets around Fenway Park and in nearby shops. There were ties for sale featuring the Red Sox logo for fifty-five cents, genuine Red Sox red socks for fifty cents, flags and pennants for a quarter, pins, placards featuring the faces of the Red Sox players, and even dolls dressed in Red Sox uniforms. Although intended for young girls and boys, more than a few made their way into the hands of young women, housewives, and matrons, sharing space in their purses to be carried around like a good luck charm and doted on like a real infant.

By noon crowds were already beginning to make their way toward Fenway Park, more than three hours in advance of the scheduled 3:15 p.m. start. Many of the reserved seats in the grandstand had already been sold, but unreserved seats in the pavilion and the center-field bleachers were still up for grabs, and there were as many standing-room tickets as the Red Sox were willing to sell.

There were two stories at work this day—the game on the field with the matchup between Wood and Johnson, and the crowd itself. Together they would change Fenway Park forever. No other game in the history of the franchise would ever have a bigger impact on the facility.

With the crowd massing on the sidewalks and spilling over into the street, at about one o'clock the Red Sox began selling tickets and opened the gates. Apart from the reserved seats in the grandstand and the box seats of those fortunate enough to have them, it was a near free-for-all as fans with tickets for unreserved seats staked out their place in the ballpark. By two o'clock the bleachers and pavilion were filled, and fans began to spill out onto the field.

No one stopped them. It was customary at the time to allow fans access to the field itself, both before and after the game. Fans routinely ambled across the outfield to reach the bleacher seats before the game and to find the exits afterward. It was not uncommon for young boys and other fans to run the bases after the game or to stand on the pitcher's mound and take a turn at pretending to be Joe Wood. The grounds crew was overwhelmed from the start, and crowd control wasn't really Jerome Kelley's job anyway, at least not when the crowd was this big. He and his men had their hands full just keeping the infield clear, shooing the hordes away so that Kelley's precious infield turf would stay free of heel prints and divots.

Today, however, as the stands filled, no one ambled anywhere. After the aisles in the stands and the grandstand decks and promenades were filled to overflowing, fans climbed over the rails onto the field, then sprinted toward their favored viewpoint. Some crowded onto Duffy's Cliff, teetering and tottering to stay upright as more and more fans squeezed their way onto the embankment. Others ringed the outfield and crowded into the open space past the grandstand along the left-field line.

The ballpark looked full, but fans continued to pour into Fenway. Once the crowd was six or eight men deep in the outfield and it was impossible for those in the back to see over the heads in front, later arrivals headed back toward the grandstand, only to find their way blocked by even more fans pouring up the ramps and onto the field. There was no place to stand except where they already were, and fans began to fill up the space in foul territory and then even behind home plate, pressing ever closer to the infield by the minute.

As the *Boston Journal* noted, "The managers of the park very badly guessed what they would be up against." Under the direction of club secretary Bob McRoy, the Red Sox kept selling tickets until it became patently obvious that if they sold any more there would be no room on the field to play the game. With perhaps as many as ten thousand fans still milling around outside the park, looking in vain for scalpers,

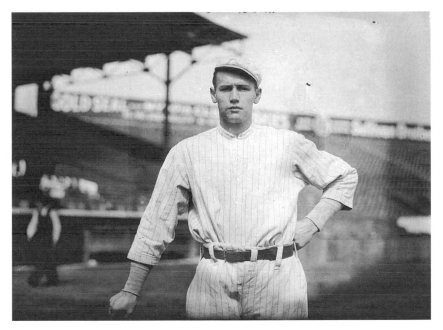

ILLUS. 13 Smoky Joe Wood was nearly unbeatable in 1912, going 34–5 in the regular season and winning another three games in the World's Series.

George Grantham Bain Collection, Library of Congress Prints and Photographs Division

ILLUS. 14 After injuries sidelined Bill Carrigan and Les Nunamaker, rookie catcher Hick Cady stepped in. With Cady behind the plate, Boston pitchers, particularly Joe Wood, thrived. Cady served as Wood's personal catcher for the last half of the 1912 season and in the World's Series.

George Grantham Bain Collection, Library of Congress Prints and Photographs Division

ILLUS. 15 Two young phenoms, Smoky Joe Wood (left) of the Red Sox and Jeff Tesreau of the New York Giants, squared off in game 1 of the World's Series at the Polo Grounds. On this day Wood outpitched his rival to win 4–3.

George Grantham Bain Collection, Library of Congress Prints and Photographs Division

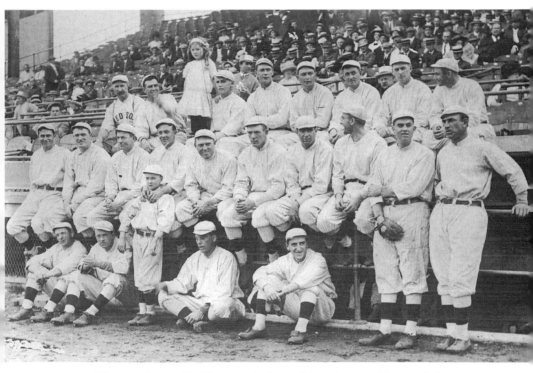

ILLUS. 16 The 1912 Boston Red Sox pose in front of their dugout at Fenway Park during the World's Series. Top row (left to right): Joseph Quirk (trainer), Tris Speaker, Joe Wood's sister Zoe, Joe Wood, Hick Cady, Pinch Thomas, Buck O'Brien, Hugh Bradley, Duffy Lewis. Middle row: Harry Hooper, Bill Carrigan, Steve Yerkes, Olaf Henriksen, Clyde Engle, Les Nunamaker, Charley Hall, Larry Gardner, Ray Collins, Jake Stahl. Front row: Heinie Wagner, Hugh Bedient, mascot, Larry Pape, Marty Krug.

George Grantham Bain Collection, Library of Congress Prints and Photographs Division

ILLUS. 17 On Boston's Newspaper Row and in other large cities all across the country, newspapers provided re-creations of the World's Series for the convenience of fans. Operators behind the board received telegraph reports of the game and within seconds, fans knew what had taken place hundreds of miles away.

George Grantham Bain Collection, Library of Congress Prints and Photographs Division

ILLUS. 18 Player-manager Jake Stahl (center) leads the Red Sox on a long march across the field from the clubhouse to the dugout at the Polo Grounds in New York before a World's Series game. *Courtesy of the Print Department, Boston Public Library*

ILLUS. 19 The Red Sox pose for a team picture in front of the grandstand early in the 1912 season. Not all grandstand seats have been installed, indicating that this photograph was taken before opening day, likely just before or after the exhibition game versus Harvard. *Courtesy of the Print Department, Boston Public Library*

ILLUS. 20 Fenway Park, 1912 World's Series. To accommodate more fans, bleacher seats were constructed on the third-base line, on Duffy's Cliff, and even more seats placed in front of the embankment. As a result it would be impossible to hit a home run over the fence in left field during the World's Series. Umpires decided that any ball hit over the short fence into the crowd, off the wall, or even into Lansdowne Street would be a ground-rule double. *Courtesy of the Print Department, Boston Public Library*

ILLUS. 21 The Royal Rooters were the best-known group of fans in the country. They sang and cheered from the first pitch to the last.

Courtesy of the Print Department, Boston Public Library

ILLUS. 22 After their seats at Duffy's Cliff were given away before game 7, the Rooters tried to take the field and sit behind home plate. Mounted police helped herd them off the field. The Rooters were so upset that most did not attend the pivotal game 8. *Courtesy of the Print Department, Boston Public Library*

ILLUS. 23 "The Royal Rooters and the Cossacks of the Fens." After their seats on Duffy's Cliff were given to other fans, the Royal Rooters rioted. This cartoon, which refers to the police as "Cossacks," reveals the allegiance of the artist.

Collection of the author

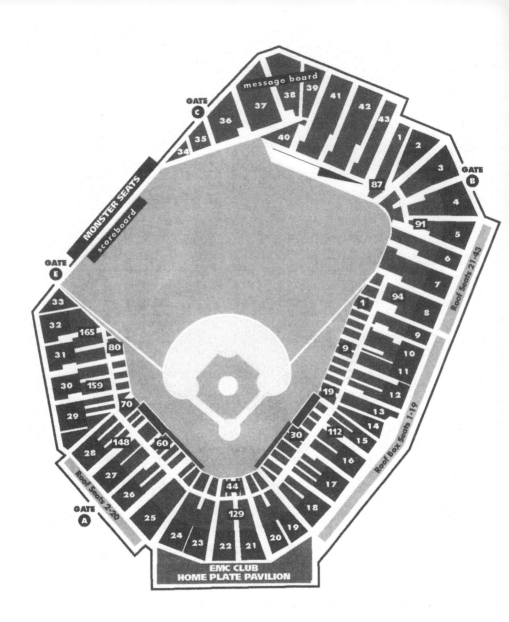

ILLUS. 24 Fenway Park today. Roughly speaking, the original grandstand stretched from section 28 through 15, the pavilion from section 14 thru section 8, and the center-field bleachers from section 39 thru 43. The third-base stands, from section 29 thru 33, and the right-field bleachers, section 1 thru 7, were added in September 1912 for the World's Series. *Courtesy of Boston Baseball*

they forced the gates closed just before 3:00 p.m. Now all they had to do was clear the field to prevent a riot.

Most of the players had retreated to the clubhouse, but as game time approached and they tried to take the field they found the dugouts packed with fans, some squeezed on the benches and others sitting on the railings and hanging off the roof. The players stood on the infield, surrounded by fans as though they were in a boxing ring, trying to play catch but most of them just gazing in wonder. None of them had ever seen anything like it before. No one had.

Meanwhile Joe Wood pushed his way onto the field, ball in hand, looking like a lost little boy in need of a playmate, searching in vain for a place to warm up. Although it had long been customary to warm up along the sidelines, over the course of the season Red Sox pitchers had begun to take their warm-up tosses deep in right field, where there was a bit more room. But now that was impossible, for as Paul Shannon observed, fans were "lining the banking of the left field fence some 20 feet deep, hanging on the tops of fences and straddling the back of the bull." He was referring to a bull-shaped sign advertising Bull Durham tobacco on the center-field end of the left-field wall that jutted out just far enough to allow a dozen or so fans to ride it bareback, the first fans ever to watch a game at Fenway Park, not atop the wall or in front of it or inside the scoreboard, but actually on the wall itself in fair territory.

Wood finally decided to warm up the old-fashioned way. Hick Cady paced out sixty feet in foul ground between the diamond and the dug out and, with fans barely an arm's length away, Wood slowly began warming up. Walter Johnson did the same on the opposite side of the field.

It was like trying to play catch on the subway platform at Park Station during rush hour. The crowd cleared a narrow corridor between the pitchers and their catchers, and the batteries started throwing the ball gingerly back and forth, Wood and Johnson taking care not to smack anyone in the jaw as they reached in their wind-up or throw the ball wild and knock someone unconscious. As they did the crowd peppered each man with questions and comments that each did his best to ignore, and heads turned back and forth en masse as the mob followed each toss and marveled at the speed of each pitch seen up close.

After a few moments each man was ready, but it was impossible to start the game with the crowd so close. Club officials, the grounds crew, do-gooders, and cops all tried to herd the throng back away from the edge of the infield, but the fans ignored each entreaty, no one willing to give up his or her hard-won space. Finally, mounted police took the field and roughly cleared fair territory and the baselines, although a ring of spectators six or eight deep still ringed the infield and decided to take their chances with foul balls. For the most part, however, they gave the players a wide berth and remained thirty or more feet from fair territory.

Players from neither team were able to reclaim their own dugouts. "So thickly were the spectators massed," wrote Webb, "that the players' pits were abandoned, the contestants bringing their war clubs out almost to the baseline." In other words the players simply sprawled on the grass halfway between the baselines and the stands, like kids gathered around a makeshift diamond on the sandlots, waiting for their ups.

Even though the crowd ringed the outfield, except in left—where fans stood not only on Duffy's Cliff but in front of it—they did not dramatically impinge on fair territory. How many were in the park? When asked by Mel Webb, Bob McRoy insisted that there were no more than twenty-nine thousand fans in the park, a figure that seems absurd and may well have been used simply to dispel any safety concerns. Paul Shannon noted that the crowd was "conservatively estimated by vice president John I. Taylor, who had a long expertise in taking care of big throngs at the old Huntington avenue park, at 35,000, though several others put the figure 5,000 higher." In fact, no one will ever know precisely how many fans squeezed, cajoled, or otherwise bribed their way into the park that day, but it seems reasonable to assume that Taylor's figure was more accurate, for several crowds in the previous few weeks had pushed thirty thousand without any fans left standing in foul ground behind the plate. Regardless, it is safe to say that no other game was ever played at Fenway Park under such conditions. Yet despite the mass of humanity and cramped conditions, only five fans found the conditions so uncomfortable that they asked for a refund, and only one, a young boy, was hurt by a foul ball. This game was not for those who viewed the game as merely a pleasant pastime, but for those who loved the game for its passion.

Some fifteen minutes after the scheduled 3:15 starting time, umpires Tommy Connolly and Bertie Hart gathered representatives of both teams at home plate to go over the ground rules. After some discussion they decided that unless a runner was particularly fast and an outfielder inordinately slow, there would be no triples or home runs. Any hit that made the crowd would be ruled a ground-rule double. That rule, combined with the proximity of the crowd to the field, which drastically reduced the amount of foul ground, made the task of Joe Wood and Walter Johnson just a little more difficult, and the possibility that the matchup might fall flat a little more likely. A few routine fly balls that fell into the crowd for ground-rule doubles could break a game open, and the lack of foul ground seemed likely to give hitters an extra chance or two. In the stands James McAleer summed up the feelings of everyone when he was overheard saying before the game that "it is going to be a great fight between two great pitchers. I wish the score might be 1–0 and that we might make the one."

While Johnson, in the minds of most, was the champion and Wood the challenger, the smart money was on Wood. Pitching at home gave him a bit of an edge, but even more important was the surrounding cast. There wasn't a player in the Washington lineup who was better than his Boston counterpart, either offensively or defensively. That alone was enough to make Wood the favorite.

When Wood took the mound at the start, Fenway positively rumbled, the singing of the Royal Rooters silenced by the sound of thirty thousand throats. When he poured his first pitch, a fastball, past Washington's center fielder Clyde Milan, the crowd roared and the stands shook. In the press box on the roof of the grandstand, nearly a century before the phrase "pitch count" made its way into the lexicon of the game, Herman Nickerson of the *Journal*, Paul Shannon of the *Post*, Mel Webb of the *Globe*, and other local baseball scribes began charting each pitch as if it were a move in a chess game between two grandmasters—as indeed it was. On this day nothing was overlooked. Perhaps no other game in the history of baseball to date had ever been covered with such thoroughness.

Milan took Wood's second pitch for a ball and then hit a bouncer in the hole. Larry Gardner ranged far to his left, but couldn't quite reach it. Charlie Wagner did and smothered it, but realizing he had no chance to throw the runner out, he held on to the ball as Milan, a poor man's Tris Speaker, streaked past first base with a base hit.

Milan, who would lead the league in 1912 with eighty-eight stolen bases, knew full well the trouble Wood had holding runners on base and how much it bothered him to do so. Wood had gotten better at holding runners on since spring training, particularly with Cady behind the plate, but daring base runners still made him nervous. Batting second, Washington third baseman Eddie Foster stepped in. Wood got a quick strike and then threw over to first. He preferred not to do so, particularly because Clyde Engle, not Jake Stahl, whose ankle often seemed to act up against better pitchers, was playing first base.

Joe Wood, like McAleer, was also thinking that one run might be the difference in the game. He was determined to hold Milan close. He threw to first a second time and then got another strike, then threw to first twice more before Foster fouled one back, the crowd behind the plate ducking and sprawling out of the way. Wood went to first again, then threw a ball, then threw to first once, twice, four times in a row, Milan diving back in safe each time as the crowd grew restless and tense. Then, with the count 1-2, Wood got the payoff.

Foster hit a comebacker straight to the pitcher. He captured it clean, spun, and threw toward Wagner who was racing toward second base. Milan, after ten pickoff attempts, got a poor jump and was just beginning his slide when Wagner's relay whistled by his ear on its way to first. Engle pulled it from the air as Wagner turned a neat double play.

The crowd cheered, knowing how rare it was to double up Milan. Wood looked relieved and now could return to his full wind-up. He was a different pitcher then, and he struck out Danny Moeller to send Boston up to the plate. Wood had kept Washington from scoring, but including his throws to first, it had taken him twenty-four tosses to get three outs. In another age, his manager would already be thinking about the bullpen, but in 1912 the thought never crossed Jake Stahl's mind. The game belonged to Joe Wood and Walter Johnson and no one else, no matter how many innings it went.

The Red Sox hitters were also thinking that it might be a one-run game, and in the first, after working the count to 2-2, Harry Hooper hit a weak flare straight to shortstop George McBride. Johnson then got a strike on Yerkes, but the Boston second baseman, who seemed to hit only when the crowds were largest, rapped a sharp ground ball down the third-base line. Eddie Foster tried to backhand the ball, but only knocked it down, and Yerkes made first base. With Speaker up, Boston fans shook Fenway Park to its foundations.

Speaker pulled Johnson's first pitch hard and long and foul into the crowd along the first-base line, the roar of excitement at the sound of the bat striking the ball quickly dissipating as the crowd peeled away from the path of the ball. Then, with the count 2-1, he ripped a ground ball down the first-base line. Chick Gandil fielded it cleanly and tossed to second to put out Yerkes, but Speaker reached first.

Now it was Johnson's turn to keep the runner close, and he alternated strikes to Lewis and throws to first before Speaker broke for second, but Johnson and catcher Eddie Ainsmith were prepared. The throw to second and the tag beat Speaker.

The first inning was over, but the tone was set: every pitch would be a battle. Wood retired Washington easily in the second on ten pitches, but in Boston's half, with one out, first Gardner and then Engle slapped hard base hits through the left side and Boston had men on first and second.

One hit could make a man a hero, but Johnson had made a living off of stifling a reach for the stars. He overpowered first Wagner and then Cady, getting each on weak pop-ups, and through two innings the score on Fenway's left-field wall told the story, 0–0.

As the hitters for each team sprawled along the grass between the crowd and the field, they all agreed on one thing—it was hard enough to hit either Wood or Johnson on a normal day, but on this one it was even harder. Each man was on his game, and the hitter's background, usually fine in Fenway, was made much more difficult by the surging crowds in center field. The contrast between the ubiquitous straw hats and white shirts and the dark jackets of the fans made a poor background for hitters. That still afflicts Fenway Park and is the reason a portion of the center-field bleachers is blocked off during day games even today. After the game home plate umpire Tommy Connolly would admit that he'd had a hard time seeing the ball, and his infield counterpart, Bertie Hart, would say that he'd found the background around the infield so poor because of the crowd that all he could see was "the pitchers making their motions and the catchers putting up their hands." Although the bad visibility would not cause any errors, several ground balls just managed to make it past the infield that otherwise might have been caught, probably owing to the late reaction of the fielders trying to pick the ball up out of the crowd.

In the early innings the game moved like the early rounds of a boxing match between two heavyweights of equal ability as each club probed the other with jabs, only to be repulsed. In the third George McBride drove a pitch from Wood over Duffy Lewis's head and onto the Cliff, which Lewis could not climb because of the crowd, for a double, and he moved to third on a sacrifice. When Walter Johnson, a fine hitter, hit a sharp ground ball, McBride broke for home on contact. But Wood stabbed Johnson's hard grounder and flipped the ball to Cady. McBride braked hard and tried to scramble back to third, but Gardner and Cady chased him down. The Senators went on to put two more men on base. Wood ended the threat by fanning Moeller, but through three innings he had already thrown nearly sixty pitches. In the fourth Speaker walked and took second on a fielder's choice but was left stranded, and in the fifth, after Ainsmith walked and Walter Johnson beat out an infield hit, Duffy Lewis and Tris Speaker nearly collided going after Clyde Milan's fly ball. At the last second Speaker pulled up and Lewis cut in front, stuck his glove up, and managed to hang on.

Johnson, apparently getting stronger, fanned the side in the bottom of the fifth, dispatching Wood on only four pitches for the final out. Washington threatened again in the bottom of the inning when former Red Sox infielder Frank Laporte drove a ball that bounded into the crowd between Speaker and Hooper for a double, but Wood escaped the jam by striking out Roy Moran.

Entering the sixth inning, the game was still scoreless, but although neither team had pushed across a run, Johnson seemed to have the edge. Wood was using more curves and seemed to be saving his best fastballs for when he needed them most. Meanwhile Johnson, as he had demonstrated in the fifth, seemed to be settling in, his fastball a straight stream of milk from his hand to the plate.

Johnson got two quick outs in the sixth, bringing up Speaker. He blew a fastball past the outfielder on the inside, and then broke a rare curveball in on his hands for strike two. After wasting a pitch, Johnson came back with a fastball over the outer half.

The pitch beat Speaker, but he still got the fat part of the bat on the ball, lacing a line drive over Foster's head at third. Speaker ran hard out of the box, but the ball made the crowd before Roy Moran could gather it up, and Speaker loped into second with a ground-rule double. It was no cheap hit—even if Moran had gotten to the ball before the crowd scooped it up, he probably would have had no play on Speaker.

Now the Boston crowd came to life again, for they knew that a base hit of almost any kind would be certain to score Speaker. Over the years they had grown accustomed to seeing Duffy Lewis, who led the Red Sox in RBIs, do just that.

Then the Senators made a mistake. Knowing that the right-handed-hitting Lewis was a pull hitter, they sent their outfield around toward left. With any other pitcher on the mound, it was the smart move, but with Johnson on the mound, perhaps not. Over the last two innings he had overpowered Boston's hitters—and even Speaker had been late getting around on the ball. Not even a dead pull hitter like Lewis could get around on Johnson.

Lewis worked the count to two balls and a strike when Johnson poured a high fastball over the outside corner. Lewis flailed at the pitch, and as Mel Webb described it in the *Globe*, "He could not get his bat around far enough to hit to his accustomed field. Instead the ball shot off to right field, and without much fire on it." It soared through the air, in the parlance of the day, like a "dying quail."

Paul Shannon captured best what happened next.

The bleachers rose en masse as the ball sailed over the head of first baseman Gandil and down towards the right field fence.

Like a deer the fleet footed Moeller raced for the fence, trying to corral the sphere in its course and thereby retire the side. One stride more and the game might well have gone into extra innings. But Moeller's desperate run was all in vain.

Though his outstretched fingers just touched the elusive leather it dropped safely and fell at his feet, Speaker scoring from second and Lewis getting second.

Moeller in fact even dove for the ball, but could not make the catch.

Boston led 1–0. The potential difference between victory and loss, Wood's winning streak and defeat, and the crown as the King of the Pitchers, was only a scant inch or so, if that.

With his throne in sight, Wood seized the day, striking out the first two Washington hitters in the seventh inning on only six pitches before getting Johnson to ground out to third. Johnson too settled down in the seventh and did not give up a base runner. After watching one Johnson pitch pass by for a strike, one of the Washington players was overheard to call out to Wagner, "Why don't you hit it?" Wagner stepped out, turned his head, and replied, "I can't see anything except a streak," before grounding out weakly. Washington threatened in the eighth when Eddie Foster singled and stole second, and for a moment it looked as if the game would be tied, for Chick Gandil hit a near mirror image of Speaker's earlier double with a line drive over Engle's head at first, but the ball curved foul. Although he then hit a pop-up foul off third that on any other day would have been an out but on this day made the crowd, Wood finally got him on a weak infield fly.

In the ninth inning, as the Rooters and the crowd chanted and swayed back and forth as one, Washington almost broke through again. Laporte hit a hard shot past Gardner at third for a single, and then Moran dropped a bunt, sacrificing him to second. All at once the singing and chanting stopped, and for the first time all game the crowd fell silent, knowing a hit would tie the game, as Moeller stepped to the plate.

All eyes were on Joe Wood, and Wood went with his best, a fastball. For the first time all game it was possible to hear the sound as it smacked into Hick Cady's mitt, but the pitch missed the plate for a ball. Fastballs had gotten Wood this far in his career, and at this moment there was no other thought in his mind besides reaching back and throwing as hard as he could, his wind-up starting as soon as Cady flashed the sign. Moeller fouled off three straight, but on the fourth pitch the crowd again heard the ball collide with Cady's mitt. Moeller shuddered, the bat frozen to his shoulder, and umpire Tommy Connolly's right arm shot up in the air. Moeller spun away from the plate, out on strikes.

Now the crowd could taste it, and so could Wood, and Cady hardly had to put a sign down. Ainsmith topped the first pitch he saw, then swung through another. With the count 0-2, he watched one pass, and this time the umpire's arm stayed at his side, making the count 1-2.

Then, for the 121st time in the game, Wood toed the rubber, took the sign, and threw. Ainsmith waved at the ball, Cady's mitt caught the sound, and the catcher rose from his crouch in triumph as Connolly called Ainsmith out. Jake Stahl raced to embrace Wood, and Fenway Park burst open like a fat man loosening his belt after a big meal. The crowd poured onto the field, and in seconds Wood was enveloped as he was half-carried and half-pushed by his teammates toward the Boston dugout.

With his thirtieth victory—making him an ungodly 30-4 for the season—and his fourteenth win in a row, Wood came away with Johnson's AL record of sixteen straight wins still within reach. In every way the game had lived up to its billing. Johnson had given up only five hits while throwing 103 pitches, including throws to first, and Wood had thrown 121 pitches while giving up six hits, but Boston's finest had struck out nine to Johnson's five, and Johnson's record fell to 29-10. The *Washington Post's* Joe Jackson wrote that "the result proved nothing save that luck broke with Wood," and even *Sporting Life* offered that "Johnson . . . pitched the best game," but no one in Boston agreed. "The challenger," wrote Mel Webb, "went down before the challenged." "All hail to Joe Wood," wrote Shannon, "uncrowned king of American League pitchers!"

WOOD BETTER MAN YESTERDAY
Johnson Not Quite His Equal—Their Match One That Will Never Be Forgotten

As the throng of happy fans stayed on the field and celebrated, and Joe Wood finally let a smile escape from his lips in the clubhouse, James McAleer, Robert McRoy, and John I. Taylor surveyed the mob that had filled every nook and cranny of the ballpark. Looking around, they could not help but share the same thoughts. After smiling for a moment at both the result of the game and the amount of money they had earned over the preceding one hour and forty minutes, each man next thought ahead to the World's Series. Watching the mayhem on the field and the logjams in the aisles and in front of each exit, they surely wondered how precisely they were going to accommodate the crowds that were certain to come in October. "Oh," wrote Tim Murnane a few days later, "for a ballpark large enough to accommodate all the people who would gladly pay double to see the World's Series."

Fenway Park, less than a season old, was already too small.

◆ 10 ◆

Giants on the Horizon

Baseball fans who visit Fenway Park next week to see the new
American League Champions perform will be surprised at the
changes that have been made since the team went away . . . The
work is being rushed and, according to the contractors, will be
finished a few days previous to the opening game of the big series.

—*Boston Globe*

THE LIGHTS WERE on late in Red Sox offices on the evening of September 6. As Robert McRoy supervised the counting of receipts following Wood's victory over Johnson he could hardly believe it. Never before in the history of the Red Sox had a single game, or a single series, been more lucrative. The first-place Red Sox and Wood's winning streak were the reasons, of course, but the mechanism was Fenway Park. Crowds in excess of 30,000 fans had turned out in the past at the Huntington Avenue Grounds, but with fewer than 2,500 higher-priced grandstand seats and so many twenty-five-cent admissions, even when the outfield was ringed with people and the stands were sagging beneath the weight of the crowd, it was impossible to take in more than $8,000 or $9,000 for a single game.

Not so at Fenway Park, where admission to the grandstand, which held nearly fifteen thousand fans when one included standing-room seats, ranged from seventy-five cents for unreserved seats to $1.25 for reserved seats in the first ten rows and $1.50 for a box seat. Another eight thousand fans paid fifty cents to sit in the pavilion. The only twenty-five-cent tickets were those in the bleachers and an unknown number of standing-room seats elsewhere in the park. Only God and Robert McRoy knew what everyone else had paid to stand on the field, for there were certainly some who had paid full price for a seat elsewhere but simply couldn't get to their seat or chose not to.

After the series finale on Saturday, which the Red Sox lost 5–1 before a crowd of twenty thousand, local newspapers tried to guess just how much the Red Sox took in, both for the entire series and for the Wood-Johnson contest. The Red Sox never released an official tally of receipts, but it is safe to conclude that, on September 6 alone, the club must have taken in, conservatively speaking, at least $15,000 and perhaps as much as $20,000, while receipts for the other three games of the series probably totaled more than $10,000 for each contest. In less than a week the Red Sox grossed around $50,000, nearly the cost of their player contracts for the entire season. Clark Griffith left Boston with Washington's share of the gate, a hefty check for almost $20,000. He was delighted and gave Walter Johnson an extra $500 for his role in bringing out the crowd.

President McAleer was not so generous with Joe Wood, who found nothing extra in his pay envelope, but a few days later, when speaking of Wood, McAleer said, "When my boys make good I am willing to pay the money." He was referring to Wood's next contract, and in 1913 Wood's salary would indeed more than double, to $7,500. For the present, however, the best pitcher in baseball was also one of the best bargains in the game.

As the Red Sox players made their way to Chicago for an extended road trip that would take them away from Fenway Park for nearly three weeks, McAleer, McRoy, and John I. Taylor pondered both their fortune and their good fortune. The Giants may have been on the horizon, but so were some gigantic crowds—and some enormous challenges. All three men knew that something had to be done, and quickly, to maximize their profits during the World's Series. As the Washington series had made abundantly clear, Red Sox fans were already half-mad with excitement. Even at inflated World's Series prices, Boston fans could fill Fenway Park on their own. But with New York only a few hours away by train, thousands of Giants fans were certain to make the trek to Fenway Park, and the Red Sox had to reserve some seats for them as well. A certain number of tickets had to be made available to both leagues, other AL and NL teams, the players of both teams and their families, former players, club employees, local VIPs like the Royal Rooters, club vendors and advertisers, city, state, and county politicians, the archdiocese . . . the list went on and on and on.

The solution was obvious. Several weeks before, they had called on architect James E. McLaughlin and contractor Charles Logue and asked both to prepare plans to accommodate larger crowds. Now the men had a little less than three weeks to make Fenway Park bigger.

No one was more familiar with the park than McLaughlin, and during the course of his design of Fenway Park he had, at various times, already created drawings that included seats in the two most obvious locations—the empty space between the grandstand and the left-field wall and the open space in right field between the pavilion and the center-field bleachers. The former area, which McLaughlin dubbed "the Third Base Stand," could provide seating for as many as another 5,000 fans, while the latter area could hold 4,500. It was a relatively easy process for McLaughlin to resurrect his basic plans for seating in these areas (see illustrations 9 and 11).

The Red Sox, in fact, had always hoped to add concrete stands along the left-field line but had put those plans on hold in the event that they gained possession of the small wedge of land adjacent to the park on Brookline Avenue. It had been for sale, but the price was too dear for McAleer and Taylor, and it had fallen into the hands of investors. All around Fenway Park, in fact, investors were suddenly snatching up property that a year or so earlier had gone wanting.

An extra 9,500 seats, however, still wasn't enough. McAleer and Taylor directed McLaughlin to maximize seating throughout the facility, and McLaughlin came up with a plan almost overnight. In addition to seats along the third-base line and in right, he designed accommodations for another 1,200 fans in seven rows of bleacher seats on Duffy's Cliff. And since the base of both the center-field bleachers and the new right-field bleachers stopped about five or six feet above the field, there was room to create three new rows of seats for another 1,200 fans that skirted the edge of the field from the center-field end of the left-field wall in front of the center-field bleachers to nearly all the way around to the grandstand. Roughly speaking, these seats

stretched from in front of section 34 of the bleachers today to the foot
of the grandstand in front of section 8. McLaughlin also created two
additional rows of box seats in foul territory wrapping from the near
end of the new third-base stands, around behind home plate to the
pavilion in right field, from section 8 to section 30 of the grandstand
today, a total of 122 boxes that could accommodate another 900 fans.
The end result was seating for a total of 11,600 fans, bringing the seating capacity of Fenway Park to 36,100—38,600 when one included
standing-room space at the back of the grandstand.

All these new seats would, of course, impinge upon the field. In
left field the seats required the construction of a low plank fence in
front of Duffy's Cliff, which removed both the Cliff and the left-field
wall from play and dramatically reduced the distance needed to hit a
ball over the fence in left field. In this new configuration a home run
would now presumably only have to cross the new, much lower, and
much closer barricade in front of the wall, and not the full height of
the wall and cliff itself, which was approximately thirty-five feet.

The new seats in center field had a similar impact: the addition of
benches and a fence in front of the bleachers cut the distance to the
stands by some twenty or twenty-five feet. In right field the change
was even more dramatic. The front edge of the new grandstand more
or less followed the path of the preexisting fence, but three new rows
of seats that sat directly behind a low fence cut from the center-field
bleachers to the right-field pavilion, roughly from section 42 to section 8 today (cutting off the right-field "belly"). This left an open space
some thirty feet wide between the right-field seats and the fence and
drastically cut the distance from home plate to right field from nearly
400 feet at its farthest point to only about 360 feet, and the distance
was much closer as the fence angled toward the line. There the impact
was even more striking. According to McLaughlin's original design,
the seats along the right-field line were supposed to run in front of the
pavilion, intruding onto the field and making the distance down the
line far shorter than left field—certainly less than 300 feet, and probably only about 270 or 280 feet from home plate. But in the end a portion of this final stretch of seats would not be built, and the distance
down the right-field line at the foul line would not be affected.

One section of the new fence included a feature that today's fan would recognize as unique to Fenway Park. The stockade fence in dead center field, presumably because it was part of the hitter's background, was painted green, the first time that color scheme was used in Fenway. The rest of the fence that ran from center to right was not only unpainted but also not impenetrable. The bottom eighteen inches or so of the fence was made of horizontal plank stockade fencing, but the rest of the fence was wide open, topped only by a rail. Balls that rolled to the fence would be stopped by the planks, but those that bounced higher than eighteen inches, unless they ricocheted off the top rail, could go through or over the fence.

Foul territory behind home plate and the infield at the foot of the existing stands was similarly decreased to accommodate the installation of the two new rows of box seats, a total of 122 boxes averaging eight seats per box. These seats were roughly equivalent to the dugout box seats that were added in 2003. The distance from fair territory to the stands had originally been some sixty feet, but the addition of the new seats cut that distance to less than fifty feet. All told, the new arrangement of seats for the World's Series cut the amount of fair territory in Fenway Park by more than 10 percent, and foul territory even more than that. These new accommodations created the most dramatic set of changes in the history of Fenway Park, alterations that helped hitters at the expense of pitchers. Fenway Park would be transformed from a facility that had been nominally a pitcher's park to one significantly more accommodating of offense. This change did not necessarily work to the advantage of the 1912 Red Sox, but that was not a concern. *Everything* was secondary to profit.

There was not enough time to build any of these new seating areas in concrete and steel. The decision was made to turn back the clock and build the new stands, like the existing right-field pavilion, out of wood—plain white pine, the cheapest and most abundant material available. And just as the center-field bleachers rested on wood piers, so would the new stands along the third-base line and in right field, to ensure that the work was completed by the time the Red Sox returned from their road trip. Even though building with pine would create a significant fire hazard and render the stands less than perma nent, this would be no ad hoc construction project. Design loads and other engineering specifications for such structures were published and readily available, and McLaughlin had already done similar work in designing the right-field pavilion. He had little more to do than adapt his earlier plans to scale. As soon as the Red Sox went on the road the work began almost immediately.

That was where Charles Logue and his crews of carpenters and laborers came in. While Boston's train chugged its way toward Chicago, surveyors got to work immediately laying out foundations and driving stakes all over the field to position the new stands. Logue brought stationary, fuel-powered ripsaws, crosscut saws, and power boring machines on-site. As soon as the first of hundreds of truckloads of lumber were delivered to the park, dozens and dozens of carpenters and laborers got to work. For the next two and a half weeks the sounds of saws and hammers echoed through the Fenway almost nonstop and the smell of sawdust was omnipresent.

As work went on in every corner of the ballpark Kelley and the grounds crew were charged with readying the field for the postseason. Most of their work was devoted to the infield, where they dug up the pitcher's box and replaced the soil. With cooler weather on the horizon, they would finally have an opportunity to spend some time repairing Kelley's precious turf. As one report stated, "New dirt [was] added and rolled out hard so that the infield will resemble a billiard table in regard to smoothness."

The result would change Fenway forever. Although the new stands, made of wood, were not technically "permanent structures"—the life span of untreated pine is generally no more than a decade—the new third-base stands along the left-field line and the right-field bleachers would remain in place for many years after the 1912 World's Series. The third-base stands would eventually burn in 1926, but the right-field bleachers, though getting more rickety by the year, even as portions were repaired, would remain in place until the 1933–34 reconstruction. These adaptations for the World's Series of 1912 locked into place Fenway Park's now-familiar angular profile of quirky nooks and crannies that have since proven so popular and given the park so much of its character. Subsequent creation and renovation of field-level seating, bleachers, and grandstands, both during the 1933–34 reconstruction and after, has done little more than duplicate or enhance the adaptations first made to accommodate the 1912 World's Series.

The Red Sox probably would have added stands in right and along the left-field line at some point anyway, but had the work not been rushed to be completed in time for the World's Series, it is likely that the stands would have been built in concrete and steel and according to a more unified design. It is doubtful that many of the irregularities that fans have since grown to appreciate and consider an essential part of Fenway's character would have been created.

While the Red Sox played in the West, they were doing more than just playing out the string. There was still Joe Wood's winning streak to play for, the chance to officially clinch the pennant and win one hundred games, plus the opportunity to gain a psychological edge over the Giants. Even so, Stahl, for the first time all year, began to lift his foot from the accelerator. Young pitcher Ben Van Dyke was added to the squad and would soon receive a tryout. Players who normally would have played through minor injuries or maladies now received the occasional day off as Stahl recognized the importance of keeping everyone healthy.

But there would be no rest for Joe Wood, at least not until he either set the record or blew his arm out trying. He wanted the mark and took the mound next with only three days' rest against Chicago. Although he faded badly at the end and had to turn the game over to Charley Hall in the ninth after giving up two hits and not recording an out, he nonetheless escaped with a 5–4 win, his fifteenth in a row.

The Red Sox were on a roll, and their subsequent sweep of the White Sox gave them thirteen wins in their last fourteen games. Only once since early June had they lost as many as two games in a row. All of a sudden their lead over the rest of the league was approaching fifteen games.

That lead increased in St. Louis, although the Sox finally dropped a game when they lost the front end of a doubleheader to the Browns on September 15, but Wood continued his mastery over the Browns with a 2–1 win in game 2, tying Johnson's AL mark with his sixteenth win in a row, eliminating Washington from the pennant chase, and virtually clinching a tie for the pennant for Boston.

The record was in sight, but Wood was exhausted. He looked gaunt, and one report noted that he had "a slight case of tonsillitis and is far from feeling right." Another noted that he had to work "uncommonly hard" to beat the Browns and that by the end of the game "his uniform was as wet as if he had been dipped in a river."

With the Red Sox one victory—or one loss by the Athletics—away from clinching the pennant, Stahl began making tangible plans for the Giants. The Sox traveled to Cleveland on September 16, and after they dropped a doubleheader to start the series Stahl sent both Charlie Wagner and Bill Carrigan, the vaunted "Board of Strategy," back to Boston. He told reporters that neither man would play until the Sox returned home, presumably to allow each to rest up for the postseason.

But there may have been more to it than that. Wagner had been fighting some undisclosed illness for the previous week, and Stahl had begun to use Cady more and more often. With Wagner and Carrigan suddenly riding the pine together, and given what would transpire both later in the 1912 season and in 1913, Stahl might have felt that the two were beginning to undermine his authority. Sending both men back to Boston was a convenient excuse to get them out of the way. Besides, the Giants were playing in New York. He had Carrigan and Wagner make a side trip to New York to scout the opposition.

After a day of rain the Sox dropped a second doubleheader to Cleveland on September 19, the first time all year they had lost as many as four in a row. It hardly mattered. As the Sox were watching the rain fall the White Sox beat Philadelphia to deliver the pennant to Boston.

The Sox were in their hotel when they got the news. While the players toasted one another long into the night, Stahl and McAleer met with the press and delivered the expected platitudes, Stahl saying, "The boys worked together as one family"—albeit a somewhat dysfunctional one, given the ongoing rift between the Knights and the Masons. He then stated the obvious when he added, "We have never slumped and we have never had any sensational winning streak, but have just gone ahead and won a majority of our games." He emphasized the fact that over the next week or ten days he planned to get everyone some rest. After the Sox returned to Boston some players, like Larry Gardner, would even be allowed to leave the club and visit family in Vermont. McAleer was even more obvious, saying, "We had the ballplayers and without the men we couldn't have pulled through." Apart from these statements, the team kept the party private, knowing that when the Sox returned to Boston there would be a more public celebration.

The only player unable to relax and enjoy the moment was Joe Wood. He had a bad cold, and Murnane noted that while "the other players looked bright and happy after they had won the championship . . . Joe was still under a strain, which began at Boston when he gave Walter Johnson his great whitewash." His pursuit of the record was beginning to weigh on him, and Stahl did not pitch him in Cleveland, giving his right arm an extra day of rest, both to help him reach the record and to give him a break before the postseason. With as many as three more games left to pitch before the end of the regular season, Wood had his eyes on Rube Marquard's major league record of nineteen consecutive victories. He also had a shot at winning thirty-five games, which would have been third-best in AL history at the time, behind Jack Chesbro's forty-one wins in 1904 and Ed Walsh's forty in 1908.

The Sox took a steamship across Lake Erie from Cleveland to Detroit on the morning of September 20 for the series with the Tigers. It was a rough crossing, and when they staggered down the gangplank just a few hours before the game few felt much like playing.

It showed. Although Wood seemed fine at the start and retired the first eight men he faced, with two out and none on in the third inning, as Charles Young wrote in the *Post*, Wood suddenly "went wrong." He began both to pitch and behave like a rank amateur.

He first walked the pitcher, Bill "Tex" Covington. Losing the pitcher to a walk, particularly a pitcher like Covington, enraged Wood, and he followed by walking leadoff hitter Donie Bush.

He didn't blame himself—he blamed home plate umpire Silk O'Loughlin. Feeling that he was being squeezed on his drop ball, Wood began yelling at O'Loughlin from the mound, loudly berating the umpire, telling him the calls were the "rawest deal" he had ever received. The reporters in the press box heard every word, for there were only about three thousand spectators at the game. Red Corriden stepped in next, and Wood almost lobbed a pitch toward the plate, trying to throw the ball down the middle. Corriden's bat stayed on his shoulder, O'Loughlin's hand stayed down at his side, and now the bases were loaded.

With each additional pitch he threw, Wood become more enraged. He was losing it, and he knew it. When the dangerous Sam Crawford came up, he tried pitching for real again, but Crawford walked as well—Wood's fourth consecutive base on balls—and Covington strolled home.

Now Ty Cobb was at bat, and Wood worked him carefully. Cobb finally lofted a towering fly to short left as the Detroit base runners, with two outs, went tearing around the bases. Marty Krug, filling in for Wagner, went back on the ball but demonstrated why he was only a utility man. He dropped it, and two more men scored to put Wood down 3–0.

The game, he knew, was lost, and so was the record. Now Wood let go, raging at his own players, steam coming out of his ears and bitterness streaming off his tongue. At first base that was all Ty Cobb needed to see. There was no one in the game better at taking advantage of a player who had lost his cool.

As Wood toed the rubber Cobb danced off first, feinting toward second again and again. A flustered Wood threw to first base over and over, a little harder each time, getting more distracted and angrier by the second. When Cobb finally took off Wood was so disconcerted that he never even threw the ball but watched helplessly as Cobb took second unimpeded.

Wood managed to get the third out, but the damage was done. And even though Boston fought back to take a 4–3 lead in the fifth, the Red Sox played indifferently in the field and gave the runs right back when both Engle and Speaker made errors. Wood hung in for the entire game, but his winning streak ended at sixteen games. The defeat was his first since July 4 and only his fifth of the year.

NO RECORD FOR WOOD

First Beating In 78 Days
Four Straight Passes Aid In His Undoing

Wood himself didn't have much to say after the 6–4 loss, but Stahl didn't pull any punches. "Defeat was the best thing that could come to Wood," he said. Then, alluding to the pitcher's demeanor during the game, he added dismissively, "Another week of thinking about his pitching record and he would be fit for a nurse." Now perhaps Wood could finally focus on getting healthy for the World's Series.

All the Red Sox wanted to do was go home, but they had one more game to play in Detroit. After the debacle the previous day Stahl went with his usual lineup, minus Wagner and Carrigan. The Sox responded by playing a tight game and entered the eighth inning leading 11–2.

Detroit's Donie Bush led off the inning with a hot smash down the third-base line. Larry Gardner dove for the ball, something he seemed to do nearly every game. Over the course of the season the Vermont native had earned a reputation as one of the best third basemen in the league, the near-equal to Philadelphia's Frank "Home Run" Baker.

In fact, Gardner was also one of the best players on the Red Sox team. Although Wood, Speaker, Lewis, Hooper, Wagner, and even Carrigan all received more press and history, for some reason, has since all but ignored him, Gardner was more than just a tenor in the Red Sox Quartet. He hit fifth in the Boston batting order and was one of the most consistent performers on the team. In fact, the decision to move him permanently to third base was one of the keys to Boston's success. Rather quietly, he had emerged as Boston's best power threat and best base runner after Speaker. Despite hitting behind Duffy Lewis, who led the club in RBIs, Gardner was the next-best run producer on the team. As Paul Shannon wrote, "Gardner has been Boston's man with the 'cleanup wallop,' having broken up more games and done more timely hitting this season than any man on Jake Stahl's team." Based on his performance, Gardner, not Lewis, probably should have been hitting fourth in the batting order.

But his glove had proven to be the real revelation. Gardner had come up as a second baseman, and although he had a strong arm, while playing second he seemed stiff and slow and had trouble turning the double play. When he was transferred to third, Gardner's quick first step, a skill he had gained from hours playing hockey as a boy and in the off-season, gave him surprising range. Despite the diminutive size of baseball gloves at the time, Gardner was also adept at catching the ball one-handed, stabbing line drives and hot ground balls cleanly with only his glove hand—something few other infielders could do—and leading Tim Murnane to note later that "no man ever had a better left hand." Although Gardner is not quite in the class of Red Sox Hall of Fame third basemen Jimmie Collins and Wade Boggs, for a time he was nearly their equal.

Gardner was from Enosburg Falls, Vermont, then a prosperous dairy farming community on the Missisquoi River in northwestern Vermont, a region that supplied milk to New York and Boston. The son of a Quebec immigrant and an American-born mother, he had captained his high school team, pitching them to the state championship. After a year playing semipro ball in and around Enosburg Falls, he had gone on to attend the University of Vermont, where he majored in chemistry and was a teammate of Ray Collins.

Playing third base, shortstop, and a little outfield, Gardner swung the bat from the left side, a trait he developed while playing hockey. Even today most hockey players, particularly Canadian hockey players, tend to use a hockey stick left-handed, a practice that often translates into swinging a baseball bat from the same side. He was a star at the University of Vermont and after the 1908 season left college one year early to sign with the Red Sox, who farmed him out to Lynn for most of the 1908 season. He reached the Red Sox for good in 1909 and finally became more or less a regular in 1911.

But in 1912 he became a star. When he dove for Donie Bush's hard ground ball his teammates and the scribes in the press box thought little of it, for they had grown accustomed to seeing Gardner make such plays. But this time, either Gardner slightly misjudged the ball or, more likely, it took a bad hop. Instead of finding the ball with his glove, then springing to his feet and throwing the runner out, Gardner was struck on his bare right hand when the ball skipped back on him.

His little finger snapped at the joint. Although the bone was not broken, the joint was dislocated, and the bone was jutting through the skin, leaving the top half of his little finger at nearly a ninety-degree angle. As Gardner doubled over in pain, Stahl and the Red Sox rushed to his side.

He left the game immediately. A physician who was called to the ballpark snapped the painful dislocated joint back in place and dressed the wound, placing the finger in a splint and taping it to

Gardner's ring finger to hold it in place. The Sox went on to win the contest, 11–4, but the return trip to Boston was less joyous than they had envisioned.

Gardner's availability for the World's Series was suddenly in doubt. His injury had less than two weeks to heal, if it did at all. And if Gardner, who had played almost every inning of every game thus far, could not play, the Red Sox would have no choice but to insert Clyde Engle into the lineup. Engle was a player with no bat, no glove, no power, no speed on the bases, and no range whatsoever in the field, and thus could hurt the Red Sox in nearly every way possible. Every man on the team knew that the loss of Gardner could tip the balance in the World's Series.

GARDNER'S INJURY EVENS THE ODDS

Still, by the time the Red Sox made it back to Boston on the afternoon of September 23, the city was in a mood to celebrate the pennant and worry about the World's Series later. The Sox were scheduled to arrive at South Station at 2:55 p.m., but the train was an hour late. By the time it crept up track 13, the band in the train shed was running out of breath and the crowd of well-wishers, which had swelled to several thousand, was running out of patience. To prevent people from being crushed the police had even spread a rumor that the players would actually disembark at Dewey Square, sending part of the mob tearing that direction.

To avoid the massive crowd the players snuck out the baggage car and were pushed, shoved, and lifted into a line of waiting automobiles—all except Larry Gardner, who was caught in the mob until a few fans recognized him because of his bandaged hand and helped him join his teammates. Led by Honey Fitz Fitzgerald and a host of Royal Rooters, including the ubiquitous Nuf Ced, the Red Sox paraded to Boston Common. It was, noted the *Post* accurately, "a reception such as few Presidents have received." All the way up Summer Street to Washington Street a solid bank of humanity clogged the way. Estimated to be as large as two hundred thousand, the crowd made downtown Boston resemble lower Manhattan some fifteen years later when that city welcomed Lindbergh after he flew the Atlantic. It took nearly an hour for the entourage to inch through the horde to Boston Common, where another crowd of ten thousand fans already occupied every available space, boys hanging off streetlights and filling the trees like so many starlings. Once they arrived, Stahl and many of the players spoke, or tried to, through a megaphone, but few could hear a word. Nevertheless, when Joe Wood was introduced and gave a small wave, "the crowd went simply crazy." The World's Series was less than two weeks off, and Boston was mad with anticipation, everyone desperate for a ticket.

That was a problem, for tickets were not yet available. After the Giants had refused to play the Red Sox in the World's Series after the 1904 season, the American and National Leagues had reached an agreement that required their champions to meet after the end of the season. But that was as far as it went. The specific schedule and details of the Series were subject to negotiation. A few days earlier the National Commission, which consisted of Ban Johnson, NL president Thomas Lynch, and commission president August Herrmann, the owner of the Cincinnati Reds, announced that they would meet at the country home of Giants owner John Brush in Pelham, New York, with representatives of the Giants and the Red Sox to discuss plans for the Series. When the Red Sox arrived back in Boston, McAleer was preparing to leave for the meeting.

As the Red Sox discovered when they went to the ballpark the following day, in their absence McAleer and the rest of the organization had been busy. Fenway Park was almost unrecognizable.

Work had gone on in all corners of the park, and the air smelled not of peanuts and cigars but of sawdust and pine sap. The new third-base stands and right-field bleachers were rising and well on their way to being completed. Seven rows of bleacher seats now covered Duffy's Cliff, two new rows of box seats intruded onto the field at the foot of the grandstand, and a low, plain wood fence fronted three rows of seats that encircled the outfield. For the first time in its history, Fenway Park was fully enclosed, the field completely surrounded by grandstands or bleacher seats. The field was unquestionably smaller, and felt smaller still, but during the four-game series against the Yankees its shrunken size had little impact on the game. Work slowed while the two clubs played—no one wanted to watch a game to the accompaniment of saws and hammers—but there was no longer any doubt that the field would be ready for the World's Series.

McAleer and McRoy left for New York at midnight on September 25 to meet with the National Commission. By the time they returned to Boston two days later, plans were complete. Boston had lost two coin tosses—heads to the Giants' tails—giving New York both home-field advantage and their preferred starting date of October 8 (the Red Sox had preferred October 7). Two umpires from each league were selected to work the Series, and the schedule was set. Beginning on October 8, the Series would be played on consecutive days, not including Sunday, October 13. If all seven games were played and it did not rain, the Series, if played to its full complement of games, would conclude on October 15. Owing to the proximity of Boston and New York, the site of the Series would alternate for each game, beginning with game 1 in New York. Each contest would start at 2:00 p.m., leaving plenty of time to get the game in before darkness. To ensure that there would be no repeat of the crowded conditions at Fenway Park during the confrontation between Joe Wood and Walter Johnson, the National Commission decided that "spectators will not be permitted to encroach or stand on the playing field at any point." The erection of temporary stands, like those already going up in Boston, was permitted. All such seats had to be fronted "with a strong three-foot railing," they could "not be less than 235 feet" away from home plate in left and right field, and the center-field seats could "not be less than 275 feet from home plate."

But as would soon become clear, the players themselves had not been consulted concerning any facet of the Series whatsoever. A fledgling players' association had just been formed but was still impotent, and it had not been called upon to represent their interests. Even if it had been, the men who owned baseball were loath to give the players any role in the management of the game. The owners were the kings and the players lowly serfs, an arrangement the kings rather enjoyed.

Other decisions made in regard to the schedule, the distribution of receipts, and ticket sales would also have an impact on the Series in ways no one could yet imagine.

First, the National Commission considered the impact of a post-

poned game on the schedule; it decided that "a scheduled game, postponed for legal cause, called before it becomes a regulation game or
terminating with the score tied, shall . . . be played on the grounds for
which it was scheduled." Second, the commission decided that "the
players' pool of receipts shall be restricted to 60 percent of the receipts of the first four games after the deduction of the commission's
ten percent . . . *regardless of whether one or more of such games ends in
a tie.*"

The main reason for the meeting with the National Commission,
however, was to discuss the sale and distribution of tickets. One year
before, tickets for games in both New York and Philadelphia had been
sold directly to speculators in enormous blocks and then resold to the
public by scalpers at exorbitant prices. The problem had been most
pronounced in New York, and Ban Johnson had even called for the
expulsion of the Giants from the major leagues over the issue. That
didn't happen, but the National Commission was determined not to
run into the same problem in 1912. The commission—or at least the
two-thirds of the commission that did not include Ban Johnson—
wanted to handle ticket sales itself.

Johnson thought differently—the Red Sox, after all, had already
started the process of ticket distribution by asking fans to produce
rain checks to prove they were true followers of the club. At length,
the commission decided that it would handle ticket sales for all games
at the Polo Grounds, but would buckle to Johnson's will and allow
the Red Sox to distribute and price their tickets as they saw fit. Commission president August Herrmann announced that since Robert
McRoy "has had experience in several World's Series, the Commission could not have a better man in charge." But as everyone would
soon learn, McRoy's World's Series experience overseeing ticket arrangements as Ban Johnson's secretary while sitting at his side was
quite a bit different from supervising the sale of nearly one hundred
thousand tickets from the offices of Fenway Park. That brash statement of support would soon be proven wrong.

For the time being, however, fans in both cities were delighted to
learn that they could finally start getting tickets in their hands. In
New York only box seats and some eight thousand reserved grandstand seats would be sold in advance, with an allowance of two seats

per purchaser for each game. The remaining tickets, nearly thirty thousand per game, would be sold only on the day of the game, and the purchaser would be required to enter the park immediately.

In Boston, however, Robert McRoy came up with a much more complicated scheme. First, the Red Sox, like the Giants, changed the pricing scheme throughout their home park. Box seats were priced at $5 per game; grandstand reserved seats at $3; the new third-base stand at $2; the pavilion, right-field bleachers, and the Duffy's Cliff and outfield seats at $1; and the center-field bleachers at fifty cents. Although the tickets were pricier than during the regular season, at a time when the average wage was $20 a week, gas cost seven cents a gallon, and steak sold for twenty-three cents a pound, tickets were not out of reach for most fans. McRoy planned to sell all reserved seats in advance. That now included not only the box seats and the entire grandstand but the new third-base stand and the three rows of $1 seats that skirted the edge of the field. The remaining seats would be sold on the day of the game, but McRoy also announced, somewhat cryptically, that he would "consider" mail applications, whatever that meant. The end result was that for the World's Series the Red Sox would be selling more tickets than ever before at new prices in an entirely new way. Although the new system would increase the potential receipts from a single game to about $70,000, more than three times the amount for a sellout during the regular season, in retrospect it almost ensured that things would get screwed up. But the potential for profit caused them to overlook the possibility of problems.

For now, Boston fans were just glad to have everything worked out so they could finally make some plans for the Series. The Red Sox, with a victory over the Yankees, earned win number one hundred for the season behind Joe Wood's two-hitter, a game that seemed to answer any concerns over the condition of his arm. The Sox were clearly ready to play out the string, as were the Giants, who finally crawled over the line themselves on September 26 and clinched the pennant everyone had ceded to them in June. The Red Sox left for their final road trip to Washington and Philadelphia on September 27 and would not return to Boston until after the season ended in Philadelphia on October 5. Unlike other World's Series participants, who often played an exhibition or two against a select squad of all-stars before "the Fall Classic," the Sox planned to work out privately before heading to New York.

The World's Series was more than a week off, but the Giants, a ball club that was as much about reputation as talent, already loomed over the proceedings. Given their schizophrenic performance during the 1912 season—playing the first half as if they were the greatest team ever to don a uniform and the second half as if sleepwalking—no one was quite certain how they would perform.

In many ways—on paper and based on recent performance, for example—the Red Sox appeared to be the stronger club, though not by much: Boston was the narrow favorite among the gamblers and sporting men who put money behind their opinion. For example, entertainer George M. Cohan, a Giants fan, was nevertheless already on record as having put down $10,000 on the Sox. New York's performance in recent weeks had done little to move the odds, for as the *Globe* noted in late September, the Giants were "not hitting, and every fan realizes it is a bad thing for a team to go into a post season series while the men are suffering from a batting slump. In the second place, the slab work of Mathewson and Marquard did not look good to observant fans." There were rumors, in fact, that Marquard's second-half slump was due to personal problems. Earlier in the season he had been carrying on with a beautiful young actress, Shirley Kellogg. He had slumped, as sportswriter Otto Flotto noted, because "he was thrown down by Shirley Kellogg, an actress who had promised to marry him. The rube took this so to heart that his mind was always a thousand miles removed from his work."

Many observers viewed Joe Wood as the difference maker. Walter Johnson, who more than any other man knew what it was like to pitch against Wood, favored Boston, calling the Boston pitcher "the gamest twirler I ever tackled in a game that was for blood." Grantland Rice, the dean of American sportswriters, wrote on the eve of the Series that Wood gave Boston the edge because "Wood on form might master and overpower any man McGraw sent against him . . . look for Wood to win the deciding game at the end." These words would prove prescient.

Most other "impartial" sportswriters—that is, those who did not work for New York or Boston papers, such as Jacob Morse of *Base-*

ball magazine, Flotto of the *Denver Post,* H. G. Salinger of the *Detroit News,* and W. A. Phelon of the *Cincinnati Times,* and others—agreed with Rice. Hugh Fullerton, whose syndicated column appeared nationwide, was perhaps the most notable of these men. He created a firestorm in New York, where his work appeared in the *Times,* when he wrote before the Series that "Boston has a better team, playing better ball and with a better system than New York . . . Boston excels New York individually in seven of nine positions." Fullerton gave the Giants the edge only with Larry Doyle at second and with catcher Chief Meyers. "Mark this," concluded Fullerton. "[The] New York team is not a 'game' club. From here it looks all Boston." New York fans howled, and the staid *Times* reprinted more than a dozen letters from outraged Giants fans, one of whom asked, "If Mr. Fullerton is being hired by the Red Sox in order to increase the odds against the Giants and make them lose courage, why doesn't he come out and say so?"

Their complaints were not without merit. Since the birth of the franchise as the New York Gothams, the history of the New York team had been drawn in brash, bold strokes. Their nickname allegedly dated back to their first championship in 1888 when owner-manager Jim Mutrie was so overcome with joy and excitement that he blurted out, "My Big Fellows! My Giants! We *are* the People!" In fact, the name had been in use since 1885, but the Giants, as their name inferred, were the kind of team that was easy to mythologize. That was one reason the Giants were perhaps the most representative club of the era, epitomizing baseball at the turn of the century, and for the first decade or so after, in their personality, their style of play, their role in the game, and the personalities they put on the field.

Even after factoring in their second-half struggles, it was hard to dismiss a team that at one point had been 56-13 on the season and that had a starting pitcher, in Rube Marquard, who had won nineteen games in a row, and a spitballer, Jeff Tesreau, who as a rookie in 1912 had emerged over the last half of the season and blossomed into New York's most dependable starting pitcher. He had won seventeen games and was the hottest pitcher on either team, winning eight games in September, including seven in a row and a no-hitter against Philadelphia on September 6.

The Red Sox, knowing full well what they were up against, had their own spitball ace, Buck O'Brien, throw batting practice over the final weeks of the season so they could become accustomed to the offerings of Tesreau. Ironically, McAleer, as manager of the St. Louis Browns in 1909, had had the first crack at Tesreau when the Missouri native was still a teenager, but turned him down. Although the burly young pitcher had plenty of stuff, it wasn't until he added a spitball to his arsenal at the suggestion of Giants coach Wil Robinson that he reached the big leagues, leading the *New York Times* to comment that "Tesreau has curves which bend like barrel hoops and speed like lightning." Entering the Series, Giants fans looked at Tesreau the same way Red Sox fans looked at Wood.

And then there was Christy Mathewson. While not quite the pitcher who had won thirty-seven games in 1908, he still went 25-12 in 1912 and was still among the best six or eight pitchers in the game. Beyond that, Mathewson was also baseball's most respected and admired player. A graduate of Bucknell College, where he sang in the Glee Club, belonged to the literary society, and played football, Mathewson was held up as everything most other ballplayers were not after he reached the major leagues in 1900. He was educated, refined, polite, and fair-minded, a model of clean living and good sportsmanship, just the figure the game needed to slough off its reputation as a haven for the hard-living, the hard-drinking, and the foul-mouthed. Mathewson helped make the game of baseball more acceptable to the middle class—in short, he was the polar opposite of his manager, John McGraw. But beneath his squeaky clean veneer, Mathewson was no pushover. He was also a tough-as-nails competitor who used a fastball, impeccable control, and a pitch he called the "fadeaway"—a screwball—to dominate hitters. Connie Mack called him "the greatest pitcher who ever lived. He had knowledge, judgment, perfect control and form. It was wonderful to watch him pitch when he wasn't pitching against you."

Offensively, Giants captain and second baseman Larry Doyle, while no Speaker, would, like Speaker, win the Chalmers Award as the most valuable player in his league for 1912. Catcher Chief Meyers hit nearly .360 and was the only regular over the age of thirty. The rest of the Giants, like first baseman Fred Merkle, third baseman Buck Herzog, and outfielders Red Murray, Beals Becker, Fred Snodgrass, and Josh Devore, were almost mirror images of each other. They could all run, they all knew how to handle the bat and work pitchers for a walk, they were all adept at the hit-and-run, and they all knew how to put pressure on the opposition.

But the man who gave Giant backers the most confidence was their manager, John McGraw, the one they called "little Napoleon," who at 5'7" was still the biggest and baddest Giant of them all. "McGraw," said Giants coach Artie Latham of his boss, "eats gunpowder every morning for breakfast and washes it down with warm blood." While in truth he was not so raw and uncouth, he did not mind if others thought so as long as that perception helped to win ball games. And as long as McGraw was in the New York dugout, no one felt completely comfortable picking the Red Sox to win. Connie Mack, who managed in the major leagues for longer than anyone else, perhaps described him best when he once said, "There has been only one manager—and his name is McGraw."

"Pugnacious" is a word that seemed invented to describe the square-jawed manager. He viewed each game of baseball as a life-and-death struggle that demanded—even required—the use of every possible tactic, legal or not, to win.

He first made his mark as a third baseman with Baltimore of the American Association in 1882, and he remained with the team when they joined the National League a year later. If the Giants were the team of the turn of the century, the Orioles had certainly been the team of the 1890s. McGraw learned the game from its master, Orioles manager Ned Hanlon, and that meant not only learning how to do all the little things the game valued at the time—stealing, bunting, sacrificing—but all the things that players could get away with when there was only one umpire on the field. Hanlon's charges learned to cut the corners when running the bases, trip the opposition, and berate, intimidate, and sometimes even fight the arbiters. Hanlon taught McGraw how to get the most from his team, even if that meant occasionally using his fists on his own players, like some early-day Billy Martin. The comparison is appropriate, for McGraw's managerial genealogy, which begins with Hanlon, continues to the present. McGraw himself had many protégés, including Casey Stengel, who in turn mentored Billy Martin. In fact, McGraw's managerial line can be traced forward through the recently retired Cubs manager, the combative Lou Piniella.

McGraw was also fiercely loyal, but even more importantly, his teams won, which earned his players money, not an insignificant factor at a time when no contract was guaranteed, careers could end in an instant, and life spans were short. As a result, his players usually responded with the same hard-nosed attitude that McGraw exhibited himself. A McGraw team played hard, tough, aggressive baseball, intimidating the opposition before the game with their swagger and then wearing them down with their relentless pressure. Every base runner was a threat to steal, every slide was hard, and every challenge was answered in kind. Apart from his pitching staff, McGraw didn't need, or even particularly want, big stars on his team. It was not necessarily their raw talent but the way McGraw's team played that was the reason for their success.

The managers may have been the biggest difference between the two teams. Although Jake Stahl was respected, McGraw was revered, and while Stahl shared both some of the responsibility of the position and the credit, in some quarters that was seen as a sign of weakness. As one writer commented in *Sporting Life*, "In the important matter of experience New York has an advantage as Manager McGraw has been through the World's Series mill twice and his present team once, whereas it is an entirely new experience for manager Stahl and his team." To win the Series the Red Sox would not just have to defeat the Giants, which seemed plausible, but *beat McGraw.* That was a far more daunting challenge.

One other factor made the Giants a particularly formidable opponent for the Red Sox—the rebuilt Polo Grounds, New York's home park. *Baseball* magazine called it "the mightiest temple ever erected to the goddess of sport and the crowning achievement among notable structures devoted to baseball." It was easily the most intimidating place to play in the major leagues. Although the Red Sox had gained some experience playing there in their series with the Yankees a few weeks before, they had yet to play in the park when it was full of Giants partisans, who responded to McGraw's tactics like a lynch mob cheering on the hangman. Boston's Royal Rooters, with their bands and songs and whistles and drums, were cute, and when singing "Tessie" they could be particularly annoying (they had rightly received credit for unnerving the Pirates during the 1903 World's Series), but they were not menacing. The fans in the Polo Grounds treated the opposition like the Christians whenever the lion entered the arena.

The dimensions of the Polo Grounds also made it unlike any other field in baseball. It was essentially a horseshoe, only 277 feet down the line in left and 256 feet in right, but from where the line met the fence the stands angled away perpendicular to home plate, making the power alleys more than 400 feet from home. Over the course of the 1912 season the Red Sox had adapted and become adept at playing in the smaller confines of Fenway Park, now made even smaller by the addition of McLaughlin's extra seats. The Polo Grounds was a radically different place. Outfielders had to play somewhat deeper to cover the gaps, leaving plenty of room for hits to fall in, and the Giants used this to their advantage, scurrying around the bases with abandon. In a short series the Red Sox had precious little time to adjust—one misplayed ball or out-of-position outfielder could cost them the Series—and the possibility of playing as many as four games in the Polo Grounds, versus three at Fenway Park, did not make the task any easier.

And if all that were not intimidating enough, on September 28 a story out of Chicago was. Former Giants manager and sportswriter Horace Fogel was the frontman for a syndicate of investors and served as the president of the Philadelphia Phillies. He made a public accusation that the National League, through its umpires, had fixed the 1912 pennant race to ensure that the Giants would reach the World's Series.

"Go among the players of the other teams," he challenged, "and see how quick they will tell you that New York gets the best of the umpiring . . . the reason for it is that the umpires are afraid of McGraw and the influence the New York club has with the President of the league. Then go ask each club owner how many games his team lost to New York this year that would have gone the other way if the umpires had not given the Giants all the best of it in any close decision." He then went on to say that the umpires were easily swayed by the promise of extra pay during the World's Series.

Fogel did not stop there. He also charged that other teams in the National League intentionally took it easy on the Giants, most specifically the St. Louis Cardinals, whose manager, Roger Bresnahan, had played for McGraw. Indeed, the Giants had won an inordinate number of close games during the season, going 32-14 in such contests, and the Cardinals had been only 7-15 against the Giants. But then again, all good teams generally have good records in one-run games. Fogel's own Phillies had finished only 5-17 versus New York, although Fogel blamed the umpires for at least six of those defeats.

NL president Thomas Lynch was quick to refute the charges, but Fogel did have a point. Just as Ban Johnson owned portions of some American League teams, there were some interlocking financial interests between teams in the National League as well, with some owners owning stock in clubs other than their own. Termed "syndicate baseball" by the press, such arrangements had undermined the integrity of the game in the late 1890s and now threatened to do so again.

The National League bristled over the charges, and even though they receded into the background as the Series approached, pending an investigation after the season, they still cast a shadow over the Series. As soon as it ended the NL would act, slapping down Fogel swiftly and banning him from baseball entirely without thoroughly refuting the charges. Still, on the precipice of the World's Series, the whispers that the Giants had an "in" with umpires could not have set well with the Red Sox. Beating the Giants and McGraw would be hard enough even on a level playing field. If it were tilted toward New York . . .

Unfortunately, it would not be the last time there was talk that the 1912 World's Series might not exactly be played on the square. There was, after all, a great deal of money to be made on the Series by the players, the National Commission, the two leagues, and the ownership of the two teams. Baseball was a game, and the national pastime, but when played for money it was business . . . serious business.

· 11 ·

The Gathering of the Clans

The peculiar conditions of the major league races of the 1912 season,
the great rivalry between the two leagues, the many unknown quantities
entering into this conflict between two teams, one of which has had,
and the other lacks, experience in World's Series contests, all have
combined to make the 1912 World Championship Series the subject
of an amount of comment, speculation, analysis and gossip equaled
only by the Athletic-Giants series of last year, to the delectation,
and perhaps also confusion and disgust, of the reading public. Of
partisan claims, predictions and gush there has been a perfect flood;
of sane conservative and non-partisan analyses, only a rivulet.

—A. H. C. Mitchell, *Sporting Life*

THE LETTERS ADDRESSED to Wood, all bearing New York
postmarks, started to arrive at Fenway Park in late September, as the Sox played the Yankees after they returned from
their road trip. Two were full of misspellings, as if the author—or
authors—was trying to disguise his upbringing and background, and
the signatures were either missing or illegible. But their meaning was
clear.

"Look out for us. We're gunning for you," read one. "You better
stay in Boston, where you are among friends," cautioned another.
More disturbing were the letters that were less obtuse. One stated
boldly, "You will never live to pitch against the Giants in the World's
Series. We are waiting for you when you arrive in town." Another was
written in red ink—like blood—and the salutation included a drawing of a knife and gun.

Joe Wood tried to laugh them off. He was in the public eye, and even then public figures attracted all kinds of odd threats and unwanted attention. Although he was not overly concerned, the letters were still disturbing, and with each new letter his anxiety increased. It was virtually impossible to track down the authors. If they were serious, there was little Wood or anyone else could do to remain safe apart from staying in his hotel room and remaining cautious. As the crowds who sometimes waited for him on his porch at his home in Winthrop demonstrated, players were much more accessible then than now. If someone truly wanted to hurt Wood or any other player, there was little to prevent them from doing so. If he was not careful, Fenway Park could be his mausoleum.

Wood did his best to ignore the threats as the Sox played out the string, but the letters did underscore just how important the Series was to some people and how much money was at stake. The letters were almost certainly sent by gamblers rather than by fans who simply hoped the Giants would win. They probably had no intention of harming Wood but hoped the letters would prove intimidating and influence the odds. As George M. Cohan had already demonstrated, bets of $50,000 or more—the equivalent of more than $1 million today—were commonplace, and men died in the street every day over much smaller sums. Millions of dollars would change hands over the course of the 1912 World's Series in New York and Boston alone. Apart from a heavyweight boxing championship, the World's Series was the premier gambling opportunity of the era, offering the same opportunities for gamblers that the Final Four, the Kentucky Derby, and the Super Bowl do in combination today, yet all wrapped up in one single event and an orgy of speculation that took place over the course of less than two weeks.

It is impossible to overstate the role that gambling played in baseball over the first two decades of the twentieth century, or to overstate the degree to which gambling was viewed by most of the people in and around baseball as, if not completely innocuous, at worst a necessary evil. Gambling fueled the game, putting people in the stands and money in the pockets of everyone—players, owners, and sportswriters.

It was present everywhere baseball was played, as much a part of the game as chewing tobacco and booing an umpire. And baseball was played virtually everywhere, in every town and city across the land, from professional contests to those between semipro or town teams. Every fan and everyone else connected with baseball knew that, on occasion, gambling probably affected the outcome of a game. Yet just as some view the impact of baseball's recent performance-enhancing drug scandal as a wash because "everybody was doing it," most baseball fans and many of those inside the game took the same attitude toward gambling in 1912. Besides, most of them liked to put a bet or two down themselves. Not until 1920, when the fix of the 1919 World's Series was revealed and organized baseball suddenly "discovered" that the game was infused with gambling, did the pursuit have any kind of lasting stigma attached to it. Before then, even the most notorious gamblers, including some who later helped mastermind the Black Sox scandal, such as Arnold Rothstein of New York and Boston's Sport Sullivan, were accepted members of the baseball community. Rothstein, in fact, was once a business partner of Giants manager John McGraw, while Sport Sullivan openly consorted with the Royal Rooters and was known to every Boston player.

Wood turned over the letters to McAleer, and the Boston owner contacted the authorities, but as the Red Sox traveled first to Washington and then to Philadelphia, Wood and his teammates were, by and large, more concerned with other matters. They wanted to stay healthy and get some rest before the Series. During the final week of the regular season Stahl gave every regular some time off. Wood, in fact, received the longest period of rest he'd had all year, not pitching for seven full days before taking the mound against the Athletics on October 3. He was not sharp when he returned, striking out only five and giving up eight hits and three runs in eight innings, but then again, he didn't need to be as the Sox romped to a 17–5 win.

The final days of the season were not entirely uneventful. Charlie Wagner's wife gave birth to their third child, a son, and in Washington Bill Carrigan split a nail on a foul ball—a painful injury but one that was not expected to affect his availability for the World's Series. John McGraw also made an appearance in the nation's capital, doing a little personal scouting. He watched the Sox beat Washington, 12–3, on October 1 as Duffy Lewis went four-for-six and Hugh Bedient scattered seven hits. Still, McGraw remained confident. When a reporter asked him whether the 1912 Giants were as good as the team that had lost to the A's in the 1911 Series, McGraw told him to "go back over the records, and I think you'll find that in every case where the same team has played in the World's Series in consecutive years, it was a stronger aggregation the second time than it was the first." That wasn't entirely true, but McGraw liked the way it sounded, and if it gave his team added confidence, it was worth stretching the truth.

The best thing that happened over the final days of the season for the Red Sox was the return of Larry Gardner. To everyone's relief, he healed quickly and rejoined the club in Philadelphia, his finger still tender but otherwise feeling refreshed from his visit to Vermont. He was pleased to discover that when he taped his little finger to the ring finger of his right hand he could bat and throw without much difficulty, and despite the layoff he exhibited little rust. On the final day of the season he cracked two hits and played errorless ball. On the precipice of the World's Series, both teams appeared to be as close to full strength as possible.

GARDNER HELPS RED SOX WIND UP WITH A VICTORY

Back in Boston, work continued at Fenway Park and Robert McRoy struggled to get tickets to the appointed parties as the appointed parties struggled to get tickets. The Royal Rooters, in particular, wanted a block of at least three hundred tickets at the Polo Grounds for game 1. As was their custom during any World's Series, they intended to travel to New York en masse, parade to the ballpark together, and sing and cheer in the stands accompanied by their band. But according to the way tickets were being allotted, there was no way for the group to secure so many seats together without the cooperation of the Giants, and the Giants were not particularly eager to give the Rooters any help—they were less than thrilled with the idea of several hundred Boston fans driving everyone batty with their incessant singing of "Tessie" and other annoyances. The Rooters, accustomed to special treatment, begged McAleer to intercede, and he promised to look into the matter.

Meanwhile McRoy and his staff spent every waking moment

sorting through stacks of ticket applications and trying to ascertain whether the applicants had sufficient standing to make them worthy of receiving reserved seats in advance. It was a long, laborious, complicated process, one that required them to first ascertain whether the applicant, by way of rain checks, was a regular at Fenway Park, and then they had to determine the number of tickets requested and at what price. McRoy intended to send fortunate applicants a card by mail informing them that they were eligible to purchase tickets. The buyers then had to redeem the card at Fenway at the time of purchase. All tickets were being sold in blocks of three—one for each game in Boston—since according to the schedule set by the National Commission, no more than three games were scheduled to be played in Boston. No single-game ticket purchases were allowed in advance.

The notices were sent out on October 2, and all over Boston hardcore fans, waiting anxiously for the mail to arrive in one of two daily mail deliveries, were hoping to find an envelope with the return address of Fenway Park. Ticket distribution began at Fenway Park the following morning at 9:00 a.m. and was scheduled to continue each day until the start of the Series in Boston. The ball club expected to sell out all the box seats and the grandstand in advance, as well as a significant portion of the third-base stands—a total of some fifteen thousand tickets for each game. Each individual ticket was keyed to the number of each game played in Boston (game 1, game 2, or game 3).

There was dissatisfaction from the start on the part of applicants who felt wrongly denied, less well-heeled fans who did not have access to the advance sale and now had to make plans to stand in line for hours on the day of the game to secure tickets, and even the ticket holders themselves. On their way to and from the park they were hounded by fans and scalpers willing to pay top dollar. The Red Sox hoped to prevent scalping by insisting that they had a record of precisely who had purchased each seat, but that did little to slow the trade in tickets.

The Rooters were having a rough time as well. New York owner John Brush, in poor health, turned McAleer's request down cold. He blamed the National Commission, telling McAleer that since the commission was handling the sale of tickets for the Giants, he "had no justification" to secure tickets for the Rooters. Besides, the Red Sox had already received an allotment of two hundred tickets per game. That was true, but the club had already distributed those tickets.

The Rooters were desperate. Together they had more than $100,000 to bet on the Red Sox, and they needed to get to New York, where Giants fans were begging for action, before the Series got under way and the odds changed. With Wood lined up to pitch game 1—and in the opinion of the Rooters he was a lock to win—once the Sox went ahead in the Series, New York money was almost certain either to dry up or to demand unrealistic odds. If the Giants came to Boston trailing in the Series, New York backers would keep their money in their pockets.

Never fear. The Rooters had friends in high places. Mayor Fitzgerald stepped in on their behalf and appealed to both the chairman of the commission, August Herrmann, and Ban Johnson by telegraph. Both men were savvy enough to realize that keeping the mayor of Boston and the Rooters happy was good business, although neither man was particularly thrilled with allowing the Rooters to feel even more important than they already did. They represented the past, and neither McAleer nor McRoy felt it necessary to continue to kowtow to the group, whose members acted like they owned Fenway Park and operated the team. But on October 3 Johnson cabled Fitzgerald, "Have instructed Sec. Heydler to provide 300 tickets for you and Boston rooters." The Giants weren't happy and still balked at turning over the tickets, but Johnson—and the Rooters—eventually prevailed.

Fenway Park was nearly ready. In the week since the Red Sox had left town the new stands had been completed, and as one report noted, Jerome Kelley and his crew had put the field "in the best possible shape. The diamond has been re-graded, every pebble has been hand-picked and heavy rollers have been hauled back and forth over the infield and baselines until the surface is as smooth as a table." To guard against inclement weather, Kelley's staff kept the infield covered with a heavy canvas when they were not working on it. He planned to leave it on until the beginning of the Series, removing it only to accommodate the practice session the Sox planned to hold two days before the start.

The biggest change to the park since the Red Sox had left town was obvious on the roof of the grandstand. The original press box could barely accommodate more than a dozen men—and even then, not very comfortably. For the World's Series, hundreds of writers planned to descend on Boston and New York—several representatives from each of the daily papers in each city as well as correspondents from regional papers and major newspapers and wire services all over the country—not to mention copy boys and various underlings. Clearly the size of the existing press box was woefully inadequate. Either it had to be expanded or seats that would otherwise be occupied by paying fans had to be taken out of circulation. In the Polo Grounds that was exactly what the Giants had to do—they turned over box seats behind home plate to the press.

McAleer shuddered at the thought of losing the income from such pricey seats. To accommodate the crush they decided instead to expand the press box atop the Fenway Park grandstand. One observer later described the new press box as looking like an extended trolley car. The modest original structure, only about thirty feet long, was torn down and replaced by a press box nearly ten times larger, one that stretched from above what is now section 16 around behind home plate to section 25. Compared to the original press box, which looked like a hastily built shed, the new facility was much more handsome. The open-air side facing the field was supported by vaulted columns every ten or twelve feet and was set precisely on the edge of the grandstand roof. Writers in the first of two tiered rows were able to peer almost straight down into the stands. Their view of the field was unimpeded.

There were other reasons to make the change. Anyone who was anyone in the baseball writing community was covering the Series, and the club certainly wanted to put on its best face. The writers representing the nearly two dozen daily newspapers in Boston and New York were among the best and best-known writers in the country at the time and included many legendary figures known to many fans even today. Some, like Murnane and Sam Crane of the *New York Evening Journal*, both of whom were often referred to as the "deans" of American baseball writing, were former players whose relationship with the game reached back to its dark ages. After graduating from

Holy Cross prep school, Murnane began his playing career in 1869, and in 1872 he became a big leaguer when he joined the Middletown (Connecticut) Mansfields in the National Association. Over the next twelve years he played for a number of teams, and in 1876, while playing for Boston, he was credited with the first stolen base in the history of the National League. Crane's career started only a few years later. The Massachusetts native abandoned his studies at the Massachusetts Institute of Technology in favor of baseball, eventually joining National League Buffalo in 1880 and playing throughout the decade before, like Murnane, becoming a sportswriter. He covered the Giants for the *Journal* and was as closely identified with the club as McGraw, whom he counted as a close friend.

Murnane's Boston contemporaries included colleagues Mel Webb and Lawrence McSweeney of the *Globe*, Paul Shannon of the *Post*, Herman Nickerson of the *Journal*, A. H. C. Mitchell of the *American*, Ralph McMillen of the *Herald*, and Jack Morse and F. C. Lane of the Boston-based *Baseball* magazine. All these names were as familiar to Red Sox fans of that era as figures like Peter Gammons, Gordon Edes, Steve Buckley, Amalie Benjamin, Tony Massarotti, and John Tomase are to Red Sox fans today.

Crane's cronies in New York included Fred Lieb of the *New York Press*, Bozeman Bulger of the *New York Evening World*, Damon Runyon of the *American*, Heywood Broun of the *Tribune*, Dan Daniel of the *New York World Telegram*, Joe Vila of the *Sun*, Sid Mercer of the *Globe and Advertiser*, and others, supplemented by writers with more national reputations like Atlanta's Grantland Rice, Chicago's Hugh Fullerton and Ring Lardner, Washington's Joe Jackson, Francis Richter of *Sporting Life*, J. G. Taylor Spink of *The Sporting News*, and Cincinnati's William Phelon. Ring Lardner and Damon Runyon would go on to become important literary figures, Lardner as a humorist and writer of short stories and Runyon as a chronicler of Broadway — his work later inspired the show *Guys and Dolls*. To many of these men writing and reporting on baseball, under a daily deadline, was a writing workshop without peer.

They were all giants of the field, trailblazers and pioneers, and every day they fought it out with each other in the press box as vigorously as the ball clubs battled on the field, pushing each other to ever more hysterical and breathless fits of prose and occasional poetry as each writer tried to stand out among the others and win for his paper the dedication and loyalty of a growing cadre of readers. While their prose, by today's standards, often appears overwrought, overwritten, and florid, it's important to keep in mind that their reporting filled a role that today is filled not only by newspapers but also by radio, television, and Internet coverage. One hundred years ago the newspapers provided the only coverage of the games available anywhere but in the park itself. Most fans knew about their team from what they read in the newspaper, and the writers had to describe not only what happened but how it happened, allowing the reader to visualize the play. Just as today more fans follow baseball online, in print, or through broadcasts than in person, in 1912 far more fans followed baseball in the papers than in person or by any other method.

Just as it was for the players, the regular season was but a warm-up for the writers to the World's Series, where the stakes and their duties increased exponentially. In the days before the Series their workload increased dramatically. The amount of space allocated for baseball in many newspapers doubled and tripled. Nearly every writer had to write lengthy and detailed analyses of the players and management of both teams, drumming up interest in a Series for which interest was already high, feeding the public's insatiable appetite for the smallest shred of inside information that might give them an edge when putting down a bet. Once the Series began, each writer was responsible not only for a game story or column each day but for background features and analysis, detailed play-by-play accounts, notes columns, and dispatches for magazines like *Sporting Life* and *The Sporting News*, for which many served as local correspondents. On a word count basis, no contemporary newspaper lavishes as much verbiage on a World Series today as many of these papers did then.

And it did not stop there. The public's appetite for baseball news was unquenchable. Other sports, like boxing and horse racing, were of intermittent interest, but baseball was part of the national conversation. What happened yesterday on the field and what would happen tomorrow was a discussion that could take place between two people regardless of class, race, sex, or religion. During the World's Series baseball bumped news of murders and wars and strikes off the front page as every publication scrambled to set itself apart from the competition. To that end virtually every Boston and New York paper had contracted with one or more players from each team, or with other well-known players, to provide inside accounts of each Series contest. The *Boston Post*, for example, published such accounts under the bylines of Cy Young, Ty Cobb, John McGraw, and Heinie Wagner. The *Herald* countered with Walter Johnson and Larry Gardner. Wood, Speaker, Larry Doyle, Mathewson, Jeff Tesreau, and Rube Marquard were also all under contract to provide daily accounts of the Series, and if a lesser-known player had a big day, the papers threw money at him after the game in exchange for an exclusive first-person account to appear in the paper the next day.

These stories have confounded naive historians and readers for years. They were, in fact, almost never written by the players themselves. In most instances they were not even based on anything beyond a brief and cursory interview but were primarily fictitious reports written on the fly. While fascinating and often entertaining—their stilted use of the English language made even the most uneducated player sound as if he had just graduated from elocutionary school—their historical value as accurate representations of the thoughts of the bylined players is, like most ghostwritten accounts, almost negligible. Their rampant use by historians either unaware of their specious origins or unconcerned about their questionable veracity has infected more than one well-intentioned history of the game. In fact, after the 1912 World's Series the National Commission, distraught over the way the accounts tended to point fingers and scapegoat, causing "open ruptures" between teammates, threatened to ban the practice altogether. Top name players like Tris Speaker, Joe Wood, Ty Cobb, and Christy Mathewson and managers like Stahl and McGraw earned as much as $3,000, as one reporter described it, "for mere use of their name above articles they were supposed to have written but which were written by expert newspapermen." For the right price, few cared what words were put in their mouths. But this World's Series would need no embellishment. What actually happened was far better than the hyperbole of any imagination.

By today's standards, Fenway Park's new press box was spartan, with few of the amenities the press receives today, and the writers' coverage of the games, while lengthy, was often incomplete. With the press box open to the elements except for a roof, writers in the first row got wet if the wind was blowing in, and in an era with no instant replay, each depended on his own eyes to write an accurate account of the game. That is why their accounts nearly always differ. It could be extraordinarily difficult at times to determine, not what happened, but precisely how. Eyes could look only one place at a time, and if a writer glanced away and missed a play, he often made up for it by writing what he *thought* happened, turning line drives into ground balls and vice versa, or what he thought made a better story.

There were nearly as many telegraph operators in the press box as reporters, for it was through their efforts that the stories of the writers made their way back to the home office and were then flashed instantly all around the country. In cities large and small, many newspapers operated scoreboards during the Series, ranging from large and complex boards that included lineups, used lights to indicate hits and errors, and featured ersatz runners in silhouette that moved around the bases, to more modest affairs, including configurations that were little more than a man and a chalkboard writing out the play-by-play. Even more complicated tableaus were created in theaters. Some even hired actors in uniform to move from one ersatz base to another to "re-enact" the Series before stage sets of bleacher-filled stands. In the Polo Grounds one hundred extra telegraph wires had been strung to accommodate the press, with a like number in Boston. Tim Murnane estimated that nationwide "over 10,000 telegraph operators will be engaged on the afternoon of the games in helping to relay the bulletins . . . nothing outside a presidential election is followed with such widespread interest."

At the Mechanics Building in Boston, where the Boston Electric trade show was taking place, preparations were under way for yet another way to present the Series. The *Globe* and New England Telephone and Telegraph combined efforts and installed ninety "loud speaking telephones" around the hall to broadcast the games from both Fenway Park and the Polo Grounds. Although it would not be until August 5, 1921, that a baseball game was first broadcast over the radio, such "telephone broadcasts," which began in the 1890s, provided a similar service. It is not known who provided the voice-over for the broadcast or whether it was made on-site or re-created from telegraph reports, but the management of the trade show did promise that the broadcast would appear in "clear distinguishable tones." It may well have been the first time the World's Series was broadcast in this fashion. The *Globe* also hired more than a dozen young female telephone operators to staff a phone bank. Homebound fans could call at any time during the game and get the score and an update.

As the writers covering the Series prepared to descend on New York and Boston, the Giants readied themselves for New York. In Philadelphia they had taken two of three from the A's to end the regular season with a stellar 105-47 mark, one and one half games better than the Giants' mark of 103-48. Athletics manager Connie Mack, an American League partisan to the core, then accommodated the league champions by giving them the run of Shibe Park to conduct practice. Only once before had two teams with more than 100 victories apiece met in the World's Series; the combined total of 208 victories between the two clubs was one short of the record set by the 1906 Cubs and White Sox, which had combined for 209 wins.

When the Sox returned to Boston the evening of October 5, Jerome Kelley stripped the canvas off the diamond, and the Sox held two secret workouts, one on Sunday afternoon and another the following morning. Wood's death threats aside, they were relaxed, confident, and excited. Wood himself exhibited no fear and did not take any special precautions. His family was visiting, and his six-year-old sister Zoe was his constant companion, even appearing in a team photo.

The Sox had every reason to look forward to the Series, for no matter how it ended, each player was certain to become rich — many of them would have their pay doubled. With crowds of approximately thirty-eight thousand expected in the Polo Grounds, and only slightly less in Boston, Series receipts were likely to set a record. Each player was guaranteed to make a minimum of nearly $3,000, and the winners would make even more. The Giants were so concerned about the number of fans who might descend on the Polo Grounds that a few days before the Series they dispatched a crew of carpenters to reinforce the stands.

CLANS ARE GATHERING FOR WORLD'S SERIES

The Red Sox left for New York at 1:00 p.m. on October 7, followed shortly by the Royal Rooters and other Boston fans, who had secured a train of their own. The "Boston Royal Rooters Special" was identified by a banner hung from the outside of one of the three private parlor cars. As the Giants played and lost an exhibition against the Yankees to benefit the sailors of the fleet, the train sped to New York. Nuf Ced McGreevey himself moved through the train handing out cards with song lyrics, satiric turns on popular ditties of the day designed to drive the Giants to distraction. It was a rolling party the whole way down. Some Rooters wore pennants "fashioned into appropriate headgears" and carried "dignified little Red Sox billikens," precious dolls dressed as Red Sox.

The Red Sox arrived just before the dinner hour and made their way quietly to the Hotel Bretton Hall on Broadway, the biggest uptown hotel in the city, between Eighty-Fifth and Eighty-Sixth Streets on the Upper West Side. It was barely three miles from the Polo Grounds, but as Hugh Fullerton noted, it was "so far from the Great White Way that not a glare touched their eyes." The Rooters, disappointed that officials of the city of New York had not given them a permit to hold a full-fledged parade on their arrival, still gathered on the street with their band. As "Tessie" echoed through the canyons of midtown Manhattan, they marched in lockstep to hired cars waiting to carry them to their hotels, most choosing to stay at the Marlboro on Broadway and Thirty-Sixth Street, a bit closer to the action. They were among the first to arrive of what Tim Murnane called "the dyed in the wool enthusiasts, men who would rather watch a game than eat, who would go through fire and water or rush a pile of ticket speculators, if occasion called for it, to see a World's Series like this." As soon as they unpacked they fanned out and began roaming hotel lobbies all over midtown, looking for New York money.

It was not particularly easy to find, for the return of Gardner to the lineup in the season finale had begun to skew the odds back Boston's way, variously reported as between 7–5 and 10–8, numbers that made many New York backers nervous. Still, some could not resist putting money down anyway, the odds be damned. On Wall Street,

then the center of gambling in New York, one unnamed Boston spec-
ulator reportedly made a single bet of $30,000.

Although the start of the World's Series was still nearly twenty-
four hours away, as soon as the Giants' exhibition against the Yankees
ended in the late afternoon of October 7 fans began queuing up on the
streets around the Polo Grounds. As the Giants' groundskeeper and
his crew searched the park for stowaways who had tried to hide inside
the park after the exhibition, others stood in line for tickets. Darkness
fell, and by 9:45 p.m. there were already thousands of fans standing
on line, sitting on boxes and leaning against the wall, waiting for tickets. As a precaution, police were called in to maintain order. People
kept arriving all night, and the police tossed out anyone trying to cut
in line, looked under boxes for truants, and rousted any boys under
the age of sixteen. By dawn the impatient were paying the oppor-
tunistic as much as $10 for their place in line. Just before the ticket
office opened at 9:00 a.m., the line stretched some twenty blocks—
nearly two miles—down Eighth Avenue to 155th Street, then down
Broadway to 145th, then on Edgecombe to 138th Street. Many were
speculators. Despite all their precautions, as soon as the tickets went
on sale the Giants discovered that they were absolutely powerless to
prevent those who had acquired tickets early from working the back
of the line, selling what they had at a nice profit, or to keep scalpers
from scooping up tickets from the early arrivals who had stood in line
for just such an opportunity. Those desperate for tickets were paying
as much as $15 for a $1 seat and $125 for the precious few box seats
that were available on the street.

BASEBALL FRENZY GRIPS AND BINDS NEW YORK

The speculators weren't the only ones making money. Nearly three
hundred baseball writers were ensconced at the Hotel Imperial. Over
the past twenty-four hours they had discovered that in order to get
an interview, as the *New York Tribune* reported, "some of the long
green has to be flashed." The going rate was $2 a word. Even Christy
Mathewson refused to part his lips unless paid to do so. It was cheaper
for the writers to make the quotes up, and many did.

On the morning of the game there was still a great deal of speculation over precisely who would pitch for the Giants. Wood, everyone assumed, would pitch for Boston. This led some writers to assume that "McGraw might as well waste a pitcher" opposite the Red Sox star, much as Jake Stahl had avoided pitching his best opposite Ed Walsh earlier in the year. If that was the case, Marquard seemed likely to get the nod, but others argued that "McGraw will not concede a Boston victory in such a manner." Tesreau, the hot hand, was widely believed to give the Giants their best chance at victory, but McGraw was being cagey. Mathewson had not pitched in twelve days, the longest layoff of his career, and some concluded that he was either injured or had been ordered to rest so he would be fresh for the first game and available to pitch in as many as four of the seven games. Despite some signs of encroaching age, Mathewson, at age thirty-one, was still a terrific pitcher, one McGraw well remembered for his magnificent performance in the 1905 World's Series. Mathewson had led the Giants to victory in five games over the A's, winning three games—all by shutout—in what was still the greatest pitching performance in World's Series history.

When the gates opened shortly after noon the crowd spilled into the Polo Grounds in a flood. News that war had broken out in the Balkans drew only disinterested shrugs—fans were far more concerned about the impending war between the Red Sox and Giants than a conflict halfway around the world. It was a perfect day for baseball, at least in October—sunny but cool and breezy—and the stands filled quickly. All the big shots were there, from Massachusetts governor Eugene Foss and Boston mayor Honey Fitz Fitzgerald and his New York counterpart, William Gaynor, to, as noted in the *Times*, "all the photographers west of the Mississippi, baseball luminaries like Ty Cobb, Walter Johnson and Detroit manager Hughie Jennings, to Ban Johnson, the rest of the National Commission," and "well-known actors, actresses, Wall Street speculators, sporting men, pretty girls, their good looking mothers and clergymen."

The Royal Rooters, true to form, arrived together in a parade of twenty automobiles. When they marched into the Polo Grounds led by McGreevey, *Sporting Life* reported, "they made as much noise as the 39,000 Giant rooters"—just the kind of notice the Rooters lived for and loved to clip and add to their scrapbooks.

Honey Fitz, resplendent in his silk hat and Prince Albert jacket, leapt from his box seat beside Mayor Gaynor, raced across the diamond, and preened before his constituents. Then he grabbed a megaphone and led his supporters in a series of cheers before closing with "Sweet Adeline," his signature tune.

Meanwhile the Red Sox and Giants also took the field. The Giants wore long maroon sweaters that one reporter noted made them look "like a party of arctic explorers." The Red Sox were also bundled against the chill and wore similar sweaters, in bright red, although the sun soon warmed everyone enough that the outerwear was quickly removed. Unlike in some recent years, neither team wore a special uniform for the Series: the Sox wore their usual road grays and the Giants their standard home uniforms. Boston took batting practice off Larry Pape, and he did his job well, for the Sox rocketed pitch after pitch down the line and into the nearby stands, fair and foul. At the same time Christy Mathewson warmed up before the stands.

As 2:00 p.m. approached a large gate opened in center field. A limousine appeared and lumbered across right field, finally parking behind a short fence recently erected down the line, in foul territory. Inside was New York Giants owner John Brush, wrapped in a blanket to ward off the chill. An invalid due to locomotor ataxia, a disease of the nervous system, he would watch the Series from the comfort of his car through the glass windows.

A few moments later the four umpires, Silk O'Loughlin, Bill Klem, Charlie Rigler, and Billy Evans, took the field, and they were joined around home plate by Stahl and McGraw. As the *Times* reported, "The combatants held a 'love feast' and all shook hands as if they were all the Board of Directors of a bank." The Polo Grounds was full to the brim, and there was also a large crowd atop Coogan's Bluff, peering into the park from on high.

The batteries were announced on the scoreboard, and the crowd realized for the first time that the Giants were starting, not Mathewson, but Jeff Tesreau, who began warming up. McGraw hoped his sleight of hand might throw the Red Sox off, but it mattered little to Boston. Their lineup stayed the same no matter who pitched for the opposition. With Wood on the mound for the Red Sox, Hick Cady, not Bill Carrigan, was Jake Stahl's selection to catch for Boston. That was what had worked for most of the 1912 season, and that was what Stahl and the Red Sox hoped would work in October as well. For despite the millions of words printed by the gallon over the previous week extolling the virtues of this player or that one, comparing the performances of everyone from the team trainer to the bat boys, Boston's best hope for vanquishing the Giants and winning the World's Series came down to only one man, Joe Wood. If Wood could pitch in October the way he had pitched from April through September, it did not matter at all who the Giants pitched opposite him, or even who Wood faced. Wood, at his best, was the best. It was that simple.

Tesreau and his teammates took the field, and the rookie pitcher, dubbed "the Bear Hunter" by sportswriter Damon Runyon owing to his build (he had never hunted a bear in his life), loomed over the mound as he took his warm-ups. As he did a herd of photographers rushed the field, much to the consternation of home plate umpire Bill Klem, and set up in foul ground along the baselines.

Klem, who ruled the game with an iron hand, wasn't having any of it. He tried to shoo the photographers off the field, but they did their best to ignore him. It took seven or eight minutes before he got them to move far enough back to start the game.

Harry Hooper stepped in to face Tesreau, Bill Klem ordered the two teams to "Play ball!" and the Series was on. After the delay, the big pitcher had a hard time finding the plate, and Hooper led off with a walk. Sox fans hoped for an early rally, but Tesreau quickly found his spitball, darting from the knees to the ankles as it crossed the plate, and retired the rest of the Red Sox easily.

Compared to Tesreau, the slender, baby-faced Wood looked like a schoolboy, but when he threw his first pitch the Giants suddenly realized what they were up against. The rest had served Wood well. His fastball was at its crackling best, and left fielder Josh Devore went out quickly on strikes. But with two out, Wood began to show some nerves, giving up a single and a walk before getting Fred Merkle to pop out to end the inning.

Tesreau quickly settled in. He didn't give up a hit through five innings as the Sox came nowhere close to scoring and squandered the only chance they had. After Larry Gardner led off the second by reaching on an error by New York shortstop Art Fletcher, Jake Stahl bunted into a force-out. Charlie Wagner then made a bad play worse by botching a hit-and-run play, leaving Stahl, who still didn't run well on his weak ankle, out by a mile at second base. The Rooters groaned at witnessing such sloppy play.

Meanwhile Wood scuffled. He had plenty of speed, but was not quite sure where each pitch was going. In the third the Giants reached him for two runs when, after a one-out walk to Devore, Larry Doyle popped a fly to short left.

In Fenway Park no fielder on the left side had much to worry about from the sun, which was generally over his right shoulder, but the orientation of the Polo Grounds was different. Magnetic north was in line with the first-base line behind the grandstand, making left and left-center the sun field.

Both Larry Gardner and Heinie Wagner drifted back for the looping fly, but when they looked up they saw only the sun. Duffy Lewis dashed in, but he was playing deeper than at Fenway and also got a late start because of glare from the sun. As Doyle tore around the bases the ball landed free. He collected a single, and Devore made third base on a ball that had not even traveled 150 feet in the air. Doyle went to second on the throw. It was the kind of play that could change a ball game.

Wood bore down and struck out Fred Snodgrass, but that brought up Red Murray. In the 1911 World's Series Murray had been pathetic, going hitless in twenty-one at-bats and earning an acerbic nickname he detested, "the Hitless Wonder." This time, however, he was no such wonder, for he smacked the ball up the middle for a base hit, scoring both Devore and Doyle. Cady, taking Speaker's late throw, then gunned the ball to second, where Murray was trying to take the extra base. The throw beat the runner, but Wagner and Murray collided violently. They jumped up and started jawing at each other before base umpire Billy Evans got them to knock it off, but the damage was done. The Giants led 2–0.

Tesreau carried the 2–0 lead into the sixth, and after he retired Steve Yerkes to start the inning he was only eleven outs away from victory and perhaps immortality as the first pitcher to hurl a no-hitter in the World's Series. Then Speaker smacked a fly ball into the gap in left-center. Snodgrass, the center fielder, and Devore both closed on the ball, but neither called for it, or perhaps both did. The two men nearly collided, but neither caught Speaker's drive. "The ball belonged to Devore," wrote Ring Lardner later, "but Josh was scared away by Fred's rush." The ball ticked off Snodgrass's glove and rolled to the fence. On another day Speaker might have collected an inside-the-park home run, but he hadn't run hard out of the box and only landed at third.

Now McGraw, in retrospect, made a mistake. Nursing a two-run lead, instead of playing the infield in to cut the run off at home, he kept the infield back, conceding the run. Lewis hit a routine grounder to third, and Speaker scored easily, making the score 2–1.

Wood held it there, and in the seventh Tesreau got Stahl to ground out to open the inning. Wagner and then Cady each followed with a single, and suddenly the Bear Hunter seemed to shrink. Joe Wood, one of the best-hitting pitchers in baseball, came to the plate, and Stahl and Bill Carrigan, coaching first base, let him swing away. He grounded to Doyle, but the second baseman fumbled the ball. Instead of hitting into a double play, Wood made first and Wagner stood on third.

Tesreau suddenly seemed to be a different pitcher, and in a sense he was. The Red Sox had been watching him closely all game long and discovered that Tesreau was tipping his pitches. Like most spit-ballers—indeed, like most pitchers of the era—Tesreau went to his mouth to moisten his fingers before every pitch. But each time he planned to throw a spitball, he allowed his hand to linger near his mouth for an extra split-second, just long enough to let the Red Sox know he was loading up the ball. They stopped swinging at the pitch, which dipped toward the ground like today's split-finger fastball. And now Tesreau, with a runner on third, was half-afraid to throw the pitch anyway, worried that his catcher might not be able to handle it. Nuf Ced McGreevey, sitting with the Rooters behind third base, ordered the band to play "Tessie," the old war hymn. The song—and a bit of foreknowledge by Harry Hooper—worked its magic once more. Hooper laid off the spitters, and with two strikes, he swung at a fastball and lifted a soft pop foul back of the plate. New York catcher Chief Meyers—so named because of his Native American heritage, and not the fastest man in the majors—raced after it, but the ball trickled off his fingers. Hooper then took advantage: armed with the knowledge that Tesreau was throwing him yet another fastball, he smacked a double over the first baseman's head, scoring Wagner and making the Rooters apoplectic. When Steve Yerkes followed with a clean single to center, Tesreau, who had been invincible, suddenly was not, and the Red Sox, trailing 2–1 only a few moments before and counting the outs until their train left for Boston, now led 4–2.

The game sped to the finish. After Boston was finally retired, Wood took care of the Giants in the bottom of the seventh. Doc Crandall took over for Tesreau, and then both pitchers shut down the opposition in the eighth. Boston took the field in the bottom of the ninth still clinging to a 4–2 lead and needing only three more outs. Then, just when it looked as if the game was over, it was not. As the *New York Tribune* later noted, "Nine tenths of the excitement was compressed in the last half of the ninth inning."

For most of the game New York hitters had been patient. As Damon Runyon noted, the Giants, under the instructions of McGraw, "tried waiting him [Wood] out." But now, with young Wood presumably anxious to escape with a victory, McGraw changed tactics and told his hitters to swing at the first good pitch. Red Murray, up first, obliged. He hit the ball sharply to right field—but right at Harry Hooper, for the first out.

All over the Polo Grounds Giants fans stood and started plotting their escape to the exits, but they hardly had time to do so before Fred Merkle fought off a fastball and dumped it just over the infield for a single. Buck Herzog followed him to home plate and wasted little time, reaching out to swing at a pitch off the plate, dropping another single to right field. Suddenly the winning run, catcher Chief Meyers, was at home plate, and Giants rooters, who had been outgunned all game by Boston's more exuberant fans, went off.

Every fan was on his or her feet, and a litter of seat cushions rained down on the field. Wood suddenly seemed small and nervous as Chief Meyers, New York's leading hitter with a .358 average for the season, stepped in. Wood was teetering, and every one of the nearly forty thousand fans in the ballpark knew it.

So did Meyers. He swung at the first pitch and drove it hard to right. It made the wall and kicked off the concrete barrier directly back to Hooper. Merkle scored, and Hooper's strong throw home kept Herzog at third, but Meyers went to second on the play.

McGraw called time-out, and Stahl took advantage of the break to walk to the mound and speak to his pitcher.

McGraw had a decision to make. Meyers represented the winning run, and he knew he had to replace the slow-footed catcher with a faster base runner. But Art Fletcher was due up, and the shortstop had been helpless against Wood's fastball. Lardner later wrote that he "had looked all afternoon like a high school freshman." Even though Fletcher had struck out only twenty-nine times all year, he had already gone down swinging against Wood twice. McGraw's best left-handed bat on the bench, outfielder Beals Becker, was also his best available base runner, and if he pinch-hit for Fletcher and the Giants tied the game, he had little faith in the fielding of Fletcher's backup, shortstop Tillie Schaefer.

Becker thought he was being called out to hit and had his bat in hand when McGraw first waved him onto the field, only then learning that his manager wanted his legs. Becker ran onto the field to replace Meyers, and Fletcher prepared to face Wood in the biggest at-bat of the game. Said Becker afterward, "I'd a darn sight rather been in there hitting instead of running."

It was, as the *Times* noted, "a question of whether Wood's nerves were steel or cast iron"—and whether his arm, after 344 innings in the regular season and eight more on this day, could still throw a baseball faster than any man alive, or at least fast enough to get two more outs. Boston brought the infield in, knowing they had to cut off the run at the plate. A ground ball anywhere but directly at a fielder would tie the game. So would a fly ball, and a base hit would win it for New York.

Wood worked carefully and threw to second base several times to steady his nerves and keep Becker close, for although the Red Sox could weather Herzog crossing the plate, Becker's run would mean defeat. Fletcher let the first pitch pass, and Bill Klem's strike call echoed through the ballpark as Boston's Rooters cheered and the rest of New York groaned. Then Wood blew a pitch over the middle, and Fletcher fouled the fastball straight back.

Wood, wrote Hugh Fullerton, "was white around the gills," gasping for air, living on fumes. His arm may well have been on fire, for on his next pitch Cady called for a curve and Wood did not shake him off. Fletcher flailed at the pitch and missed it, striking out for the third time.

Now all that stood between Wood and victory was pitcher Doc Crandall. McGraw, coaching third, made no move for a pinch hitter. The pitcher, who in the past had occasionally filled in on the infield and as a pinch hitter, was a better hitter than some men in the regular lineup. In 1910 Crandall had hit a robust .342 and led the team in slugging, and in 1912 he had hit .313.

The at-bat took forever. Wood needed every ounce of his strength, and he abandoned the stretch for the full wind-up. Off third base, McGraw's voice rang out, exhorting Herzog to feint and dash and try to unnerve the pitcher, while Christy Mathewson, coaching at first base, also called out to Wood and tried to distract him from his task.

It almost worked, for one pitch by Wood sailed directly at Crandall's head, sending him to the ground. Cady had to leap to his feet to knock down the ball and prevent a wild pitch and tie game.

And then the count was full, 3-2, two out, the score 4–3, and men on second and third, forty thousand fans in the Polo Grounds screaming each other hoarse, an exhibition hall in Boston filled with fans gathered around an electric megaphone, crowds along Boston's Newspaper Row watching the electronic scoreboards, telegraph operators listening intently, farmers in small towns watching a boy with a piece of chalk reach to mark on slate, and everyone, everywhere, watching and waiting for the next pitch.

Then Wood wound up and threw the ball, a small white dart he aimed at Cady's glove, "one of the swiftest pitched balls," wrote Runyon, "they have ever seen delivered and which was straight as a foot rule." The ball was waist high, in, over the plate.

Crandall swung and missed.

Next stop, Fenway Park.

• 12 •

Home Sweet Home

There were plays in the field which simply lifted the spectators out
of their seats in a frenzy. There were others which caused them to
want to sink through the hard floor of the stand in humiliation.
There were stops in which the fielders seemed to stretch like
India rubber and others in which they shriveled like parchment
that has been dried. There were catches of fly balls that were
superhuman and muffs of fly balls which were "superawful."

—John B. Foster, *Spalding's Official Baseball Guide*

WHILE NEW YORK fans slipped back into their seats and
turned away disgusted, their cheers brought to a dead
stop by Wood's last pitch, from the third-base stands the
Rooters spoke as one. Within moments they poured out of the stands
and onto the field, dancing behind their band and singing with all
their might. They continued the impromptu parade outside the ballpark and made a successful charge to the top of Coogan's Bluff, a conquering army of sorts, the escarpment their San Juan Hill with both
McGreevey and Fitzgerald vying for the role of Teddy Roosevelt.
By the time the Rooters gave ground and poured into their cars, the
Polo Grounds was empty. As they passed the Bretton Hall Hotel they
all piled out and resumed the parade, this time for the benefit of the
Boston players, who had already made it back to the hotel and were
preparing to leave.

Later that night the Rooters marched once more, this time to
Grand Central Station to catch their overnight train back to Boston,
the New Haven Railroad's *Owl*. Although the train boarded at 10:00

p.m., it did not leave the station until three hours later, which allowed passengers to settle in for a good night's sleep. Even then, to provide a smooth ride for sleeping travelers, the train made the trip to Boston at a top speed of only thirty-six miles per hour, arriving at South Station at 7:00 a.m. The Rooters were joined on the train not just by their New York counterparts but by those writers covering the Series who had a tight deadline and could not take an earlier train.

The players of both teams and writers not on deadline took an earlier train, the New Haven Railroad's *Gilt Edge Express*, which ran between New York and Boston. Because that train was scheduled to leave just before 6:00 p.m. — to arrive in Boston around 11:00 p.m. — passengers were forced to scramble to get from the ballpark to their hotel and then to the station as fast as possible after the game. For the rest of the Series all interested parties would travel in this fashion between the two cities — combatants on the field, in the stands, and in the press box, but fellow passengers and companions each night on the trains.

When the Red Sox arrived at Grand Central Station they were forced to run a gauntlet as a crowd of New Yorkers pelted them with rocks and other debris. New York police simply looked the other way, and Buck O'Brien was badly cut on the face when struck by a stone. Still, despite some lingering bad blood after game 1, during the trip the members of both teams let their guard down a bit. Both teams' players realized that while they were pitted against one another on the field, off the field they were united against the men who owned baseball.

Sometime during the journey from Boston to New York the players began talking to one another, and perhaps after perusing the most recent issue of *Sporting Life* or being tipped off by one of the writers on the train or by a fan or family member, they became aware of the decision by the National Commission a few weeks earlier in regard to the division of the World's Series money. They learned that they would share in the proceeds of the first four games only, regardless of whether one of those games ended in a tie, with the remainder going to management, shared by the National Commission and the two participating teams. For the players, who already felt that they should receive the lion's share of the proceeds, the question in regard to the tie game was hardly insignificant. As recently as 1907, in fact, a Series game had ended in a tie. The players, while powerless, were acutely aware of their rights—or lack thereof. It was an era of reform, and players were becoming increasingly political. The recent millwork-ers' strike in Lawrence, Massachusetts, had gained the widespread sympathy of the public, and players in both leagues were increasingly disgruntled at being treated like serfs. Mineworkers and chamber-maids had more rights than major league ballplayers.

The issue of the tie game was brought to the attention of the Gi-ants' Christy Mathewson, the uncrowned monarch, the players' moral leader, and a man of honor beyond reproach. Mathewson agreed that the ruling was patently unfair, and he was determined to do some-thing about it.

The next morning Mathewson, who was staying with the rest of the Giants and most of New York's entourage of writers at the Cop-ley Square Hotel, spoke with Sam Crane of the *New York Evening Journal* and voiced his complaint. Crane, an old ballplayer himself, was sympathetic. He knew, better than most, that while players were relatively well compensated during their careers, those careers were brief. Once players' skills had eroded or they became injured, they were discarded like yesterday's newspaper. At a time when the aver-age life span was just over fifty, few players, even those with a college education, were able to start a successful second career after retiring from baseball. Crane had been lucky to become a journalist. Many other old ballplayers ended their lives as clichés, working menial jobs and mourning days gone by over shots of rye.

The contrast between players and owners was telling. The mem-bers of the National Commission were crying poor mouth, but they were staying at Boston's newest and most expensive hotel, the opu-lent Copley Plaza. It had opened for business a little more than a month earlier. The players were picking up the tab.

When the two men finished speaking Crane returned to his room and started writing. Mathewson, he wrote, "insinuates, or rather threatens, that if the players' share is curtailed in future games the Na-tional Commission will find itself left flat by one club or the other. . . . Mathewson's present complaint is the commission's refusal to allow the players to share in any playoff game in case there is a tie in any game of the first four played." He then quoted Mathewson directly: "There are many of us who think we are entitled to a share of all the games played. The Commission makes rules without consulting us or letting us know their intentions." While Mathewson did not threaten specific action, he was clearly speaking for the players of both teams and made it clear that the players were united by both their anger and their determination to have the inequity resolved. They were keenly aware that the immense crowds in Boston and New York promised to bring in a record-setting amount of money. The players, not James McAleer, John Brush, or Ban Johnson, were the reason for that.

As Mathewson spoke with Crane, Fenway Park was becoming the most popular piece of real estate in Boston. The streets surrounding the ballpark were already choked with some five thousand fans who had spent the night in gigantic lines that stretched out in every direction from the eight ticket booths on Jersey Street. From there they spread, spiderlike, up Van Ness Street (then still referred to as "Auto Road"), Boylston Street, Ipswich Street, and Brookline Avenue. Some in the crowd had gone directly from South Station to Fenway Park. While the crowd sipped from flasks and sang "Tessie" and other favorites all night long, enterprising boys sold sandwiches, coffee, cigars, and mugs of milk and ran errands. Tickets finally went on sale at 9:00 a.m., and the team began rushing fans inside before they could slip their tickets to scalpers. By 1:00 p.m., just as the Red Sox were taking the field for batting practice, the line was suddenly gone. Thousands more who had arrived later that morning and seen the long lines had assumed that the game would be sold out. They had turned around and left, deciding to follow the game for free at Newspaper Row or in the comfort of a theater. But now, although few realized it, the crowd was gone and seats were still available without waiting. The first World's Series game at Fenway Park would not quite be a sellout.

Inside the park tensions were high and tempers short. Fifteen minutes before the start of the game the crowd turned a bit chaotic. Some fans with tickets for the center-field bleachers broke through a gate and, chased by police the whole way, squeezed their way into some of the seats rimming the outfield. But there were more escapees than wardens, and once they made it into the stands it was hard to determine who belonged and who did not, and most made it safely. At home plate the ubiquitous Mayor Honey Fitz presented a car to Jake Stahl, a gift of the subscribers to the *Boston American*, a fully equipped "White 30," and Charlie Wagner was given a silver bat. As soon as that ceremony ended the Royal Rooters, craving attention like a hitter craves base hits, marched in behind their band through the center-field gate between the left-field wall and the center-field bleachers. They then paraded to their place in the stands, most on Duffy's Cliff, where the Red Sox had agreed to reserve a block of seats in the Rooters' name. More enterprising fans who made the instant decision to become Royal Rooters in order to get better seats for free followed them through the gate and sent the police chasing after still more scofflaws. At the same time the Elks Club band, already stationed in the center-field bleachers, decided to play. For much of the day the antics of the crowd made Fenway seem more like the venue of a college football game than a baseball game. First the Royal Rooters band and then the Elks Club band would break out in song, each trying to play louder and faster, often playing the same song at the same time but not so often on the same measure, as their constituents sang and waved pennants and made everyone who was not from Boston want to cover their ears and hide.

Although the addition of the extra seats made it the biggest official crowd in Fenway history—30,148—by the start of the game a handful of seats were still available on Duffy's Cliff and fans at the top of the center-field bleachers still had room to stretch out. The weather, although fall-like, was fine, mostly overcast but with an intermittent swirling wind blowing out to left field. Fenway Park was a gem, the green grass the only splash of color on the gray day.

Just before 2:00 p.m. head umpire Silk O'Loughlin called Jake Stahl and John McGraw to home plate to exchange lineup cards and discuss the ground rules. The decisions made in the next few moments were perhaps the most important in the World's Series. The new seats that ringed the ballpark had changed everything. Fenway Park itself would exert as much influence on the Series as any player.

The umpires had been given what the National Commission deemed "supreme authority" over matters such as the ground rules, and the recent additions to Fenway Park necessitated some changes from the rules that had been in effect during the regular season. With the new bleachers on Duffy's Cliff and several rows of seats now intruding onto the field in front of the Cliff and encircling the outfield, both the Cliff and the left-field wall were now out of play entirely. As the Red Sox and Giants had taken batting practice O'Loughlin and the other umpires had watched closely as fly balls that were routine outs only a few weeks before now landed in the crowd, and dozens of practice balls had already been lost to young boys. As the umpires and managers discussed the situation, everyone agreed that if balls hit over the new, much closer, and much lower left-field fence were allowed to be home runs, there might be as many as five or six in each contest. That would turn the game into a travesty and, if it benefited New York, perhaps even cause a riot by disgruntled fans dizzy from watching Giants run around the bases. That would not do at all.

Since they could not move the fence back, O'Loughlin decided it was only fair to rule that any ball that landed over the low rail fence and in the crowd would not be a home run at all. Instead such hits would be good for only two bases, a ground-rule double. Whether or not the ball hit the wall and bounced back onto the field or even cleared the wall and landed on Lansdowne Street was insignificant. *Any ball* that went over the temporary fence installed in front of the Cliff would only be a double, even one that cleared the left-field wall on the fly, like Hugh Bradley's first-ever Fenway Park home run in April and the handful that had subsequently cleared the barrier. No matter how far the ball was hit, the only possible home runs hit to left field would have to be of the inside-the-park variety, and given that the distance to the fence had been greatly reduced, one of those was not very likely. Had the 1975 World Series been played under the same ground rules, for example, Carlton Fisk's game-ending home run in the twelfth inning of game 6, perhaps the best-known home run in Red Sox history, would have only been a double. Then again, so would Bucky Dent's blast in the 1978 playoff against the Yankees.

Stahl and McGraw readily agreed to the changes. The integrity of the game had to be preserved, and O'Loughlin had come up with a commonsense solution. Home runs over the wall were still so rare that few writers covering the Series even saw fit to mention the change, and no one complained about the rule during the Series.

Fortunately, that specific ruling would have little impact—no ball hit during the Series would clear the left-field fence atop the Cliff, although a significant number of otherwise routine fly balls would become doubles. But then O'Loughlin made another ruling that would have a much greater impact.

The new shorter and lower fences in center and right field created a problem as well, particularly the fence in right. During the regular season any hitter who struck the ball over the right fielder's head had a fair chance of getting at least a triple, if not an inside-the-park home run. That was impossible now. Not only was the fence shorter, but instead of being a solid stockade fence, like the one in dead center, the fence that stretched around to right field was a plank fence only eighteen inches tall topped by a rail three feet off the ground, leaving an eighteen-inch gap between the planking and the rail, similar to the kind of fence used on a farm to contain pigs. During batting practice the umpires had noticed that even though the new fence was much closer, no one had hit the ball over it and only a few balls had even bounced that far.

O'Loughlin, perhaps feeling some sympathy for the hitters after his ruling in regard to left field, ruled that if a ball either was hit over or even *bounced over* the low three-foot-high stockade fence in center field, it would be a home run. But in right field the ball would be a home run not only if it cleared the fence or bounced over it, but also if it went *through* the gap between the planks and the rail. Thus, during this World's Series at Fenway Park, balls hit over the fence in left field could not be home runs, but balls that bounced over or through the fence elsewhere would be. Fenway Park, already made smaller by the addition of the extra seats, became dramatically smaller. The ground rules would have an immediate, dramatic, and lasting impact on the Series.

The first World's Series game in the history of Fenway Park was, wrote the *Herald*'s R. E. McMillen later, both "the best of games" and "the worst of games," a fine mess of baseball that included tremendous plays and stupendous gaffes, fabulous base running and horrendous mistakes, a game with more mood swings than a patient at the nearby State Lunatic Hospital at Danvers. It was a ball game that, as the *Tribune* noted, "wrecked the hearts of thirty-five thousand fans and tore the nerves of the players to shreds," and one that, in the end, both counted and didn't matter, decided nothing and changed everything. Joe Jackson, writing in the *Washington Post*, commented later, "Viewed critically or judged as an artistic exhibition, the affair was impossible." In other words, it was a rather typical game at Fenway Park, where no lead was safe and the ballyard itself played a role in just about everything that happened.

McGraw, to no one's surprise whatsoever, selected his old standby, Mathewson, to start for New York. Jake Stahl countered with lefty Ray Collins, for it was widely believed that the Giants lineup had a bit of trouble with left-handed pitching and, as yet, left-handed pitchers were not thought to be a liability in Fenway Park. That characteristic would develop later, after the introduction of the lively ball in 1920 made the left-field wall a more inviting target for right-handed hitters and sluggers like Jimmie Foxx took advantage.

THRILLS, THROBS, SIGHS, SMILES

How They Mixed It Up At Yesterday's Game
Big Crowd Gets Its Money's Worth Every Minute

Collins took the mound, O'Loughlin called out for the game to begin, and with the noise of the crowd reaching a crescendo, outfielder Fred Snodgrass, leading off for the Giants, took Ray Collins's first pitch for a strike. He swung at the second and hit the ball solid to left field, where it went up as a rather routine fly ball but came down and was swallowed by a sea of hands on Duffy's Cliff. During the regular season Duffy Lewis might have either caught the ball or retrieved it in time for a play at second, but not anymore. Snodgrass collected a ground-rule double.

Collins left him stranded, but in the Boston half Mathewson was not so fortunate. Hooper led off with a single, and then, after he stole second, the Giants played hot potato. Steve Yerkes smacked a soft line drive to shortstop Art Fletcher, who not only failed to hold on to the ball but missed a chance to double up Hooper, who misjudged the hit and was already on his way to third. Both men were safe. When Tris Speaker then dropped a perfect bunt down the third-base line,

Mathewson made no attempt to field it but walked behind it until it rolled to a stop, hoping it would go foul while eyeballing Hooper and keeping him at third. That filled the bases. Groundouts by Lewis and Gardner and a single by Stahl gave the Red Sox a quick 3–0 lead.

The Giants should have gotten one run back in a hurry. With one out in the second, Buck Herzog rapped the ball far and deep to right field, way over Hooper's head, and the ball took a long bounce to the rail fence—a sure home run if it had not hit the top rail with a crack and bounced straight back. Had it gone either over or through the barrier, Herzog would have had a home run, but now he only made third. Fortunately for New York, the issue became moot when Chief Meyers cracked a bad-hop ground ball off Larry Gardner's face and Herzog scored to make it 3–1. Gardner's cheek began to swell almost immediately, and for the rest of the Series he would look like a prize-fighter after a bad night.

In the middle innings the two clubs traded runs as each did its best to give the other the game. New York shortstop Art Fletcher, with one bad play already to his credit, kept it up, having a perfectly wretched day in the field. One day after striking out three times, Fletcher made several other miscues, such as dropping a perfect peg to second base that should have caught Harry Hooper and helping Boston to a run. However, Fletcher saved his best work—from Boston's perspective—for the eighth inning.

In the top of that inning with the score 4–2, it looked at first as if the Giants had put the game away and tied the Series. It began with Duffy Lewis lending the opposition a helping hand by dropping Fred Snodgrass's leadoff fly ball. Larry Doyle then singled, and after a force-out put runners at first and third, Red Murray hit a slashing drive to deep left. Once again, a few weeks earlier Lewis, maybe playing deeper, might well have tracked the ball down and made a fine running catch. But on this day, with the close crowd, the ball was past him in a flash and into his namesake bleachers for a double, scoring Snodgrass.

That was enough for Stahl. The Giants had been hitting Collins hard all day, and at various times the Boston manager had had both Joe Wood and Charley Hall warming up in front of the third-base stands, the only place left in the park where there was room for a pitcher to throw. He called on Hall, and the rescue pitcher nearly saved the day. He got Fred Merkle to pop out foul to Carrigan, who was catching this day instead of Cady. Buck Herzog then lifted another twisting foul toward the first-base stands. As is well known to generations of fans who have sat in the grandstand, a wind blowing in through the stands pushes such foul balls back toward the field, even today. Had Carrigan caught the ball, the Giants would have been out of the inning, but the catcher struggled to track the twisting fly. The ball hit the catcher's glove and then, as Hugh Fullerton wrote, "rimmed around like a golf ball on a long putt" before dropping out. Carrigan cursed loudly as the ball fell, and Herzog was free to hit again.

He made Boston pay. Once more a long fly was sent toward left. The ball ricocheted off the stockade fence in left-center for a double, two runs scoring. The Giants were suddenly ahead, 5–4, and only six outs away from tying the Series with Christy Mathewson, who had pitched better than the score, looking strong.

Matty got two quick outs in the eighth before Fenway Park and Art Fletcher combined to save the day for the Boston. A few innings before, when the sun peeked through the clouds, John McGraw had made a switch, sending diminutive left fielder Josh Devore to right and right fielder Red Murray to left because Murray had trouble with the sun field. Now the sun was gone, but McGraw had not bothered to have the two men switch back to their original places. Duffy Lewis lofted a routine fly ball Murray's way, and the outfielder drifted back on the ball, which, pushed by the wind, headed to earth some twenty feet shy of the wall.

Of course, because of what Sam Crane disparagingly referred to as "the temporary little low circus seat stand erected behind left field," that meant that the ball was actually dropping just over the temporary fence. Murray staggered back and, not sure of precisely where the fence was, leapt up for the fly ball just as he backed into the low rail. Devore, nearly half a foot shorter than Murray, might not have even tried for the catch, but the taller man did, and the ball and Murray entered the stands together. Murray flipped backward over the fence and tumbled headfirst into the stands.

Duffy Lewis pulled up at second base, but no one more than ten

feet away from Murray was quite sure whether or not the outfielder
had caught the ball. Murray himself didn't know. After landing on
his head, he was dazed and only semiconscious, and Boston fans were
not particularly eager to help him up. Umpire Bill Klem, manning the
left-field line, had a good angle on the play, however, and was relatively certain that the ball had landed free. In a matter of seconds he
dashed over to where Murray had disappeared and looked for the ball.

It was not in the groggy outfielder's glove, and Klem, quickly ascer-
taining that it had not been caught—at least not by Murray—ruled
the hit a double. After a minute or two a hatless Murray returned
to the field—an enterprising Royal Rooter had taken advantage of
the situation and obtained a souvenir—and was given a fine ovation
by the Boston crowd, both for his effort and because it had been for
naught. The game was delayed another minute while Murray was
given a spare cap and a moment to make sure his head was still attached to his neck.

After watching the delay from the mound, Mathewson turned
around to face Larry Gardner, who hit a hard ground ball to Art
Fletcher at short. The infielder didn't move, and that was the problem. It should have been the end of the inning, but the ball, wrote the
New York Times, "went through his hands and legs as it would a ladder." Lewis scored, and the game was tied, 5–5.

The ninth inning went fast, and the game entered extra innings,
but night was falling quickly. Sunset would be just after 5:00 p.m., and
the sun, which had peeked in and out of the clouds until midgame,
was now hidden behind a thick bank of low clouds, a harbinger of
rain. Players on both teams began to play quickly, taking chances
they would not have taken earlier in the day, desperate for the game
to end before it was called. Fred Merkle led off the tenth for New
York with a long drive to left-center, and by the time Duffy Lewis
ran the ball down Merkle, who ran hard from the start, was at third
base. Two batters later, McGraw pulled Art Fletcher in favor of pinch
hitter Moose McCormick, who came through, hitting a fly ball to left
that scored Merkle easily. Now New York led 6–5, and Mathewson,
still in the game, needed only three outs to collect a win and knot the
Series.

Steve Yerkes opened the tenth by grounding out, bringing up Tris

Speaker. He had hit the ball hard all game but thus far had but one hit, his first-inning bunt. Standing at the plate with his bat held low and flat, like Ty Cobb, this time he swung away and hit the ball square.

The liner rocketed to center field and came within an eyelash of making it over the fence for a home run, but to New York's good fortune, it smacked against the fence and then rolled away from the center fielder. Speaker tore toward first but nearly stumbled when first baseman Fred Merkle, using a trick that dated back to John McGraw's days with the Orioles, "accidently" wandered in his path. Speaker managed to stay on his feet, however, then rounded second and was nearly at third when Snodgrass's throw came in to short-stop Tillie Schaefer, who had taken over for Art Fletcher. Speaker appeared to be slowing up as he approached third, but when he looked over his left shoulder and saw Schaefer bobble the ball, he suddenly sped up. As he did, third baseman Buck Herzog got in his way, caus-ing Speaker to take a bad step and nearly fall once again before he careened toward home.

Tillie Schaefer's throw had Speaker beat by ten feet, but when catcher Artie Wilson, set up just in front of the plate, tried to catch the ball and spin to his left to put the tag on Speaker, he couldn't hang on to it and the ball rolled free. Speaker, twisting out of the way be-hind home, slid past without touching the plate. As Silk O'Loughlin leaned over the proceedings with his hands at his sides, Wilson real-ized that he didn't have the ball, Speaker realized that he had missed the base, and both men suddenly sprang into action. Wilson grabbed the ball and dove toward Speaker as Speaker, from his knees, launched himself toward home, his right hand reaching out. An instant be-fore Wilson reached him, Speaker slapped home to tie the game, 6–6. Speaker was given a triple on the hit, and an error was charged to Wilson.

Speaker jumped to his feet and, limping badly, let O'Loughlin have it, claiming in the most profane terms that first Merkle and then Her-zog had blocked his path and he had the sprained ankle to prove it, but O'Loughlin claimed not to have seen anything illegal. Speaker then took up his case with base umpire Charlie Rigler, but Rigler hadn't seen anything either. Speaker limped off, still complaining, waving his arms in the air in frustration as the Giants smirked.

Mathewson was gassed, but McGraw decided to stick with his pitcher, win, lose, or draw. The pitcher tried to wiggle out of the jam and, after toeing the rubber, stepped off and threw to Merkle at first, making an appeal that Speaker had missed first base, but his plea was denied. Then Mathewson took a deep breath, dug deep, and threw.

Even the bands were tired now, and it was almost too dark to read the music anyway. Fenway Park was nearly silent as he released the pitch, but the crack of the bat as Lewis sliced the ball to right brought the crowd to its feet.

It was as if Fenway Park was suddenly some billiard table and every ball hit some new trick bank shot. Once again, the Red Sox lost a home run by an eyelash as Lewis's hit found the two-by-four-inch railing and fell back onto the field. Lewis pulled up at second base with another double, incredulous. Gardner, his eye now black from his earlier encounter with the ground ball, tried to win the game with a smash through the hole on the right side, but Larry Doyle reached out with one hand, knocked it down, then threw him out. Stahl then grounded out and the game was still tied.

As the teams exchanged positions Speaker stopped Buck Herzog near the pitcher's mound, blocking his way like a matador stopping a bull. The two men jawed at one another for a minute and then nearly came to blows until first Larry Doyle and then John McGraw himself came out and kept Herzog from trying to knock Speaker down again, this time with his fist. Jake Stahl, having seen enough of Charley Hall, who had walked four in two and two-thirds innings, made the only move he had left and replaced Hall with Hugh Bedient.

By then, as Damon Runyon wrote, it was 4:45 p.m. and "somber dusk was shrouding Fenway . . . lights were popping up in the windows of houses beyond the wall and electric signs were commencing to twinkle on the roofs of distant buildings." The two clubs were exhausted, yet both knew they needed to work quickly—Silk O'Loughlin had informed each manager that he would call the game at the end of the inning. The Giants got Snodgrass and Becker on in the eleventh on a hit-by-pitch and a walk as Bedient showed nothing but nerves, but both men, desperate to reach scoring position, were cut down stealing. The Red Sox worked quickly in their half as well, swinging at almost everything. When Mathewson threw his 128th and final pitch of the game to Hugh Bedient, he topped the ball back to the mound for the third out in the eleventh inning. Silk O'Loughlin waved his hand and the game was over.

It was a tie, 6–6, but although it was not yet obvious, for Boston it was far better than kissing your sister. The tie contest—slowly, inexorably, and irrevocably—tilted the advantage Boston's way. As the National Commission had decided earlier, a tie game would be made up in the city in which it had been played. So instead of getting on a train to New York, the teams would stay in Boston for another game at Fenway the next day, and New York's home-field advantage was now less pronounced. Moreover, if the Series was extended because of the tie, Joe Wood might be available to pitch in not just three but four games. So could Tesreau, but the Sox, after discovering that he was tipping his pitches, were not afraid to face him again.

Fenway Park had done its job. While the vagaries of the ballpark's recent makeover had taken away several potential long hits and created several others, at the most critical time it had also accommodated Boston's eighth-inning comeback and helped the home team avoid a loss. And now they would get to play game 2 again.

That night, however, more than just the outcome of the game was on the minds of the players. Precisely the situation Mathewson had described to Sam Crane earlier that day had taken place, a tie game, and after the game Mathewson again discussed the issue with his teammates. He explained to them that if the Series went to its full complement of games, the owners were in line to receive a windfall of somewhere between $70,000 and $80,000. While the players were still likely to receive a record payout, none of them were happy at the prospect of playing an extra game without compensation—no one liked to work for free. Mathewson, knowing that he needed as much support as possible before approaching the commission with a complaint, decided he would bring up the issue with the Red Sox before deciding how to proceed. Meanwhile, they would all keep playing.

After using Collins, Hall, and Bedient in game 2, Stahl had little choice but to pitch Buck O'Brien, the pride of Brockton and 20-13 during the regular season, in game 3. McGraw, on the other hand, was always looking for an edge and remained circumspect. Even though he would later have both Tesreau and Marquard warm up before the game, the Red Sox expected his choice to be Marquard and planned accordingly. They knew that it would take more than Tesreau and Mathewson to beat them. Marquard would have to pitch at some point, and for the Giants to win he would somehow have to recapture the magic that had led him to nineteen straight wins to start the season. McGraw had tried everything to get him to return to form and had used him sparingly in September, hoping the rest would help, but in limited duty he had shown few signs of regaining his form. The Royal Rooters, in particular, salivated at the opportunity to see Marquard on the mound, for after the tie game New York fans were surprisingly confident and Boston backers had found plenty of New Yorkers eager to bet on game 3 at even money.

On the morning of October 10 Jerome Kelley awoke, heard rain dripping from the eaves outside his bedroom window, and rushed to Fenway Park. All morning, as the rain slowly turned to drizzle, he supervised his crew in the now-familiar task of trying to make the field at Fenway Park playable. Just before noon, with the game still in doubt but the sun just starting to peek through the clouds, Kelley had his men peel back the canvas they had put in place over the infield the previous evening so the umpires could inspect the field. They nodded their approval, and as the clouds skidded off thousands of Bostonians who had heard that tickets had gone wanting for the tie game left for lunch and did not return to work. Those who had purchased tickets in advance were notified in the morning papers that even though the first game at Fenway had ended in a tie, they should use their tickets marked "game 2" for the next contest. In the event the tie caused a fourth contest to be played at Fenway, fans with reserved seats were told that they would need to present their game 3 ticket stubs to acquire tickets. An already confusing situation was getting even more convoluted.

The crush at Fenway Park was tremendous as more than twenty thousand fans converged and tried to buy a ticket in the final two hours. This time the precious pasteboards disappeared before the line in the street had reached its end, and those who could not manage to find a ticket were forced to improvise. Signs and streetlights that offered any kind of view of the park were commandeered and sagged under the weight of boys and young men willing to risk their lives for a view of the ball game, and a number of enterprising fans even scaled the outside of the left-field wall and watched the game perched precariously on its top edge, the first to sit there since the first game of the season. Others sat atop the fence in extreme center field near the flagpole. An enterprising garage owner on Lansdowne Street erected bleachers on the roof, similar to the seats that have been erected on rooftops adjacent to Chicago's Wrigley Field. Even the bull-shaped sign on the left-field wall was commandeered again. In the *Globe* an unnamed female reporter wrote that "the great palpitating sea of faces was like one huge round blackboard of life."

The Rooters indulged in the usual shenanigans before the game, but there was little other pomp and circumstance beyond the presentation of a Chalmers automobile to Tris Speaker, his reward for being named the league's most valuable player. His New York counterpart, Larry Doyle, had received his car before the first game of the Series, and Speaker waved Doyle over to join him in the car. The NL MVP complied, and the New Yorker received a polite ovation, but then Speaker surprised everyone by starting the engine, putting the car in gear, and taking off, turf flying off the rear wheels as they spun in the mud and Jerome Kelley cringed. According to the *Times*, "Speaker shattered all the Boston speed laws by whirling around the baseball field at such a clip that the crowd's heart was in its mouth for fear that both joy riders would be pitched out." Before the day was over the record crowd of 34,624 would experience many more "heart in the mouth" moments.

The first two games had come down to the last pitch, and so would the third. Buck O'Brien, the thirty-year-old rookie, was better than Joe Wood had been in game 1 and gave up only two runs, one in the second after Red Murray—again—led off with a double and scored on Herzog's sacrifice fly, and a second run in the fifth when Herzog planted one in the stands in left and then scored on Art Fletcher's single. Apart from that, O'Brien's spitball and the occasional fastball and curve kept the Giants off balance as he scattered only six hits and three walks in one of the better pitching performances of the Series.

Unfortunately for Boston, Rube Marquard, who had cost the Giants some $11,000 to sign several years before and had been considered a complete bust until his record-breaking streak at the start of the 1912 season, only to turn bust again, improbably turned back the clock. He was once again pitching like the man who could not be beat, using a fastball nearly as dominant as that of Joe Wood. Through eight innings he scattered five hits and struck out six, shutting out Boston while not allowing a man past second base. Only once did the Red Sox threaten, when Jake Stahl walloped one to deep left-center, nearly knocking the men off the bull, a ball that would have been a home run in most ballparks and might have even been one in Fenway Park, albeit of the inside-the-park variety, were it not for the ground rules that held Stahl at second base. In the eighth Stahl, watching the game slip away, became desperate. In the words of Ring Lardner, he "began to rush the militia," using two pinch hitters, a rarity at the time, batting for both Bill Carrigan and O'Brien. Yet neither replacement could crack Marquard. Hick Cady then took over behind the plate, and Hugh Bedient came on to pitch the ninth.

In his relief appearance in game 2, Bedient had started out by hitting the first batter, and he did so again, plunking Buck Herzog. Cady saved him by cutting down Herzog on a steal attempt, but then Chief Meyers singled, bringing up the much-maligned Art Fletcher. Fletcher hit a flare toward center field, and the lumbering Meyers, eager to give Marquard an insurance run, took off from first without giving a thought to the possibility that the ball might be caught.

Tris Speaker was in center field, and no man in baseball played the position better. In a play that in another context would probably still be talked about today, he chased down Fletcher's drive, then pulled up, checking on the runner. Meyers, oblivious, was charging toward third. Speaker could have beaten the husky catcher to first base had he chosen to, but there was no need. Besides, when he stopped short his ankle, hurt while trying to avoid Herzog the day before and now wrapped in adhesive tape, started to give way. He threw to first for the double play, and Boston was out of the inning.

Despite the fact that Boston was only three outs away from defeat, not a fan in the stands or perched atop anything made any move to leave. All year long the Red Sox had shown a propensity for making late-inning comebacks, and even as the sun began to dip below the horizon and long autumnal shadows made it hard for fans to track the ball—now darkened by grass stains and tobacco juice—no one left the ballpark. If a season at Fenway had taught them anything, it was that no game was ever, ever over.

Speaker led off. He could barely walk, but the Giants did not know that, and it stayed a secret when he popped up to Fletcher for the first out. Duffy Lewis then stepped in.

He had collected Boston's first hit in the second inning, when he looped a line drive to right, but he was hardly feeling confident. The pull hitter had been late on Marquard all day. This time he was not only late but weak.

The ball bounced harmlessly to the hole between first and second. Fred Merkle, still playing Lewis to pull, was well off first base and went after the ball, which might well have been more easily caught by Doyle. Lewis broke from the box quickly, but Marquard, probably thinking Doyle would field the ball, hesitated before breaking toward first. Merkle threw to the pitcher racing to the bag, but Lewis beat him to the base and was safe.

For the first time all day Marquard seemed to crack, visibly upset both at himself and at Merkle for not covering first and with Merkle for fielding the ball. He knew it was the kind of mistake that could cost a pitcher a ball game, the kind of bad break that had turned the second half of his year into a nightmare.

Now he had to face Larry Gardner with a man on, and he had to throw from the stretch. He knew better than anyone else that after more than 120 pitches his fastball was beginning to fade. Marquard threw, and Gardner, swinging from the left side like he was playing the wing in a hockey game on a pond in his native Vermont, took a wrist shot at an inside fastball.

It rocketed down the right-field line in a flash, past Merkle, then hit the ground with overspin and almost seemed to speed up as it skipped and bounded to the corner. The ball hit the fence at the edge of the pavilion and bounded into deep right field, where Josh Devore tore after it. Lewis was off with the pitch, and Gardner was chasing after him.

Charlie Wagner was coaching third, but he hit seventh, only two spots after Gardner. Just as Gardner hit the ball Tris Speaker had gone out to take Wagner's place so he could warm up in case he got a chance to hit.

As Lewis approached third he saw two men in Red Sox uniforms—

Wagner, waving him around, and another, Speaker, not doing anything. Confused, Lewis started to slow.

Behind him, Larry Gardner was running with his head down, thinking he probably had a triple, but as he approached second and looked toward third, he saw Lewis slowing down. Afraid he was being held up, Gardner put on the brakes.

Now Wagner got Lewis's attention, and the outfielder, not the fastest man in the world, took off for home. He still had plenty of time, for the throw was just on its way to the infield. Lewis scored easily, but by then Gardner had stopped at second. He could have walked to third, as Devore foolishly threw toward home, not third, and when Fred Merkle tried to cut the throw off the ball skipped away. But Gardner hesitated and then stayed where he was.

The crowd roared and booed, happy that Boston scored but disappointed that Gardner only made second. Had Lewis not slowed down, Gardner might have scored himself when the relay got away from Merkle.

It was too late, although Gardner was still in scoring position. A single could tie the game.

Jake Stahl was up next, and he hit the ball hard, a comebacker straight at Marquard, but the pitcher made a nice play, knocking the ball down.

Now Gardner became the real goat. Upset at himself and frustrated, he decided to try for third. Marquard, a left-hander, scooped up the ball and threw a fastball to Herzog at third base. He dropped to his knee, blocking Gardner from the base, and tagged him out. Once again, as the cheers quieted, a smattering of boos was heard in the crowd.

STUPID WORK ON BASES

On first base Jake Stahl called time and waved to the bench, calling for Olaf Henriksen to pinch-run. The manager was almost out of players and didn't have a clue who would play first base if the Sox managed to take the lead—maybe Joe Wood?—but that was not his concern now. Henriksen could run, he could not, and Boston needed to score.

It seemed not to matter when Charlie Wagner, up next with the game on the line, bounced the ball to Art Fletcher. The Giants short-stop fielded the ball cleanly for once, flipped to first, and the Giants began to walk off the field, the game over.

But it was becoming hard to see as the moisture on the field after the rain began to turn to mist. Fred Merkle, trying to track the dark-ened ball against the crowd, backlit by the still bright sky, lost the ball, then found it and stabbed at it. But the ball bounced out of his mitt—barely the size of a garden glove and with hardly any pocket—and Wagner was safe.

Olaf Henriksen, on the roster only because of his speed, didn't know that. With two outs, he was running with the pitch and run-ning hard, as he should have been, and had already rounded second base when he realized the ball was free. Now, like a kid on the sand-lots, he just kept going. Merkle picked up the ball and made a strong throw to Herzog, and for a moment plate umpire Bill Evans, respon-sible for the play at third, hesitated. Then he put out his arms, palms down. Henriksen was safe, and Boston was somehow still alive, and the crowd, which had cheered and groaned and cheered and groaned, now got a chance to cheer again as Hick Cady stepped to the plate.

If Lewis's hit had unnerved Marquard, Gardner's smash and now Merkle's errors left the pitcher staring into the face of pure oblivion. The entire inning—indeed, the entire game—was playing out like a condensed version of his whole schizophrenic season. He and his roommate, right fielder Josh Devore, had spent much of the second half of the year consoling each other. Devore, as Runyon noted later, "had been taunted and joshed by the big town fans this season until his boyish heart was almost broken." The diminutive outfielder, who ran well but had no power, had, like Red Murray, been judged a failure during the 1911 World's Series, and a certain element among the fans at the Polo Grounds had done their best to remind him of that. In fact, few Giants followers thought he deserved a permanent place in the lineup.

Hick Cady stepped in. Cady let Marquard's first pitch pass wide, and Wagner lit out for second, hoping to draw a throw that would allow Henriksen to score, but the Giants let him go, willing to let the winning run reach scoring position rather than risk letting the tying run cross the plate.

Now the decision was McGraw's. With first base open, Marquard did not have to pitch to the catcher. Although the use of the intentional walk was extremely rare at the time, it was still an option. Hugh Bedient, a poor hitter, was due up, and Stahl's only option was to use another pitcher as a pinch hitter, something he had not done all year long.

The Giants manager did not move, and Marquard wound up and threw.

Cady swung from his heels and drove the ball deep to right-center field. In the stands, hats were in the air and hugs were in the offing as Fred Snodgrass in center and Devore in right both angled back for the ball, and as the space between the two men closed Henriksen danced across the plate and Wagner whirled around third. In the regular season, with the outfielders playing somewhat deeper, it would have been an easier catch, but now the wind was pushing the deep drive, and in pushing it the wind also held the ball up. The two outfielders converged, and with his last stride Devore cut in front of Snodgrass, raised his hands over his head, and reached out for the ball.

"Anyhow," wrote Ring Lardner a few moments later, almost out of words to describe it, "he caught up with the flying thing, grabbed it and held on." Devore gathered the ball in like a split end catching a pass over his shoulder, smothering the ball with both hands and then pulling it to his chest. In the center-field bleachers and in right, where they could see the ball and see right-field umpire Charlie Rigler signaling an out, the cheers stuck in the throats of Sox fans as Devore took a few stumbling strides, then got control and turned to run back to the dugout without breaking stride. But those watching from the grandstand, where the dark ball in the dimming light was almost impossible to see, saw Snodgrass and Devore slowing down and Wagner following Henriksen home, then heard cheers and felt the crush of a happy crowd turning toward the exits. Few thought to look at the scoreboard to confirm what their eyes told them had just happened.

Half the fans did not know it, and some would not know it until reading the newspapers the next morning, but Devore had indeed caught the "flying thing." The Red Sox had not won 3–2. The game had gone to the Giants, 2–1, and the Series was now tied in every way possible, one game for Boston, one game for New York, and one game tied.

GIANTS WIN, 2–1 DEVORE SNATCHES
VICTORY IN NINTH

It was back to New York.

Giant Killers

I doubt if the game has ever produced two gamer teams than the
Giants and Red Sox . . . When it's over both teams will realize that
it was a baseball war to the bitter end. As I have said all along, the
teams are evenly matched. Not the most skillful teams that ever
played for the big money, but rather fighters with the punch.

—Tim Murnane, *The Sporting News*

THE STRUGGLE FOR "the championship of the universe,"
wrote Ring Lardner after game 3, was on "even terms."
No kidding. As the players hurriedly dressed and rushed to
South Station to catch the *Gilt Edge Express* to New York, the two
clubs, both exhausted but one also exhilarated and the other exasperated, were spent. They had just played three games in which every
pitch in every inning had mattered and in which the fortunes of both
teams had swung back and forth so many times that fans had nearly
gotten whiplash just from watching.

The past seventy-two hours had decided nothing but this: the 1912
league champions were the two most closely matched teams in baseball—certainly in that season, probably in the short history of the
World's Series, and perhaps for all time. And now, after three games,
the World's Series would be a best-of-five, not best-of-seven, affair.
As R. E. McMillen of the *Boston Herald* wrote, whichever team won
game 4 would have an enormous advantage because "to the loser
falls the big task of gathering in three out of four of the remaining
games," a daunting prospect for any team so closely matched with its
opponent.

The Giants were confident, for as Sam Crane noted, they "have met the enemy, so to speak, bowed to them in defeat, fought them to a standstill and then overcame them." In other words, the Giants felt that they had momentum, that they had weathered all that the Red Sox could throw at them and survived, and they were looking forward to taking command back on their home turf.

The Red Sox, on the other hand, were not so ebullient. The main reason for that was Tris Speaker's ankle. His catch of Fletcher's drive had proven costly. When he boarded the train he was hopping on one foot, his ankle swollen and sore, a sight that sent gamblers racing to take advantage of such inside information. Even before the train pulled out of the station, Red Sox trainer Joe Quirk began working on the most valuable player's most valuable asset. He and everyone else knew that if Speaker could not run he could not play, and if Speaker could not play the odds of the Red Sox winning the Series were slim. As the train rumbled toward New York Quirk worked on the ankle nonstop, alternately soaking the appendage in hot water and Epsom salts, then trying to massage away the swelling. The Red Sox and their followers hoped that the weather forecast, which called for rain, was correct. If game 4, scheduled to be played on a Friday, was postponed and the rain fell on Saturday as well, the Series would not resume until Monday, as Sunday baseball was banned in New York as well as Boston. By then, they hoped Speaker would be healed.

But all hope was not lost. Regardless of the condition of Speaker's ankle, Boston still had Joe Wood. And for all their bluster on the train, the Giants had not yet proven they could beat him. If they could not do that, they were not going to beat the Red Sox.

While Speaker was having his ankle treated, players from both teams ate in the dining car and then retired, some to their seats and others to the neutral ground of the smoking car, where a passable truce between the two teams was in effect. Christy Mathewson and Buck Herzog approached knots of Red Sox players and let them know their concerns over the division of Series receipts, seeking their support. They did so quietly, for they did not want to alert the managers of either club to their activities. It was widely known that Jake Stahl owned a piece of the Red Sox, and most players assumed that McGraw owned a piece of the Giants. Each manager was representative of ownership and unlikely to look upon any sign of dissension with understanding. Bill Carrigan agreed to represent the Red Sox, and before the train pulled into New York Mathewson asked the National Commission, whose members were all riding on the train as well, for a meeting. They agreed, albeit without enthusiasm.

But Bill Carrigan, perhaps fearing some retribution from his manager, backed out. Mathewson went into the meeting alone.

The result of the meeting, which was short and abrupt, was no surprise. On all issues involving player rights the owners were the hammer and the players, even Mathewson, mere nails. In no uncertain terms August Herrmann told Mathewson that the rule restricting the player's share to the proceeds of the first four games, regardless of any ties, was the rule, and that was that, end of discussion. Mathewson then asked, as a compromise, if the commission would allow the players to play an exhibition against one another after the Series at a neutral location so they could make back the money for the tie game that way. This idea too was smacked down and dismissed out of hand. In fact, if the commission had its way, they wanted to make 1912 the last season in which the two World's Series contestants would split what Herrmann called "the good things of the World's Series," the players' share. He wanted every player in the league to see some Series swag.

He was not being beneficent. If every player in the league stood to make $500 or so each year from the World's Series, ownership could use the postseason bonus as an excuse to lower salaries across the board. "I am getting tired of the exorbitant and greedy demands of a few ballplayers who do not know when they are lucky," sniffed Herrmann.

When Mathewson met with a delegation of players from both teams and spread the word of the result of the meeting, as *Sporting Life* later reported, "the player delegation retired in an angry mood . . . with threats of a strike." But the players had virtually no public support. Fans weren't paying attention to the scant few paragraphs most newspapers gave to the issue, and the mainstream baseball press generally took the side of management. *Sporting Life* called the players' position "an unfair demand." With no time to organize, the players knew they were on their own. Unlike the Lawrence millworkers, they were not going to receive any support from the International Workers of the World. If a player went on strike, he could be banned from the major leagues for life and could do nothing about it.

That was the reality of the situation, and as the players discussed the matter among themselves they began to realize that if the National Commission would not agree to their demands, they might have to take action themselves. By the time the train pulled into New York players on both clubs were united against management, determined to try to revisit the issue, and, as would become clear, determined to earn back some of the money they felt had been stolen from them—and there were ways to do that without going on strike. For the time being, however, they were still determined to do their damnedest to defeat each other.

It was raining when the two clubs arrived in New York, and it rained most of the night and was still drizzling at dawn. Players from both teams looked out the windows of their hotels and apartments and hoped for a postponement. They worried that the weather would hurt the gate. Since this was the fourth game of the Series, unless the commission caved to their demands, it would be their last chance to reap a financial harvest from the proceedings. Or at least their last chance according to the rules.

In midmorning the four umpires made their way to the Polo Grounds to inspect the field. Although the clouds were low and dark and heavy, the rain had stopped. Only a smattering of fans stood in line waiting for tickets. As the players had feared, most fans thought the game would be called and either stayed home or went to work.

The diamond itself was covered by a tarpaulin, but there were puddles in the outfield, and any place not covered by grass was pure mud. Still, after some discussion the arbiters decided that the game would be played. Word spread quickly, and by 11:00 a.m. several thousand fans were in line for tickets and more were streaming to the park from every direction. Any fears that the weather would hold down the crowd proved to be unfounded. In fact, it probably had the opposite effect, as fans who had despaired at the notion of waiting in long lines all morning suddenly decided to take a chance at getting a ticket. By game time more than thirty-six thousand fans had crowded into the park.

After the histrionics of the first three games, game 4, aided perhaps by the absence of the Rooters and their incessant singing and banging of objects together, unfolded rather quietly. Boston's loudest and best-known fans, by and large, had stayed behind in Boston. Many had thought the game would surely be canceled because of the weather, while others stayed behind because the next day was Columbus Day, a holiday almost on a par with St. Patrick's Day for the overwhelmingly Catholic group. Boston, for the first time ever, was having a parade to celebrate the day. Although some individual members of the group made the trip, this time they did so without the accompaniment of their band, something Giants fans, Giants players, and aficionados of music appreciated.

Jeff Tesreau took the mound for New York under leaden skies. What enthusiasm the partisan crown could muster under the cold and damp conditions quickly went by the wayside as Hooper opened for Boston with a single. Yerkes followed with a bad bunt, and Chief Meyers scooped up the nubber, which barely made it into fair territory. He threw the ball away, however, and the Red Sox seemed likely to score. But Speaker, playing with his ankle heavily taped and moving cautiously, hit a ground ball to short and was doubled up at first for a double play. Another ground ball ended the inning for Boston, and Joe Wood took the mound.

It took about thirty seconds for Wood to announce his presence, punching out game 3 hero Josh Devore, who led off for the Giants. Even though Larry Doyle followed with a single, Snodgrass grounded out into a force play, then got too cute on first base. Acting like he was Ty Cobb, he danced off the bag and dared Wood to do anything about it. The pitcher, as if annoyed, picked him off, flicking the Giant away like a spot of lint on his shoulder.

The Bear Hunter knew he was in trouble and was suddenly as skittish as a mouse. Larry Gardner, knowing what was coming from Tesreau, opened the second with a triple to right. On a dry field the drive would probably have been a home run, for not only did the heavy ground slow the ball down but Gardner had to take care running the bases—the tarpaulin that had covered the infield had not been completely effective. A few moments later he danced home with the first run of the game when Tesreau, rattled, uncorked a wild pitch. Boston led, 1–0.

For the next five innings, wrote Hugh Fullerton, "New York had about as much chance to score as a sober man has to sleep on the midnight to Boston." Wood was rarely in trouble, and whenever it seemed he might be, Charlie Wagner, playing his best game of the Series, made one spectacular play after another. Wood, perhaps still tired because of all the time he spent warming up during game 2, used his fastball only when necessary and spent much of the game mixing in his drop ball and changing speeds. On the dark day virtually every commentator noted how difficult it was to see the ball after the first inning or so, when the mix of mud and saliva turned home plate umpire Charlie Rigler's choice of baseballs into a decision between dark, darker, and darkest. But that worked against the Red Sox at the plate, and despite knowing what was coming, they found it hard to score. Boston finally added a second run in the fourth when Jake Stahl, after botching a sacrifice bunt and reaching base on the fielder's choice, surprised everyone by stealing second, moved to third on Wagner's grounder, and then scored on Hick Cady's base hit. Wood led 2–0, a margin that, for him, was nearly insurmountable.

Still, the Giants tried. In the seventh Merkle, unable to hit what he could not see, struck out to start the inning, bringing up Buck Herzog. According to Fullerton, "He seemed helpless with the dark ball, but fouled it into the stand and a new ball was thrown out." Home plate umpire Charlie Rigler was out of baseballs. He retrieved some more and tossed Wood a "pearl," a brand-new white one. It was like the lights went on—Herzog singled and then went to second on an out. Art Fletcher found the new ball to his liking as well and followed with a double down the right-field line, Herzog just making it home under Cady's tag. The score was now 2–1.

Jeff Tesreau was up next, but McGraw knew the Giants were running out of time. He called on his pinch hitter par excellence, Moose McCormick. McCormick, who could not run or do much else, was made to pinch-hit, once saying, "I never worried when I went to the plate. I always thought this when I was asked to bat for another, 'Well, if I fail, no fault can be found with me, for if everybody on the team had been hitting I would never had been called on.'" He came through, singling off Steve Yerkes's shin. McGraw, knowing his club might not have another chance to score, waved Fletcher, who had slowed rounding third, toward the plate.

The Boston second baseman scrambled after the ball in short right, picked it up, and threw home, where Hick Cady crouched before the plate, blocking it like a fallen tree with Fletcher still fifteen feet from home. "Fletcher," wrote Paul Shannon in the *Post* later, "saw the cause was lost and that his only hope lay in knocking the ball out of the hands of the catcher . . . therefore he hurled himself straight at the catcher, not with feet forward . . . but sideways, so the big catcher received the full force of the collision." Cady held on, and Fletcher, noted Shannon, "got the worst of it." Both men tumbled to the ground, Cady absorbing the blow with his ribs but applying the tag and sending Fletcher over his shoulder in a somersault. When Fletcher opened his eyes he found Cady, enraged, bent over him, ready to tear him apart. McGraw rushed to the aid of his player, Tris Speaker raced in to back up Cady, and umpire Charlie Rigler got between all four of them and was finally able to convince everyone to cool off.

The Giants' last chance came in the eighth when, with two out, Snodgrass reached on an error and Red Murray singled, bringing up Fred Merkle with two on. After the batter drove a long ball foul into the stands, Cady called time to settle Wood down, and Stahl joined them both on the mound for a conference. Even though Wood often professed that he felt no fear on the mound, his teammates knew better. Harry Hooper later recalled that at times Wood got so worked up that he couldn't even speak. Fortunately, he was adept at channeling his fear into his performance. Given a chance to take a few breaths and steady himself, Wood poured the ball past Snodgrass for a strikeout to end the threat.

As he walked back to the Boston dugout a fan delivered what the *Times* called the "tribute de luxe" to Wood. The box seats in the Polo Grounds were adorned with flowers, and a smitten young woman plucked a handful of posies and tossed them to Wood as he stepped into the dugout, the flowers landing on his head and shoulders like a laurel wreath.

The Red Sox tacked on an insurance run in the top of the ninth off relief pitcher Red Ames when Wood himself knocked home Gardner with a single, making the score 3–1. The Giants began wondering what was on the dinner menu in the dining car of the *Gilt Edge Express.* They went out quickly in the ninth. Wood, whom the *Tribune* afterward called a "mighty magician and apostle of necromancy far too potent for the pigmy bats of the Giants," had his second victory of the Series after scattering nine hits and this time striking out only eight. When he left the field the New York crowd that had hoped to jeer his demise instead stood and gave the Boston pitcher some well-earned cheers. Of his 108 pitches, only 28 had been called a ball by umpire Charlie Rigler.

JOE WOOD, THE GIANT–KILLER, BESTS TESREAU AGAIN, 3–1

Once more the players dressed quickly after the game and were ferried to Grand Central Station to make the train back to Boston. Speaker, still hobbled, traveled once again between the two cities soaking his ankle in warm water. The palm of Hick Cady's glove hand was black and swollen, the price of catching Joe Wood all year long, but this time the Red Sox were the ebullient ball club, while the Giants were tight-lipped and grim. They had been in the lead all season long, and now, for the first time all year, it looked like they were licked.

Fenway Park was shrouded in fog the next morning, a low dense cloud that soaked everything and blocked out the sun, but once the decision was made to play the game and the gates opened at noon, another record crowd pressed its way into the park. McRoy and McAleer somehow found a way to squeeze an extra fifty-nine fans into every nook and cranny to set another attendance record, trumping the mark set only two days before. Many fans were already half in their cups, for the Columbus Day parade was winding through Boston and more than 100,000 people were on the streets.

Despite the dank weather, as the players on both teams scanned the morning paper—the Red Sox reading every eager word about Wood's victory the day before and the Giants flipping through in search of the funny pages—they were heartened to learn that they were rich. The players' share of receipts from the first four games totaled $147,571.70 on a paid attendance of 138,006, bettering the record set the previous year by the Giants and the A's. The winning club would divvy up 60 percent of that sum, meaning the champions would earn about $4,000 a man and the losers nearly $3,000. It was nice to know a check was in the offing, but at the same time the players knew that the tie game was bringing the owners a windfall they had done nothing at all to earn. The more the players thought about it and talked with each other, the more steamed they became. It just wasn't right. The National Commission was stealing about $1,000 a man, enough to buy a new automobile.

Christy Mathewson was McGraw's choice as pitcher for game 5, but Stahl had not only Ray Collins warming up before the game but also, in something of a surprise, Hugh Bedient and Charley Hall. Most observers had expected him to select the veteran Collins over the rookie Bedient, even though the Giants had hit Collins hard in his earlier start.

As game time approached Stahl kept scanning the sky. Although the fog had lifted a bit, it was still dark—as dark as it had been in New York the day before. Stahl had noted how hard it had been to see the ball, particularly when Wood threw a fastball.

Collins was a control artist. Bedient did not throw as hard as Wood—no one but Walter Johnson could claim that—but he threw harder than any other Boston pitcher, and that helped him to a record of 20-9 for the season. That wasn't bad for a rookie, though Bedient, like every other Boston pitcher, suffered in comparison to Wood. He used a slow wind-up and then threw across his body, a deceptive motion that made it seem as though he threw even harder than he did. His fastball, thought Stahl, combined with the dark day and a dark baseball, made Bedient his best bet to shut the Giants down. Although control problems had plagued both of his earlier relief appearances in the Series, if Bedient could find the plate Stahl believed that he could give the Giants real trouble. With a one-game lead in the Series, Stahl could afford to gamble, and if the rookie stumbled Collins and Hall would be ready.

John McGraw had no such luxury. Although some pressed him to turn to Marquard with only one day's rest, McGraw resisted the temptation. Besides, Mathewson had already won more than three hundred games in a Giants uniform, and even if he no longer had the stuff that had once made him the best in baseball, he still had the heart of a champion. McGraw knew that Matty would give everything he had.

When the batteries were announced, there was a buzz around Fenway Park, for not only did Bedient get the start for Boston, but so too did Hick Cady behind the plate. Thus far in the Series Stahl seemed to have decided that Cady would catch Wood and Carrigan would catch everyone else. The veteran had been behind the plate when both Collins and O'Brien had pitched, but now the manager went with Cady. It might have been just a hunch on Stahl's part, but Stahl may also have gotten wind of the fact that Carrigan had again agreed to represent the Red Sox in a meeting that Mathewson was trying to set up with the National Commission to discuss the players' grievances over the tie game. That was like trying to take money out of both Stahl's pocket and that of his father-in-law. In any event, Bill Carrigan's World's Series was over. He would spend the remaining games coaching first base.

As game time approached the raucous crowd grew more restless and nasty. All Series long the Boston crowd in the center-field bleachers had been razzing Giant center fielder Fred Snodgrass unmercifully, reminding him of his play in the 1911 World's Series. In game 3 of that Series Snodgrass had spiked Philadelphia third baseman Frank Baker. A's fans thought he had done so deliberately, and when Snodgrass appeared on the street after the game he was hooted and hissed and his life was threatened—one newspaper report even indicated that he had been shot. Fortunately, the report was false, but Snodgrass was petrified. McGraw saw the toll that the threats were having on his center fielder, and when the Series was delayed for almost a week by rain he sent Snodgrass home to regain his nerve. Ever since, fans had viewed Snodgrass as soft and something of a coward. They let him know it, and he heard every word.

The Boston crowd had detected his weak spot, and as Snodgrass and the Giants warmed up before the game the outfielder's rabbit ears kept growing. He finally blew up and jawed back at the crowd, but only managed to further incite the Boston partisans. When a ball strayed near the stands and a couple of fans tumbled over the low fence to retrieve it, Snodgrass, his temper growing hotter by the minute, threw a fastball at the interlopers like they were part of a carnival game. This really set the crowd off, and a few moments later so many had pressed against the fence to razz Snodgrass that it gave way and a hundred or so Boston fans tumbled onto the field. The police ushered them back into the seats, and the grounds crew came out and secured the fence, but Snodgrass would not spend another second in Fenway Park without the fans in center field doing everything in their power to drive him to distraction. After the game the *Herald* noted that the crowd "greatly affected his batting" during the game—Snodgrass went hitless—and offered that "no man is capable of doing his best when the crowd is riding him." If that was the case, Snodgrass had more trouble in his future.

As Bedient took the mound and began to throw his final warm-up tosses McGraw and the Giants were eager to face him. The Giants manager expected the young pitcher to show his nerves and cautioned his team to be patient. In his first two appearances Bedient had been unable to find the plate. McGraw was convinced that if they gave Bedient the opportunity, he would beat himself.

Leading off for New York, little Josh Devore made McGraw look like the genius he was. As McGraw hooted and hollered at Bedient from the third-base coaching box, the Boston pitcher was wild high, and Devore worked a walk. Doyle, up next, tried to be patient as well, but Bedient's fastball, like Wood's, had a "hop" to it. Doyle swung at a ball that looked like it was coming in waist high, but he hit underneath the pitch as it passed by his armpits, sending up a high foul that Lewis caught in the narrow space between the baseline and the third-base stand. Fred Snodgrass, up next and determined to silence the Boston crowd, then bounced a pitch to where ground balls died on the Fenway Park infield, the glove of Charlie Wagner, and the shortstop turned a neat double play.

The two clubs parried one another for the first few innings, each threatening but neither team scoring as both Mathewson and Bedient seemed overly cautious and a bit off their game. With each at-bat, however, the pitchers seemed to settle down. The game was still scoreless when Harry Hooper stepped to the plate to lead off the bottom of the third. Mathewson did not know it, but during this at-bat he was facing more than just a dangerous left-handed hitter. He was also pitching against architect James E. McLaughlin, builder Charles Logue, and the ballpark they had created together, Fenway Park.

On his second pitch Mathewson threw one wide. Hooper hit the ball flush but late, slicing a line drive to the right of Buck Herzog. The third baseman, playing off the line, dove but could not reach it. The ball hit the ground in shallow left and started skipping to the corner with New York left fielder Josh Devore, hoping to cut the ball off and hold Hooper to a single, in pursuit.

There was, noted Ralph McMillen of the *Herald*, "a shade of English on the ball," and the drive skipped and rolled innocently toward the left-field corner, where the foul line met the wall. Left-field umpire Bill Klem watched closely as Boston fans, screaming and hanging over the third-base stands, saw the ball bound by Devore, now a certain double.

The new third-base stands met the left-field line at an angle about thirty feet from the left-field fence, then, instead of running parallel to the foul line, angled back slightly away from the field. Although James McLaughlin's drawing of Fenway Park with the new arrangement of seats for the World's Series showed the fence running in front of the Duffy's Cliff bleachers and meeting those stands, cutting the left-field wall off from the field of play completely, what Charles Logue built was not exactly what McLaughlin drew. To accommodate the construction of the new third-base stands and allow fans easier access to the seats on Duffy's Cliff, instead of extending across the foul line to meet the stands the fence stopped where the bleachers themselves did, *at* the foul line. That left what McMillen accurately described as a "pie-shaped open space between these stands and the Lewis Ledge [Duffy's Cliff] seats" (see illustration 9).

For the Red Sox this pie-shaped piece of real estate and its narrow entrance way would prove to be a banquet, but for the Giants the slice of property the *New York Tribune* later dismissed as an "ugly triangle" was pure food poisoning. The ball skipped into the space and rattled around like it was in a pinball machine, glancing off the tall board fence that covered the end of the new stands, rolling up the small exposed wedge of Duffy's Cliff to the wall, then clattering back and forth between the fence, the bleachers, and the third-base stands. Meanwhile Hooper was rounding first and racing to second.

Devore raced into the triangle, with umpire Bill Klem close behind him to make sure the ball remained accessible. If it became wedged against the bottom of the fence or bounced beneath the bleachers, Klem would have no choice but to rule the hit a ground-rule double.

It did not. Devore scrambled into the piece of pie, spotted the ball, and then, completely out of sight of most of the press box and everyone else in the park except for those far across the field in the stands along the first-base line, picked it up. He wanted to throw, but from his vantage point he could not see third base or extend his arm to throw. Devore was forced to take a few quick steps out from the piece of pie and into the outfield where everyone, including Harry Hooper, who was now well on his way to third, could see him. "When the relay finally reached the infield," wrote McMillen, "Hoop was resting comfortably on the final hassock" (third base), and the Boston crowd was shaking the park to its foundations.

Fenway Park had never been more friendly to the Boston cause. With a strong assist from McLaughlin and Logue, the ballpark had just made the difference in the game. Hooper's hit may well have been the key at-bat for the entire Series, for it left the Red Sox in position to win the game and put themselves only one game away from a world championship.

Mathewson, who rarely allowed anything to bother him, seemed taken aback, as if he could not believe that Hooper's bouncing little line drive had resulted in a triple, and Buck Herzog went out to the mound to steady him. Steve Yerkes stepped to the plate. In center field the crowd pelted Snodgrass with a constant barrage of abuse, and the center fielder edged a few steps closer to home plate. Hooper ran well, and Snodgrass knew that if Yerkes hit the ball to center, his only chance to catch Hooper at the plate would be on a short fly ball.

His opening day heroics notwithstanding, Yerkes had been considered the weakest link in Boston's batting order for the rest of the season, and the player least likely to drive the ball for extra bases. But thus far in the Series he was doing better than he had any right to. Playing the best baseball of his career at the best possible time, Yerkes was outperforming his New York counterpart, NL MVP Larry Doyle, by a wide margin.

Mathewson threw, and Yerkes connected, driving the ball over Fred Snodgrass's right shoulder toward left-center field. The outfielder was slow to react—they were saying some really awful stuff to him in center field—and then the ball hit the left-field fence near where it met the center-field fence and caromed away. Snodgrass ran a gauntlet of verbal abuse as he tracked the ball along the fence, and by the time he ran it down and threw it back in to shortstop Art Fletcher, Yerkes was on his way to third, where he avoided Herzog's tag on the relay with a beautiful hook slide to the outfield side of the base. Hooper walked home, and Boston led, 1–0.

Trailing 1–0 had not overly concerned the Giants, but trailing 2–0 did. With the heart of Boston's batting order coming to the plate, McGraw moved the infield in to cut off a potential second run at the plate. He also sent pitcher George Wiltse to warm up in foul ground along the right-field line. Desperation had replaced confidence.

Tris Speaker knew his role. He got a good pitch and hit it hard, a ground ball that under normal circumstances would have knocked in a run. But this one was hit directly to Larry Doyle.

Yerkes, running on contact, lit out for home. "It was a tense moment," reported the *Times* later. "The crowd jumped to its feet as the hot bouncer steamed toward Doyle, who set himself to check its course.

"Shame on Larry! Set as he was for the ball the sphere didn't even tarry to flirt with his hands as he dug them into the dirt. The place where he dug was not the place where the ball passed." In other words, Doyle missed it, the hard ground ball going right between his legs. Yerkes, who would have been out by a mile had Doyle fielded the ball cleanly, danced home. Even though Speaker killed the rally when he forgot about his sore ankle and tried to take second, only to be thrown out by right fielder Red Murray, Boston now led 2–0.

That was it. Pitching with a lead, Bedient, who had seemed nervous early, was now the epitome of calm as one Giant after another came to the plate and lifted an easy fly to the Boston outfield. Mathewson, too, seemed changed by the outburst—not another Boston hitter reached base the remainder of the game as he slammed the door.

New York's only real chance to do any damage against Bedient came when Merkle hit a ground-rule double into the Duffy's Cliff bleachers to lead off the seventh and later scored on Larry Gardner's error. Bedient just yawned and got back to work, however, retiring the next seven hitters without incident. The Red Sox won, 2–1.

WITH BEDIENT PITCHING THE GAME OF HIS LIFE, RED SOX WIN, 2–1

"Four hundred and ten years ago today," wrote Hugh Fullerton after the game, "Mr. Columbus discovered America and this afternoon Mr. McGraw and some other millions of more or less transient New Yorkers discovered to their astonishment that the Boston Americans possessed more than one pitcher." Hugh Bedient's performance left the Red Sox only one win away from a world championship, and the Giants were now in the precarious position of needing to defeat Boston in three straight games.

The young pitcher was lauded after the game, a Giant killer suddenly equal in status to Wood. In the *Globe* Wallace Goldsmith drew the pitcher as an actual giant of lore and legend, equal in size, next to Fenway Park, as the Prudential Center tower is today and crushing the baseball Giants beneath his grandstand-sized feet. As far as the championship aspirations of the Giants were concerned, the cartoon was no exaggeration. If they were to come back and win the Series, the Giants would somehow have to play David to the Goliath the Red Sox had become.

Now the Giants, who had been so confident only a few hours before, turned on each other. Larry Doyle, he of the critical eighth-inning error, berated Fred Snodgrass for misplaying Yerkes's triple, and some members of the New York press unloaded on McGraw for not managing aggressively early in the game, when the Giants had had a few opportunities to put pressure on Bedient.

The Giants left immediately after the game for New York since the next day, Sunday, was an off day—the first of the Series, due to the Sunday baseball ban. Meanwhile the Red Sox, who did not intend to leave for New York until Sunday evening, stayed in Boston.

It might have been better if the Red Sox had not had time to stop and think. Over the next twenty-four hours the Red Sox players, manager Jake Stahl, and owner James McAleer had a chance to ponder the variables, and that might have been the worst thing that could have happened.

No matter where you went, from McGreevey's saloon in Roxbury to the Oak Room at the Copley Plaza Hotel or the lobby of the Hotel Bretton Hall in New York, and no matter who was talking, from bartenders and sportsmen to newsboys, ballplayers, and chambermaids, if you were a baseball fan in either Boston or New York on Sunday, October 13, 1912, there was only one question on everyone's lips: who would the Red Sox pitch against the Giants on Monday? Not until 1948, when Sox manager Joe McCarthy selected Denny Galehouse to pitch the playoff game against the Cleveland Indians in Fenway Park, would the choice of a starting pitcher by a Boston manager be more controversial.

Nearly everyone, except Bedient, was ready—Wood, Collins, and O'Brien—and there were sound reasons to select any of them. By Monday Ray Collins would have four full days of rest and Buck O'Brien three, and both had pitched effectively against the Giants earlier. In the *Herald*, Ralph McMillen speculated that "it looks very much like Buck O'Brien" and pointed out that Collins had warmed up before game 5 and would probably do the same in game 6. In the *Post*, Paul Shannon also thought Stahl would pick O'Brien, writing that, "while with Wood in the box the Boston team would not have the slightest doubt of the issue, the players are anxious to see the Buck return to the rubber and redeem himself." But in the *Globe*, Tim Murnane reported that "Joe Wood is anxious to go again." Although he cautioned that "Wood with two days' rest will not be at his best," he admitted that one reason not to pitch Wood was that if Wood were to pitch the contest and then lose, "the Giants would be in the stronger position" for the rest of the Series. In addition, if Stahl held Wood back a day, then Bedient might also be available for game 7. The players, in their various ghostwritten columns, were blandly magnanimous, evincing confidence in victory no matter who pitched. The *New York World* reported that "opinion was about evenly divided" among the Red Sox players over who would pitch, and another report suggested that half "the boys" expected Wood to take the mound and half either Collins or O'Brien. Their preference probably split along ethnic and religious lines between the KCs and the Masons. Everything else did, and this situation was no different.

There were many reasons for Stahl to pitch Wood. For one, Wood wanted the ball, and that was not insignificant. He had carried the Sox this far and felt he deserved to have the ball in his hand when they won. For another, many observers believed that whenever a team had a chance to win a championship, they should do so with all due haste. That meant using the best pitcher if at all possible. Although, after pitching on Friday, Wood would have to pitch on only two days' rest, that was not a major concern. In his last start he had handled the Giants after only two days' rest between games 1 and 4, and Wood had lost only five times all season, no matter how much or how little rest he had. Were he to lose on Monday, in theory he might still pitch the finale on Wednesday, and no one thought he could lose twice, not even when pitching on one day of rest. These were the days when pitchers were ironmen, and little thought was given to the future.

But that argument also assumed that Wood's arm was healthy. No one, apart from Wood himself, knew if that was the case. While he had appeared stronger in his two World's Series appearances than he had late in the regular season, his change of speed and his dependence on "drop" balls during game 4, as noted in the press, were either red flags for a sore arm or a sign that he was becoming a pitcher, not just a thrower, one who had successfully changed his approach to keep the Giants off balance.

Although the question of who Stahl would select to pitch made great conversation, the Red Sox, needing only one more win, had the Giants on the run, and most players were anxious for the Series to end regardless of who pitched. The season had been long, and the finish was in sight. Some players were already making plans to leave for their homes directly from New York after Monday's game—Charlie Wagner had a new son to spend time with, and Bedient, Hall, and Collins all had new brides waiting at home. The Giants were down on the ground; it was time to step on their neck and put them out of their misery. All Stahl had to do was make a decision.

If in fact the decision was Stahl's to make. When Stahl and the Red Sox boarded their train for New York at five-thirty Sunday evening, the manager may well have learned that the choice was not his alone.

Barely a hundred fans saw the club off, for most of the Rooters had already left for New York. "The boys feel pretty sure of the result," quipped Stahl as he boarded the train. The question of who would pitch was still up in the air, but as he climbed aboard Joe Wood told a New York reporter, "I am ready to pitch tomorrow if wanted, but I have not heard yet whether I am to be called on."

James McAleer had stayed in the background for much of the Series, allowing his manager and his players to do most of the talking for the team, saying little more than that he had faith in his club and expected to win. But McAleer was under some financial pressure— he had gone into debt to buy into the team, and the other investors in the club were at least as concerned with dollars and cents as with hits and runs. Although the World's Series had been lucrative so far, everybody could do the math: every additional game the Red Sox played meant money in the bank because, from game 5 forward, the players didn't get another dime. Ten percent of the gate went to the National Commission, and the Sox and Giants split the rest, giving the Sox around an extra $30,000 for each game played—nearly half their operating expenses for the year.

That was something to consider. If the Series ended with game 6, the two teams were leaving as much as $60,000 on the table. Not that anyone was suggesting that the Red Sox should throw the game . . . but if you owned a piece of the Red Sox there *were* worse things than losing game 6 and making an extra $30,000.

There is a baseball axiom that if a team is concerned about anything other than winning, it is destined to lose. On the train ride to New York the evidence suggests that the Red Sox—both players and management—thought the Series was in the bag and may well have started to be more concerned about money than they were about winning.

Although they would not receive any more of the proceeds from any of the games, the players still had ways to pick up some extra cash on the Series. Few were shy at all about gambling. It was an open secret that players often bet on baseball, a practice no one was much concerned about as long as it stayed quiet and as long as the players did not bet against themselves or their own teams and did not try to fix games. Joe Wood, for example, loved to gamble and liked few things more than wagering on his skills with a cue stick in a billiard hall. Almost a decade later both he and Tris Speaker would admit to betting on baseball. In the wake of the Black Sox scandal, the incident may have played a role in Wood's premature retirement after the 1922 season, a year in which he hit almost .300 for the Cleveland Indians as an outfield regular after injuries forced him to give up his pitching career.

The disagreement with the National Commission over the tie game left most players thinking they were due a little more, and making a smart bet or two was one way to recoup what they felt had been unfairly taken from them. Although the odds had tilted in Boston's favor — the Sox were now overwhelming favorites to win the Series — there was still money to be made on game 6, particularly if Wood, who they felt could not lose, was on the mound and Marquard, who had renewed Giants backers' confidence in him, was pitching for New York. As the train chugged to New York making money not necessarily winning the game — became more and more important.

McAleer, only one year removed from the manager's chair, was not shy about making "suggestions" to Stahl, but he was careful to do so privately. He did not second-guess his manager in public or offer ideas through the press. In turn, neither was catcher Bill Carrigan shy about expressing his opinion to either man. The owner himself wasn't altogether certain who deserved the most credit for Boston's big season — Stahl or the "Board of Strategy," Wagner and Carrigan. Both Hugh Fullerton and Fred Lieb reported, as Fullerton put it the day before the game, that "Stahl is being advised in this Series by Jimmy McAleer and they will have to see how the pitchers look tomorrow."

Somewhere between Boston and New York, McAleer and Stahl sat and discussed who to pitch in game 6. In all likelihood their discussion fell along the lines outlined above, taking everything into consideration and hashing through every argument. Stahl, despite being a part owner himself, argued for Wood. McAleer, with Carrigan whispering in his ear, knew that, while winning game 6 and the Series in New York would be great fun, if the Sox were to lose, then pitching Joe Wood in game 7, winning in Boston, and putting another $30,000 in the owners' pockets would be even better. Damon Runyon, for one, judged that to be the probable case, writing later that the chance for an extra gate was part of "the baseball calculations of the local directors of the game."

By the end of those calculations, and reportedly over the objections of Stahl, one name emerged: Buck O'Brien was chosen to start the game, a selection that may not have been entirely about winning.

When the players reached New York they checked in together at the Hotel Bretton Hall. Tim Murnane, who rode on the train with the team, as did most other Boston writers on the off-day journey, later noted that, "after a time he [O'Brien] retired to his bed, anxious to be in shape for what he considered to be the chance of a life—to win the fourth game and the championship." This account is an indication, if Murnane is to be believed, that by that time Buck O'Brien knew he would get the ball the next day.

It remained to be seen, however, whether O'Brien, like Wood and Bedient before him, could stake his claim as a Giant killer in his own right. Or whether the Giants, flat on their back under Boston's boot and barely breathing, might make a last stand and extend the Series. Over the next three days the baseball world would find out—and all hell would break loose in Fenway Park.

14

Last Stand at Fenway Park

No individual, whether player, manager, owner, critic or spectator who
ever went through the World's Series of 1912 will ever forget it. Years
may elapse before there is a similar series . . . From the lofty perch
of the "bleacherites" it was a series crammed with thrills and gulps,
cheers and gasps, pity and hysteria, dejection and wild exultation,
recrimination and adoration, excuse and condemnation . . .

— John B. Foster, *Spalding's Official Base Ball Guide*

B Y BREAKFAST Joe Wood was ready to spit blood. He had
learned that O'Brien was pitching that afternoon when everyone knew that it was he who deserved the honor. Wood
was not happy, and not shy about letting everyone know. It was an
affront not only to his competitive heart but to his wallet as well.
Wood's brother Howard, whom everyone knew by his nickname Pete,
had reportedly put $100 down on the game, betting on his brother and
perhaps even using his brother's money. Another friend of Wood's
supposedly bet another $500 on his behalf. And now Wood wouldn't
even get a chance to take the ball and make back his money.

He was not the only player who was upset. The Masons were together on this one in support of Wood, just as the KCs were behind
O'Brien. By the time the Red Sox made it to the Polo Grounds the
team that had played well together, even if they had not particularly
liked one another, was starting to come apart.

There was no question who the Giants would pitch. Rube Marquard was the logical solution, and even though McGraw floated a

rumor that he had a sore arm, trying to throw Boston off, no one fell for it.

As the Red Sox loosened up for the contest on another gray day at the Polo Grounds the division between the two factions on the club deepened. When Stahl posted his lineup not only was Buck O'Brien pitching, but Hick Cady would serve as his catcher. For the fourth game in a row Bill Carrigan would man the first-base coaching box.

Now Carrigan was mad as well, and his anger probably incited some of the other KCs. It had been bad enough that Cady had usurped his role and become Joe Wood's personal catcher, and Carrigan had kept his mouth shut—publicly anyway—when Stahl chose Cady to catch Bedient, but this was too much. He considered himself Buck O'Brien's personal catcher. The two men were close friends and had even gone to Mass together on Sunday before leaving for New York. Carrigan confronted Stahl, but the manager wouldn't hear it.

Stahl's confidence in Cady, both behind the plate and in the batter's box, had only grown over the course of the Series, and in September, while Carrigan had been briefly sidelined with the split nail and had joined Charlie Wagner in scouting the Giants, Cady had caught O'Brien and the duo had been fine together. O'Brien had won, and Cady had no trouble with his spitball, but now the KCs were as steamed as the Masons. Suddenly every man on the team had a gripe about one thing or another.

When Marquard took the mound just after 2:00 p.m. the Red Sox were a divided team. The Rooters were out in force, as more than six hundred had ponied up $15 apiece to cover the expense of taking the train to New York together—a price that included everything but their hotel rooms—and several hundred more Boston backers had traveled independently to New York. The New York crowd was a bit subdued before the game as the Boston fans went through the usual histrionics, and there was still a smattering of empty seats in the nether reaches of the ballpark. The Polo Grounds was some six thousand spectators shy of capacity, as many New Yorkers expected the Giants, whose cause was next to hopeless, to fold.

But this was a different ball club than the one the Red Sox had played thus far in the Series. After the loss to Bedient, McGraw concluded that his team had been too passive, playing it safe and waiting for something to happen. Hell, the Red Sox were using a rookie catcher and two rookie pitchers, and his club had stolen only five bases the entire Series. It was time to fight, and before the game McGraw addressed his team like a union organizer on a soapbox, exhorting them to play aggressive baseball — swinging at the first pitch, stealing every base possible, and taking the fight to Boston. In short, it was time to play old-style Baltimore Orioles in-your-face baseball. McGraw believed that "if you catch a man from behind you take the heart out of him," and now that was exactly what the Giants had to do to the Red Sox.

Everything started out fine for Boston. Harry Hooper, leading off, worked the count full before knocking a ground ball past Marquard. Larry Doyle got to the ball, but Hooper had an infield hit.

As Yerkes stood in the batter's box, Hooper feinted off first, trying to distract Marquard, but the left-handed hurler caught Hooper leaning and fired to first. Hooper broke for second, then saw what was happening and managed to get caught in a rundown for a moment, but suddenly there was no place left to run and first baseman Fred Merkle slapped the ball on Hooper's thigh and he was out. Yerkes then lifted a routine fly ball out to center, but Speaker worked a walk from Marquard. The pitcher was having a hard time finding the plate.

Speaker, more cautious than Hooper but with his ankle feeling better, stole second, and when Duffy Lewis hit a sharp liner to left it looked as if Speaker might score, but Josh Devore raced in and caught the ball shin high to end the inning. Although the Red Sox had not scored, they had put pressure on the Giants, and Marquard, as Hugh Fullerton later noted, seemed "wabbling and uncertain." It seemed only a matter of time before Boston would break through against Marquard and the Giants would begin to fold.

The bottom of the inning started quietly too — sort of, for John McGraw, coaching third for the Giants, and his cohort, Wil Robinson at first, unleashed a barrage of insults and distractions at O'Brien from the start. They had tried the same thing against Bedient, to no effect, but they had better ammunition to use against O'Brien, who was quicker to anger anyway. Word of his romance with Connie Mack's daughter had made the rounds, and some found his singing in the Red Sox Quartet somewhat less than manly. There was little respect for the thirty-year-old rookie who only a few years before had been working in a shoe factory. He was just a semipro punk.

Josh Devore led off against O'Brien and grounded meekly to third. Then Larry Doyle topped a spitball and beat out the slow roller to second.

Now it was Doyle's turn to dance off base, and he stole second, but O'Brien didn't seem bothered, striking out Fred Snodgrass. His spitball was working fine, dropping just as it should, this time causing Red Murray to top the ball, another bleeder that hung up in the long grass of the Polo Grounds infield before Charlie Wagner could grab it. The Giants now had men on first and third with Fred Merkle at the plate.

It was the kind of situation McGraw's team thrived on—two quick runners on the corners—and he had both men take huge leads, putting pressure on O'Brien, while he and Robinson continued their tirade. O'Brien worked carefully, trying to keep Murray from breaking toward second and giving Doyle a chance to steal home if Cady tried to nab Murray.

Once, twice, three times O'Brien threw to first, and each time Murray made it back free, only to dance off the bag again as soon as Stahl returned the ball to the pitcher. Then, as Murray left the bag once more, O'Brien appeared to begin his wind-up, then stopped and feinted a throw to first, cocking his arm, starting to throw, then stopping as Murray dove back in.

According to Damon Runyon, "for a full ten seconds none of the Giants seemed to gather the import of the act." Then "the hoarse bellow of Robinson rolled across the diamond."

From the first-base coaching box Giants coach Wil Robinson nearly jumped out of his shoes. "Balk," he started sputtering, looking first toward home plate umpire Bill Klem and then to base ump Billy Evans. "Balk! Balk!"

Evans, in the best position to see the play, immediately looked at O'Brien's feet. If his foot was not on the rubber, a fake throw was legal, even to first base. But if his foot was on the rubber, it was a clear balk, an attempt to deceive the runner. If a balk was called, both Murray and Doyle would be allowed to advance, giving the Giants a 1–0 lead.

As Evans later recalled, he was "standing directly behind O'Brien when he made the slip," but when he looked at O'Brien's feet, "I was really in doubt myself'" over whether the pitcher had committed an infraction. Evans erred on the side of caution and made no call.

But Robinson kept yelling, and now so too did McGraw, the other Giants, and the fans around the infield. According to Evans, home plate umpire Bill Klem "hesitated several moments before motioning the runners to advance." Doyle ran home, Murray ran to second, and McGraw and Robinson started blasting away again at O'Brien as the partisan crowd roared.

In the field-level press box behind the home plate screen the play looked bad, at least to those sportswriters who were actually watching when it took place. Balk calls, while rare, were usually made when the pitcher made an inadvertent move while his foot was on the rubber. Stopping in mid-wind-up to fake a throw to first base with a foot on the rubber was something professional pitchers simply did not do. Fullerton called it "bone-headed, grammar school baseball."

As the crowd howled and hooted, Evans asked O'Brien, "What in the world were you thinking about?"

"Bill," O'Brien answered back, "I thought my foot was off the rubber." The feint to first was not a mistake but something O'Brien had planned to do, only to have Klem — much farther from O'Brien than Evans — rule that the move was a balk.

O'Brien was shaken by the call. He started overthrowing the ball, and the spitter, instead of dropping, began to stay straight.

Now O'Brien, wrote Lardner, "worked in a trance . . . he blew, and never in history did anybody blow harder . . . a 10-year-old girl with a bat in her hands could have gone up to the plate and made a base hit." It wasn't a ten-year-old girl but Fred Merkle who was up next. He doubled to deep right, and then Buck Herzog did the same to deep left, and in a flash the score was 3–0.

The other Sox didn't help matters. When Gardner went after Chief Meyers's "slow ugly grounder" to Wagner, he left third base uncovered, which allowed Herzog to advance to third while Meyers beat Wagner's throw to first. As O'Brien, now afraid to do anything that might be ruled a balk, toed the rubber, McGraw ordered a double steal, and Meyers, a slow runner, got a good jump. Cady threw to second as Herzog broke for the plate. Steve Yerkes cut the throw off short and made a quick return throw home, but threw the ball away. Herzog scored, Meyers went to third on the play, and then he scored when Art Fletcher made a perfect bunt. When O'Brien finally ended the inning by picking Fletcher off first—no balk this time—it was 5–0. The Giants and some of the Royal Rooters hadn't even sat down yet. On the Boston bench Joe Wood sat tight-lipped, his jaw clenched, quietly seething.

The Sox tried to battle back, scoring twice in the second when Clyde Engle doubled in two runs, but then, with Ray Collins pitching in relief of O'Brien and Rube Marquard settling down, they played the final seven innings as if they could not wait for the game to end. The first two innings had taken an hour to play—an excruciating amount of time for the era—but after that players from both teams swung at the first pitch and the game ended in a tidy one hour and fifty-eight minutes. Tim Murnane commented that "the game was simply over after the fourth inning" and that "the players on both teams acted as if rather tired."

O'BRIEN GOES UP IN THE AIR

Five Runs Off Moist Ball Twirler In First Give New York Easy Victory

Immediately after the game, as some Boston players bolted to the clubhouse and others sat stone-faced and angry on the bench, Stahl and McGraw were asked by National Commission chairman August Herrmann to join him on the field. The commission had decided that, since the second game had been a tie, if the Giants beat Boston the next day it would be only fair to have the winner of a coin toss select the location of the final game.

As the Rooters surrounded the three men ten deep around the pitcher's mound, Herrmann tossed a silver dollar in the air. Stahl called out, "Tails," and the coin landed face down.

"Where will the game be played?" asked McGraw, knowing the answer already.

Happy to have won something, Stahl smiled and said, "In Boston." But he still hoped it would not be needed.

Stahl's decision to use O'Brien over Wood was the subject of little criticism, perhaps because the press knew—or guessed—that the decision had not really been his to make. O'Brien, on the other hand, was excoriated after the game, particularly in New York, where several reports intimated that he had been hungover, but that may well have been sour grapes from New York sportswriters who had lost bets themselves on the game and were none too eager to return to Boston. Murnane, for one, found the rumors in regard to O'Brien being drunk preposterous—he had sat with him on the train to New York and had seen him go to his room the night before. Murnane later referred to those who would perpetrate such stories as "slander mongers . . . microbes that thrive in the dark, but who die when the truth of sunlight is flashed across their paths."

O'Brien's only real crimes—apart from being an Irish Catholic on a team on which half the roster was intolerant—were the balk (the first in World's Series play), the fact that all five runs scored with two out, and plain bad luck. Most observers overlooked the fact that three of the six hits O'Brien gave up never left the infield, that Gardner made a mental error and Yerkes a real one with the bad throw, that the balk call might not have even been correct, and that after the second inning both teams played like the game was already over. But others did pay attention. Among the touts and sportsmen who made it their business to watch such things closely, some began to wonder if Boston had put forth a full effort.

When the final out was recorded and the electronic baseball boards on Boston's Newspaper Row went dark, fans began showing up at Fenway Park, looking for tickets. For much of the next twenty-four hours it would be chaos in the Fenway Park ticket office and bedlam in the streets outside. No one in the entire country had an advance ticket for a game that no one had expected to be played and that suddenly everyone wanted to attend. All advance tickets had been sold in lots of three, one each for the three Series games originally scheduled for Boston, games 2, 4, and 6. But the tie had changed that, giving Boston an extra game and now, after the coin flip, perhaps a second extra game as well. Robert McRoy, fortunately, had tickets on hand to cover the extra games, but precisely how he would distribute them and how he would make certain those who had previously bought tickets in advance would get seats for the added game was still being worked out.

The only Bostonians who seemed happy were the Rooters in the Polo Grounds. For them the only thing worse than seeing the Red Sox lose was to see the baseball season come to an end, and Boston's loss gave them at least one more day to sing and cheer. They made their usual postgame parade around the Polo Grounds and stopped before the Boston bench. A few players were still lingering, grim-faced, when, as the *Times* reported, some Rooters "executed a war dance around several of the players who had not yet run for cover." Then the Rooters congregated at home plate, where McGreevey and others gave speeches that spoke of certain victory in the offing.

After the players boarded their train for the return trip to Boston, ate, and the liquor started to flow, the atmosphere among the Red Sox players became poisonous as teammates looked upon one another with suspicion. It was made even worse when they all learned that a last-ditch effort by Mathewson to get them all some money from the tie game had been shot down once more by the National Commission—this time the members of the commission claimed to have no authority to change the rules the commission itself had enacted. At the same time the players and press learned that Theodore Roosevelt, the presidential nominee for the Progressive Party, had been shot in Milwaukee. Although Roosevelt's wound was minor—in fact, he went on to deliver a ninety-minute speech with the bullet harmlessly lodged in his chest—the news only added to the mood of distrust and disgust permeating the club. Their whole damn world seemed to be spinning off orbit.

Then the lid came off. Pete Wood, angry over losing the bet he had made on his brother Joe, confronted O'Brien. Angry words were exchanged, and the confrontation exploded into violence, O'Brien emerging from the scuffle with a blackened eye. Yet another report claimed that the combatants were O'Brien and Joe Wood himself, that after Wood made a crack about O'Brien's balk O'Brien knocked Wood out cold with a straight right to the jaw, and that Cady and Bill Carrigan were also pulled into the fray. The *Herald* reported the next day that there were rumors of "several three cornered battle royals" after the loss, indicating that even more players were involved. The two groups circled each other the rest of the trip, angry and wary. By the time the Red Sox made Boston they were sick of the Series and sick of each other, but at least they were home. Perhaps Fenway Park would prove a tonic to what ailed them.

After hearing about and probably witnessing some of the brouhaha on the train, the Giants were suddenly feeling optimistic. They liked their chances. The Red Sox were starting to fray at the edges, and they did not think Wood could beat Tesreau a third time, particularly with his own club divided behind him. McGraw, who had seen everything in his life in baseball, knew that as long as the Red Sox were beating up on each other they weren't thinking much about beating his ball club.

A crowd the *Times* described as "larger than on previous home days" began to line the streets around Fenway, and as the sun went down and the night turned cold and crisp, the temperature dropping to near forty degrees, Robert McRoy opened the ticket office and started selling. There simply wouldn't be enough time to sell all the tickets by the start of the game if he kept the ticket office closed until morning. As the night stretched on, rumors rippled up and down the line and then spilled into local taverns about Roosevelt, fights between players, anarchists, thrown games, shifting odds, and everything else imaginable.

Confusion reigned. Those fans who could not prove they had purchased reserved seats to earlier games were only allowed to buy either unreserved seats or the seats in the few areas of reserved seats that had previously gone unsold in advance. Those who had bought tickets in advance and still had the stubs to prove it were allowed to buy tickets at the same price as before, but McRoy could not promise anyone the exact same seats—the club had kept track of buyers, but not the precise location of their seats. At 1:00 a.m. exhausted ticket sellers convinced him to close the office for the night so they could get some sleep. Several of the salesmen slept on their stools, slumped over the counter.

At dawn the next day, although the sun broke through, clouds flew across the sky on a blustery day that warned of winter. The temperature sat only a few degrees above freezing and would gain no more than another ten degrees or so over the course of the day. Newsboys stood on every corner near the park screaming "Extra!" and trying to shill newspapers whose front-page headlines were evenly divided between the assassination attempt and the World's Series, but they were left wanting. No one wanted to read about the loss in New York, and now that it was common knowledge that Roosevelt had suffered what his doctor called a "superficial flesh wound," no one much cared about the shooting either. Besides, Boston was a Democratic town, and on such a blustery day it was impossible to unfold a paper and try to read it. All anyone needed to know was that both Roosevelt and the Giants were still alive.

When the Red Sox gathered at the park about noon it was considerably cooler in the Red Sox clubhouse, with the hotheads of the previous evening now giving each other the cold shoulder. Stahl and McAleer had both seen what took place on the train, or at least its aftermath. In the press McAleer denied that Wood and O'Brien had come to blows, saying that he had been in the locker room immediately after Monday's game "and can truthfully say there was no trouble among the players," conveniently leaving out any mention of trouble on the train. Once the entire team was inside, they closed the door to the clubhouse and everyone aired it out.

The meeting wasn't civil as players questioned each other over who was trying to win and who wasn't, who had bet how much on what, why, and for what reason, and when they began to voice the hundred other slights and complaints that had built up over the course of the season, violence erupted once again. *The Sporting News* would report later that "Joe Wood and Buck O'Brien had a fist fight in the Boston clubhouse before Tuesday's game, the cause being a derogatory remark of Wood about O'Brien's balk in Monday's game," and the *Washington Post* reported that O'Brien defended himself with a bat. McAleer, Stahl, and the players were tight-lipped when they left the clubhouse, Stahl refusing to reveal what the meeting was about except to say obliquely, "We had some things to go over."

When the Sox took the field to warm up, the Giants liked what they saw—not a team but a bunch of school kids apparently taking a feud out to the playground for the second day in a row. Christy Mathewson, one of the few players who actually did his own writing, later wrote that there was obvious hostility between the Red Sox players during the Series and noted that "such friction could not help but interfere with the team-work. Reduced efficiency is the inevitable consequence of internal dissension."

The same was apparently true when it came to selling tickets. Nevertheless Fenway Park was nearly full when the Red Sox began their final warm-ups, and apart from the rumor mill and some circumspect reporting in the morning papers, most fans were oblivious to the poisonous atmosphere between the Boston players when Wood began loosening up with Hick Cady.

The Royal Rooters had yet to appear, but just then, some ten or fifteen minutes before the start of the game, the now-familiar strains of "Tessie" began wafting into the park from behind the center-field bleachers. The Rooters soon appeared on the field, marching behind the band, singing and waving their banners. The weather, meanwhile, was near-apocalyptic. One moment the bright sun would be blazing, then in the next it would give way to great waves of dark thunderheads racing across the sky in a gale that swirled as it blew into the park unchecked, from the west and north, snapping the flags taut. With the field bright and bathed in light one minute, then menacing and dark the next, the day was as dramatic and schizophrenic as the entire Series had been thus far.

Yet as the Rooters marched across the field toward their usual seats, which included most of the bleachers on Duffy's Cliff, they were stunned to find the bleachers already occupied. One Rooter, an aide to Honey Fitz, had signed for the usual allotment of tickets at noon and produced the wad of ducats to the section gatekeeper, but it was pointless — the seats were full. Nuf Ced McGreevey, Johnny Keenan, and the others all had the same thought: "What the hell is going on?"

They believed at first that their seats were occupied by interlopers, but Boston police captain Thomas Goode, charged with manning the barricade that provided access to the seats, told them that at 1:00 p.m. Robert McRoy himself had ordered Goode to "throw open the section." In a matter of minutes the seats had been filled by fans who had paid $1 for an unreserved seat. Earlier in the Series such a ticket would have given most of them a seat in either the pavilion or the third-base stands. But when they saw that the Duffy's Cliff bleachers were open — and empty — fans had streamed to the new seats, eager to experience the game from that unique perspective, just as the "Green Monster" seats in Fenway Park today are among the most coveted in the park for much the same reason.

Once before, when their singing of "Tessie" had famously driven the Pittsburgh Pirates to distraction during the 1903 World's Series, the Rooters had received credit for turning the tide of the Series. Now, with a bit of an assist from Fenway Park, they nearly did so again, this time in the opposite direction.

The Rooters, all accustomed to getting their way, piled into the narrow passageway no more than five or six feet wide at the base of the Duffy's Cliff bleachers, between the seats and the short fence that separated the stands from the field, the same low barrier Red Murray had tumbled over earlier in the Series. They first politely asked the fans in "their" seats to move. Then they insisted upon it. Then some, particularly those toward the back of the parade—where no one had much of a clue as to what was happening—chose to try to take the seats by force, but the interlopers held firm and emotions ran high.

ROYAL ROOTERS AN ANGRY LOT
BADLY USED AT BALL PARK, THEY FEEL

The two groups tussled for a few moments, and every time someone lost his or her footing the Rooters in front and the fans in the stands all risked falling like dominoes. Finally the Rooters, uncomfortably squeezed into the narrow passageway, concluded that if they could not regain "their" seats, they would watch the game from where they were—crammed in behind the fence. As one press report noted, this left those already seated in the bleachers "in a fury." Only those at the very top of the stands could still sit in their seats and see over the heads of the Rooters. For the rest, unless they too stood, their view of the field was completely blocked. Soon everyone in the bleachers had to stand to see, and no one was very happy about it.

Over the next few minutes the police, stationed at regular intervals along the fence, did what they could to keep watch over the situation. As the *Globe*'s Lawrence McSweeney reported in the most complete account of the incident, "Every time one of the men in that jamming, shoving, punching crowd of 'standees'—standers because of necessity—leaned his head and shoulders over the fence he was shoved back by a policeman." And all the while, "the turbulent rooters, already incensed by the indignity of being deprived of seats . . . [were] made more wrathful by the epithets hurled at them by those whose vision they hampered."

Out on the field, as the players made their final preparations to play, they were oblivious to what was happening. All of Fenway Park was a teeming mass of people, and while it looked like there was some kind of disturbance going on in left field, there was nothing surprising about that. Scraps in the crowd were a regular occurrence anytime the stands were full.

But just as Joe Wood walked to the mound to make his final warm-up tosses, the Red Sox prepared to take the field, and Billy Evans began to gather the combatants at home plate to go over the ground rules, someone in the mob of Rooters behind the fence—or, more likely, someone whose view was blocked by the mob of Rooters behind the fence—yelled out that the Rooters were going to be allowed to congregate in "seats of honor at the front of the grandstand."

Then came the crushing blow—the call to "jump the fence!" It was, wrote McSweeney, "like the imbecile who cries 'fire' in a theatre."

From all along the front of Duffy's Cliff, the Rooters, like rats escaping a burning ship, leapt over the fence out onto the field and began sprinting toward the grandstand. Others poured out through the little pie-shaped triangle. Then, as the police tried to block them and everyone pushed and shoved, the last twenty-five-foot section of fence just inside the left-field line "gave way before the pressing crowd and fell upon the field. Scores went with it, many being trampled upon as those behind them scrambled for a breathing space. A rush was begun. . . ." In an instant hundreds of Rooters and members of their band, some carrying instruments now twisted and bent, raced across the field toward the promised land of the grandstand.

The riot was on. Police chased the gatecrashers around the park, including four or five riding mounts, the hooves of their horses tearing up great chunks of Jerome Kelley's precious turf. Over the next few minutes, as the rest of the crowd roared at the unexpected spectacle, the players dodged the fans, and the fans sought refuge behind the players, the police slowly took control. Faced with being either trampled or beaten with batons, the Rooters slowly allowed themselves to be herded back toward left field. As they passed the third-base stands, supporters, seeing a line of policemen within their reach, were unable to resist the temptation. Wrote McSweeney, they "began a bombardment," pelting Boston's finest with "bags of peanuts, scorecards, canes and miscellaneous weapons and missiles."

Rooter Johnny Keenan, megaphone in hand, slowly began taking control of his charges, doing what the authorities could not. "Now go back behind the fence," he called out. "The police are not to blame in this matter." It was McRoy who had wronged them, he said, and he would be taken care of later. "Remember," he thundered, "two wrongs don't make a right."

Chastened, the crowd reluctantly began to fall back behind the fence once more, pulling it upright, albeit a little less straight and close than before. As they did, first Charlie Wagner and then Jake Stahl came out and implored the Rooters to stay in place. If they did not, as Wagner told them, "it means the game will be forfeited to New York, and if we don't get going right away, and if the crowd comes onto the field again, the umpires can declare the Giants the winner." It was true enough that Evans and his crew had that authority, but had they used it, what was still a somewhat comic riot of several hundred fans would surely have turned into a real one of many thousands. Still, the threat of a forfeit brought the Rooters back in line.

Grumbling and cursing McAleer and McRoy, and watched over by a small army of police, the Rooters reluctantly took up residence behind the fence, and the fans in the bleachers, having no other choice, were forced to stand on their seats in order to see the game. But many would not remain on their feet—or even at Fenway Park—for long.

The start of the game had been delayed perhaps ten minutes by the display when Billy Evans finally yelled out, "Play ball," and Joe Wood peered in and took the sign from Hick Cady as Josh Devore stepped in for the Giants. Game 7, at last, could begin.

The next few minutes were among the worst moments in Red Sox history, and some of the worst moments in the life of Joe Wood. Perhaps it was the ten-minute delay while the Rooters threw a tantrum that left his arm cold, or the lingering effects of being punched in the jaw, or the consequence of punching someone else's jaw with his golden right hand, or perhaps the impact of being struck with a bat, or a sore arm from pitching too much, or a sore head and a thin wallet due to the result of game 6, or the cold wind that blew through the stands, or a brand-new white baseball, or just some great work by the Giants, or all of these together—or just plain dumb luck. But in the next five minutes, from atop the mound at Fenway Park, Smoky Joe Wood, the pride of the Boston Red Sox and the American League, the reigning King of Pitchers, the greatest in the game, 34-5 for the season, with two World's Series wins already under his belt, without any question whatsoever absolutely, positively, no doubt about it, completely, and utterly *stank*.

It was over that fast. Wood, as Tim Murnane noted, was "cutting the ball over the heart of the plate from the jump," and his speed, as the *Herald* reported, was "lacking and his curve broke badly." In response, the Giants, swinging early and often, beat poor Joe Wood's brains in far more effectively than they had Buck O'Brien's or anyone else's all season long. Ralph McMillen, unable to resist the turn of phrase, wrote later that it was "Smokeless Joe that stepped out into the teeth of the tempest."

Devore led off by taking a strike and Wood was ahead in the count 0-1. It would be the last time that day Boston was ahead on anything. Devore hit a dribbler on the next pitch. Wagner tried to field the ball one-handed, but the Boston shortstop lost it, and Devore made first. Swinging at the first pitch, Larry Doyle then singled to right-center over Yerkes's head.

With two swift runners aboard, common sense and sound baseball strategy dictated that Wood pitch from the stretch. But if O'Brien's balk had been the mistake of a schoolboy, Wood's mistake was that of someone who had not yet been to school at all.

McGraw, determined to force the issue, called for the double steal, and Devore and Doyle gave the play away by feinting off each bag. Cady alerted Wood to the runners, and the Boston pitcher held the ball, and held it, then held it some more, and then, as Devore and Doyle danced off the bases again, Wood took a long, slow, full wind-up. Both men broke for the next base, and by the time Wood's pitch reached Cady each runner had arrived safely at his destination without sliding. Cady had no chance at either man and seemed so surprised that he dropped the ball anyway. Everyone was safe.

What was Wood thinking? Stahl didn't know either. He yelled over to the bench, and Charley Hall ran out of the dugout and out toward the outfield with backup catcher Les Nunamaker to warm up. O'Brien, on the bench, must have found it hard to suppress a smile. Who was the bonehead now?

Wagner waved his teammates in, playing to cut off the run at home, but Snodgrass swung at the next pitch and hit it to right field. Hooper raced in and tried to make a running catch at his knees but kicked the ball free. Devore and Doyle scored, and Snodgrass raced to second while Hooper retrieved the ball.

On the next pitch Red Murray, blessedly, bunted, a sacrifice straight to Stahl, and Snodgrass made third as the first baseman beat Murray to the base. Then Merkle hit a completely ordinary pop-up to short left field.

Duffy Lewis trotted in, looked up in the sky, and saw the ball go up and then, at the peak of its flight, become captured by the breeze, which sent it first this way and then that as he staggered and trotted and then ran beneath it, the ball finally dropping untouched for what Paul Shannon called "a ridiculous two-bagger." Then Lewis followed one bad play with another, making a poor throw, and Snodgrass scored as Merkle took second.

"The game was lost," wrote Paul Shannon, "for Wood had shot his bolt." But while the game was done, the pitcher was not. Hall was warming up as fast as he could but not fast enough. Buck Herzog hit a quick comebacker that Wood grabbed with his bare hand and threw to third, catching Merkle in a rundown, but Herzog was able to make it all the way to second before Merkle was put out. Then Chief Meyers singled, and then so did Art Fletcher, and Fletcher made second when Harry Hooper tried and failed to gun down Meyers when he ran to third. Jeff Tesreau stepped up to bat, anxious to help his cause, and he also singled, bringing home Meyers and sending Fletcher to third. The pitcher then capped things off by executing a double steal, taking off and getting into a rundown long enough for Fletcher to dash across the plate with New York's sixth run before Tesreau was tagged out. The inning was over, and so was Wood's day.

Accounts vary, but Wood threw somewhere between eleven and

fifteen pitches, seven of which were knocked for base hits. Meanwhile nearly every Boston player who had touched the ball or tried to had made a mistake of one kind or another, allowing the Giants to run wild, one of the worst played innings in the history of the franchise. It made people wonder, and in the stands plenty did.

Wood walked off the field, ashen-faced, to a smattering of boos and a handful of cheers, mostly from New Yorkers, but primarily to silence. Boston fans were stunned speechless. "A place at the right hand corner of the Red Sox bench was taken by a stooped, wilted figure [SWF]," wrote the correspondent for the *New York World*. "The SWF was Joe Wood." He sat, in Paul Shannon's words, with "black despair written on his face . . . the Red Sox were a beaten team and looked it."

ALL KNOCK WOOD AND GIANTS TIE WORLD'S SERIES

The game was over, for as Ralph McMillen noted accurately, "whatever the Red Sox did thereafter was spasmodic and weak." But there were still several plays worth mentioning. Larry Gardner, in the second inning, and Larry Doyle, in the sixth, both hit home runs, the first two World's Series home runs in the history of Fenway Park, but neither ball cleared a fence on the fly. Each was hit to right field and merely bounced over the low fence. And in the ninth inning Tris Speaker turned in an unassisted double play, the first of his career and the first in World's Series history by an outfielder. With Artie Wilson on second, Art Fletcher hit a liner to Speaker, who caught it and then doubled up Wilson, who had raced to third, by running in and touching second base himself. But by then Wilson and the Giants just might have wanted to get the game over with.

Jeff Tesreau was not dominant, but it didn't really matter, as the Red Sox fell, 11–4. By the end of the game only a smattering of fans were left in the stands, and the Red Sox left the field quickly, eager to forget about the game, while the Giants, knowing they had Mathewson ready, were already anxious for the final contest to begin.

The only people who lingered inside Fenway Park were the Royal Rooters. They marched across the field and then into the street, stopping several times along the way to caucus before finally congregating in front of the Red Sox offices on Jersey Street. Each time they stopped Johnny Keenan would ask for "three cheers for Secretary Bob McRoy of Chicago," his voice dripping with sarcasm, and the crowd would respond with a chorus of boos. Then he would ask for three cheers for Giants owner John Brush, and the crowd would roar its approval, driven by the circumstances to cheer for the opposition. Their point made, the Rooters finally dispersed. Larry McSweeney noted after the game that "the Royal Rooters of 1912 are a thing of the past . . . if any of them attend the final game, they will do so individually . . . there will be no parade, flying of colors, singing of songs or cheers." Over the next few days the Rooters and McRoy would battle it out in the press, Honey Fitz calling for McRoy's ouster and a boycott of the final game. McRoy and McAleer would eventually offer an apology, but by then the damage was done. The bond between the new owner, who valued money more than people, and the Boston fan base was irrevocably broken.

The talk in the taverns that night around Boston was bitter. The fans, who had been rabid beyond belief just over a week before, were now tired of the whole mess. Word of the fights and rumors of a fix — talk the disgruntled Rooters now helped propagate — coupled with Wood's dismal performance, suddenly let all the air out of the balloon. The World's Series of 1912 was crashing to earth. Nobody gave a damn anymore.

There was no great rush for tickets overnight or even the next morning, which was colder than the day before, just as windy, and cloudy with no accompanying moments of sunshine. Summer was most certainly over. The fans who did come to Fenway Park were dressed for winter. Those who wanted reserved seats were told to bring their rain check from game 7 to prove themselves worthy, but few did. On this day, if a person had the cash for the face value price of a ticket, he or she could sit anywhere in the park. By game time the bleachers and pavilion and other nonreserved sections were barely half full, if that, and even fewer fans were seated in the grandstand. The official attendance was only 17,034. Not until the final game of the 1918 World's Series — also played in Boston, at Fenway Park, under circumstances that left the fans bitter — would a World's Series game be seen by so few people.

The Giants, behind Mathewson, were sure of victory. The Red Sox, with Bedient available to pitch, just didn't want to be embarrassed and hoped the youngster could keep it close. They were playing not so much for each other now—that hope was gone—but for themselves and the simple glory that comes with a good effort. Each man on the team knew that, no matter how he felt about the man next to him, either on the field or on the bench, the difference between winning and losing the final game was worth more than $1,000, maybe more. That payout, and a man's reputation, were still worth playing for.

Without the Rooters in the crowd, there was little drama before the game, and apart from some noisemakers used by a few fans that made an odd clacking sound, it was nearly silent at the start. Fenway Park, for the first time, did not look new anymore. The day was dark, and it felt more like the last game of the season played by two clubs far out of the race than the culmination of the last eight-game World's Series in history.

Then, remarkably, a pretty good baseball game took place. Hugh Bedient and Christy Mathewson set the tone, for while some others might have thought the Series was over, neither pitcher took anything for granted. The Red Sox might have been coming apart at the seams, but Bedient had stayed out of the fray and was playing for pride. Mathewson, as always, was beyond reproach.

The Giants wanted to pull the same pranks on Bedient that they had on O'Brien and Wood, but Bedient refused to cooperate. He was not perfect, but in the first two innings no Giants reached base until two were out, and then Bedient stiffened. And despite his relative lack of experience, Bedient was better than either Wood or O'Brien at holding runners on base.

The game was scoreless until the third. Devore worked a leadoff walk, and this time the Giants showed just how valuable a base on balls could be as the outfielder moved to second and then third on two ground balls. Red Murray then lifted a foul off first that should have been out number three, but this time Fenway took the out away—the new box seats put in place for the Series left the pop-up just out of Stahl's reach. Murray then doubled to put the Giants ahead, 1–0.

They threatened again in the fourth, only this time Fenway Park provided Bedient with an enormous assist. Leading off, Herzog hit the ball hard to left, and the ball skipped into the same pie-shaped enclosure that had delivered Hooper's triple in game 5, the hit that had turned the tide for Boston and eventually delivered a victory to Bedient.

This time, even though the ball was hit by a Giant, it helped Boston. For as soon as the ball skipped into the wedge, Bill Klem, again manning the left-field line, waved his arms over his head and called the ball dead. After the earlier hit, the umpires had met and decided that it was unfair to allow the ball to rattle around an enclosure where an outfielder did not have a play while the runner raced around the bases unimpeded. If it happened again, they decided, the hit would be a ground-rule double.

Herzog had to stop at second. Chief Meyers advanced him to third on a sacrifice bunt, but he was left stranded—assist by Fenway.

Mathewson, meanwhile, was just this side of magnificent. Through the first four innings he gave up only two hits, the second one a double by Larry Gardner that handcuffed Snodgrass in center field, but Gardner tried to stretch the hit to a triple and was thrown out. It was beginning to look like the Red Sox, while playing better than they did in the last two contests, were destined to die quietly.

That changed in the fifth. Devore led off with a single, and this time McGraw sent him to second on a steal, but Cady gunned him down. Larry Doyle, up next, pulled a drive to far right, and the ball, captured by the wind, seemed destined for the seats in right field just a few yards fair, where the fence was barely three hundred feet away from home.

Harry Hooper got an excellent jump on the ball and tracked it back, as one reporter noted, "in full careen." The ball fell toward the earth just to the left-field side of where James McLaughlin's short fence in front of the right-field bleachers met the pavilion stands. Had it not been for the new stands and fence installed for the World's Series, Hooper would have been able to make the catch on the run, a nice play, but not a particularly remarkable one. But now he was running out of room, and as he approached the barrier he turned for the ball, hit the short fence, and began to flip over, much as Red Murray had fallen over the fence going for a catch in left field earlier in the Series.

Even as he began to fall back Hooper saw the ball coming at him and instinctively held up his bare hand, reaching for the ball before tumbling into the arms of grateful fans. Seconds later he emerged, holding the ball high. Over time the significance of Hooper's catch would grow until usurped by a similar catch by Dwight Evans in right field at Fenway Park in the eleventh inning of game 6 of the 1975 World Series that robbed Cincinnati's Joe Morgan of a go-ahead home run.

Even Hooper could barely believe he had held on. He later gave credit for the miraculous catch to a prayer card he had found on the ground before the game and tucked in his pocket. The Giants did not believe it and protested futilely, claiming that Hooper had either left the playing field prior to making the grab—which would have rendered his catch meaningless—or palmed it, while out of view, from a fan who had caught it. Billy Evans, manning the right-field line, was adamant. Hooper had caught the ball. Doyle left the field kicking at the dust.

Still, entering the seventh inning, the Red Sox trailed by a run, and Mathewson, needing only nine more outs, seemed unbeatable. After retiring the Sox with only three pitches in the fifth, he had worked his way out of a jam in the sixth when the Red Sox, with Speaker at first and Yerkes on third, tried a double steal. New York catcher Chief Meyers threw toward second, and Mathewson was prepared on the set play. He cut off the throw as it passed the pitcher's mound, then spun and threw to third where Herzog put the tag on Yerkes, who had broken for home and was caught scrambling back. In the press box the scribes began asking each other where they were spending the winter.

Larry Gardner led off the seventh by flying out, and then Jake Stahl lifted a short fly to left. Murray came in, Fletcher and Herzog went out, and each man looked at the others to see who would call for the ball. When no one did, it landed on the field with a soft thud and Stahl had a cheap hit.

Mathewson could see victory slipping away on such a play and lost his composure, walking Wagner on four straight pitches. But when Cady popped up, bringing up Bedient, a poor hitter, Mathewson looked like he would work out of it.

Now Stahl pulled a surprise. From second base he called for a pinch hitter. Despite the fact that Bedient had given up only a single run and five hits in seven innings of work, Boston was running out of time and needed to score. Besides, he had the best pitcher in baseball sitting on the bench—or at least someone who had been the best pitcher in baseball until twenty-four hours before. Bedient left the game having pitched Mathewson to a standoff. He was one of the few players on the Boston roster who had played over his head during the Series, a performance that seemed to herald the start of a remarkable career.

Stahl had several hitters to choose from. The best—and most experienced—was Bill Carrigan, but he had gone hitless against Mathewson in game 2, and after the events of the past few days Stahl didn't trust him. Instead he called on his only left-handed hitter on the bench, little Olaf Henriksen, Boston's little-used, Danish-born fourth outfielder, a player who had come to bat during the regular season exactly fifty-six times. He had been off the bench only once in the Series, to pinch-run in game 3.

If the World's Series was to be decided on a matchup between Christy Mathewson and Olaf Henriksen, the Giants would have accepted those odds a hundred times, secure in the knowledge that Mathewson would win the battle on at least ninety-nine occasions. But this was the one time in a hundred.

With two strikes, Mathewson got too cute and left a curveball over the plate. Henriksen swung, fighting off a pitch that fooled him. He chopped at the ball and sent it bounding down the third-base line, where it just got past Herzog, then bounced into foul territory.

Stahl, running as fast as he could, scored, and as the ball twisted away from Herzog, Henriksen made second and the game was tied. For the first time all game the stands did not sound half-empty. But after Hooper flew out, now Wood had to take the mound for Boston.

This was his chance for redemption, and he knew it. If the Red Sox were to lose this game and lose the Series, Wood would live with the ignominy of being the losing pitcher for the last two games of the World's Series, something that had never happened before. He would live with the goat horns on his head forevermore, the great accomplishment of his 1912 season washed away in defeat, just as Jack Chesbro's wild pitch that cost New York a pennant on the last day of the 1904 season had overshadowed his remarkable forty-one wins that season. Whatever had ailed Wood the day before—his arm, his head, his heart, or his wallet—was not an issue now.

He had nothing, really, but the one thing he had not shown the previous day, and that was guts. The Giants got good swings, but over the course of the season, particularly with Cady catching, Wood had learned to pitch without his best stuff. Although not at his blazing best, he was good enough, and he and Mathewson matched each other through the eighth and the ninth innings. The game entered extra innings still tied, and the longest World's Series in history kept going a little longer.

In the tenth inning, however, with one out, Wood faltered. Red Murray got around on the ball and popped it to left. Duffy Lewis went back, but that damn short fence got in the way again, and the ball landed in his namesake seats. Had they not been there—and on this day, with the stands half full, they were not even needed—he might have made the catch. But as every player knows, Fenway Park both gives and takes away, and this time it gave the Giants a cheap double. The Red Sox would have to earn this victory on their own.

Better than any other man, Tris Speaker knew that more games were lost on singles that fell in front of an outfielder than on balls hit over their heads, but he also knew that an outfielder had to make the right judgment on such hits. Fred Merkle, up next, hit a sinking liner right in front of Speaker. If he played the ball on a hop, the hit was a single and would put runners on the corners. If he tried for the catch, it would either save Wood's neck or cost his roommate both the ball game and the rest of his reputation.

Speaker sprinted all out, going for the catch, but the ball found the ground before it found his glove, then trickled away, just far enough for Red Murray to charge around third to score and for Merkle to make second on the error and to put the Giants ahead, 2–1. It now looked as if two goats of the game would be sharing the same address in Winthrop.

On the mound Joe Wood decided that if he was going to lose he was going to go out in glory. He bore down and struck out Buck Herzog on what he later said were his "hardest three pitches of the season."

But he was now spent, all exhaust and no smoke. Chief Meyers ripped a pitch up the middle, and for the first time all year Wood faced a ball that was faster coming out than it had been going in.

He reacted, throwing his bare hand at the ball. He knocked it down, picked it up, and threw to first for the last out, but he knew before he took another step that it was also the last ball he would throw that year. The ball had hit the fingers of his throwing hand flush, and they were already starting to throb and swell. He could not pitch another inning against his little sister, much less the Giants. He left the field to a smattering of polite but tired applause, thinking in his heart that he would be remembered as a loser.

Mathewson needed only three more outs to cap off the most improbable comeback in the history of the World's Series and was only moments away from winning the most important game of his distinguished career. The veteran had entered the Series almost as an afterthought, not even in the same conversation with Wood and Tesreau, yet had outpitched them both. When he had been the hero of an earlier Series—in 1905 he won three games, all by shutout—he had been young and felt indestructible. Now he was older and knew it was not so easy. That made him treasure the moment even more.

Wood was due to lead off, but he could not even hold a bat in his swollen hand. Stahl looked past Carrigan again, and his eyes settled on Clyde Engle, 0-for-2 thus far in the Series and a .234 hitter for the season. He told Engle to grab a bat.

Out in center field Fred Snodgrass had been having an uneventful day until the fourth inning, when his miscue on Larry Gardner's drive had reignited the crowd in center field. Although fewer in number than the day before, they had still spent the rest of the game reminding Snodgrass that they had not forgotten him. Now, with the game only a few pitches from ending, Snodgrass was looking forward to the silence that would come over the crowd with a New York win and perhaps starting to think about how he might spend that World's Series swag. Engle was no threat.

The Boston pinch hitter took a swing and hit under the ball, lofting what Snodgrass later called a lazy, high fly ball to left-center. Red Murray, in left, called for the ball first, but Snodgrass waved him off.

It was the kind of ball Snodgrass had tracked down hundreds of times each year and probably dropped once.

Make that twice. The ball hit his glove, bounced out before his bare hand could hold it fast, and fell to the ground. When Snodgrass followed up the error by making a weak throw, Engle, running hard, slid safe into second, then stood up, grinning, as Murnane wrote, "to the music of a thousand yells."

The players on the Boston bench began to stir, and the boy behind the scoreboard on the left-field wall slid a big white marker under the slot that was headed "ERROR." The crowds at Newspaper Row, who had started to drift away, saw Engle's name at second base, stopped in their tracks, and pushed closer. Joe Wood, sitting alone on the Boston bench, felt the noose around his neck begin to loosen, and the fans in center field heckled Snodgrass with renewed vigor as he stood, his face flushed with embarrassment and anger at himself, feeling, as he later explained, "frozen to the marrow." In the press box, from Murnane and Shannon and Nickerson to Fullerton, Rice, Lardner, and Runyon, all the writers paused from the stories they were starting to write about Mathewson's triumph, looked to their scorebooks, wrote "E-8" representing the error by Snodgrass, and circled it. They knew it was the kind of play that could change everything. The door was open a crack.

Harry Hooper stepped in next. After making the catch in right field, he felt great, but was disappointed when Stahl called on him to sacrifice. He failed to get the hit down, but with two strikes he ripped a Mathewson pitch to right-center and was thinking triple as he left the batter's box, certain he had just tied the game.

Snodgrass ran after the ball as if his life depended on it, and now he made the kind of catch a player makes only once or twice a season, one as spectacular as his previous effort had been awful. With his left hand stretched out and up as far he could reach, he caught the liner on the dead run, the grass- and tobacco-stained ball smacking into his glove, the leather fingers closing around it. Engle, unsure whether or not the ball would be caught, strayed too far off second, and when Snodgrass made the catch he had to race back. Knowledgeable fans groaned, for if he had just stayed at second, he could have tagged up and made third, and if the ball had fallen in he could have scored anyway.

Mathewson seemed disturbed once again, and now he walked Yerkes, the winning run. That brought up Speaker, Boston's best hitter, when they needed him to be just that.

Two of the greatest players in the history of the game squared off in an at-bat that could follow either to the grave, both knowing the game and the Series were on the line. Mathewson threw and Speaker popped it up.

The shallow fly drifted into foul ground almost to first base, maybe fifteen feet off the line. It was Merkle's ball all the way, but the first baseman, as one reporter put it, "turned to stone" and was inexplicably slow to react. As the ball started to drop, Mathewson, seeing Chief Meyers racing for the ball as Merkle moved like his feet were stuck in concrete, called out the name of his catcher to alert him to the fact that Merkle might not get there in time and Meyers had to. Meyers lunged as Merkle pulled up short and the ball dropped free.

As Mathewson walked back to the mound Speaker reportedly grinned and called out, "You just called for the wrong man [Meyers]. It's gonna cost you the ball game." But the fault was not as much Mathewson's as it was Merkle's.

Nevertheless, with Speaker's boast ringing in his ears, Mathewson wound up and delivered a curve. Speaker turned on the pitch and spanked it into right field for a long base hit. Engle scored the tying run, racing past home plate straight into the dugout as Yerkes slid into third and Speaker went to second on the throw.

Mathewson sagged, but he knew the game was not yet lost. He walked Duffy Lewis, setting up a force play at every base. The Boston outfielder did not run well, and if Mathewson could induce a ground ball, a double play would end the inning and the game would go on, and the Red Sox would have to send out either Collins or O'Brien, both warming up, to pitch the eleventh inning. That is, if there was an eleventh inning. The game was more than two and a half hours long already. It was beginning to get dark. Perhaps there would be another tie—and a game 9.

The World's Series that would not end seemed destined to continue as Mathewson, trying to get Gardner to hit the ball on the ground, fell behind 2-0, Meyers scooping both pitches out of the dirt. Then Gardner swung through a pitch a bit higher, at his knees, and tipped the ball back into the edge of the stands—where Fenway Park, one last time, lent the smallest of assists. The original box seats at the foot of the grandstands sat several feet up off the field, and it was impossible for a fan to lean over and swipe a foul ball from the ground without tumbling onto the field. But the temporary field-level box seats built in front were lower. An alert Boston fan hung over the rail and scooped up the ball, forcing Silk O'Loughlin to put a new white baseball in play. The count was 2-1.

Mathewson knew a walk would beat him, and his next pitch—his last—was a bit higher. Gardner jumped at it and succeeded in hitting the ball in the air to right, where Josh Devore ran to his left, then set himself and waited. The fate of the Series hung in the air.

Before Gardner had come to bat, Devore had tried to gauge just how deep he could play and still catch the ball and throw out Yerkes at the plate, and now he barely moved, waiting for the ball to come down so he could make his throw. Had the old ball still been in play, Gardner's fly might have landed twenty or thirty feet shorter or more, but this one went all the way out to where Devore stood at the extreme edge of his range.

As Devore set himself to catch and throw, Steve Yerkes placed his left foot on the base and prepared to push off with his right, waiting to see the ball in the glove before breaking for home. He did not want to score the winning run and then be called back for leaving the base too soon.

Devore caught the ball and threw it in one motion, releasing it quickly and almost falling to the ground as he followed through. Yerkes broke from the bag and ran, with clods of damp earth flying from his spikes, in a line straight toward home, watching Chief Meyers's eyes tracking the bright white ball as it sailed toward the plate, straight as a string. It hit the infield short of the plate and died in the soft ground, bouncing to the plate a half-second late, trickling in behind Yerkes as he slid over the plate, the winning run. The Series was over at last, the 3–2 score went up on the left-field wall, and the telegraph operators in the press box tapped out the result in a frenzy.

BOSTON NOW SUPREME IN BASEBALL WORLD

Suddenly the half-empty stands seemed full and erupted with shouts and songs. In seconds it seemed as if everyone had raced onto the field, where the Giants, apart from Mathewson, ran off quickly, heads down, bitter at losing a game and a Series they felt they should have won. Mathewson simply stood there for a moment, worn out and stunned, and did not seem to wake up until he was surrounded by Red Sox fans, grinning and magnanimous, slapping him on his back. He accepted their thanks with a blank face and trudged off.

Yerkes leapt to his feet and ran toward the dugout, where he was first greeted by his manager, who had been on deck, and then Wagner and Carrigan, who had been coaching first. In a moment they were all out there, incredulous and glad, hugging and shaking hands with each other and the fans, suddenly a team again, Gardner and Lewis, Hooper and Speaker, Wagner and Bedient, Collins and Hall, and O'Brien and Joe Wood, who was happier than anyone, the goat horns off his head.

Only one other Giant was left on the field, John McGraw, marching toward the Boston dugout to seek out Stahl and shake his hand. Some Boston fan could not resist and gave him a shove from behind, and the manager fell to the ground, tasting earth. McGraw stood, turned, and punched the attacker square in the face, dropping him. Then he found Jake Stahl and offered the Red Sox manager his hand.

The Red Sox, so suspicious for the last three days, were suddenly giddy, and men who would not look each other in the eye or share a seat on the train a few hours before now laughed and grinned. The heroes of the moment—Speaker, Yerkes, and Engle—were swarmed by a bevy of women and smothered in kisses, which they did not reject.

The World's Series was theirs, and they could hardly believe it. One after the other, they ducked into the dugout and then to the clubhouse. On the field, without the Royal Rooters to lead them, the celebration of the fans soon sputtered out, and as dusk fell they skipped across the field and into the stands, heading for the exits.

Despite winning only two of the five games at Fenway Park and tying another, the Red Sox had prevailed, and the keys to their success had been starting pitching, defense, timely hitting, and the occasional assist from their home field. Over time many of the questions that surrounded games 6 and 7 would fade, and Fenway Park's first season would not be remembered for the squabbles of the Red Sox but for their success, the cheers of the fans who did watch game 8 echoing longer and louder than the cheers of those who did not.

History anointed its heroes and sentenced its villains. In the days after the World's Series, Hugh Bedient, the man who mastered Mathewson and was lauded now as one of the great young pitchers in the game, the near-equal of Wood, received the most kudos, as did Yerkes and Engle and Gardner and Henriksen. But over time other heroes emerged—namely, Harry Hooper, for his superb game 8 catch of Doyle's drive, and Joe Wood, who in the end made most people forget game 7 and who won three games in the Series, a performance that underscored his 34-5 mark in the regular season. With 109 wins, the 1912 Red Sox set a club record that still stands. No Boston team has ever been better.

The goat became not Fred Merkle—who botched the foul pop-up that gave Speaker another chance—but Fred Snodgrass, if only because the loss demanded a scapegoat and the writers, somewhat inexplicably, selected him. The next morning a headline in the *New York World* read: "A $29,495 Muff Beats Giants in World's Series." Although his own teammates would absolve him of blame, baseball fans far and wide soon began to refer to his sin in shorthand as "Snodgrass's $30,000 muff," the figure representing the monetary difference between winning and losing. For the record, the extra $29,495 allowed each winning Red Sox player to take home $4,025, while each Giant received a check of only $2,566. The error and the phrase were soon carved in stone and have caused later generations to overlook most of what happened in the 1912 Series prior to game 8. By any measure it was one of the most remarkable World's Series in history. Featuring some of the greatest names in the history of the game, it was played in two settings, the Polo Grounds in New York and Fenway Park in Boston, that provided the perfect backdrops to a masterpiece.

Twenty minutes or so after Yerkes crossed the plate, Fenway Park emptied and fell nearly silent, the only sign of victory the muffled sounds of celebration taking place in the clubhouse. Ushers started scouring the stands for garbage, and in the waning light Jerome Kelley and the other groundskeepers gave the field a quick raking and pulled the canvas tarpaulin over the diamond. They would be back in the morning to begin to put Fenway Park to bed for the winter, but for now they only pulled the covers close.

In one season Fenway Park had gone from infancy through adolescence, revealing most of the quirks and much of the character that would serve it well for the next hundred seasons as it grew and evolved, almost every year, in ways both large and small. Although Fenway Park is not now the same place it was when the first fans spun through the turnstiles in 1912, it is nonetheless a treasure, a place where, from April to October each season, the history of a city and a people and a team is written, where legends have walked and legions have watched—a ballpark for the heart and the soul.

The next morning, as all Boston prepared to honor the Red Sox at a reception at Faneuil Hall, the Royal Rooters forgot their differences with McRoy and McAleer for a day and jumped back on the bandwagon. Jerome Kelley and his crew, as they did every other day, arrived at Fenway Park early and got busy.

They stripped the bunting from the stands, uncovered the infield, raked the dirt, pulled a few stray weeds, and filled a few holes here and there as the pigeons watched over them from beneath the grandstand roof. As a cold north wind whipped across Fenway Park and the dark low clouds of winter clamped down on New England, Jerome Kelley, like most other Red Sox fans, was already thinking about next year—and spring in Fenway Park.

There was a lot of work to do.

Epilogue

AFTER WINNING THE World's Series and turning in what is still the best single-season record in Red Sox history, the franchise seemed poised to begin a dynasty. With baseball's best outfield, baseball's best pitcher, two of the best rookie pitchers, emerging stars at third base and behind the plate, one of the youngest rosters in the game, and a new ballpark now fully operational, the 1913 season seemed to promise another first-place finish and appearance in the World's Series for the Red Sox.

Not so fast.

At first, all seemed well as the on-field record was backed up by a mountain of cash. According to *Sporting Life*, the Red Sox made $450,000 in profit during the 1912 season. Jake Stahl earned upward of $20,000 from his 5 percent stake in ownership, plus nearly another $15,000 in salary and his World's Series check. After making a public apology, McAleer and McRoy survived their run-in with the Rooters, when everyone appeared to forget the shenanigans that had taken place between games 6 and 7 and look toward the future.

But the simmering tensions that had threatened to pull the team apart during the 1912 season were not entirely washed away by the victory. The disagreement between Stahl and McAleer over the game 6 starter revealed a rift between the two, one that took little to reignite in 1913. Stahl, troubled by continuing problems with his ankle, was forced to retire as a player, which both weakened the team offensively and left Stahl with a little less value to the team and a whole lot less leverage. Joe Wood, after spraining an ankle in spring training, got off to a slow start and then pitched inconsistently—good one game and poor the next—as at only age twenty-three the wear and tear on his arm began to show. The Red Sox got off to a poor start, dropping three of four to open the season as the Athletics bolted ahead and everything began falling apart for Boston. After winning the pennant in 1912, the Red Sox did not spend a minute in first place in 1913.

By midseason the Red Sox were out of the race entirely and struggling to play .500 baseball. Joe Wood was on the shelf with a broken thumb, Charlie Wagner had a sore arm again, and McAleer and Stahl were hardly speaking. Stahl's contention that he, not McAleer, should be in charge of the franchise sparked a war among club investors that pitted the Chicago faction against McAleer and the Taylors. In July, soon after Buck O'Brien was sent to the White Sox in a waiver deal at Stahl's behest, the manager lost the tug-of-war. McAleer fired him and named Bill Carrigan manager, a move that put the KCs firmly in control of the ball club. The Sox played a bit better under Carrigan in the second half but still finished in fourth place, 78–71, twenty-five and a half games worse than their record in 1912 and fifteen and a half games behind first-place Philadelphia.

By then McAleer's days were numbered as well. The ticket snafu from the 1912 World's Series was not forgotten by all Boston fans, and the firing of Stahl coupled with the team's poor performance alienated the rest. Attendance dropped from 597,000 fans in 1912 to only 437,000. Investors were not happy. As soon as the season ended Ban Johnson, seeing his own investment at risk, began to engineer a sale. McAleer was powerless to stop him. In December "the assets of all Chicago interests"—meaning those of Stahl, his father-in-law, McRoy, and McAleer—were sold to Canadian Joseph Lannin.

James McAleer retired to his hometown of Youngstown, Ohio, and washed his hands of major league baseball. He never worked in organized baseball again and died in 1931 at the age of sixty-six. Of all Red Sox owners, he is, despite his long involvement with the game and the 1912 world championship, perhaps the least well known today.

Robert McRoy was more fortunate. His close ties with Ban Johnson kept him in the game, and after severing ties with the Red Sox, he joined the Cleveland Indians, serving as vice president and general manager before passing away in 1917.

Jake Stahl returned to Chicago and resumed his banking career, and although he was rumored to be part of a group that was interested in buying the Cleveland franchise, Stahl, too, never returned to the game of baseball. In 1917 he went to France to serve during World War I as a second lieutenant in the Air Bombing Division of the U.S. Army. The war apparently took a toll: shortly after he returned in 1919 he suffered a nervous breakdown. He spent two years in a California sanitarium before dying in 1922 of heart disease.

Bill Carrigan took over the Red Sox for Stahl and managed to keep his job even after the team was sold to Joseph Lannin. When the Federal League was created in 1914, an event that weakened rosters in both the American and National Leagues, the Red Sox, rejuvenated by some young pitching talent, including Babe Ruth, suddenly found themselves competitive again. They finished second under Carrigan in 1914 and bounced to the top of the American League in both 1915 and 1916, winning the World's Series each time, but using the new Braves Field, with its higher seating capacity, instead of Fenway Park. Carrigan then chose to go out on top and retired to go into banking in Maine. He was talked into returning to the Red Sox as manager in 1927, 1928, and 1929, but the team was dismal, the game had passed him by, and the ball club finished last all three seasons, making Carrigan both one of the most and least successful managers in club history. Following the 1929 season, he returned to Maine. Over the next few decades he occasionally made appearances at Fenway Park, a symbol of days gone by, before passing away on July 9, 1969.

The influence and popularity of the **Royal Rooters,** and the personal fame of **Nuf Ced McGreevey,** peaked during the World's Series of 1912. The story of the ticket debacle before game 7 was reported in papers from coast to coast. McAleer and McRoy were both forced to make a formal apology, and despite their game 8 boycott, the Rooters had still led the celebration at Faneuil Hall.

Although the Rooters were still influential enough to receive more World's Series tickets in 1914, 1915, and 1916, their preeminence among Boston fans began to wane as their members got older and were not replaced by younger Rooters. When Honey Fitz was forced to drop out of the 1914 mayoral race after a scandal over his relationship with a cigarette girl named Toodles, the group lost a staunch ally, and the opening of Braves Field moved the center of Boston's baseball uni-

verse a bit farther away from McGreevey's saloon. Without the baseball crowds, business slowed, and after the 1915 season McGreevey
was forced to close the tavern at 940 Columbus Avenue. He reopened
several blocks away where he owned some property, at 1153 Tremont
Street, on the corner of Ruggles Street, but it wasn't the same. The
Rooters attended their last World's Series en masse in 1917, but by
then the group was down to only about one hundred members. When
the Red Sox appeared in the 1918 World's Series the Rooters were nowhere to be found. Lamented the *Globe's* Edward Martin, "The crowd
did not come up to expectations . . . It is the first time any Boston
club has been in a series that 'Tessie' had not been heard from good
and proper." Indeed, only six years after the debacle of 1912, the Royal
Rooters were not even mentioned by the press during the Series.

On August 1, 1918, the U.S. Senate adopted the Eighteenth Amendment to the Constitution, prohibiting the sale of alcohol. The House
followed suit on December 17, and the amendment, after being quickly
ratified by the states, became law on January 29, 1919. Regrettably,
Nuf Ced McGreevey closed his tavern, and he eventually donated the
bulk of his collection of baseball photographs to the Boston Public
Library. He died of heart failure on February 2, 1943, and with his
death a chapter of Boston baseball history also passed, although the
recent opening of McGreevy's, a Boylston Street bar and restaurant
thoughtfully modeled after the original saloon, has once again made
Nuf Ced and the Rooters household names.

Hugh Bradley, the man who hit the first home run over the left-
field wall in Fenway Park, never hit another, and after the 1912 season he never made another appearance in the major leagues. Sold to
Jersey City after the end of the season, he resurfaced in the Federal
League in 1914, hitting .307 for Pittsburgh but failing to hit a home
run. After appearing with both Pittsburgh and Brooklyn in the Federal League in 1915, Bradley returned to the minor leagues in 1916 and
played for a variety of clubs before he retired after the 1923 season. He
settled in Worcester, Massachusetts, near his hometown of Grafton,
and died in 1949.

Although **Hick Cady** never quite lived up to the promise of his
rookie season, he remained a backup catcher for the Red Sox through
1917. Then, after injuring his shoulder in a car accident, he was traded

with Larry Gardner to the Athletics. He did not appear in a game in 1918 but did appear in thirty-four games in 1919, then played six more seasons in the minor leagues before retiring and becoming a minor league umpire. He died in a hotel fire at age sixty in Cedar Rapids, Iowa, in 1946.

After the 1912 World's Series, **Buck O'Brien,** the man who pitched the first official game in Fenway Park, seemed poised for greatness. He pitched well at the start of the 1913 season, but then faltered. When the war between Jake Stahl and James McAleer broke out into the open, O'Brien was a casualty. According to one news report, O'Brien "hadn't been strong with the Boston manager for a long time. Buck is said to have committed the indiscretion of having smeared his fist over Joe Wood's classic countenance last fall. . . . So Stahl sent O'Brien to Chicago." On July 2, 1913, O'Brien, with a record of 4-11, was acquired by the White Sox on waivers for only $5,000. He failed to win a game for the White Sox and later that year was sold to Oakland in the Pacific Coast League. After a brief stint with Memphis in the Southern Association in 1914, O'Brien eventually returned to Boston and for much of the next decade was a familiar face on semipro teams in the Boston area, pitching primarily for the Dilboy Club. He passed away on July 25, 1959, and on Fenway's golden anniversary on April 21, 1962, O'Brien's grandson, nine-year-old Tom O'Brien, threw out the first pitch.

Hugh Bedient, the hero of the 1912 World's Series, never recaptured his 1912 magic either, although he did manage to stay with the Red Sox for two more seasons, going 15-14 in 1913, then 8-12 in 1914. In 1915 he jumped to the Buffalo franchise of the Federal League and compiled a record of 16-18, but when the league folded Bedient was unable to make it back to the majors, and in 1917 he developed arm trouble. After sitting out several seasons, he returned to the minor leagues, where he spent most of his time pitching for Toledo in the American Association, before retiring after the 1925 season and returning to his hometown of Falconer, New York. There he lived on a farm and worked for the Harbison-Carborundum Corporation. He died in 1965.

Charlie "Heinie" Wagner's arm gave out during the 1913 season, and he was never the same player again. Released during the 1916 season, Wagner briefly returned during 1918 when the Red Sox were caught short during World War I, and he subsequently served several stints as a Red Sox coach, the last time for his friend Bill Carrigan. Wagner took over for Carrigan as Red Sox manager in 1930, but after the team finished last, he resigned and went to work as a supervisor in a lumberyard in New Rochelle, New York. He died of a heart attack in 1943.

After being dumped by the Red Sox in 1914 when he failed to hit, University of Pennsylvania graduate **Steve Yerkes** jumped to the Federal League and played two seasons. He then made a brief appearance with the Chicago Cubs in 1916 before returning to the minor leagues. He retired as a player after the 1923 season. Yerkes later managed in the Canadian American League, and in 1940, before buying and operating a bowling alley, he managed the Yale freshman baseball team. He appeared at Fenway Park's golden anniversary in 1962 and passed away in 1971.

Ray Collins was the only member of the 1912 starting rotation to pitch well in 1913, winning nineteen games, and he remained effective in 1914, when he won twenty games. But when he pitched poorly in 1915, he decided to retire at age twenty-nine. Collins returned to his family dairy farm in Colchester, Vermont, which he operated for most of the remainder of his life. He briefly coached the University of Vermont baseball team and served in the Vermont legislature and on the board of trustees for the University of Vermont. He died of complications following a stroke in 1970.

Larry Gardner played another dozen years in the major leagues. In 1918 he was dealt with Hick Cady to the Philadelphia Athletics, and in 1919 he was traded to Cleveland, where he was reunited with Tris Speaker and Joe Wood. Gardner enjoyed his greatest success as an Indian, knocking in more than one hundred runs in both 1920 and 1921, and proved to be a very good, but not quite great, ballplayer. After spending several seasons as a minor league manager, he returned to Enosburg Falls, then moved to Burlington, Vermont, where in 1932 he became head baseball coach at the University of Vermont. After he retired, he worked in a camera store and passed away at age ninety in 1976. Sadly, the University of Vermont baseball program, which contributed both Gardner and Ray Collins to the 1912 Red Sox, was dropped by the university after the 2008 season.

The best outfield in baseball remained intact for the next three seasons as Duffy Lewis, Harry Hooper, and **Tris Speaker** all turned down entreaties from the Federal League and in turn were able to squeeze big contracts out of Red Sox owner Joseph Lannin. But when the Federal League collapsed, Lannin wanted to roll back salaries and cut Speaker's $18,000 salary in half. Speaker held out, and Lannin traded him to Cleveland for Sam Jones, Fred Thomas, and $55,000. Once in Cleveland, Speaker continued to forge a Hall of Fame career. He retired after the 1928 season with a career batting average of .355 and was elected to the Hall of Fame in 1937. Following his retirement, Speaker had an eclectic career as a minor league manager, executive, broadcaster, and coach before dying of a heart attack in 1958.

Duffy Lewis played with the Red Sox through the 1917 season and joined the military in 1918. When the Red Sox had a glut of players at the end of the war he was traded with Dutch Leonard and Ernie Shore to the Yankees for $15,000 and four players, including pitcher Ray Caldwell. Lewis's major league career lasted until 1921, when he returned to the minor leagues. He retired from baseball in 1927. Wiped out by the stock market crash, Lewis returned to the game in 1931, becoming a coach for the Boston Braves from 1931 to 1934 before serving as the club's traveling secretary, a position he held for the Braves in Boston and in Milwaukee until 1961. He died in Salem, New Hampshire, in 1979.

Harry Hooper played with the Red Sox through the 1920 season, then was sold to the Chicago White Sox. He retired after the 1925 season. After playing several more seasons of professional baseball in California, he became active in the real estate business and also became postmaster in Capitola, California. In 1971 he was elected to the Baseball Hall of Fame, and he died of a stroke in 1974.

Although **Joe Wood** was troubled slightly by a sprained ankle during spring training in 1913, in one April exhibition against the University of Illinois Wood reportedly had terrific speed and control and struck out all twelve men he faced as his infielders, bored, turned around and watched a parade. But in his opening day start against the Philadelphia Athletics a week later Wood lasted only five innings, giving up nine hits and seven runs, his worst regular-season performance in more than a year. Two weeks later it was reported that Wood was experiencing pain in his thumb, and after slipping while fielding a bunt in a game against Detroit on May 12, Wood was telling people that the joint was broken. He missed several starts, then came back. Later he told Lawrence Ritter, "I don't know whether I tried to pitch too soon after that, or whether something happened to my shoulder at the same time. But whatever it was I never pitched again without a terrific amount of pain in my right shoulder. Never again." Wood made no mention of the arm troubles that had plagued him intermittently through the 1912 season. He reinjured the thumb on July 18, 1913, in a game against Detroit while chasing Sam Crawford during a rundown. Apart from one brief relief appearance, his season was over.

His blazing fastball was gone for good. Although he remained effective when he did pitch, Wood could not stand the pain and retired after the 1915 season. In 1917 he decided to try to make a comeback, this time as an outfielder, and the Red Sox sold him to Cleveland, where he was reunited with Tris Speaker. Wood, a fine hitter and athlete, managed to become a valuable part-time player for Cleveland, hitting .366 in 1921 and then .296 as a regular in 1922 before he retired for good, saying he had nothing left to prove. In 1923 Tris Speaker helped him secure a job as freshman baseball coach at Yale. One year later he took over the varsity and held the position until 1942.

In 1928 Wood was implicated, along with former teammates Tris Speaker, Dutch Leonard, and Ty Cobb, in the possible fixing of a game between the Tigers and the Indians on September 26, 1919. Wood cooperated with the investigation, and while he admitted to betting on baseball and holding money for other players, he denied having any involvement in the actual throwing of a game—he did not appear in the contest in question. After leaving Yale, Wood went into business with his brother in California, operating a driving range, then retired in New England. Repeated efforts by his family and others to have him enshrined in the Hall of Fame failed, and Wood died in 1985 at the age of ninety-five, the last surviving member of the 1912 Red Sox.

Tim Murnane continued to cover the Red Sox as the dean of Boston's baseball writers until he died suddenly of a heart attack at age sixty-five on February 7, 1917, while attending a production at the Schubert Theater in Boston. Much beloved by the New England baseball community, on September 27, 1917, an all-star benefit game on his behalf was held at Fenway Park. Actress Fanny Brice helped sell programs, Will Rogers performed rope tricks, and former heavyweight champ John L. Sullivan coached third base for Boston. In pregame contests Babe Ruth won the fungo-hitting contest with a drive of 402 feet, Joe Jackson made the longest throw of 396 feet, eight inches, and Ray Chapman beat everyone around the bases, circling the diamond in fourteen seconds. Before a crowd of seventeen thousand, the Red Sox, behind the pitching of Babe Ruth and Rube Foster, defeated the all-stars, 2–0, as Boston's hurlers shut down a lineup that included Jackson, Chapman, Ty Cobb, Tris Speaker, Buck Weaver, Rabbit Maranville, Stuffy McInnis, Wally Schang, and Walter Johnson. The game raised $14,000 for Murnane's widow. No Boston sportswriter before or since has ever been more beloved.

After **Charles Logue's** death, his son, Emmitt, took over the company and ran it until 1949, when his son, Emmitt Jr., took over as president until closing the company in 1972. Charles Logue's great-grandson, Jim Logue, started the construction firm Logue Engineering three years later in 1975, and in 2006 he was joined in the business by his son, Charles Logue's great-great-grandson, Kevin Logue. They are Red Sox fans.

After helping with the addition of seats to Fenway Park for the 1912 World's Series, architect **James E. McLaughlin** apparently was never called on by the Red Sox again in regard to Fenway Park. He continued his successful career as an architect focusing primarily on public buildings. His crowning achievement—apart from Fenway Park—was probably the Commonwealth Armory on Commonwealth Avenue in Boston. Other notable buildings he designed include the Quincy State Armory, Watertown High School, Dorchester High School, Boston Latin, and the Woburn Armory. In 1918 he also designed 256 houses for the U.S. Housing Corporation to provide housing for wartime shipbuilders in Quincy, Massachusetts. In 1920 McLaughlin took on a partner, G. Houston Burr, and the two went into business as McLaughlin and Burr, with offices at 88 Tremont Street. McLaughlin and his wife Mary lived on Reservoir Road in Chestnut Hill and had no children. Over the decades his contribution to Fenway Park was little noticed, and when he died in February 1966 the passing of the man who designed Fenway Park went unnoticed in Boston newspapers.

By opening day of the 1913 season the temporary seats that ringed the outfield of **Fenway Park** had been removed, as had the bleachers on Duffy's Cliff, but other seats added to accommodate the 1912 World's Series, such as the third-base stands, the right-field bleachers, and the gigantic press box, remained as permanent fixtures, even as the evolution of Fenway Park continued.

The ballpark was pressed into service for the World's Series once again in 1914, this time hosting the "Miracle" Boston Braves, who abandoned the South End Grounds for the roomier confines of Fenway Park. They swept the Series in four games and, for the first and only time, made Fenway Park the site of a no-holds-barred world championship celebration.

Although the Sox won the AL pennant in 1915 and 1916, they played the World's Series each time at Braves Field, which had a greater seating capacity than Fenway Park. It was not until 1918 that Fenway Park hosted the World's Series again. Although the Red Sox defeated the Cubs in six games, the finale at Fenway Park was not unlike the finale in 1912: the Sox won the final game, but it was played to a park at only half-capacity because a threatened players' strike had left fans disgruntled.

By then, the remaining wooden stands were beginning to show their age. Although ownership of the team had passed from Joseph Lannin to Harry Frazee, the park remained the property of the Taylor family and in its first decade was the beneficiary of very little maintenance. By the time Bob Quinn acquired both the ball club and the ballpark in 1923, the wooden portions of the park—the third-base stands, both bleacher sections, and the pavilion—were already past due for some work, the ten-year usable life of white pine having been pushed well past its limit. Quinn, although well intentioned, was underfinanced from the start, and under his ownership the decay of Fenway Park increased dramatically. The ballpark was barely ten years old and already starting to fall apart.

On May 7, 1926, two small fires broke out beneath the third-base stands but were rapidly extinguished. One day later, just after the end of the game, the wood structure, dry as tinder after more than a decade of exposure to the elements, caught fire again under suspicious circumstances. This time it burned to the ground, and if not for the heroic efforts of area workers, who ran garden hoses to the grandstand roof and doused it with water, the grandstand roof probably would have caught on fire and that might well have spelled the end of Fenway Park. The structure was saved, but instead of rebuilding, Bob Quinn used the insurance money for operating expenses. For the rest of his tenure the ground along left field beyond the grandstand sat empty, just as it had when Fenway Park was first built. Ever so slowly, the park was returning to its original April 1912 configuration.

By 1928 Quinn, desperate to stay afloat, wanted to sell Fenway and was making overtures to the Braves, proposing that the two clubs share their field in Allston, but the National League club turned him down. By then, a decade of bad luck, bad decisions, and lack of money had buried the Red Sox in the second division. Apart from holidays or visits by Babe Ruth and the Yankees, attendance at Fenway Park rarely topped more than a few thousand fans a game and sometimes was even less. No one was extolling the virtues of the park, singing its praises, or waxing nostalgic about being taken there by their father or anyone else. The ballpark was a dump.

That began to change on February 21, 1933, four days after Tom Yawkey celebrated his thirtieth birthday and received control of his family inheritance of more than $7 million. He celebrated the occasion by dropping $1.2 million on the Red Sox, buying the team and the ballpark. Over the next few seasons, as he tried to buy a championship by acquiring players like Jimmie Foxx, Lefty Grove, and Joe Cronin, Fenway Park did not miss out on his largesse.

After the 1933 season, even as the NFL's Boston Redskins played their home games at Fenway, Yawkey embarked on a renovation of the ballpark. Duffy's Cliff, which had been greatly diminished in 1926, was dug up entirely and hauled off. Lansdowne Street was held back by a concrete barrier, leaving only a subtle rise to serve as a warning track in front of a new left-field fence made not of wood but primarily of concrete and tin. As soon as the football season ended reconstruction proceeded to other areas of the park, particularly the outfield bleachers, which were torn down and rebuilt in steel and concrete.

But on January 5, 1934, a fire broke out in the wooden falsework beneath the new bleachers when "salamanders," gas-fired heaters used to help concrete cure, sparked a fire, possibly a case of arson to create a diversion for a planned payroll heist. The payroll was saved, but the fire destroyed the new bleachers.

It was the best thing that could have happened. Tom Yawkey responded with an even more ambitious renovation plan. He renovated the entire ballpark, and over the next three months more than one thousand workers toiled around the clock to ready the park for opening day.

By then Fenway Park had taken on much of the look it would retain for the next fifty years. The ballpark was painted "Dartmouth green," the facade was sandblasted, the press box and grandstand roof were rebuilt, a new scoreboard was built into the left-field wall, and the new concrete-and-steel bleachers, pavilion, and third-base stands were integrated into the main grandstand, which received a near total facelift.

Over the next few decades most changes to the park, with only a few exceptions, were incidental. Following the 1939 season, bullpens were built in right field, a move that cut down the home run distance by twenty-two feet and was widely believed to have been done to make it easier for Ted Williams, a rookie in 1939, to hit more home runs. In 1946 "skyview" seats were added on either side of the press box, and lights were installed in 1947, making it possible to play night games in Fenway Park for the first time.

In 1952 the Braves abandoned Boston for Milwaukee, Wisconsin, and the benefits of a new ballpark, built by Milwaukee County. In Boston and elsewhere major league fans and owners alike began to feel that they, too, deserved new ballparks with expansive parking lots underwritten by taxpayers—or at least some help with renovations and infrastructure. To that end, in 1958 the Red Sox asked the city to cede Lansdowne Street for expansion purposes, but they were turned down. Soon plans for a new ballpark were being floated, the most common idea being a multipurpose stadium that could also serve as a football field, to be built in either the Fenway, the South Station area, or the western suburbs. But the timing was not right: Boston's weak city government, a stagnant local economy, and anti-Boston bias at the state level left all such plans on the drawing board—and saved Fenway Park. If such a stadium had been built, Fenway would undoubtedly have been torn down.

Instead, Fenway Park was again left to deteriorate, and only the most basic maintenance took place. By the mid-1960s Tom Yawkey, frustrated with the performance of his team and the lack of financial help from local officials, began speaking openly of moving the Red Sox from Boston and abandoning Fenway Park. Sox fans yawned. On the final day of the 1965 season the smallest crowd in the history of Fenway Park, 487 fans, bothered to show up.

Then came the "Impossible Dream" season of 1967. The moribund franchise rose from the dead and won an improbable pennant. Just as older ballparks elsewhere were beginning to be introduced to the wrecking ball, a new generation of baseball fans were reintroduced to Fenway Park. Almost overnight Fenway Park went from an anachronism to an asset, and it was soon deemed worthy of preservation. As the Red Sox remained competitive into the early 1970s and attendance surged, the team began to revitalize the park, building a workout area for the players beneath the center-field bleachers, installing plastic seats in 1974, and in 1975 adding a new scoreboard and replacing the facade of the left-field wall. When the Red Sox played the Cincinnati Reds in a classic World Series that fall, the contrast between Fenway Park and the Reds' super-stadium, Riverfront Field, was obvious. Fenway was a treasure and the super-stadium an abomination. For the first time in Boston history "going to Fenway," as a trip unto itself, became at least as important as going to see the Red Sox.

Tom Yawkey died in 1976, and his wife, Jean, took over. In 1980 the team embarked on a long-overdue, multi-year plan to refurbish and modernize the park while remaining relatively sensitive to preserving its unique personality. Pilings and foundations were reinforced to support new luxury boxes on the roof, the clubhouse was refurbished, the lighting was upgraded, and the grandstand got a new roof. The plan culminated in 1988 with the construction of the "600 Club" on the grandstand roof behind home plate, which also resulted in the relocation of the press box to the structure's roof.

The 600 Club was arguably the worst addition in the history of Fenway Park. Apart from the aesthetic issues it raised—the structure changed the scale of the grandstand completely and for a time made the entire structure appear somewhat top-heavy and out of balance—it put well-heeled fans behind a massive shield of Plexiglas. It also changed the wind patterns in Fenway Park, adversely affecting home run totals. Although it would take a number of seasons before team management realized it, the new structure subtly changed the ballpark from an offense-minded park to one much more neutral. The addition of the 600 Club had one more deleterious effect as well—its construction precluded the construction of a full and complete second deck. Logistically, it became just too difficult to deconstruct the 600 Club structure and reconstruct a complete second deck during the off-season. Fortunately, however, the most egregious and aesthetically offensive feature of the structure, the Plexiglas barrier, was removed before the 2006 season.

Jean Yawkey died in 1992, and control of the team passed to the Yawkey Trust, administered by John Harrington. Even as Fenway Park began to inspire a new generation of "retro" ballparks, such as Baltimore's seminal Oriole Park at Camden Yards, before long team officials were extolling what Fenway Park was not instead of what it was. They again began to beat the drum for a new ballpark, preferably one financed on the backs of taxpayers. The team was floating the notion that Fenway Park was obsolete and irreparable, that the park made it financially impossible for the team to compete, and that any kind of renovation plan was unfeasible. The Sox proposed a new park, to be called New Fenway, a double-decked park with the same footprint to be built adjacent to the existing Fenway Park.

Although these plans got farther along than most other schemes—the local media fell for the plan with little scrutiny—when everyone crunched the numbers and came up with nothing but red it fell apart. The Yawkey Trust finally decided to quit while they were ahead—and the stock market was high—and put the team up for sale, effectively killing any plans for a new ballpark.

On March 1, 2002, the Red Sox were purchased by a group led by investor John Henry and television producer Tom Werner. At a total cost of $286,000,000, during the subsequent decade the team embarked on the most ambitious changes at Fenway Park since the renovations of 1933–34. Behind the wind of a winning team and an aggressive public relations program, the Red Sox were able to obtain cooperation from city officials that had been withheld from previous owners. This included the taking of Yawkey Way before, during, and after games and permission to construct, alongside Lansdowne Street, the "Green Monster" seats atop the left-field wall, a feature every Red Sox fan over the age of three had always thought should be built and wondered why it had not.

Under the direction of former senior vice president of planning and development Janet Marie Smith, nearly every expansion plan that had been deemed impossible by the ball club's previous administration was now found to be not only possible but affordable. A host of changes were undertaken at the park, including a reinforcement of the foundations that would make them sound, according to team president Larry Lucchino, "for another forty years." In April 2002 two rows of "dugout box seats" on the infield side of both dugouts to the backstop were built, seats that essentially mimicked those created by James McLaughlin for the 1912 World's Series. That September, Yawkey Way was turned over to the Red Sox during ball games, and the gate A concourse was expanded. In April 2003 the Green Monster seats were added, and two rows of box seats were extended from the end of the dugouts to the outfield. Later that year another large concourse was opened in right field, and in 2004 right-field roof seats were added. Nearly every year since, the park has seen some additional change—seats added here, a restaurant there—as the ballpark's exterior footprint has increased. When the "Jeano" Building, the former site of NESN on the corner of Brookline Avenue and Lansdowne Street, was annexed and renovated, more of the park itself could be turned over to seats and other contemporary amenities, and the capacity of the ballpark increased by more than five thousand spectators.

Understandably, the primary motivation for virtually all of these changes has been more financial than aesthetic. They were made to boost team revenue through an increased number of higher-priced seats and additional concession options, including bars and restaurants, in order to capture ballpark-generated revenue inside Fenway Park rather than in the surrounding neighborhood. As a result, outside vendors were forced farther away from Fenway Park's front doors, and the ballpark was turned into an ever more efficient delivery system for food, beverages, merchandise, and memorabilia. This change has come at the expense of family-affordable seats: Fenway Park is now the most expensive ballpark in the country, with the average ticket price topping $50. While these changes have unquestionably proven to be a financial boon to the club, at the same time they have priced most middle-class fans out of Fenway Park and done little to address cramped seating in the grandstands and bleachers.

From a purely aesthetic perspective, these changes are something of a mixed bag. Some features, like the Green Monster seats, seem to be an integral part of the structure (at least from the inside). Others, such as the proliferation of rooftop seats, have simultaneously both amplified the out-of-scale, top-heavy design first exhibited by the building of the 600 Club (now called the EMC Club) and, to a degree, helped ameliorate it, since the addition of limited rooftop seating adjacent to the EMC Club has softened the scale issue. Much of the exterior of Fenway Park remains visually unappealing, and the original office facade, the only part of the structure with some charm, is now festooned with all manner of banners and flags that, in combination with construction on the opposite side of the street, make it almost impossible to view the unadorned structure as it was originally intended to be seen. The effect of the adjacent renovations and construction on the Jeano property—which now extends along Brookline Avenue and wraps around Lansdowne Street—is to awkwardly reference McLaughlin's original design without either copying or honoring it.

Perhaps the most jarring and unsightly feature of the park today is the proliferation of signs and advertising, which make it nearly impossible to find a place to rest the eye without being visually bombarded by corporate messages. That, in combination with a relentless barrage of music and audio messages, has utterly changed the emotional experience of attending a game at Fenway Park. The end result is, rather ironically, that today's Fenway Park shares more in common with the retro parks designed to mimic it than with itself. The park that spawned a host of imitators has now evolved and changed to such a degree that it more closely resembles the very ballparks it inspired rather than James McLaughlin's own original design.

In the end, however, nearly one hundred years after the first fans passed through the turnstiles, Fenway Park remains. It has been saved, but it has not, except in the most general sense, been preserved. Very little of the ballpark that opened in 1912 is still visible. What little that does remain has essentially been built over, built under, and built on top of until the original design is almost unrecognizable. Yet because the changes to Fenway Park have taken place over the course of one hundred years, they do not seem as dramatic as they truly are. And what has changed the least is perhaps what matters most—the field itself, those few hallowed green acres upon which some of the greatest players and greatest games in the history of baseball have been played.

The man first responsible for that, chief groundskeeper **Jerome Kelley,** served at Fenway Park for almost another decade before being replaced by Bert Gerioux. According to the *Boston Globe* of June 8, 1921, several Red Sox players complained about the condition of the grounds. Kelley "was evidently provoked at what he considered unfair criticism" and abruptly resigned.

Acknowledgments

THE WORK OF this book was accomplished over the course of more than two decades and could not have been done without the help and assistance of a number of friends and colleagues, most notably Siobhan and Saorla, who support my work in every way, every day. My biggest thanks go to the staff of the Boston Public Library, particularly Henry Scannell, John Devine, Aaron Schmidt, John Dorsey, and the staffs of the Microtext Department and Print Department, whose collections house the greatest archive of Red Sox history in existence. Thanks also to my occasional researcher and assistant, Denise Bousquet, for her studious fact-checking of numbers, to Jim and Kevin Logue for their cooperation, and my two most trusted readers, my good friends and colleagues Richard Johnson and Howard Bryant. Editor Susan Canavan, production editor Beth Burleigh Fuller, designer Brian Moore, agent John Taylor Williams, and Hope Denekamp of Kneerim and Williams Literary Agency all helped this project evolve from a two-paragraph proposal into a fully realized work.

Writing it has been a privilege.

Bibliographic Notes and Sources

W RITING A BOOK about any aspect of Fenway Park poses some special challenges. While it is a place that many feel they know intimately, it is also a place that few people truly know very well in its original state, which is the main focus of this book. There is no single comprehensive trove of primary resource material in regard to the building of Fenway Park in the form of original architectural drawings or construction notes. Given the length of time that has passed since Fenway Park was built, this is not completely surprising, and it is important to note that it is only in the last forty or fifty years—since 1967—that Fenway Park has been viewed as a special place. Before then, there was little historical interest in the ballpark. James McLaughlin, its architect, is obscure even to local architectural historians, and from what I have been told the Red Sox discarded virtually all files in regard to the first three decades of their history shortly after Tom Yawkey purchased the club in 1933—long before this kind of material was valued by historians, researchers, or memorabilia collectors.

For these reasons my main sources throughout this book, in regard to not only Fenway Park but also the 1912 season and the 1912 World's Series, are newspaper and periodical accounts written during the time period it covers. I consulted thousands and thousands of individual newspaper and periodical stories during this project, which began in earnest in 2008 and occupied the bulk of my time for the next two and a half years.

The major newspapers consulted for this project include the *Boston Globe, Boston Post, Boston Journal, Boston Traveler, Boston Herald, Lowell Sun, New York Times, New York Tribune, New York World, New York Journal,* and *Washington Post,* and I also consulted the weeklies *The*

Sporting News and *Sporting Life* and the monthly *Baseball* magazine. A few of these papers, such as the *Globe* and the *Times*, are available online. Others are accessible through microfilm. In the latter case I have generally used the files maintained by the Boston Public Library, the Widener Library at Harvard University, the W. E. B. Du Bois Library at the University of Massachusetts in Amherst, the New York Public Library, and the National Baseball Hall of Fame Library. *Sporting Life* and *Baseball* magazine are also accessible through the LA84 Foundation's online library. I accessed other newspapers from other areas of the country through newspaperarchive.com. In most instances I used this source to access wire and syndicated reports in regard to the 1912 season and the World's Series, as well as most of the reports by newspaper reporters like Sam Crane, Hugh Fullerton, Ring Lardner, and Grantland Rice, whose stories were distributed nationally and appeared in many newspapers all around the country. Rather than select from one of several obscure sources, I instead reference the date of their report in the text, which is more useful to researchers. I also conducted more contemporary newspaper research through newslibrary.com and proquest.com. I consulted the microfilmed scrapbooks of Duffy Lewis, Joe Wood, and Nuf Ced McGreevey held by the Boston Public Library, the Bill Carrigan scrapbook in the archives of the Sports Museum of New England, and my own archives created over the last twenty-five years during the writing of numerous books and articles on baseball history — including my collection on Fenway Park, which began in earnest in 1987 when I was asked to write the official seventy-fifth anniversary history of the park for *The Official 1987 Red Sox Yearbook*.

In regard to newspaper reports, I tend to source the most important stories directly in the text itself, referring to either the newspaper or the reporter by name (for example, "according to Paul Shannon in the *Post* . . ."). For readability, as this is a popular history and not an academic one, I do not always source the precise date of the newspaper account used, but researchers who wish to track down these stories should be aware that most useful game stories, then as now, appear in print the day after the date of the game in question.

Particularly important sources and stories are listed individually in the chapter notes, but I have made no attempt to create a bibliographic citation for every story consulted or to create formal footnotes. In most instances—and particularly for the World's Series—I re-created the games by using multiple newspaper accounts, sometimes from as many as a dozen sources or more. Thus, a specific accounting would have been both challenging and confusing—sometimes I would have had to cite a half-dozen or more sources for a single sentence. As such, these accounts are composites—multiple original accounts of the same events and rarely 100 percent consistent with one another. To the best of my ability I have tried to be as accurate as possible, but it is certainly possible that another author, using these same sources, would arrive at a slightly different interpretation of events. That is the nature of the process. Although retrosheet.org and baseball-reference.com do not yet maintain "game logs" and box scores for regular-season games during the 1911 or 1912 season, both do maintain substantial day-by-day accounts of the regular season. I consulted these accounts throughout the book for scores and schedules, game logs of the World's Series, and various other statistical information.

All dialogue used in this book is taken from a previously published source. Anything that appears in quotation marks is from a written document. Absolutely no dialogue has been created, invented, or surmised, although in a few instances in which different sources reproduce dialogue about a specific event that is not identical, I have used my own judgment to create a composite statement. Neither have I made significant use of the ghostwritten player accounts that appeared in most newspapers during the 1912 World's Series. As noted in more detail in my chapter notes, with few exceptions (such as those authored by Christy Mathewson and Eddie Collins), the veracity of such accounts, most of which were written by newspaper reporters with little to no input from the bylined author, should be considered dubious at best.

Selected Books

A. J. Reach and Company. *The Reach Official American League Baseball Guide.* Philadelphia: A. J. Reach Company, 1912.

Alexander, Charles. *John McGraw.* New York: Viking Press, 1988.

———. *Our Game: An American Baseball History.* New York: MJF Books, 1991.

Angell, Roger. *Season Ticket.* Boston: Houghton Mifflin, 1988.

Benson, Michael. *Ballparks of North America: A Comprehensive Historical Reference to Baseball Grounds, Yards, and Stadiums, 1845 to Present.* Jefferson, N.C.: McFarland Publishing, 1989.

Berry, Henry, and Harold Berry. *The Boston Red Sox: The Complete Record of Red Sox Baseball.* New York: Macmillan, 1984.

Boston Red Sox. *Official Media Guide,* various editions.

———. *Official Scorebook Magazine,* various editions.

———. *Official Yearbook,* various editions.

Cobb, Ty. *Busting 'Em and Other Big League Stories.* New York: Edward J. Clode, 1915.

Gay, Tim. *Tris Speaker: The Rough-and-Tumble Life of a Baseball Legend.* Guilford, Conn.: Lyons Press/University of Nebraska, 2007.

Ginsburg, Daniel E. *The Fix Is In: A History of Baseball Gambling and Game Fixing Scandals.* Jefferson, N.C.: McFarland Publishing, 1995.

Golenbock, Peter. *Fenway.* New York: G. P. Putnam's Sons, 1992.

Hirshberg, Al. *The Red Sox: The Bean and the Cod.* Boston: Waverley House, 1947.

———. *What's the Matter with the Red Sox?* Cornwall, N.Y.: : Dodd Mead and Company, 1973.

Johnson, Dick, ed., text by Glenn Stout. *Ted Williams: A Portrait in World and Pictures.* New York: Walker and Company, 1991.

Johnson, Dick, and Glenn Stout. *Red Sox Century.* Boston: Houghton Mifflin, 1999.

———. *Yankees Century.* Boston: Houghton Mifflin, 2002.

Jones, David, ed. *Deadball Stars of the American League.* Dulles, Va.: Potomac Books, 2006.

Kaese, Harold. *The Boston Braves.* New York: G. P. Putnam's Sons, 1948.

Keene, Kerry, et al. *The Babe in Red Stockings.* Champaign, Ill.: Sagamore Publishing, 1997.

Lieb, Frederick. *Connie Mack: Grand Old Man of Baseball.* New York: G. P. Putnam's Sons, 1945.

———. *The Boston Red Sox.* New York: G. P. Putnam's Sons, 1947.

———. *Baseball as I Have Known It.* New York: Coward, McCann & Geoghegan, 1977.

Lowry, Philip. *Green Cathedrals.* Reading, Mass.: Addison-Wesley, 1992.

Macht, Norman L. *Connie Mack and the Early Years of Baseball.* Lincoln: University of Nebraska Press, 2007.

Mack, Connie. *My 66 Years in the Big Leagues.* Philadelphia: John C. Winston, 1950.

Murdock, Eugene. *Ban Johnson: Czar of Baseball.* Westport, Conn.: Greenwood Press, 1982.

Nash, Peter J. *Boston's Royal Rooters.* Charleston, S.C.: Arcadia Books, 2005.

Neft, David S., and Richard Cohen. *The Sports Encyclopedia: Baseball.* New York: St. Martin's Press, 1997.

Ritter, Lawrence. *The Glory of Their Times.* New York: Macmillan, 1984.

Seasholes, Nancy S. *Gaining Ground: A History of Landmaking in Boston.* Cambridge, Mass.: MIT Press, 2003.

Seymour, Harold. *Baseball: The Early Years.* New York: Oxford University Press, 1960.

———. *Baseball: The Golden Years.* New York: Oxford University Press, 1971.

Thomas, Henry W. *Walter Johnson: Baseball's Big Train.* Lincoln, Neb. : Bison Books, 1998.

Thorn, John, and Pete Palmer, eds. *Total Baseball.* New York: Harper/Perennial, various editions.

Voigt, David Q. *American Baseball,* vols. 1–3. Norman: University of Oklahoma Press, 1983.

Walton, Ed. *Red Sox Triumphs and Tragedies.* New York: Stein and Day, 1980.

Zingg, Paul. *Harry Hooper: An American Baseball Life.* Urbana: University of Illinois Press, 1993.

Notable Articles

"Careless Players Make Blunders, O'Brien's Balk Reminds Many Leading Athletes of Costly Mistakes" by Billy Evans. *New York Times,* December 8, 1912.

"Commission Rules for World's Series." *New York Times*, September 30, 1912.

"The Engineering Features of the Athletics' Baseball Park" by Mark Monaghan. *Proceedings of the Engineers Club of Philadelphia*, paper 1067, 1911.

"Fans Could Not Have Undergone Strain Longer." *Syracuse Herald*, October 10, 1912.

"Forever Fenway" by Glenn Stout. *The Official 1987 Red Sox Yearbook.*

"The Grand Exalted Ruler of Rooters' Row" by Glenn Stout. *Sox Fan News*, August 1986.

"The Great Wall of Boston" by Jack Mann. *Sports Illustrated*, June 28, 1965.

"The Greatest Pitcher on the Diamond Today" by F. C. Lane. *Baseball*, September 1912.

"Hugh Bradley the Hero. . . ." *Boston Post*, April 27, 1912.

"If You're Going to Fenway Park Next Week, This Will Show You Where Your Seat Is, If You're One of the Lucky 6,500." *Boston Globe*, October 4, 1912.

"Jimmy McAleer and the 1912 World Series" by Mike Kopf. www.robneyer.com/book_05_Serious1912.html.

"McAleer Winds Up the Red Sox Deal." *Boston Journal*, September 16, 1911.

"New Home of the Red Sox; Plant Ideal in Equipment and Location." *Boston Globe*, October 15, 1911.

"Prevent Players from Being 'Expert Writers.'" *New Castle* (PA) *News*, October 22, 1912.

"A Reinforced Concrete Baseball Grandstand." *Engineering Record*, Vol. 66, no. 1, July 6, 1912.

"The Red Sox as Seen by a Rip Van Winkle." *Boston Globe*, September 5, 1912.

"Red Sox Deal Goes Through. . . ." *Boston Globe*, September 16, 1911.

"Royal Rooter" by Glenn Stout. *Boston Herald*, October 3, 1993.

"To Develop New Baseball Park in the Fenway." *Christian Science Monitor*, September 25, 1911.

"A War in Red Sox Camp." *Sporting Life*, July 12, 1913.

"Warring Factions Slump Boston Team." *New Castle News*, May 13, 1913.

"Why We Lost Three World Championships: Part 3" by Christy Mathewson. *Everybody's Magazine*, October 1914.

"Work on Pavilion and Grounds. . . ." *Boston Globe*, December 3, 1911.

Special Collections

Bill Carrigan (1883–1969) Archives. Sports Museum of New England.

Harold Kaese (1909–1975) Collection. The Boston Tradition in Sports Collection, Boston Public Library (call number GV742.K343A2). A reporter for the *Boston Transcript* and *Boston Globe*, Kaese wrote more than seven thousand daily columns, now available in microfilm form. The collection also includes correspondence, clippings, notebooks, manuscripts, press guides, programs, rule books, photographs, and other sports-related material. Although Kaese's primary interest was baseball, the files also cover local college football, golf, track and field, squash, handball, boxing, and tennis.

George Edward "Duffy" Lewis (1888–1979) Collection. The Boston Tradition in Sports Collection, Boston Public Library (Microtext Department). A scrapbook of items on the Red Sox left fielder.

Michael T. "Nuf Ced" McGreevey (1867–1943) Collection. The Boston Tradition in Sports Collection, Boston Public Library (call number GV865.M29A3). Donated by the well-known owner of the Columbus Avenue tavern Third Base, this collection consists of more than 170 photographs of professional baseball in Boston and personal scrapbooks from the 1890s to 1912. Originally displayed at McGreevey's saloon, the photographs form the largest collection of its kind

"Smoky Joe" Wood (1889–1985) Collection. The Boston Tradition in Sports Collection, Boston Public Library. Scrapbooks of material on the early Red Sox pitcher.

Online Resources

baseballalmanac.com

baseballfever.com. Researcher Bill Burgess maintains a remarkable archive of biographical information on American baseball and sports writers.

baseball-reference.com

bioproj.sabr.org

RedSox.com

retrosheet.org

Notes

Introduction

Portions of the introduction appeared in somewhat different form in the magazine *Boston Baseball*.

The precise spelling of both Michael T. "Nuf Ced" McGreevey's surname and his nickname have always been uncertain. Period newspaper dispatches used "Nuf Ced" and "Nuff Said" and "McGreevey" and "McGreevy" interchangeably. For consistency, I have chosen to use the nickname "Nuf Ced" exclusively. Both spellings of both names appear on period advertisements, but a photograph of the front of Third Base dating from 1903 clearly states, "M. T. McGreevey and Co." The same spelling of the surname appears on U.S. census records for both McGreevey and his relatives and has always been used by the Boston Public Library in bibliographic records. I used "McGreevey" in the text for *Red Sox Century* and in other earlier work, and that spelling still seems most common among Internet search engines. The surname itself is derived from Mac Riabhaigh, lords of Moylurg in County Roscommon. In the thirteenth century they were subdued by the MacDermots, eventually to disperse throughout Ireland. Over time the Gaelic surname Mac Riabhaigh was corrupted and anglicized, appearing in some locations as Kilrea or MacIlrea, in others as MacGreevy, Mac Creevey, Magreevy, McGreavy, McGreevy, Creevy, or in other similar combinations. By the nineteenth century the name was common in such disparate locations as Sligo, Ulster, Down, and Antrim.

Although in recent years several publications have chosen to use the spelling "McGreevy," and that is the name that now appears on a tavern on Boylston Street based on Nuf Ced's original saloon, in 1993 McGreevey's granddaughter, Anna Thompson, his only direct descendant, told me that she was certain the correct spelling was "McGreevey," evidence that I find particularly compelling. Others are free to disagree (after all, in regard to Nuf Ced, *some* kind of argument seems wholly appropriate), but I have chosen to retain that spelling throughout.

Prologue

Background information on Jerome Kelley is taken from Boston city directories and U.S. census records.

"Busy Days at Red Sox' New Ball Park," *Boston Globe,* January 28, 1912, reports that Kelley had removed the sod "at the end of the 1911 season," which was October 6, 1911, and presumably before the charity soccer game of October 15, 1911.

The "Huntington Avenue Base Ball Grounds" sign appears in earlier photographs of the Huntington Avenue Grounds but is absent in photographs from 1911.

Chapter 1: 1911

"Red Sox Drop Two Games": *Boston Post,* September 4, 1911.
Ban Johnson's role in the creation of the Boston franchise in the American League and the

early history of the club are discussed in greater detail in Glenn Stout and Dick Johnson, *Red Sox Century* (Boston: Houghton Mifflin, 2000), and Eugene Murdock, *Ban Johnson* (Westport, Conn.: Greenwood Press, 1982).

Information on Francis Dana can be found in *The Biographical Directory of the United States Congress* at: http://bioguide.congress.gov/scripts/biodisplay.pl?index=D000021.

Although today we refer to the postseason championship as the "World Series," in 1912 it was still referred to as the "World's Series." I have chosen to use that term throughout.

Players' backgrounds are taken from various clippings, bioproj.sabr.org, and the player scrapbooks cited in the Bibliographic Notes and Sources.

"fairly cool head": "Has Faced the Big Fellows," *Boston Globe*, July 29, 1908.

According to baseballalmanac.com, since 1881, both Hooper and Lewis were among the first seventy-five major league ballplayers from California, a state that has since sent hundreds of players to the major leagues. Tris Speaker was only the fifteenth Texan to play in the majors. Joe Wood was born in Missouri, the birthplace of many major leaguers, but he was only the second from Kansas City, on the state's western border. Both states have since sent hundreds of players to the major leagues. In contrast, the New England states, such as Maine and Vermont, sent many players to the majors before 1920 but have since sent very few.

The division on the team between its Catholic and Protestant members is mentioned in many accounts, ranging from Fred Lieb, *Baseball as I Have Known It* (New York: Coward, McCann & Geoghegan, 1977), to Tim Gay, *Tris Speaker* (Guilford, Conn.: Lyons Press/ University of Nebraska, 2007), and in many different press accounts, such as "Warring Factions Slump Boston Team," *New Castle News*, May 13, 1913, which provides perhaps the most comprehensive delineation of the split.

Although from today's perspective it seems almost impossible that there could be such enmity between any group of Protestants and Catholics in the United States, I remind the reader that until very recently social intercourse between Protestants and Catholics in Ireland was extremely limited—and often violent.

"Fading Is the Last Chance of the Crippled Sox," *Boston Post*, September 6, 1911.

"McAleer Will Own Half of Red Sox," *Boston Journal*, September 13, 1911.

"No Decision at Conference," *Boston Journal*, September 15, 1911, and "Red Sox Deal Not Perfect," *Boston Globe*, September 15, 1911, detail the meeting at the Algonquin Club.

"Red Sox Deal Goes Through . . . ," *Boston Globe*, September 16, 1911; "McAleer Winds Up the Red Sox Deal," *Boston Journal*, September 16, 1911; and many other articles during this time period, including accounts in both *The Sporting News* and *Sporting Life*, chart the sale of the club to McAleer.

In "Progress and Prestige of the National Game," *Boston Globe*, March 12, 1911, Johnson states his desire for more modern ballparks throughout the league.

"New Home of the Red Sox; Plant Ideal in Equipment and Location," *Boston Globe*, October 15, 1911, provides seating capacity and a drawing of the park by illustrator J. C. Halden for McLaughlin, showing an early design.

"To Develop New Baseball Park in the Fenway," *Christian Science Monitor*, September 25, 1911, notes the groundbreaking on September 25, although I found no reference to any kind of formal ceremony.

"For Development": *Boston Globe*, September 30, 1911.

"The park was considered": "Red Sox Move Up to Fourth Place," *Boston Globe*, October 8, 1911.

Chapter 2: Hot Stove

I culled background information on James McLaughlin and his family from U.S. census records, World War I draft registration records, and Boston city directories.

"a compromise between Man's Euclidian": John Updike, "Hub Bids Kid Adieu," *The New*

Yorker, October 22, 1960. Updike's famous essay is apparently the source for subsequent observations that the layout of Boston streets is responsible for Fenway's misshapen dimensions. As various Sanborn Insurance maps show, this contention is incorrect: the streets bordering Fenway Park were laid out according to a basic grid pattern.

Background information on Charles Logue and the Charles Logue Building Company was provided by James Logue, his great-grandson, and Kevin Logue, his great-great-grandson, of Logue Engineering, in the form of both interviews and clippings provided by the family.

For background on architectural training, see Daniel D. Reiff, *Houses from Books: Treatises, Pattern Books, and Catalogs in American Architecture, 1738–1950: A History and Guide* (State College: Pennsylvania State University Press, 2001).

For background information on the history of concrete construction, see R. E. Shaeffer, *Reinforced Concrete: Preliminary Design for Architects and Builders* (New York: McGraw-Hill, 1992).

As can be seen in Ray Stubblebine, *Stickley's Craftsman Homes: Plans, Drawings, Photographs* (Layton, Utah: Gibbs Smith, 2006), the brickwork of one Stickley-designed home in particular, designated as number 106 (p. 390), is particularly evocative of Fenway. An anomaly when compared to Stickley's other work, this structure not only uses Tapestry brick work but reveals some of the design shapes that were used, on a different scale, in Fenway. (Tapestry brick was a patented style made by Fiske and Company of New York.) This design was originally published in January 1911, when McLaughlin was at work on the design of the ballpark.

Ray Stubblebine, *Gustav Stickley and the Craftsman Home: An Exhibition Presented by the Craftsman Farms Foundation* (brochure, n.d.).

"Rather than using McLaughlin's other public buildings as a reference for his design inspiration at Fenway Park, I have often thought that the more arts and crafts treatment of the Fenway Studio Building by Parker and Thomas, 1905, at 30 Ipswich Street, a couple blocks east of Fenway Park, was on his mind when designing the main elevation. There is a somewhat similar diagonal patterning in stucco and brick on the two facades." E-mail communication of October 5, 2009, to the author from Dr. Keith Morgan, past president of the American Society of Architectural Historians and editor of *Buildings of Massachusetts: Metropolitan Boston* (Charlottesville: University of Virginia Press, 2009).

For basic background information on not only Fenway Park but other ballparks of the era, see Michael Benson, *Ballparks of North America: A Comprehensive Historical Reference to Baseball Grounds, Yards, and Stadiums, 1845 to Present* (Jefferson, N.C.: McFarland Publishing, 1989), and Philip J. Lowry, *Green Cathedrals* (Reading, Mass.: Addison-Wesley, 1992).

"New Home of the Red Sox": *Boston Globe*, October 15, 1911.

Details of the sale of the Red Sox are taken from period newspapers as well as from *Sporting Life*, November 1911 through January 1912; the latter details the financial involvement of Stahl and his father-in-law. For a somewhat more detailed overview of the transaction, see Mike Lynch, "A Question of Ownership," February 26, 2010, http://www.seamheads.com/2010/02/26/a-question-of-ownership.

Most of the construction details, seating capacity figures, and other data concerning the construction of Fenway Park appear in "A Reinforced Concrete Baseball Grandstand," *Engineering Record*, Vol. 66, no. 1, July 6, 1912, pps. 20–21, which is a detailed description of the specific engineering used at Fenway Park during its construction written for the engineering and construction industries. To my knowledge this article has never been cited in any previous book or article published on the construction of Fenway Park. Also useful was Mark Monaghan, "The Engineering Features of the Athletics' Baseball Park," paper 1067, *Proceedings of the Engineers Club of Philadelphia* (1911); "Stadium of Syracuse," *Engineering Record* 57 (1908), pp. 78–81, which discusses period building methods and procedures; and *Engineering and Contracting* 36, no. 2, which describes the engineering and construction procedures used during the 1911 renovation and rebuilding of the Polo Grounds.

Background information on period excavating machinery and methods was gleaned from Allan Boyer McDaniel, *Excavating Machinery* (New York: McGraw-Hill, 1913).

In the late 1970s and early 1980s I spent several years in both commercial and residential concrete construction as a laborer, form carpenter, and foreman supervising the placement of rebar, building slabs, poured concrete walls, "tilt-up" walls, sidewalks, curbs, slabs, and other common types of concrete construction. My own experience in this field was invaluable in translating technical information into layman's terms and decoding period drawings and photographs. My good friend and fellow Red Sox fan Paul Valiquette of Alpha Concrete in North Hero, Vermont, was also kind enough to answer a number of important questions in regard to concrete construction techniques.

Photographs of Fenway Park that appear on the Library of Congress website (www.loc.gov/rr/print/catalog.html) provide useful construction details, as do the photographs and Sanborn Insurance maps of the Fenway Park area that appear in the Boston Public Library's online exhibition "Sports Temples of Boston: Images of Historic Ballparks, Arenas, and Stadiums, 1872–1972" (www.bpl.org/online/sportstemples).

The wheeled concrete dumpers, chutes, and manpower used to pour the seating deck are shown in a photo that appeared in the *Boston Globe* on December 21, 1911. The guy derrick used at Fenway Park for the erection of steel is clearly visible in a photograph in the *Boston Globe* on January 28, 1912. It is possible that the paucity of published photos of Fenway during construction is due, at least in part, to lack of access by newspapers other than the *Globe*, which may have enjoyed special access because of the influence of the Taylor family. For this reason I have tended to use more reports on the ballpark from the *Globe* than from other Boston newspapers.

"Work on Pavilion and Grounds": *Boston Globe*, December 3, 1911.
"Winter of Old Days Returns": *Boston Globe*, January 7, 1912.
"Busy Days at Red Sox' New Ball Park": *Boston Globe*, January 28, 1911.

Chapter 3: Hot Springs

I gleaned much of the information about spring training from the 1912 Bill Carrigan scrapbook held by the Sports Museum of New England. Although the provenance of the scrapbook is uncertain, my friend and colleague, curator Richard Johnson, believes that it may have been maintained by Bill Carrigan's younger sister. Most of the scrapbook's clippings are from either the *Boston Post* or the *Boston Globe*, although some are of uncertain origin. In addition, some of the *Globe* clippings are apparently from editions of the *Globe* that are not reflected in the online record of the newspaper. I consulted the Carrigan scrapbook, which covers the entire 1912 season, for the entirety of this book, as well as the Joe Wood scrapbook, the Duffy Lewis scrapbook, and the Nuf Ced McGreevey scrapbooks retained on microfilm by the Boston Public Library in its Boston Tradition in Sports Collection. These various scrapbooks are the sources for any uncredited newspaper quotes, as many of the clippings in them do not include the original source and some may be from newspaper editions that were not preserved in the microfilm record of the newspaper. I have also consulted other Boston newspapers, primarily the *Boston Journal* and *Boston Post*, in this section.

Photos published in contemporary newspapers clearly show that the main grandstand deck was poured long before the treads were added. I created the Fenway Park construction timeline from the period documents cited earlier, brief notes in newspaper stories, newspaper photos, and my own knowledge of construction procedures.

More useful background on Red Sox activities in Hot Springs can be found in Tim Gay, *Tris Speaker* (Guilford, Conn.: Lyons Press/ University of Nebraska, 2007), and Paul Zingg, *Harry Hooper* (Urbana: University of Illinois Press, 1993).

"Stahl Plans Long Hike": *Boston Globe*, March 7, 1912.
"Red Sox Walk, and That's All": *Boston Globe*, March 23, 1912.
"Boston Team Lucky": *Boston Post*, April 6, 1912.

The arrangement between Jake Stahl and Charlie Wagner is best described in "A Curious Situation," *Baseball*, November 1912.

Information on Majestic Park appears at Arkansas Diamonds: The Ballparks of Arkansas and Their History, http://ballparks.baseballyakker.com. As stated on the website: "Majestic Park was built in 1909 by Boston Red Sox owner John Taylor, who wanted his own field for spring training in Hot Springs. The city was a hot spot for spring training from the 1880s to the 1940s. Before Majestic Park was opened, the Red Sox and whoever else was training there had to share Whittington Park, the only other usable field in the city."

The website also notes that Taylor held the team's 1908 spring training at West End Park, the home field of the Little Rock Travelers, members of the Southern Association. To pay for the field Taylor gave the Travelers a prospect, twenty-year-old Tris Speaker, who went on to play 127 games that season with Little Rock , batting .350. By season's end the Red Sox had already re-signed him, and the fear of losing another good young player may have been one reason Taylor chose to build his own park for spring training. With the exception of 1911 and 1919, the Red Sox spent spring training there every year through 1920.

The name Duffy's Cliff did not come into widespread use until midseason. By the World's Series, however, it was used in advertising, game reports, and cartoons. Earlier in the year it was simply termed "the bank," or "the embankment." Other nicknames, such as "Lewis's Ledge," did not stick.

Chapter 4: Opening Days

"The sight of the great, mildly sloping stands": "The Red Sox as Seen by a Rip Van Winkle," *Boston Globe*, September 5, 1912. This article, which appeared without a byline, is written from the conceit of an old-time fan who has awoken to see Fenway Park for the first time. Although it was written in September, the sense of wonder at the new park is indicative of the response when the park was first opened.

The train route and reception are described in period newspapers and the *Ohio Public Utilities Commission 1914 Railroad Map of Ohio.*

The Copley Square Hotel was built in 1891 and was the Back Bay's first hotel.

The description of Fenway Park during the exhibition game against Harvard on April 9, 1912, and on opening day, April 20, 1912, is derived from a close study of descriptions from Boston newspapers, examination of photographs and drawings reproduced in the newspapers and other sources, such as insurance maps, and information culled from "A Reinforced Concrete Baseball Grandstand," *Engineering Record*, Vol. 66, no. 1, July 6, 1912, pp. 20–21. Since complete architectural plans no longer exist, some distances and measurements, as indicated in the text, are approximate, for many of the specific dimensions of these 1912 structures, such as the center-field bleachers, are unknown, as far as I have been able to determine, and the photographic record of the park both on the day of the Harvard game and on opening day is far from complete. The best photographic record of the park in 1912 was taken just prior to the 1912 World's Series and is retained by the Library of Congress, but by then many changes to the original structure had already been made. It is quite possible, and even desirable, that subsequent research will provide more specific detail. Information on the Huntington Avenue Grounds can be found in Philip J. Lowry, *Green Cathedrals* (Reading, Mass.: Addison-Wesley, 1992).

Although today there are standards for the construction of bleacher and stadium seating, they were not in place in 1912. In contemporary bleacher construction seats are generally set at a thirty-degree angle. If the left-field embankment at Fenway Park was forty-five degrees, it would have been extremely difficult for overflow crowds to stand upright, for the embankment was not terraced. This leads me to conclude that the embankment extended from the wall toward the field from between fifteen and twenty feet.

"Invite Old Timers": *Boston Journal,* April 4, 1912.

"Boston 2, Harvard 0": *Boston Globe,* April 10, 1912.

In the *Boston Globe,* April 10, 1912, Wallace Goldsmith's drawings from opening day show men on the left-field wall and the unfinished state of the wall.

According to the *New York Times,* Dana Wingate of Harvard died at age thirty of tuberculosis in Saranac Lake, New York. Both the Harvard and Exeter baseball programs still give an annual award in his memory.

For more background on the rivalry with the New York Yankees, see Glenn Stout, *Red Sox Century* (Boston: Houghton Mifflin, 1999) and *Yankees Century* (Boston: Houghton Mifflin, 2002).

"Sox Open to Packed Park": *Boston Globe,* April 21, 1912.

Many teams have made the claim that they were the first to use an "electric" scoreboard, but depending on the definition the claim is almost meaningless. Although it is unknown how the first scoreboard at Fenway Park operated, photographs reveal that no lights were used. In all likelihood descriptions of the scoreboard as being either "electronic" or "electric" refer both to the method by which the scoreboard operators were contacted from the press box and the mechanical operation of certain aspects of the scoreboard itself. In their book *Baseball: The Golden Years* (Oxford University Press, 1971), historians Harold and Dorothy Seymour state that the first electric scoreboard was invented by George Baird of Chicago in 1908 and that it "instantly recorded balls, strikes and outs," while all other information was operated manually. Previously, scoreboard operators like those at Harvard University's football stadium were communicated with by way of hand signals from the press box. Buzzer systems such as the one described later became commonplace; they were eventually replaced by telephone systems. Several Wallace Goldsmith cartoons show scoreboard operators peering out of the slots on the scoreboard, and a cartoon drawn during the 1912 World's Series clearly shows that the operator was visible to pedestrians on Lansdowne Street, one of whom Goldsmith shows asking the operator for the score. When Fenway's scoreboard was changed during the 1933–34 reconstruction the Red Sox made the claim that the new scoreboard was the first to use lights—red designating balls and outs and green for strikes.

Chapter 5: The Wall and the Cliff

What with the vagaries of press coverage, it is extraordinarily difficult to determine what took place during a baseball game of this era with absolute certainty. To do so a researcher must compare a variety of press accounts and hope for either a consensus or a layering of detail that creates a complete portrait. The first game at Fenway Park provides a perfect example of this quandary, as no two descriptions of many plays are quite the same. Both Steve Yerkes's first hit at Fenway and Tris Speaker's game-winning hit in the eleventh are described in a variety of ways and with different levels of detail in each newspaper account of the contest. Speaker's hit, for instance, is variously described as a hit to center, a hit to third, a hit to short, and a hit through the hole. In general I tend to side with the account that provides the most detail. In the instance of Yerkes's hit, the *New York Times* notes "Zinn's falling on the left bank" in pursuit of the drive, while in regard to Speaker's hit the *Boston Journal* adds that "the big centrefielder was across the bag and Yerkes over the pan before Chase received the throw"—that is, the throw from Dolan, indicating an infield hit.

Opening day accounts include "Sox Open to Packed Park," *Boston Globe,* April 21, 1912; "Fenway Park Is Formally Opened with Red Sox Win," *Boston Post,* April 21, 1912; and "Red Sox Win Opening Game at Fenway Park," *Boston Traveler,* April 21, 1912.

Information on Lewis, Speaker, Wood, Cady, Wagner, Stahl, Hooper, O'Brien, and Gardner and other profiles and vignettes of notable Boston players that appear throughout the book generally make use of information from *Deadball Stars of the American League,* edited by David Jones (Dulles, Va.: Potomac Books, 2006), and from http://bioproj.sabr.org, supplemented with period newspaper and scrapbook reports. Although these sources were invaluable for basic biographical data, such as place of birth and death date, many provide only limited insight into the career or personality of a player, beyond the recitation of annual statistics, and most of them lack details about the 1912 season. The profile of Bill Carrigan, for example, notes that he "caught the majority of innings for the 1912 pennant winners." The next sentence notes that he had only seven at-bats in the World's Series, yet does not explore that discrepancy. The reason, as noted in the text, was the emergence of Hick Cady. As far as I have been able to determine, no previous account of Red Sox history has made note of Cady's emergence or its impact on the 1912 season.

Additional information on Lewis appeared in an "as told to" series that he did with Joe Cashman of the *Boston Daily Record* in January 1951. His putouts rose from 203 in 125 games in 1911 to 301 in 154 games in 1912.

Fielding statistics are from baseballreference.com.

"Bradley's Terrific Smash Good": *Boston Globe*, April 27, 1912. See also "Hugh Bradley the Hero," *Boston Post*, April 27, 1912.

The proposed Hal Chase trade is detailed in "New Chase Deal Planned," *New York Times*, May 23, 1912.

"Braves Battle Uphill to a Tie," *Boston Globe*, May 23, 1915, mentions other early home runs over the wall. I was later able to confirm Rube Oldring's home run.

A more contemporary account of opening day and Bradley's home run appeared in the *Boston Herald*, April 17, 1992.

I spent a great deal of time trying to determine the specific origin of the use of the phrase "Green Monster" in regard to Fenway Park. Although William Shakespeare often used the phrase "green-eyed monster" to denote jealousy, despite the way the wall has made some visiting sluggers feel, there appears to be no connection. In a search of all available online newspaper resources through Proquest and newspaperachive.com, as well as in my own hard-copy print research over the past twenty years—indexes that survey literally billions of articles (although the major Boston dailies are not indexed in these sources before 1980, many other Massachusetts newspapers are) and not, significantly, the major Boston dailies—the earliest reference I have found for the use of the phrase "Green Monster" in regard to the left-field wall at Fenway Park dates back to a story distributed by United Press International on August 24, 1960. One day earlier the Cleveland Indians had come from behind to beat the Red Sox 3–2 in ten innings, and they scored the winning run on two doubles off the wall, the first by pitcher Jim "Mudcat" Grant and the second by Cuban rookie shortstop Mike de la Hoz. The story states that "the right-hander [Grant] pounded a double off the left field wall then scampered home as rookie shortstop Mike De La Hoz also stoked a two bagger off the Fenway Park's Green Monster." One year later, on August 2, 1961, the Angels dropped a doubleheader to the Sox at Fenway Park, 7–2 and 8–7, during which the Sox hit twelve balls off the left-field wall. In his game story for the *Long Beach Press Telegram* that appeared the next day, "Red Sox Chinese Handball Court Too Much for Angels," Ross Newhan wrote: "The Boston Red Sox put a black border—or more properly, a green one, around the Angel's fine July record by sweeping a doubleheader . . . And the reason Bill Rigney is looking doubly green this morning is because of the green monster that stretched across left field at Fenway Park. It is the American League's answer to the [Los Angeles] Coliseum's Chinese screen." In a 2010 e-mail exchange, Newhan informed me that he has no recollection of when he first heard the phrase used or first used it himself.

Jack Mann's 1965 *Sports Illustrated* story on the Red Sox and the left-field wall, "The Great Wall of Boston," makes no mention of the phrase. In fact, the phrase did not appear in *Sports Illustrated* until October 16, 1967. The Associated Press story of October 3, 1967, referenced in the text states that "the Cardinals, who flew in late Monday, are due to see Fenway and the 'green monster' as the handy left field wall is known, Tuesday afternoon." It is interesting to note that the author found it necessary to explain the phrase, which indicates that it was then unknown to most readers. Subsequent AP stories throughout the Series continued to use the phrase, and after that date it is more likely to be used in regard to Fenway than to either Art Arfons or Oakland Hills in newspaper databases. Searches in books through Google's book search function and my own library find no book references to the phrase before the 1970s, and even before the 1980s usage was relatively rare. Although it is certainly possible that someone could find the phrase used in print sources earlier than those cited here, the larger point remains. Like the misleading phrase "Curse of the Bambino," which dates back to 1986, the use of the term "Green Monster" is of relatively recent vintage. Anecdotally, when I first moved to Boston in 1981 the most common term for the left-field wall was still simply "the wall." Significantly, in Benson's *Ballparks of North America*, his entry on Fenway Park makes no mention of the "Green Monster," but only three years later, in 1992, Philip Lowry's entry on Fenway Park in *Green Cathedrals* does use the phrase, suggesting that it began to come into regular use around 1990. I suspect, however, that as more period newspapers become available in a searchable format, subsequent researchers may well find the phrase used in print to describe the left-field wall before 1960.

"Silk the Arbitrary": *Boston Globe*, May 1, 1912.

Chapter 6: Home Stand

For a history of Kenmore Square, see Grahm Junior College Memorial Page at http://www.grahmjuniorcollege.com/Kenmore_Square.html. Although Kenmore Square was usually called Governor's Square until 1932, to avoid confusion I have chosen to refer to it as Kenmore throughout this book.

Estimates of the range and depth of outfielders is based on both observation and an examination of photographs and videos. When running from first to second, most players take eleven or twelve full strides to cover eighty feet or so when stealing a base (ninety feet minus the length of their lead off base) or a stride or two less when running through the base. Through observation, I have noted that most outfielders catching a long drive on the run, depending on speed and stride length, have a range of thirteen to nineteen strides while pursuing a fly ball, for an effective range of between 100 and 150 feet. Given his speed, it seems reasonable to presume that Speaker was at the upper range. A photograph available at http://www.vintageball.com/files/1912_Sox_album3.jpg, although in poor condition, shows the right-field fence before it was altered for the World's Series. Clearly, the distance to this fence before the construction of the right-field bleachers was nearly four hundred feet. For more on my methodology here, see http://verbplow.blogspot.com/2009_05_01_archive.html. Estimates of how deep outfielders play today are from aerial photographs taken during games. Contemporary outfielders generally play at least three hundred feet from home plate in right and center field at Fenway Park, and often even a bit deeper than that.

"Georgia Peach Specked": *Boston Globe*, May 10, 1912.

"Browns Always at Wood's Mercy": *Boston Globe*, May 12, 1912.

A Google Earth image of Fenway Park taken on April 8, 2008, clearly shows that in April the sun is in almost direct alignment with the right-field line.

Chapter 7: The Big Trip

F. C. Lane, "The Greatest Pitcher on the Diamond Today," *Baseball*, September 1912. Although Lane's article did not appear until later in the season, given magazine deadlines, it was probably written in June.

Information on Joe Wood is taken from sources previously cited and various clippings, including "Joe Wood the Wizardly Perplexing Pitcher of the Red Sox," *Boston Globe*, September 15, 1912.

Wood's nickname "Smoky" did not come into widespread use until September, following the matchup with Walter Johnson.

Joe Wood discussed his off-field life in *Baseball Digest*, May 1981.

It is interesting to note that even after Wood injured his arm in 1913, which effectively ruined his pitching career, when he did pitch he still threw virtually as hard as he did before his injury.

His problem was not his fastball but the pain produced when he threw it: Wood could barely raise his arm after pitching a game. He described the pain as being in the shoulder joint—almost certainly a rotator cuff tear.

Much of the impression we have of Wood today stems from the recorded interview he gave Lawrence Ritter in his classic oral history *The Glory of Their Times* (New York: Macmillan, 1984). Ritter's book—the first of its kind in baseball—does a terrific job capturing the mood and tenor of the age, but in places its veracity is questionable, for the players interviewed are speaking from memory and, understandably, tend to be self-serving. Ritter, while well intentioned, did not know enough baseball history at the time to ask many of the questions that beg to be answered today. Most of his interviews are occasionally wrong on the facts, and transcripts held by the National Baseball Hall of Fame reveal that in some instances Ritter's editing of the interviews made them less than authentic. His interview with Wood is emblematic of these problems: there is no mention of the controversy during the 1912 World's Series or the betting scandal that later drove Wood from baseball, even though Ritter's book also includes interviews with Rube Marquard, Harry Hooper, and other period players. For these reasons, I chose to make only limited use of this source.

For more on Bill and Tom Yawkey, see Glenn Stout and Dick Johnson, *Red Sox Century* (Boston: Houghton Mifflin, 1999).

"If they give me the chance . . .": *Olwein (Iowa) Daily Register*, April 25, 1913. According to *Baseball Digest*, the quote was from a clipping in a scrapbook maintained by Wood and quoted Johnson as saying, "Nobody can throw harder than Joe Wood." Wood later told Roger Angell, "I don't think anybody was faster than Walter Johnson."

For more on Walter Johnson, see Henry W. Thomas, *Walter Johnson: Baseball's Big Train* (Lincoln: University of Nebraska Press, 1998).

Chapter 8: Home Safe

For more on Harry Hooper, see *Deadball Stars of the American League,* edited by David Jones (Dulles, Va.: Potomac Books, 2006), and Paul Zingg, *Harry Hooper* (Urbana: University of Illinois Press, 1993).

The story about Buck O'Brien and Connie Mack's daughter appears in Norman L. Macht, *Connie Mack and the Early Years of Baseball* (Lincoln: University of Nebraska Press, 2007).

"It's All Red Sox": *Boston Globe,* July 4, 1912.

For population data, see Campbell Gibson, *Population of the 100 Largest Cities and Other Urban Places in the United States: 1790–1990* (Washington, D.C.: U.S. Bureau of the Census, Population Division, 1998).

"Sox Get Two Tiger Pelts": *Boston Globe,* July 13, 1912.

The Day (New Haven, Connecticut), October 5, 1915, discusses the makeup of the "Board of Strategy" and states that during the 1912 World's Series Wagner, Carrigan, and Stahl met twice each day to plot strategy and discuss the events of the game.

Ty Cobb, *Busting 'Em and Other Big League Stories* (New York: Edward J. Clode, 1915), is one of many sources that make note of the internal dissension on the 1912 Red Sox.

For a good midseason summation of the Red Sox, see "Baseball Now on Homeward Route," *Boston Post*, July 21, 1912, and "Thrilling Success of the Boston Red Sox Team . . . ," *Boston Globe*, July 21, 1912.

"Our Sox Going Good": *Boston Globe*, July 22, 1912.

While growing up, I was an amateur pitcher. I recall first experiencing shoulder pain when pitching as a fifteen-year-old in a fifteen- to seventeen-year-old summer league, my first season throwing from the major league distance of sixty feet, six inches. Nevertheless, I was still effective and even threw a no-hitter. But something was not right in my arm, and a little over a year later, pitching in a fall league, the pain eventually became so bad that I could neither brush my teeth nor brush my hair with my right arm. A visit to the doctor, in which a barium solution was injected with a hypodermic needle into my shoulder so the doctor could track the blood flow in my shoulder via an X-ray television monitor, confirmed that I had a class 4 tear of the rotator cuff. This was in 1975, and apart from invasive surgery, which could cause even more damage, there was no treatment available at the time. My baseball career was over, and for the next seventeen years my arm continued to bother me—although I eventually regained my range of motion, it remained weak and I could not sleep on my right side.

At age thirty-three, I was able to take advantage of medical advances. A physical trainer began a rehabilitation program for my shoulder consisting of lifting very light weights to build up the rotator cuff muscles. One year later, after doing some additional research on my own, I began a "pre-hab" shoulder exercise routine, joined an over-thirty adult baseball league, and began pitching again. Over the next nine seasons I pitched around five hundred innings and was never again bothered by shoulder trouble. Unfortunately, this knowledge was not available during Joe Wood's career.

Chapter 9: Heavyweights

"deadly 'snap ball'": "Wood's Strong Wrist Great Aid in Pitching," *Sporting Life*, November 30, 1912. The article quotes Johnson from a conversation held the previous May.

"Red Sox Celebrate with a Double Win": *Boston Globe*, August 15, 1912.

"[Johnson] had a chance to win the game": *Sporting Life*, September 7, 1912.

"No More Moonlight Baseball, Silk": *Boston Globe*, August 28, 1912.

"Tell Wood," [Griffith] sneered: *The Sporting News*, September 12, 1912.

Two pictures and one drawing reveal the space beneath the stands referred to by Murnane in regard to the August 17 game against Detroit. One is the photograph of Charles Logue standing at the end of the grandstand behind third base. One can see the ground directly behind Logue beneath the stands and what appears to be a wire-covered gap. The second is a photograph of the dugout from *Engineering Record* that clearly shows the wire-covered gap stretching in both directions from the end of the dugout. James E. McLaughlin's artist rendering of the park from 1911 also shows a space beneath the box seats past the dugout apparently covered by wire fencing.

The proposed sale of Johnson is described in "Far Too Little, Says Griffith," *Boston Globe*, August 30, 1912.

For more on the feud between Johnson and McGraw, see Eugene Murdock, *Ban Johnson* (Westport, Conn.: Greenwood Press, 1982), and Charles Alexander, *McGraw* (New York: Viking Press, 1988). Johnson's reaction is quoted in Murdock's book.

"Wood and Johnson in Pitching Duel Today": *Boston Globe*, September 6, 1912.

Accounts of the September 6 game are taken from a number of sources, most notably the *Boston Globe*, the *Boston Journal*, the *Boston Post*, *Sporting Life*, *The Sporting News*, the *Washington Post*, and the *New York Times*. As was customary in any game of this era, descriptions in individual newspapers varied to some degree—in this instance most dramatically in the pitch-by-pitch account of the game. The *Globe*, for instance, describes Wood as throwing twenty-four pitches in the first inning, including ten to first, while the *Journal* puts the number at nineteen with seven throws to first. Although I have taken descriptions from various accounts, for pitch-by-pitch description I have depended on the *Globe*, which published not only a table listing the pitches of both Johnson and Wood but also a pitch-by-pitch narrative, a detailed at-bat narrative, and a generally more detailed game story than can be found in most other sources.

Emil Rothe, "The War of 1912: The Wood-Johnson Duel," SABR Research Journals Archive, www.research.sabr.org/journals/war-of-1912.

"Wood Better Man Yesterday": *Boston Globe*, September 7, 1912.

The gate receipts are discussed in "Griffith Took Away $16,000," *Boston Globe*, September 8, 1912.

Chapter 10: Giants on the Horizon

On September 8 the *Globe* speculated that receipts for the four games totaled $44,000, but admitted that its calculations were "not official figures." *Sporting Life* estimated Washington's take as $18,000. The American League also received a portion of the receipts for each game.

In "Work on Pavilion and Ground Goes on Apace," *Boston Globe*, December 3, 1911, Tim Murnane speculated that team payrolls varied from $50,000 to $85,000 per year.

The first print mention of the expansion of Fenway Park for the World's Series that I have found appeared in a Tim Murnane dispatch dated August 26, 1912, in *The Sporting News*. Murnane was the Boston correspondent for the magazine.

The details of the bleacher construction are taken from John Butler Johnson, Morton Owen Withey, and Terence Hanbury White, *Materials of Construction* (London: John Wiley and Sons, 1918), and "Grandstand and Bleachers of the Pittsburg Athletic Company," *Concrete Engineering*, May 1909.

McLaughlin's diagram of the seats showing the additions made for the postseason appears in one of his drawings under the title "If You're Going to Fenway Park Next Week, This Will Show You Where Your Seat Is, if You're One of the Lucky 6,500," found in *Boston Globe*, October 4, 1912, and in slightly different form elsewhere.

Several photographs not reproduced in this book owing to reprint costs bear mentioning, particularly in regard to the insight they provide about the changes made for the World's Series. Getty editorial image 51475552 (available at: http://www.gettyimages.com/detail/51475552/Archive-Photos) shows the Fenway outfield, from left-center field to right-center field, taken from the perspective of home plate, apparently either just prior to a World's Series game or at the end of the regular season. The low wall fronting right field contained advertising, and the center- and right-field bleachers were separated by an alleyway at least twenty feet wide. Another Getty photograph (editorial image 53550663), taken near the end of the regular season from the roof of the grandstand, shows that construction was not yet complete in the left-field corner. Before the World's Series a fence was constructed from the end of the third-base stands to the left-field wall, paralleling the third-base line and creating the small triangle that later figured so prominently in several plays during the World's Series. A photograph available at http://www.vintageball.com/files/1912_Sox_album3.jpg shows the right-field fence before it was altered for the World's Series. Clearly, the distance to this fence before the construction of the right-field bleachers was nearly four hundred feet.

Wood's condition is mentioned in "Joe Wood Not Quite Himself," *Boston Globe*, September 15, 1912, and "Red Sox Make Pennant Certain," *Boston Globe*, September 16, 1912.

Jealousy over the "Board of Strategy" in 1912 is reported in "Warring Factions Slump Boston Team," *New Castle* (Penn.) *News*, May 13, 1913.

"Rousing Welcome for Red Sox," *Sporting Life*, September 23, 1912.

"Wild Acclaim for Red Sox," *Boston Globe*, September 24, 1912.

"Welcome Champions," *Boston Post*, September 24, 1912.

The arrangements made by the National Commission in regard to the World's Series were widely reported in local newspapers on September 26, as well as in *Sporting Life* and *The Sporting News*. See "World Series Opens . . . ," *Boston Globe*, September 26, 1912, and "Commission Rules for World's Series," *New York Times*, September 30, 1912.

"Go among the players": "Says Pennant Race Is 'Fixed,'" *Boston Post*, September 29, 1912. For a more sober accounting, see Harold Seymour, *Baseball: The Golden Years* (New York: Oxford University Press, 1971).

For background on John McGraw, see Charles Alexander, *John McGraw* (New York: Viking Press, 1987). On Mathewson, see Ray Robinson, *Mathewson: An American Hero* (New York: Oxford University Press, 1994), and Philip Seib, *The Player* (Cambridge, Mass.: Da Capo Press, 2004).

Chapter 11: The Gathering of the Clans

In recounting the story of the World's Series in chapters 11 through 13, I have depended on newspaper accounts from papers in Boston and New York, primarily but not exclusively the *Boston Globe, Boston Post, Boston Journal, Boston Herald, New York Times, New York Tribune,* and *New York World*, as well as *Sporting Life* and *The Sporting News*. Since game stories generally appear the day after the a game is played, for space reasons—with a few exceptions—I do not reference individual stories here unless a source provided unique information.

It is sometimes important to disclose not just the sources used but those not used. I did not use *New York Post* sportswriter Mike Vaccaro's fanciful account of the 1912 World's Series, *The First Fall Classic* (New York: Random House, 2009). I always prefer to do my own research rather than utilize the work of another author on the same subject anyway, but the book's lack of sourcing, the questions raised by Keith Olbermann on his MLB blog and by others over its accuracy, and the author's admission that he created dialogue used throughout the book render it untrustworthy as a source for any serious work of history.

The threatening letters appear in an unsourced newspaper account, "Wood Threatened by Mail . . . ," dated October 7, in the Joe Wood scrapbook.

"Has $50,000 to Bet on Red Sox," *Boston Globe*, September 10, 1912.

"300 Fans Still Waiting," *Boston Globe*, October 3, 1912.

"Gardner Helps Red Sox Wind Up with a Victory": *Boston Post*, October 6 1912.

For background on the buildup to the World's Series, see "Nine and Fans Eager . . . ," *Boston Globe*, October 7, 1912; Hugh Fullerton, "Two Sides to a Big Story," *New York Times*, October 7, 1912; "Clans Are Gathering for World's Series," *Boston Globe*, October 7, 1912; "Hub Rooters in New York," *Boston Globe*, October 8, 1912; and "Fans in Thousands Come to New York," *New York Times*, October 8, 1912.

For the National Commission's views on players writing ghostwritten accounts, see "Prevent Players from Being 'Expert Writers,'" *New Castle* (Penn.) *News*, October 22, 1912.

"Baseball Frenzy": *New York Tribune*, October 7, 1912.

"Base Ball by 'Phone,'" *Boston Globe*, October 8, 1912, describes the telephone broadcast.

Although retrosheet.org and baseball-reference.com both indicate that Chief Meyers's ninth-inning double was hit to left field, multiple newspaper accounts state that it was hit to right field. Since several of these accounts note that Boston right fielder Harry Hooper fielded the hit, I have chosen to go with that account.

"I'd a darn sight": "Mayor Declared This a Holiday," *Boston Globe*, October 9, 1912.

Chapter 12: Home Sweet Home

For train information, see the website of the New Haven Railroad Historical and Technical Association (www.nhrhta.org) and Fred Lieb, *Baseball as I Have Known It* (New York: Coward, McCann & Geoghegan, 1977).

"insinuates, or rather threatens": Sam Crane, "Fans Could Not Have Undergone Strain Longer," *Syracuse Herald*, October 10, 1912. Reports on the dissatisfaction of the players also appeared in several other sources, particularly *Sporting Life* and the *Washington Post*, although Sam Crane appears to be the only daily reporter to have pursued the story with alacrity.

"Thrills, Throbs, Sighs, Smiles": *Boston Globe*, October 10, 1912.

Box score reports for each game list umpires as being assigned to either home or field (infield, left field, or right field).

The bleachers on the garage roofs outside Fenway Park are shown in several Wallace Gold-smith drawings reprinted in the *Globe* during the World's Series. For the best, see "Impressions of a World's Series Game . . . ," *Boston Globe*, October 11, 1912.

Before embarking on this project, I was unaware of the role played by cloudy weather in the selection of a pitcher during this era. On darker days, most baseball people believed, a fastball pitcher was preferable to any other kind. The logic behind that belief was that after only a few batters the ball would darken with grass stains and tobacco juice and be difficult to see in good light—and even more so on a day without shadows.

"Giants Win, 2–1": *New York Times*, October 11, 1912.

Chapter 13: Giant Killers

"Joe Wood, the Giant-Killer": *Boston Journal*, October 12, 1912.

"With Bedient Pitching the Game of His Life, Red Sox Win, 2–1": *Boston Globe*, October 13, 1912.

Although Joe Wood always refuted claims that he or his brother fought with Buck O'Brien, either during the train ride to Boston or before game 7, reports of an altercation and/or dis-sension on the team over the decision to have O'Brien pitch game 6 appear in multiple sources, including *The Sporting News*, October 24, 1912; Ty Cobb, *Busting 'Em and Other Big League Stories* (New York: Edward J. Clode, 1915); "Trouble in Red Sox Ranks," *Des Moines News*, October 16, 1912; "Wood and O'Brien in Fight Before Game," *Washington Post*, October 15, 1912; and Christy Mathewson, "Why We Lost Three World Championships: Part 3," *Everybody's Magazine*, October 1914. According to Mathewson, "No one was more positive than 'Smoky Joe' Wood that we would lose. Wood had been given to understand he would pitch the next game. He had beaten us before, and accordingly he gave $500 to a friend and had him bet on Boston to win the next game . . . The sequel comes on a train going to Boston that night. Strolling into a car where O'Brien was sitting, Wood walked up to him and announced: 'Well, you're a fine joke of a pitcher! Put the game on a platter and handed it to the Giants, didn't you?' O'Brien growled something. Then one thing led to another and an altercation ensued. This was one of the causes that engendered fric-tion in the Red Sox; and such friction could not help but interfere with the team-work. Reduced efficiency is the inevitable consequence of internal dissension. In fact, next year we saw a world's-champion transformed into a second division team."

Fred Lieb, *Baseball as I Have Known It* (New York: Coward, McCann & Geoghegan, 1977), is the main source for the story about the conversation between Stahl and McAleer. Lieb notes that Wood's brother had placed a bet on the game. The fact that Lieb covered the Series as a young reporter gives his account some credence, but other aspects of his retelling of the final few games are, like much of his book, inaccurate. For example, he has the conversation between Stahl and McAleer taking place during a "leisurely Sunday daytime trip" to New York, but the Red Sox left on their usual 5:30 p.m. train. His description of the snafu with the Royal Rooters tickets before game 7 contradicts the newspaper reporting at the time: Lieb claims that Wood was forced to wait a half-hour, while newspapers reported nearly unanimously that the delay was ten minutes. Since this is approximately the same amount of time Wood would have waited between innings in any game, it is doubtful that the delay was solely responsible for his performance.

Although some accounts written well after the fact state that Devore caught Cady's drive with his bare hand, I could find no contemporaneous account that mentions it—such reports have about as much credibility as those that suggest that Devore faked the catch. Later writers may have confused this catch by Devore with either Hooper's catch of a ball hit by Devore later in the Series, which was caught barehanded, or reports that refer to Devore making the catch with "one hand." At the time, given the gloves in use, one-handed catches—particularly one-handed catches made on the run—were unique enough to be mentioned in news accounts.

A report in *Sporting Life* on October 19, 1912, states that Mathewson brought up the issue of the division of playoff receipts with the Red Sox "on the train to Boston on the night of October 10, the day after the 11 inning tie game." However, there was no such train, as the two clubs had traveled to Boston on the night of October 8 and remained in Boston for game 3 the next day. In the context of the larger story, the author was probably referring to the train to New York on the evening of October 10. Both the *New York Tribune* and the *Boston Herald* of October 16 refer to another meeting with the National Commission on October 15, leading me to conclude that there were at least two meetings between the commission and Mathewson in regard to the issue.

There is one particular error in Mike Vaccaro's *The First Fall Classic* (New York: Random House, 2009) that bears correcting, and I mention the discrepancy here so that readers of both books will know why our accounts differ so drastically. Vaccaro describes Hooper's key game 5 triple in some detail. But he misplaces the hit in center field and even details how outfielder Fred Snodgrass first came in on the ball "two steps," then went back, and then had to retrieve the ball after it became stuck in a "tiny hole" at the extreme end of the bleachers in center field, leading to a colorful and extended argument between Giants manager John McGraw and umpire Silk McLoughlin.

None of this took place. As multiple newspaper sources, baseball-reference.com, and retrosheet.org all agree, and as I describe in the text, the ball was not hit to either center field or even left-center field—it was hit down the left-field line and bounced into the small "pie-shaped" triangle of open ground between the third-base stands, the Duffy's Cliff bleachers, and the left-field wall, roughly the location just beyond the roll-up garage door that occasionally vexes left fielders in Fenway Park today. There it was indisputably retrieved by Giants left fielder Josh Devore. Vaccaro evidently confused the pie-shaped triangle of Ralph McMillen's description with the much larger space in center field between the left-field wall and the center-field bleachers, where the flagpole stood. Although this center-field space had been in play for most of the season, the accommodations made for the World's Series blocked this area off with a stockade fence. It is also important to note that neither of these "triangles" is the same as the current "triangle" that exists in Fenway Park just to the center-field side of the bullpen. Later in the book Vaccaro also confuses Hooper's misplaced hit with a later triple by Steve Yerkes. These are but two illustrations of why I chose not to use this volume as a source.

It is also interesting to note that when McLaughlin's accommodations for the World's Series were first built, this area was much larger and extended to the far end of the new third-base stands. At some point between the end of the regular season and the start of the World's Series, however, a fence much closer to the foul line was created, presumably to prevent balls from rolling out of sight at the end of the third-base stands.

Chapter 14: Last Stand at Fenway Park

"I thought my foot was off the rubber": Billy Evans, "Careless Players Make Blunders, O'Brien's Balk Reminds Many Leading Athletes of Costly Mistakes," *New York Times*, December 8, 1912.

"Royal Rooters An Angry Lot": *Boston Globe*, October 16, 1912.

"All Knock Wood": *New York World*, October 16, 1912.

"Boston Now Supreme in Baseball World": *Boston Globe*, October 17, 1912.

Epilogue

"A War in Red Sox Camp," *Sporting Life*, July 12, 1913, and "Warring Factions Slump Boston Team," *New Castle* (Penn.) *News*, May 13, 1913, outline the breakup of the 1913 Sox.

"hadn't been strong with the Boston manager": *Chester* (Penn.) *Times*, August 7, 1913.

Subsequent changes in Fenway Park through 1987 are outlined in Glenn Stout, "Forever Fenway," in *The Official 1987 Red Sox Yearbook*. Major changes after 1987 are described at redsox.

com. It is interesting to note that the property on the corner of Brookline Avenue and Lansdowne Street was not purchased by the Red Sox until 1980, to house NESN (New England Sports Network). The lot was first built on in 1913, when former New Hampshire governor John Smith purchased the property. Over the years it served as the home to dealerships for Packard and Cadillac automobiles, Boston's first television station, WMEX radio, a retail store owned by golfer Francis Ouimet, the real estate firm Jeano Inc. (for which Joe Cronin served as president), a bowling alley, and several other businesses.

Each year major league baseball calculates a "Fan Cost Index" measuring the total price for a typical family of four to see a game. The FCI includes the price of two children's tickets, two adult tickets, four small soft drinks, four hot dogs, two small drinks, two programs, and parking. In 2010 Fenway Park's FCI was $334.78, making it the most expensive ballpark in the major leagues.

"Jerome Kelly [*sic*] Resigns," *Boston Globe*, June 9, 1921.

Boston Red Sox 1912 Statistics

BATTING

NAME	POS	G	2B	3B	AB	AV.	BB	H	HR	OBP	OPS	R	RBI	SB	SH	S%
Neal Ball	2B	18	2	0	45	.200	3	9	0	.250	.494	10	6	5	1	.244
Hugh Bedient	P	41	0	0	73	.192	13	14	0	.314	.506	11	7	0	6	.192
Hugh Bradley	1B	40	11	1	137	.190	15	26	1	.275	.581	16	19	3	7	.307
Jack Bushelman	P	3	0	0	3	.000	1	0	0	.250	.250	1	0	0	0	.000
Hick Cady	C	47	13	2	135	.259	10	35	0	.324	.710	19	9	0	7	.385
Bill Carrigan	C	87	7	1	266	.263	38	70	0	.359	.656	34	24	7	8	.297
Eddie Cicotte	P	9	0	0	13	.154	4	2	0	.353	.507	1	1	0	0	.154
Ray Collins	P	27	1	0	65	.169	12	11	0	.308	.492	8	2	0	3	.185
Clyde Engle	1B	58	5	3	171	.234	28	40	0	.348	.647	32	18	12	6	.298
Larry Gardner	3B	143	24	18	517	.315	56	163	3	.383	.832	88	86	25	16	.449
Casey Hageman	P	2	0	0	0	.000	1	0	0	1.000	0	0	0	0	0	.000
Charley Hall	P	34	4	2	75	.267	4	20	1	.321	.734	10	14	0	3	.413
Olaf Henriksen	OF	44	3	1	56	.321	14	18	0	.457	.868	20	8	0	2	.411
Harry Hooper	OF	147	20	12	590	.242	66	143	2	.326	.653	98	53	29	21	.327
Marty Krug	SS	24	2	1	39	.308	5	12	0	.386	.797	6	7	2	3	.410
Duffy Lewis	OF	154	36	9	581	.284	52	165	6	.346	.754	85	109	9	31	.408
Les Nunamaker	C	35	5	2	103	.252	6	26	0	.313	.652	15	6	2	3	.340
Buck O'Brien	P	37	1	1	94	.138	6	13	0	.190	.360	4	6	0	4	.170
Larry Pape	P	13	1	0	17	.235	2	4	0	.316	.610	1	1	0	0	.294
Doug Smith	P	1	0	0	0	.000	0	0	0	.000	.000	0	0	0	0	.000
Tris Speaker	OF	153	53	12	580	.383	82	222	10	.464	1.031	136	90	52	7	.567
Jake Stahl	1B	95	21	6	326	.301	31	98	3	.372	.801	40	60	13	17	.429
Pinch Thomas	C	13	0	0	30	.200	2	6	0	.250	.450	0	5	1	1	.200
Ben Van Dyke	P	3	0	0	4	.250	0	1	0	.250	.500	0	0	0	0	.250
Heinie Wagner	SS	144	25	6	504	.274	62	138	2	.358	.717	75	68	21	14	.359
Joe Wood	P	43	13	1	124	.290	11	36	1	.348	.784	16	13	0	6	.435
Steve Yerkes	2B	131	22	6	523	.252	41	132	0	.312	.629	73	42	4	25	.317
TEAM TOTALS			269	84	5,071	.277	565	1,404	29	.355	.735	799	654	185	191	.380

Statistics provided for: Games (G), Doubles (2B), Triples (3B), At-Bats (AB), Batting Average (AV), Bases on Balls (BB), Hits (H), Home Runs (HR), On Base Percentage (OBP), On Base Percentage + Slugging Percentage (OPS), Runs (R), Runs Batted In (RBI), Stolen Bases (SB), Sacrifice Hits (SH), and Slugging Percentage (S%)

PITCHING

NAME	G	W	L	%	ERA	GS	CG	IP	H	BB	K	SH	SV	HB	ER	R
Joe Wood	43	34	5	.872	1.91	38	35	344.0	267	82	258	10	1	12	73	104
Ben Van Dyke	3	0	0	.000	3.14	1	0	14.1	13	7	8	0	0	1	5	10
Doug Smith	1	0	0	.000	3.00	0	0	3.0	4	0	1	0	0	0	1	1
Larry Pape	13	1	1	.500	4.99	2	1	48.2	74	16	17	0	1	2	27	36
Buck O'Brien	37	20	13	.606	2.58	34	25	275.2	237	90	115	2	0	10	79	107
Charley Hall	34	15	8	.652	3.02	20	9	191.0	178	70	83	2	2	4	64	85
Casey Hageman	2	0	0	.000	27.01	1	0	1.1	5	3	1	0	0	0	4	5
Ray Collins	27	13	8	.619	2.53	24	17	199.1	192	42	82	4	0	2	56	65
Eddie Cicotte	9	1	3	.250	5.67	6	2	46.0	58	15	20	0	0	1	29	34
Jack Bushelman	3	1	0	1.000	4.70	0	0	7.2	9	5	5	0	0	0	4	4
Hugh Bedient	41	20	9	.690	2.92	28	19	231.0	206	55	122	0	2	3	75	93
TOTALS	105	47		.691	2.76	154	108	1362	1,243	385	712	18	6	35	417	544

Statistics provided for: Games (G), Wins (W), Losses (L), Winning Percentage (%), Earned Run Average (ERA), Games Started (GS), Complete Games (CG), Innings Pitched (IP), Hits (H), Bases on Balls (BB), Strikeouts (K), Shutouts (SH), Saves (SV), Hit Batsmen (HB), Earned Runs (ER), and Runs (R)

FIELDING

NAME	P	G	PO	A	E	DP	TC/G	%	RF*	C	TC	PB
Steve Yerkes	2B	131	244	323	34	39	4.6	.943	0.00	567	601	–
Joe Wood	P	43	41	110	4	2	3.6	.974	3.95	151	155	–
Heinie Wagner	SS	144	332	391	61	43	5.4	.922	0.00	723	784	–
Ben Van Dyke	P	3	2	1	1	0	1.3	.750	1.88	3	4	–
Pinch Thomas	C	8	42	14	2	1	7.3	.966	0.00	56	58	1
Jake Stahl	1B	92	853	49	18	37	10.0	.980	0.00	902	920	–
Tris Speaker	CF	153	372	35	18	9	2.8	.958	0.00	407	425	–
Doug Smith	P	1	0	0	0	0	0.0	.000	0.00	0	0	–
Larry Pape	P	13	1	17	1	0	1.5	.947	3.33	18	19	–
Buck O'Brien	P	37	10	83	5	1	2.6	.949	3.04	93	98	–
Les Nunamaker	C	35	166	33	6	3	5.9	.971	0.00	199	205	6
Duffy Lewis	LF	154	301	23	18	4	2.2	.947	0.00	324	342	–
Marty Krug	SS	11	15	19	4	3	3.5	.895	0.00	34	38	–
Marty Krug	2B	4	4	7	1	1	3.0	.917	0.00	11	12	–
Harry Hooper	RF	147	220	22	9	6	1.7	.964	0.00	242	251	–
Olaf Henriksen	OF	11	10	0	1	0	1.0	.909	0.00	10	11	–
Charley Hall	P	34	9	59	3	0	2.1	.958	3.20	68	71	–
Casey Hageman	P	2	0	0	0	0	0.0	.000	0.00	0	0	–
Larry Gardner	3B	143	167	296	35	16	3.5	.930	0.00	463	498	–
Clyde Engle	1B	25	209	8	5	11	8.9	.977	0.00	217	222	–
Clyde Engle	2B	15	25	27	5	3	3.8	.912	0.00	52	57	–
Clyde Engle	3B	11	9	18	3	1	2.7	.900	0.00	27	30	–
Clyde Engle	SS	2	5	6	0	0	5.5	1.000	0.00	11	11	–
Clyde Engle	RF	1	0	1	0	0	1.0	1.000	0.00	1	1	–
Ray Collins	P	27	3	45	2	0	1.9	.960	2.17	48	50	–
Eddie Cicotte	P	9	3	16	2	2	2.3	.905	3.72	19	21	–
Bill Carrigan	C	87	413	102	16	7	6.1	.970	0.00	515	531	10
Hick Cady	C	43	249	56	3	4	7.2	.990	0.00	305	308	3
Hick Cady	1B	4	31	1	0	2	8.0	1.000	0.00	32	32	–
Jack Bushelman	P	3	0	4	1	0	1.7	.800	4.70	4	5	–
Hugh Bradley	1B	40	354	21	4	13	9.5	.989	0.00	375	379	–
Hugh Bedient	P	41	6	67	2	1	1.8	.973	2.84	73	75	–
Neal Ball	2B	17	13	25	3	1	2.4	.927	0.00	38	41	–
TEAM TOTALS		4,109	1,879	267	210	4.2	.957		4.40	154	5,988	6,255	20

Statistics provided for: Games (G), Putouts (PO), Assists (A), Errors (E), Double Plays (DP), Total Chances per Game (TC/G), Fielding Percentage (%), Range Factor (RF), Chances (C), Total Chances (TC), and Passed Balls (PB—pertains only to catchers)

JOE WOOD IN 1912

DATE	OPPONENT	STARTING PITCHER	SCORE	W/L	H	K	BB
4/11	@New York	Caldwell	5–3	1-0	7	2	3
4/16	@ Philadelphia	Krause	9–2	2-0	13	11	1
4/23	Washington	Groom	2–6	2-1	8	7	7
4/27	Philadelphia	Brown	6–5	3-1	7	6	1
5/1	@Washington	Hughes	1–2	3-2	6	7	4
5/7	Detroit	Mullin	5–4	4-2	11	1	1
5/11	St. Louis	E. Brown	8–1	5-2	3	11	2
5/15	St. Louis	Pelty	2–1	6-2	5	5	1
5/20	Chicago	Walsh	2–0	7-2	5	8	1
5/23	Cleveland (R)	George	6–5 (10)	8-2	2	1	0
5/25	Philadelphia	Coombs	2–8	8-3	9	4	5
5/29	Washington	Walker	21–8	9-3	11	4	0
6/2	@Cleveland	George	5–4 (10)	10-3	7	6	3
6/5	@Detroit (R)	Willett	6–8	ND	4	3	1
6/8	@Detroit	Works	8–3	11-3	6	4	3
6/12	@St. Louis	Powell	5–3	12-3	6	6	1
6/16	@Chicago	Lange	6–4	13-3	5	5	3
6/21	@New York	Quinn	12–3	14-3	9	6	2
6/26	@Washington	Johnson	3–0	15-3	3	9	1
6/29	New York	Thompson	6–0	16-3	1	4	2
6/29	New York	Thompson	6–0	16-3	1	4	2
7/4	@Philadelphia	Plank	3–4	16-4	8	2	2
7/8	St. Louis	Allison	5–1	17-4	7	8	2
7/12	Detroit	Willett	1–0 (11)	18-4	5	10	1
7/15	Detroit (R)	Works	4–6	ND	0	1	0
7/17	Chicago	Peters	7–3	19-4	6	8	2
7/23	Cleveland	Blanding	6–3	20-4	9	7	2
7/28	@Chicago	Cicotte	5–4	21-4	6	6	2
8/2	@St. Louis	Hamilton	9–0	22-4	3	5	3
8/6	@Cleveland	Blanding	5–4 (11)	23-4	13	5	0
8/10	@Detroit	Willett	4–1	24-4	7	10	2
8/14	St. Louis	Allison	8–0	25-4	4	9	3
8/16	St. Louis (R)	Hamilton	2–3	ND	0	4	1
8/17	Detroit (R)	Mullin	6–4	Save	2	0	0
8/20	Detroit	Dubuc	6–2	26-4	6	3	1
8/24	Cleveland	Gregg	8–4	27-4	7	8	2
8/28	Chicago	Taylor	3–0	28-4	6	8	0

(continues)

JOE WOOD IN 1912 (cont.)

DATE	OPPONENT	STARTING PITCHER	SCORE	W/L	H	K	BB
9/2	@New York	McConnell	1-0	29-4	8	8	3
9/6	Washington	Johnson	1-0	30-4	6	9	3
9/10	@Chicago	Benz	5-4	31-4	12	5	1
9/15	@St. Louis	Hamilton	2-1	32-4	7	8	2
9/20	@Detroit	Covington	4-6	32-5	7	8	5
9/25	New York	Schulz	6-0	33-5	2	10	1
10/3	@Philadelphia	Brown	17-5	34-5	8	6	2

Season Total	G	CG	W	L	S	H	K	BB	R	ER	ERA
	43	38	34	5	1	267	258	82	104	73	1.91

1912 FINAL STANDINGS

NL

TEAM	G	W	L	T	PCT	GB	RS	RA
New York Giants	154	103	48	3	.682	–	823	571
Pittsburgh Pirates	152	93	58	1	.616	10.0	751	565
Chicago Cubs	152	91	59	2	.607	11.5	756	668
Cincinnati Reds	155	75	78	2	.490	29.0	656	722
Philadelphia Phillies	152	73	79	0	.480	30.5	670	688
St. Louis Cardinals	153	63	90	0	.412	41.0	659	830
Brooklyn Superbas	153	58	95	0	.379	46.0	651	744
Boston Braves	155	52	101	2	.340	52.0	693	871

AL

TEAM	G	W	L	T	PCT	GB	RS	RA
Boston Red Sox	154	105	47	2	.691	–	799	544
Washington Senators	154	91	61	2	.599	14.0	699	581
Philadelphia Athletics	153	90	62	1	.592	15.0	779	658
Chicago White Sox	158	78	76	4	.506	28.0	639	648
Cleveland Naps	155	75	78	2	.490	30.5	677	681
Detroit Tigers	154	69	84	1	.451	36.5	720	777
St. Louis Browns	157	53	101	3	.344	53.0	552	764
New York Yankees	153	50	102	1	.329	55.0	630	842

1912 WORLD'S SERIES LINE SCORES

Game 1: Tuesday, October 8, 1912, at the Polo Grounds

RED SOX	0	0	0	0	0	1	3	0	0	–	4	6	1
GIANTS	0	0	2	0	0	0	0	0	1	–	3	8	1

PITCHING

RED SOX	IP	H	R	ER	BB	SO	HR	BFP
Wood W (1-0)	9	8	3	3	2	11	0	36

GIANTS	IP	H	R	ER	BB	SO	HR	BFP
Tesreau L (0-1)	7	5	4	4	4	4	0	30
Crandall	2	1	0	0	0	2	0	7
TOTALS	9	6	4	4	4	6	0	37

HBP: Wood (1, Myers)
Umpires: HP – Bill Klem, 1B – Billy Evans, 2B – Cy Rigler, 3B – Silk O'Loughlin
Time of Game: 2:10   **Attendance:** 35,730

Game 2: Wednesday, October 9, 1912, at Fenway Park

GIANTS	0	1	0	1	0	0	0	3	0	1	0	–	6	11	5
RED SOX	3	0	0	0	1	0	0	1	0	1	0	–	6	10	1

PITCHING

GIANTS	IP	H	R	ER	BB	SO	HR	BFP
Mathewson	11	10	6	0	0	4	0	45

RED SOX	IP	H	R	ER	BB	SO	HR	BFP
Collins	7.1	9	5	3	0	5	0	31
Hall	2.2	2	1	1	4	0	0	14
Bedient	1	0	0	0	1	1	0	3
TOTALS	11	11	6	4	5	6	0	48

HBP: Bedient (1, Snodgrass)   **IBB:** Hall 2 (2, Doyle, Meyers)
Umpires: HP – Silk O'Loughlin, 1B – Cy Rigler, 2B – Bill Klem, 3B – Billy Evans
Time of Game: 2:38   **Attendance:** 30,148

Game 3: Thursday, October 10, 1912, at Fenway Park

GIANTS	0	1	0	0	1	0	0	0	0	–	2	7	1
RED SOX	0	0	0	0	0	0	0	0	1	–	1	7	0

PITCHING

GIANTS	IP	H	R	ER	BB	SO	HR	BFP
Marquard W (1-0)	9	7	1	1	1	6	0	35

RED SOX	IP	H	R	ER	BB	SO	HR	BFP
O'Brien L (0-1)	8	6	2	2	3	3	0	32
Bedient	1	1	0	0	0	0	0	3
TOTALS	9	7	2	2	3	3	0	35

HBP: Bedient (2, Herzog)
Umpires: HP – Billy Evans, 1B – Bill Klem, LF – Silk O'Loughlin, RF – Cy Rigler
Time of Game: 2:15   **Attendance:** 34,624

Game 4: Friday, October 11, 1912, at the Polo Grounds

RED SOX	0	1	0	1	0	0	0	0	1	–	3	8	1
GIANTS	0	0	0	0	0	0	1	0	0	–	1	9	1

PITCHING

RED SOX	IP	H	R	ER	BB	SO	HR	BFP
Wood W (2-0)	9	9	1	1	0	8	0	35

GIANTS	IP	H	R	ER	BB	SO	HR	BFP
Tesreau L (0-2)	7	5	2	2	2	5	0	27
Ames	2	3	1	1	1	0	0	10
TOTALS	9	8	3	3	3	5	0	37

WP: Tesreau (1)
Umpires: HP – Cy Rigler, 1B – Silk O'Loughlin, 2B – Billy Evans, 3B – Bill Klem
Time of Game: 2:06   **Attendance:** 36,502

Game 5: Saturday, October 12, 1912, at Fenway Park

GIANTS	0	0	0	0	0	0	1	0	0	–	1	3	1
RED SOX	0	0	2	0	0	0	0	0	x	–	2	5	1

PITCHING

GIANTS	IP	H	R	ER	BB	SO	HR	BFP
Mathewson L (0-1)	8	5	2	2	0	2	0	29

RED SOX	IP	H	R	ER	BB	SO	HR	BFP
Bedient W (1-0)	9	3	1	0	3	4	0	33

Umpires: HP – Silk O'Loughlin, 1B – Cy Rigler, 2B – Bill Klem, 3B – Billy Evans
Time of Game: 1:43   **Attendance:** 34,683

Game 6: Monday, October 14, 1912, at the Polo Grounds

RED SOX	0	2	0	0	0	0	0	0	0	–	2	7	2
GIANTS	5	0	0	0	0	0	0	0	x	–	5	11	1

PITCHING

RED SOX	IP	H	R	ER	BB	SO	HR	BFP
O'Brien L (0-2)	1	6	5	3	0	1	0	8
Collins	7	5	0	0	0	1	0	22
TOTALS	9	11	5	3	0	2	0	30

GIANTS	IP	H	R	ER	BB	SO	HR	BFP
Masquard W (2-0)	9	7	2	0	1	3	0	34
Ames	2	3	1	1	1	0	0	10
TOTALS	9	8	3	3	3	5	0	37

BK: O'Brien (1)
Umpires: HP – Bill Klem, 1B – Billy Evans, 2B – Silk O'Loughlin, 3B – Cy Rigler
Time of Game: 1:58   **Attendance:** 30,622

Game 7: Tuesday, October 15, 1912, at Fenway Park

GIANTS	6	1	0	0	0	2	1	0	1	–	11	16	4
RED SOX	0	1	0	0	0	0	2	1	0	–	4	9	2

PITCHING

GIANTS	IP	H	R	ER	BB	SO	HR	BFP
Tesreau W (1-2)	9	9	4	2	5	6	1	43

RED SOX	IP	H	R	ER	BB	SO	HR	BFP
Wood L (2-1)	1	7	6	6	0	0	0	9
Hall	8	9	5	3	5	1	1	37
TOTALS	9	16	11	9	5	1	1	46

WP: Tesreau 2 (3)   **HBP:** Tesreau (1,Gardner)
Umpires: HP – Billy Evans, 1B – Bill Klem, 2B – Silk O'Loughlin, 3B – Cy Rigler
Time of Game: 2:21   **Attendance:** 32,694

Game 8: Wednesday, October 16, 1912, at Fenway Park

GIANTS	0	0	1	0	0	0	0	0	0	1	–	2	9	2
RED SOX	0	0	0	0	0	0	1	0	0	2	–	3	8	4

PITCHING

GIANTS	IP	H	R	ER	BB	SO	HR	BFP
Mathewson L (0-2)	9.2	8	3	1	5	4	0	41

RED SOX	IP	H	R	ER	BB	SO	HR	BFP
Bedient	7	6	1	1	3	2	0	30
Wood W (3-1)	3	3	1	1	1	2	0	13
TOTALS	10	9	2	2	4	4	0	43

IBB: Mathewson (1,Lewis)
Umpires: HP - Silk O'Loughlin, 1B – Cy Rigler, 2B – Bill Klem, 3B – Billy Evans
Time of Game: 2:37   **Attendance:** 17,034

Note: Much of the information used or adapted here was obtained free of charge from and is copyrighted by Retrosheet. Interested parties may contact Retrosheet at www.retrosheet.org. More comprehensive World Series and season statistics are available there and at at baseballreference.com.

Index